R. C. Sharma

THE LAST SAMURAI

THE LAST SAMURAI

The Life and Battles of
Saigō Takamori

MARK RAVINA

WILEY

John Wiley & Sons, Inc.

Published by John Wiley & Sons, Inc., Hoboken, New Jersey
Published simultaneously in Canada

Design and composition by Navta Associates, Inc.

For general information about our other products and services, please contact our Customer Care Department within the United States at (800) 762-2974, outside the United States at (317) 572-3993 or fax (317) 572-4002.

Wiley also publishes its books in a variety of electronic formats. Some content that appears in print may not be available in electronic books. For more information about Wiley products, visit our web site at www.wiley.com.

Library of Congress Cataloging-in-Publication Data:
Ravina, Mark, date.
   The last samurai : the life and battles of Saigo Takamori / Mark Ravina.
      p. cm.
   ISBN 0-471-08970-2 (cloth: alk. paper)
   ISBN 0-471-70537-3 (paper: alk. paper)
   1. Saigō, Takamori, 1828–1877. 2. Statesmen—Japan—Biography. 3. Japan—History—Restoration, 1853–1870. I. Title.
DS881.5.S2R35   2004
952.03'1'092—dc21

2003006646

Printed in the United States of America

10 9 8 7 6 5 4 3 2

To my parents

Contents

Note to the Reader

Dates

Prior to 1873 Japan used a lunar calendar with twelve months each of 29 or 30 days for a total year of about 354 days. Intercalary or "leap" months were used to keep this lunar calendar synchronous with the solar year. This adjustment is common with other lunar/solar calendars, such as the traditional Jewish calendar, which also uses "leap" months to reconcile lunar months with the solar year.

Following historiographic convention I have expressed lunar calendar dates in year/month/day format and converted Japanese years, but not months or days, to the Gregorian calendar. Thus, the fifth day of the eleventh lunar month of the sixth year of the Hōreki era is rendered as 1756/11/5. The letter *i* represents an intercalary or "leap" month. The date 1756/i11/5 represents the fifth day of the eleventh intercalary (or twelfth) month of 1756. In converting dates I relied on the tables in Tsuchihashi 1952.

The Japanese year began "late," and the exact Gregorian date for the Japanese New Year varied between January 21 and February 19. The Meiji government adopted the Gregorian calendar in 1873. January 1, 1873, and 1873/1/1 are the same day.

Names, Romanizations, and Spelling

Japanese words are romanized according to the modified Hepburn system used in *Kenkyūsha's Japanese-English Dictionary*. Japanese nouns do not have plural forms: thus, for example, "shogun" and "samurai" are singular or plural depending on context. I have presented Japanese and Chinese personal names in traditional fashion: family name followed by given name. For Chinese words I have used the pinyin romanization system, but I have included the older Wade-Giles system in parentheses in cases where the older version of the name is likely to be more familiar to readers.

Rendering Japanese names in English presents certain problems. In nineteenth-century Japan, important men commonly used several names. Saigō Takamori, for example, was given the name Saigō Kokichi at birth, and took the name Takamori at adulthood, but wrote poetry under the name Saigō Nanshū. Samurai and nobles received new names with promotions in rank. Thus the daimyo Hitotsubashi Yoshinobu became Tokugawa Yoshinobu after his succession as shogun. In addition, Japanese names often have more than one reading, since characters can be read in either Chinese or Japanese fashion. Yoshinobu and Keiki, for example, are simply different readings of the same two characters. In confronting these issues I have put the interest of an American readership foremost. I consistently refer to individuals by the same name, even when this is technically inaccurate. Thus I continue to refer to Hitotsubashi Keiki as such, even in referring to the period after he became shogun and received the new family name of Tokugawa. Further, where there are multiple readings of a given name, I have chosen the most distinctive reading: Thus Keiki instead of Yoshinobu, since Keiki better distinguishes him from his rival Yoshitomi. I also have used unofficial names whenever this seemed easier to remember: thus I refer to the daimyo of Fukui as Matsudaira Shungaku rather than as Matsudaira Yoshinaga. See page 256 for information on accessing variant names for major figures.

Japanese place names present different problems. The suffixes to Japanese place names are often descriptive. Shiroyama, for example, means "mountain of the castle," so technically the phrase "hills of Shiroyama" is redundant. One can correct for this redundancy by dropping suffixes, but this creates new problems. Anyone looking for Shiroyama needs to look under that name and not Shiro or Mount Shiro. There is no established solution to this problem. I have tried to avoid redundancy, but I have included such terms as "hill" or "temple" when necessary for clarity.

For daimyo domains, there are other issues. Large domains were known by several names: the name of the castle town, the name of the daimyo house, the name of the province, or the name of the region. In this work I have generally identified domains by the name of their castle town with the following important exceptions: Satsuma domain instead of Kagoshima domain; Chōshū domain instead of Hagi domain; and Tosa domain instead of Kōchi domain.

I have tried to be systematic with the translation of Japanese titles. I have employed the term "lord," however, to refer to a range of late Tokugawa figures who were powerful samurai rulers but not daimyo. Tokugawa Nariaki, for example, was a dominant force in Mito even after he formally retired in favor of his son. Alternately, Shimazu Hisamitsu never became daimyo at all but effectively ruled Satsuma through his son, the daimyo Shimazu Tadayoshi. In Tokugawa Japan there were specific terms in Japanese for fathers of daimyo and retired daimyo, but in English, for the sake of simplicity, I refer to all of these daimyolike men as "lords."

The common English translation of *Seinan sensō* is "Satsuma rebellion," but I feel that this misrepresents both the original Japanese and the war itself. The struggle extended far beyond Satsuma, and, in scale, it was far closer to a civil war than a rebellion. Rather than "Satsuma rebellion," the term is translated throughout the book as "War of the Southwest."

All translations from Japanese in the text and notes are mine unless otherwise noted.

For those interested in pronouncing Japanese, the following may be helpful. Japanese vowels are pronounced as in Italian. The macron, or long vowel mark, changes the length of the vowel rather than its sound. Thus the "o" in "Saigō," a family name, and "saigo," a word meaning "last," are both pronounced as in "Roma" or "prego." The "o," in Saigō, however, is held longer and would count as two syllables rather than one in poetry. Doubled consonants such as "kk" are similarly held longer in time.

I have included macrons for all Japanese place names except for Ryukyu, Tokyo, Osaka, and Kyoto, which are conventionally printed without them in English-language publications. I have also omitted macrons on those common nouns found in standard American dictionaries, such as daimyo *(daimyō)* and sumo *(sumō)*.

Measures

I have converted all measurements into U.S. units with the exception of *koku,* the unit used for samurai stipends. Samurai investitures, including the holdings of daimyo, were measured in *koku* of rice: one *koku* equaled 4.95 bushels or 180 liters.

Acknowledgments

I could not have written this book without the help of Haraguchi Izumi, professor of Japanese history at Kagoshima University. Haraguchi was my sponsor for a semester of research at Kagoshima University and gave me unstinting support and encouragement. His knowledge of Satsuma history is encyclopedic, and I often learned as much from a brief chat with him as I did in hours at the library or archives. But I am equally indebted to him for his help on less intellectual affairs. Haraguchi let me stay at his home until I found an apartment, let me use his office on campus, and shared his enormous private library. I am touched by both his hospitality and his interest in my research.

I owe an enormous debt of thanks to two of Haraguchi's graduate students: Adachi Kōichi and Kajiya Sadayuki. Adachi's research on samurai education in Satsuma and Kajiya's work on the Ryukyuan community in Kagoshima greatly enhanced my understanding of the world in which Saigō lived. Their research and advice pointed me both to important primary sources and recent revisionist scholarship. I owe special thanks to Adachi, who sat with me for many hours as I struggled to render Saigō's letters into English; his advice and companionship on this endeavor was a true gift.

Thanks also to my old friend Sakurai Katsumi, a specialist in *komonjo* (diplomatics) at NHK Gakuen. For some fifteen years Sakurai has been my ad hoc tutor in the intricacies of handwritten documents, and for this project he joined me in Kagoshima and Kumamoto to sort through piles of prints *(nishikie)*. Although I suspect that I have been one his slowest students, Sakurai spent hours teaching me the intricacies of *hentaigana* and then carefully checked my transcriptions. I am thankful for both his professional support and his companionship.

Yamada Shōji, director of the Nanshū kenshōkan, editor of *Keiten aijin* (a journal devoted to Saigō), and an indefatigable local historian, answered my many questions about Saigō. I am indebted to him for his time and generosity. Imayoshi Hiromu, director of the Reimeikan (Kagoshima Prefectural Museum of Culture), graciously allowed me to examine, photograph, and reproduce parts of the museum's enormous holdings. Oguchi Yoshio, curator at the Reimeikan and editor of several volumes of collected primary sources, pointed me to invaluable documents I would otherwise have overlooked. Yoshimitsu Shōji of the Reimeikan helped me photograph woodblock prints of the *Seinan sensō* and answered my many queries.

Nozoe Kōichi of the the Kagoshima City Museum of Art took me seriously when I telephoned trying to find the original of *Saigō nehan zō,* a print I had seen reproduced on the promotional calendar of a local bank. In the ensuing search he found not only *Saigō nehan zō* but also several prints that changed my understanding of Saigō and Saigō legends.

Thanks to Matsuo Chitoshi of the Shōkōshūseikan Museum for his help in finding photographs of Shimazu Nariakira and Shimazu Hisamitsu, as well as Kagoshima Castle and environs. I thank the Shōkōshūseikan for permission to reprint the photographs.

Ishihara Takenori of the Kumamoto Museum of Science (Kumamoto hakubutsukan) took time from his busy schedule to help me examine and photograph the museum's extensive collection of woodblock prints. The staff at the Tabaruzaka shiryōkan took the time to explain the details of breech-loading and muzzle-loading rifles and to answer my many questions about the Battle of Tabaruzaka.

In Kyoto I was given access to several temples and gardens where Saigō stayed, strolled, and hid. The administration at Kiyomizudera let me lazily reflect in the garden of the Jōjuin, where Gesshō was once abbot. Ōtsuka Kantetsu of the Shōrenin and a modest, anonymous monk at Shōkokuji talked with me at length about the history of their temples. I owe special thanks to Sugii Miyako, mother of the abbot at Tōfukuji sokusōin, where Saigō and Gesshō reportedly met and conspired. Despite the stifling Kyoto summer heat, she walked me through the sprawling temple grounds to show me the Satsuma cemetery behind the abbot's residence.

When I visited Saigō's house on Amami Ōshima I enjoyed the great hospitality of Ryū Masako, a descendant of Saigō's wife, Aigana. She shared with me her stories about Aigana and gave me a copy of *Tatsugō senkyochū no Nanshū ō jitsuwa denkishū,* a locally published collection of Saigō legends. I am indebted also to Yamashita Fumitake, a respected local historian, for answering questions about Amami Ōshima and to Matsuda Hideki, curator at the Amami Museum, for special access to the museum's collection.

Ōyama Yasuhiro gave me a guided tour of Okinoerabujima and shared the island's oral history. Hashiguchi Fumio, curator at the Wadomari Museum of Historical Ethnography (Wadomari-chō rekishi minzoku shiryōkan) on Okinoerabujima gave me valuable advice on island customs and history.

In the Netherlands, Joost Schokkenbroek of the Nederlands Scheep-vaartmuseum and Ingeborg Th. Leijerzapf of the Studie en Dokumentatie Centrum voor Fotografie in Leiden helped me tracked down nineteenth-century photographs of Japan and arrange for their reproduction in this book.

This biography is a different and, I hope, a better book because of the Internet and the World Wide Web. Through H-JAPAN and H-ASIA, two moderated Internet listservs devoted to history, I was able to query hundreds of Asia specialists on issues as diverse as early Japanese children's games and ancient Chinese literati. I am especially indebted, via these sites, to Par Cassel, Helen Hardacre, Earl Kinmonth, Lawrence Marceau, David Pollack, S. A. Thornton, and Donald B. Wagner. Also worthy of note are the Chinese Philosophical Etext Archive, based at Wesleyan University (http://sangle.web.wesleyan.edu/etext/index.html), and Charles Mueller's site at Tōyō Gakuen University (http://www.human.toyogakuen-u.ac.jp/~acmuller/index.html). These digital resources allowed me to track down classical references in Saigō writings with exceptional ease, and this, in turn, deepened my understanding of Saigō's thought.

Harahata Kenji brought a fresh eye to my translations of Saigō's letters, and I am thankful for his unstinting concern for accuracy, his advice on Tokyo restaurants, and his enduring friendship. At Emory University, Ho Wan-li guided my attempts to render Saigō's Chinese poetry into English. I benefited from both her enthusiasm and her strict standards.

I have had the good fortune to present parts of this work at two scholarly meetings, the Southern Japan Seminar and the Tokyo Ph.D. Kenkyūkai, where I received helpful suggestions from Izumi Nakayama, Richard Rice, Lucien Ellington, Simon Partner, Paul Dunscomb, and Edward Pratt. Henry Smith of Columbia University generously arranged to have his undergraduate seminar read an earlier draft of this book and allowed me to sit in while they discussed it. My own undergraduates at Emory also read and critiqued earlier versions. I learned much from these student critiques, especially those from Anri Yasuda and Eben Pindyck at Columbia and Minh Le at Emory.

This biography is part of a broader project to reconceptualize the Meiji Restoration. I have presented that research at several academic forums, including a conference at the Princeton Institute for Advanced Study; a conference in Istanbul on globalization, cosponsored by Emory University's Halle Institute and Bogazici University; a meeting in Leiden of the International Institute for Asian Studies; a meeting of the Historical Society in Atlanta; and a Columbia East-Asian Studies Brown Bag seminar. On that longer project I have benefited from the insights of John Boli, Martin Colcutt, Kevin Doak, Richard Doner, Martin Doornbos, Selçuk Esenbel, Karl Friday, Sheldon Garon, David Howell, Franklyn Knight, David Lurie, Marc Miller, Cathal Nolan, Greg Pflugfelder, Luke Roberts, Henry D. Smith, Leila Wice, Willem Wolters, and R. Bin Wong. Thanks also to Sasaki Junnosuke, Ronald Toby, George Wilson, Derek Wolff, Dirk Schumann, Matthew Payne, Cheryl Crowley, Kristin Gorell, and Michael Bellesiles.

Three readers evaluted this manuscript for John Wiley. Their thoughtful comments prodded me to reread, rethink, and rewrite; this is a better book for their keen attention and historical insight. Conrad Totman also read the entire manuscript as a personal favor and gave me much valuable advice. His deep knowledge of Tokugawa politics saved me from numerous errors in fact and interpretation. My editor at John Wiley, Stephen Power, and my copy editor, Kate Gilbert, helped me turn a manuscript into a book.

This book would not have been possible without a research grant from the Japan Foundation and a University Research Council grant from Emory University. I am also thankful for support from the Institute for International and Comparative Studies at Emory.

Nora Levesque and my children, Walker and Zoe, were both inspirations and distractions. I am grateful that they let me blather about the nineteenth century but demanded that I periodically return to the twenty-first.

THE LAST SAMURAI

Statue of Saigō in Ueno Park, Tokyo

INTRODUCTION

Where was Saigō Takamori's head? For one frantic morning in 1877 this question consumed the Japanese government. The Japanese imperial army had defeated Saigō's rebellion. They had reduced his army of thirty thousand fearsome, disgruntled samurai to a few hundred diehards. Then, on the morning of September 24, 1877, government forces launched a final attack on the remnants of the rebel army. Within hours, Saigō's forces were utterly destroyed. The War of the Southwest, Japan's bloodiest conflict in more than three hundred years, was over. But the government's triumph rang hollow. The imperial army had Saigō's body, but his head was nowhere to be found. Without Saigō's head the government's victory was incomplete.

Why did Saigō's head matter? In searching for Saigō's head the Japanese army was honoring one of the oldest traditions of the warrior class. The presentation of severed heads was a celebrated part of medieval Japanese warfare, and the great warrior epics are replete with descriptions of formal presentations. Samurai would take the heads of defeated warriors and offer them as tribute to their lord. In major battles the victorious army would collect hundreds of enemy heads. The heads of lesser warriors were collected in piles and displayed as grim trophies. But the severed heads of honored enemies, in legend if not in fact, were treated with deference. A famous case is that of Minamoto no Yoritomo, Japan's first shogun, and his half brother Minamoto no Yoshitsune. Originally they were allies, but Yoritomo came to distrust his half sibling and ordered his assassination. Yoshitsune was declared a rebel and a traitor, but he was, nonetheless, a noble traitor. According to a well-known tale, in 1189, when Yoritomo's men took Yoshitsune's head, they treated it with reverence. Yoshitsune's head was washed carefully. It was then placed it in a black lacquer box filled with sake for presentation to Yoritomo. When Yoritomo's officers received the head, they reportedly wept at the tragedy of Yoshitsune's youthful demise.[1]

While the presentation of heads was a decisive means of identifying defeated commanders, the greater meaning was of fealty. The severed head of an enemy general symbolized a retainer's supreme dedication to his lord, representing the risks he had taken in acquiring such a trophy. By presenting such "gifts" a samurai proved himself worthy of his lord's favor.[2] Conversely, by accepting them, a victorious commander demonstrated his superiority to lords whose retainers had been unable to support them successfully in battle.

On September 24, 1877, these medieval rituals had renewed vibrancy and power. This was an ironic, posthumous victory for Saigō. In searching for his head, the imperial army was honoring a tradition it had officially renounced. The modern Japanese army had explicitly rejected feudal concerns and symbols. The new Japanese army was based on modern nationalism, not on feudal loyalty. Imperial army soldiers were loyal to king and country, not to regional feudal lords. The 1872 edict that created the conscript army described the samurai tradition as a terrible inequity. Conscription was described as a great egalitarian project:

On the one hand, warriors who have lived without labor for generations have had their stipends reduced and have been stripped of their swords; on the other hand, the four classes of the people [samurai, peasants, artisans, and merchants] are about to receive their freedom. This is the way to restore the balance between the high and the low and to grant equal rights to all. It is, in short, the basis of uniting the farmers and the soldier into one. The people are not the people of former days. They are now equally the people of the empire, and there is no distinction between them in their obligations to the state.[3]

This new army had no reason to be interested in Saigō's head. The government, in fact, had renounced the public display of heads as an example of the cruelty of the old regime. Imperial officers did not owe the emperor severed heads as symbols of their fealty.

The defeat of Saigō should have been an occasion for celebrating the "new" Japan. The army that smashed Saigō's rebellion was an emblem of Japan's rapid transformation after the imperial restoration of 1868. The imperial army was a modern, national force. It was staffed by conscripted commoners, funded by national taxes, supplied by railroads and steamships, and connected by telegraph. The Japanese government used its most modern and fearsome weapons against the rebels. It employed, for the first time in Japanese history, land mines, sea mines, balloonborne mines, and rockets. Saigō's rebel forces were, by contrast, samurai, fighting with swords. Although they had begun the war armed with cannons and firearms, they had long since exhausted their ammunition. Swords against artillery: the battle could not have been more clearly drawn. The two armies were also fighting for two different visions of Japan. The rebels had neglected to draw up a manifesto, but their implicit cause was the restoration of samurai honor. The new government in Tokyo had abolished the samurai monopoly on military service and government offices. It had challenged one of the principal precepts of the old order: the idea that samurai alone had the courage to serve as warriors and the moral fiber to serve as government officials. The courage of Saigō and his men was beyond question. Yet when commoner conscripts and samurai met on the battlefield, the commoners were victorious. Old Japan and new Japan had met in battle. Old Japan had lost.[4]

Why then the search for Saigō's head? That the modern Japanese army should honor medieval Japanese tradition was scarcely accidental. The defense of samurai tradition was at the core of Saigō's rebellion. Saigō and his comrades had failed to restore the samurai estate through force of arms. They were determined, however, to glorify samurai tradition in death. Their demise was an almost choreographed display of courage and resolution. The rebels made their last stand in the hills of Shiroyama behind Kagoshima Castle. The castle had once been the residence of the Shimazu family, the lords of Satsuma domain, now known as Kagoshima Prefecture.

But in 1877, it was, in name if not in fact, the property of the Japanese imperial government. Saigō was sheltered in a cave in the hills, facing Kagoshima Bay. He had long ago stopped fearing death, but he was now particularly contemplative and peaceful. Reconciled to death and defeat, Saigō had spent his last days in reflection, enjoying the beautiful scenery of his birthplace. He was almost lighthearted: exchanging poems with his comrades, playing the Japanese game of go, and making jokes. Saigō's companions shared his mood. On September 22 Saigō told his followers that this battle would be their last and urged them to face the end with courage:

> As we are determined to fight to our deaths; to fulfill our moral obligations to a noble cause [taigi meibun]; and to die for the imperial court; so let your mind be at peace and be prepared to make this castle your [final] resting place. It is vital to bestir yourselves yet even more, and to be resolved not to leave for posterity any cause for shame.[5]

On the following night, according to legend, Saigō gave leave to all those not prepared to die. The men who stayed were not merely loyal; they also were determined to die with Saigō. On the evening of September 23 the rebels celebrated their imminent deaths. Under a bright moon they drank sake, sang songs, and exchanged poems about honor, loyalty, and death.[6]

The imperial army began its final assault attack at 3:55 A.M. The rebels defended their hilltop positions but were rapidly beaten back by superior force. By 5:30 A.M. the imperial army had destroyed the rebels' fortifications. The army moved artillery into these positions and began to concentrate fire on the valley below. Saigō's force was reduced to about forty men. At roughly 7:00 A.M. Saigō and his troops descended the hill to face the Japanese army and die. Saigō was surrounded by his closest and dearest allies: Kirino Toshiaki, Murata Shinpachi, Katsura Hisatake, and Beppu Shinsuke. Halfway down the hill, Saigō was shot in the right hip. The bullet passed through his body and exited at his left femur. Saigō fell to the ground. According to legend, Saigō composed himself and prepared for seppuku, samurai ritual suicide. Turning to Beppu he said, "My dear Shinsuke, I think this place will do. Please be my second (kaishaku)." Saigō then calmly faced east, toward the imperial palace, and bent his head. Beppu quickly severed his head with a single, clean stroke and passed the head to

Saigō's manservant Kichizaemon, who fled and hid it from the approaching army. The ritualized death of a fallen hero was complete. Saigō had died a model samurai. *Nishikie,* colorful woodblock prints that served as tabloid journals, expanded on this legend in spectacular fashion. Saigō was shown, glorious and noble, pushing a sword into his abdomen.[7]

Saigō's autopsy tells a different story. Shot through the hip, Saigō would have been unable to sit calmly and discuss his death with Beppu. And although Saigō's head was severed with a clean cut, there were no wounds to his abdomen. Crippled and probably in shock, Saigō had been unable to dispatch himself with traditional samurai honor. These facts did little to alter the legend of Saigō's glorious death. With each retelling, Saigō's composure grew greater, his soliloquy to Beppu longer, and the poignancy of the moment more intense. Because Saigō had come to represent samurai valor, his death had to represent samurai tradition. Physiology notwithstanding, tradition demanded that Saigō sit on a shattered hip and serenely ask Beppu to help him die. Saigō had become a legend, and the Japanese media decided to print the legend, not the man.[8]

The death of Saigō meant the death of an entire conception of the Japanese polity. Saigō and his men had fought for the tradition of local independence. Although Saigō's followers could tolerate commoner-soldiers in Tokyo, they could not accept the power of Tokyo to challenge samurai privilege in Satsuma, their home domain. The *Tokio Times,* writing for an English-language readership, described this transformation in the language of American history:

> [T]he idea of national integrity has been stated and established. Widespread throughout the empire it is accepted and appreciated, as never before, that this is one country;—not a bundle of semi-sovereign and jealous powers, but a nation. In this respect the moral of the strife coincides strikingly with the lesson of the civil war in America. There, as here, one of the vital issues was the question of the relation of the state to the central authority, and the result in both cases has vindicated the claims of the latter to be the superior and final arbiter. That this, an "inevitable crisis," here as in America, has been fairly met and satisfactorily adjusted is matter for congratulation.[9]

The *Hōchi shinbun* focused on the collapse of samurai power:

From the time when the feudal system was replaced by the present form of government, the power of the *shizoku* or ancient military class has rapidly decreased. The resistance of Saigō to the rulers of the empire was an attempt of the shizoku to regain their old status of military control in national affairs. . . . [T]herefore the present victory is not simply a suppression of Saigō's rebellion alone, but is a universal triumph over the old feudal idea of the supremacy of the shizoku everywhere.

The editorial was celebratory: "Are not all the people of our country rejoiced to hear such good news as this?"[10]

Many Japanese were, in fact, less than congratulatory. Even the *Hōchi shinbun* acknowledged that Saigō had "sustained his fame until the last . . . died without shame, and closed his eyes in peace with the full satisfaction of vengeance." To the government's dismay, Saigō had come to represent all that was commendable in the samurai estate. Despite a formidable government propaganda campaign, Saigō remained immensely popular. He was widely seen as the model samurai: loyal, courageous, fearless in the face of death, incorruptible, fair, and compassionate. Saigō had held himself above commoners, but as a compassionate leader, not a tyrannical overlord. For Saigō, samurai authority demanded benevolent leadership. It allowed no margin for imperiousness. A good samurai ruled not to advance himself but to serve heaven. As servants rather than masters, samurai were obliged to live simple, frugal lives. For Saigō, frugality and modesty were moral imperatives. Saigō was famous for his love of simple clothing, and even as a high-ranking minister he avoided frock coats and elaborate court dress. According to legend, Saigō once visited the imperial palace dressed in a simple cotton kimono and straw sandals. When he was leaving the palace, he was stopped by a guard who assumed that such a shabbily dressed figure must be an intruder. Saigō identified himself, but the guard did not believe him until Iwakura Tomomi, a senior court noble, confirmed his identity. In an era of turmoil, Saigō's reputation for simplicity and honesty was enthralling.[11]

Saigō's appeal extended to his political opponents. One of Saigō's principal defenders was the educator and author Fukuzawa Yukichi, who was Japan's premier exponent of Western ideas and values. His celebration of Western-style education, *An Encouragement of Learning,* was the most widely read volume of the 1870s in Japan. Fukuzawa thought Saigō's defense of samurai privilege was reprehensible. But Fukuzawa was still more incensed by the government's propaganda, which he saw as vilification of a noble man. In passionate defense of Saigō, Fukuzawa argued that Saigō had rebelled not to seize power but in response to the government's tyranny. Fukuzawa opposed violence but saw Saigō as a victim of autocracy. "We must feel compassion for Saigō," he wrote, "for it was the government that drove him to his death."[12]

While the intelligentsia defended Saigō in essays, the populace defended him through legend and rumor. According to popular mythology, Saigō did not perish on the hills of Shiroyama. Instead he fled to China, where he was collecting his forces for a second attack that would purge Japan of injustice and corruption. By some accounts, Saigō was hiding in India, gathering forces for his return. These rumors began soon after Saigō's defeat and continued, unabated, for decades. In 1881 the streets of Osaka were flooded with pamphlets describing Saigō's flight to an island off the coast of India. Readers took these pamphlets seriously. As a local newspaper observed, no one seemed to believe that Saigō was actually dead. These Saigō survival legends rebounded in 1891. The occasion was Russian crown prince Nikolai's visit to Japan. Saigō, according to the revised legend, was actually in Russia and would return to Japan, with Nikolai, on a Russian battleship. Once back in Japan, Saigō would seize power, purge corrupt officials, revise Japan's unequal treaties with the Western powers, and lead an invasion of Korea. This rumor was so earnestly received that when Saigō did not appear, Tsuda Sanzō, a Japanese constable, suspected foul play and attacked the crown prince.[13]

So powerful was Saigō's appeal that he was transformed into a demigod even before his death. Most Japanese newspapers dutifully reported the defeat of Saigō the "traitor" and celebrated the victory of the Japanese army. But Saigō's enormous popularity leaked through the constraints of government censorship. In the popular mind, Saigō's defeat was actually part of his ascent to the heavens. In Osaka, tales of Saigō's ascent to the stars first appeared in August 1877, while Saigō was in eastern Kyūshū. In the early morning of August 2 a comet appeared in the southwestern sky. On August 3 the *Ōsaka nippō* newspaper reported that when examined with a telescope, this "bright star" revealed a portrait of Saigō: healthy, fit, and in full imperial army uniform. This story swept through the city, and night after night people stood on their laundry-drying platforms to get a better look at the celestial hero. Woodblock prints soon appeared showing Saigō,

Kagoshima shiritsu bijutsukan

Saigō in the Heavens
Zokushō Saigō boshi no zu in the Kagoshima shiritsu bijutsukan

ensconced in a star, looking down at Japan from the heavens. The prints, true
to the newspaper story, showed Saigō in formal uniform. This is an intriguing detail: the government had declared Saigō a traitor, but they had failed,
in the popular imagination, to strip him of rank. The association of Saigō
with the comet was strengthened by the Japanese predilection for word play,
since the period term for comet, *hōki boshi,* also could be read as "rebellious
star," in reference to Saigō's insurrection.[14] As news of these "Saigō sightings"
spread, the rumors grew more intense. By the time the story reached Tokyo,
the Saigō comet had become an object of veneration, and people were

climbing to their roofs to get a better look. There were serious injuries as roof boards collapsed under the weight of Saigō watchers.[15]

Saigō's ascent to the heavens was supported by other astronomical phenomena. In August and September 1877 the earth and Mars were in unusual proximity, and Mars glowed with exceptional brightness. On August 19 the *Chōya shinbun* reported that Saigō, burning with anger, had been transformed into the planet Mars. That same month the Japanese press reported that the American astronomer Asaph Hall had discovered a satellite around Mars. For Saigō loyalists this moon was none other than Saigō's loyal companion Kirino, who had accompanied his friend into the heavens.[16] By September the transformation of Saigō into Mars was a common theme of popular prints. Edward Morse, an American zoologist and a keen observer of Japanese society, noted these prints in his journal:

> In riding through the streets [of Tokyo] one notices the crowds in front of the picture shops, which are bright in color from the war prints. The Satsuma rebellion [Saigō's rebellion] furnishes the themes for the illustrators. The pictures are brilliant in reds and blacks, the fig-ures of the officers in most dramatic attitudes, and "bloody war" is really depicted, though grotesque from our standpoint. One of the pictures represents a star in heaven (the planet Mars), in the centre of which is General Saigo, the rebel chief, beloved by all the Japanese. After the capture of Kagoshima he and other officers committed *hara kiri*. Many of the people believe he is Mars, which is now shining with unusual brilliancy.[17]

Another type of Saigō image was deeply religious. In *Saigō nehanzō,* or nirvana prints, Saigō was shown as an enlightened being preparing to transcend physical existence. Still in military dress, he is surrounded by common Japanese—men and women, young and old—who are praying intensely for his return to the corporeal world. These prints were based closely on depictions of the death and transcendence of Siddhartha, the founder of Buddhism. Like the Buddha, Saigō is peaceful as he faces death. Instead of disciples, Saigō is encircled by representatives of all walks of life, including shopkeepers, newspaper vendors, geisha, and monks. To cement the parallel with the Buddha, a horse, a dog, a cock, and a snake grieve as well: like Siddhartha, the prints suggest, Saigō strove for the salvation of all

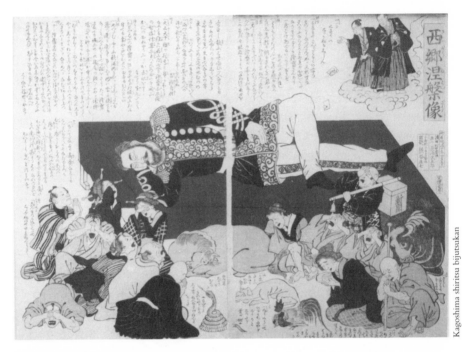

Saigō Attains Nirvana
Saigō nehanzō in the Kagoshima shiritsu bijutsukan

sentient beings. For a Japanese audience this was roughly equivalent to depicting Saigō on the cross, although the *Saigō nehanzō* lacked any sacrilegious overtones. Saigō could be a Buddha without impugning the dignity of the historical Buddha, Siddhartha.[18]

These strange transformations were symbolic but powerful. In nineteenth-century Japan the boundary between the world of the living and the world of the dead was porous and indistinct. The souls of powerful men outlasted their physical bodies. Ghosts were serious concerns. Most Japanese believed that the souls of the deceased returned to the world of the living each summer for a brief visit. Japanese villages staged folk dances called *bon odori* every July or August to welcome these ghosts. Dressed in cotton summer kimono, villagers would dance to the sounds of singing, hand clapping, drums, gongs, and flutes. These festivities can be traced to the ritual appeasement of angry spirits, although the ghosts of farmers were commonly less feared than the ghosts of warriors. In some villages, the souls of the dead, once properly welcomed by their relatives, were thought to join in the dancing.

Powerful souls such as Saigō's were matters of special concern, and a potent soul such as Saigō's could be expected to exact punishment on his enemies. By Japanese tradition such potent ghosts could be appeased only when their enemies enshrined them as gods *(kami)* and made appropriate ritual offerings. The most famous case of a wrathful kami is Sugawara Michizane (845–903). An administrator, a poet, and a scholar of great distinction, Sugawara rose beyond his birth status to the second-highest post in the imperial administration. In 901 he was falsely accused of treachery by his enemies and was reassigned from the capital, Kyoto, to a demeaning provincial post. There he died two years later, separated from his family and friends. In the years following his death, Sugawara's enemies began to die under mysterious circumstances: hunting accidents, lightning strikes, and unexplained illnesses. These tragedies were widely attributed to Sugawara's spirit. Sugawara's ghost was finally appeased in 947 when, by imperial decree, a shrine was erected to honor the scholar and poet. Sugawara became a god—Tenman daijizai tenjin, commonly known as Tenjin. Tenjin is a strangely dualistic deity. He is widely associated with scholarship. To this day students preparing for high school and college entrance exams commonly purchase amulets at Tenjin shrines. But he also is a potent and wrathful deity, a manifestation of the Thunder Lord (Raikō), who smites his enemies.[19] Such concerns were clearly on the mind of the artist who created the nirvana print *Saigō nehanzō*. The commoners in the print are praying for Saigō's return "even as a ghost," but the priests, mindful of the dangers of a wrathful spirit, are praying for his soul to find repose so he will not return as a vengeful spirit.

Saigō's transformation into a celestial being was thus a modern gloss on an ancient tradition of ghosts and gods. And if a poet and administrator such as Sugawara could wreak havoc on his enemies, what might Saigō's rivals expect? The Japanese government could not quite admit to fear of Saigō's ghost, but they could not ignore his enduring appeal to the Japanese public. Saigō had become a symbol of principled resistance to the imperial government. The Japanese intelligentsia had embraced him as honorable and incorruptible, as a symbol of everything the "new" Japan was not. The public remained enamored of tales of Saigō's survival. Even as a dead man, Saigō was dangerous. Rather than fight Saigō's legend, the government ultimately embraced it. On February 22, 1889, Saigō was pardoned of all crimes against the state and restored to imperial court rank. His pardon was part of a general amnesty commemorating one of the new state's crowning achievements: the promulgation of the Meiji constitution on February 11. No longer a rebel, Saigō was rapidly transformed into an exemplar of Japanese virtue, celebrated in school textbooks.

The pardon of Saigō enshrined his status as Japan's favorite rebel. Saigō was a traitor, but he was now an imperially approved traitor. These contradictory impulses—rebellion and reverence for authority—had long shaped Saigō's life. His strange status as a revered rebel and a loyal traitor had also shaped his death.

Saigō's rehabilitation was years away on the morning of September 24, 1877, but the search for Saigō's head foreshadowed the Meiji government's change of heart. It is not surprising that Saigō's comrades sought to hide his head. They were determined to deny the Meiji government the triumph of possessing it. What is surprising is the government's response. Even without Saigō's head, the state could be quite sure that Saigō was dead. They had a huge cadaver (Saigō was nearly six feet tall) with a distinctive scar on the right arm: this was certainly Saigō's body. But the Meiji state was fighting against a legend who had, in the popular press, begun his ascent to heaven even before his death. A physical victory against Saigō's body was incomplete without a symbolic victory over the Saigō legend. The search for Saigō's head was emblematic of the government's deep ambivalence toward the legacy of samurai tradition and its confusion over what to revere and what to vilify. To understand the search for Saigō's head is, at one level, to understand how Saigō came to represent samurai valor and how the Meiji government grappled with the samurai culture. Where, then, was Saigō Takamori's head on September 24, 1877, and why did it matter? Those are the questions we will now seek to answer.

Chapter 1

"POWERFULLY SENTIMENTAL"

Saigō's Early Years in Satsuma*

Saigō's Birthplace

Saigō was born in Kagoshima, a castle town and the capital of Satsuma domain. Kagoshima was, depending on one's perspective, a primitive backwater or Japan's gateway to the world. Viewed from the shogun's capital of Edo (now Tokyo) or the imperial capital of Kyoto, Kagoshima was remote in the extreme: it lay at the far southwestern corner of Kyūshū, the southernmost of the four main islands of Japan. Ōsumi, one of the three provinces that comprised Satsuma domain, means "big corner": if Kyoto and Edo were the center of Japan, then Satsuma was at the periphery. The overland route from Edo to Kagoshima was nearly a thousand miles; the speediest couriers took two weeks to bring news from Edo. Natives of Satsuma spoke a dialect of Japanese virtually unintelligible to the rest of Japan. Popular literature reinforced this image of Kagoshima as primitive. In his famous collection of erotic fiction, Ihara Saikaku described Satsuma as "remote and backward."[1]

---

*This description of Saigō in his youth is from the recollections of Ōkubo Toshimichi. See *STZ* 6:631.

On the other hand, Satsuma was a link to the outside world. Before the 1630s traders coming up from China often made their first stop in Satsuma, and the domain became an entry point for new goods and technologies. The Japanese word for sweet potato, for example, is *satsumaimo,* or "Satsuma potato": the tuber was brought to Japan from China through Satsuma. (In Satsuma, however, term is *karaimo,* or "Chinese potato.")[2] Guns also first arrived in Japan through Satsuma, specifically the island of Tanegashima in 1543. An early Japanese term for matchlock was *tanegashima,* reflecting the weapon's point of arrival. When nineteenth-century students from Satsuma produced one of the first Japanese-English dictionaries, *satsuma jisho,* or "Satsuma dictionary," was briefly a term for Japanese-English dictionary.

Satsuma's extensive contact with the world outside Japan had a political dimension as well as a geographical one. The domain had a special relationship with the kingdom of the Ryukyus, now the Japanese prefecture of

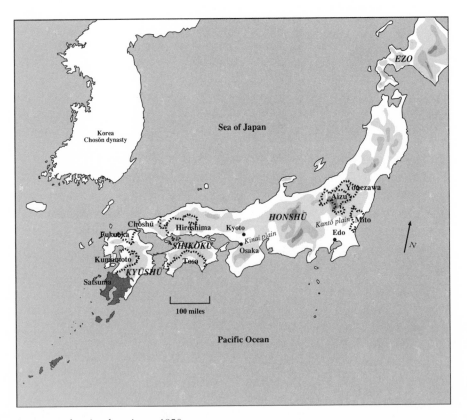

Satsuma and major domains, c. 1850

Okinawa. Satsuma conquered the Ryukyuan capital of Naha in 1609 and thereafter demanded tribute from the Ryukyuan kings as a sign of their sub-jugation. The daimyo of Satsuma, the Shimazu house, used this relationship to elevate their status within Japan: they were the only daimyo house to receive an oath of fealty from a foreign king. Externally, however, the Shimazu took great pains to conceal their power over the Ryukyus. The great value of the kingdom was as an economic bridge to China. According to Chinese diplomatic protocol, the Ryukyuan king was a Chinese vassal, and Satsuma had no desire to imperil trade by challenging this relationship. Thus Japanese officials in the Ryukyus concealed all signs of their presence before the arrival of Chinese diplomatic personnel: they left the capital, Naha, for a nearby village and ordered the Ryukyuans to hide all records of their presence. Chinese diplomats suspected that something was afoot but never disputed the arrangement.[3] The Shimazu were not alone in handling foreign trade. The Tokugawa shogunate entrusted trade with Japan's trading post in Pusan, Korea, to the Sō house of Tsushima domain, and the Matsumae house of Matsumae domain managed trade with the northern frontier of Ezo. But the Shimazu's position was uniquely prestigious: the shogunate ordered them to "rule" over the Ryukyuan kingdom.[4]

In Kagoshima itself there was a sizable Ryukyuan embassy, known as the Ryukyukan, which handled diplomatic affairs between the governments. The Ryukyuan community was probably never more than a few hundred people, but it had a marked impact on the city. A nineteenth-century visi-tor from Edo reported that people took no notice of Ryukyuans but greeted travelers from Edo with quiet laughter.[5] Small as it was, the Ryukyukan community was nevertheless one of the largest foreign com-munities in Japan. In the seventeenth century the Tokugawa shoguns had drastically restricted travel to and from Japan. Japanese who left Japan were barred under penalty of death from ever returning, and oceangoing ships were prohibited. Dutch and Chinese merchants were restricted to Nagasaki.[6]

The Shimazu were distinctive in other ways as well. Not only did they receive foreign ambassadors, but also they were the oldest surviving warrior house in Japan. Few daimyo families could comfortably trace their lineage past the 1500s. Most of the daimyo of the early modern era rose from lower status during the intense civil warfare of the fifteenth and sixteenth cen-turies. Even the ancestors of the Tokugawa shoguns were but a minor warrior family in the 1540s. The Shimazu, by contrast, traced their lineage as warlords back to Japan's first shogunate, the Kamakura regime (1185–1333). In 1185 Minamoto Yoritomo, Japan's first shogun, appointed Koremune Tadahisa as a military steward *(geshi)* over Shimazu *shō,* a large investiture in what is now Kagoshima Prefecture. In 1197 he promoted Tadahisa to military governor *(shugo)* of the province, and the following year Tadahisa changed his family name to match his investiture. This is where the Shimazu daimyo began their genealogies. Remarkably, historians have traced the Shimazu back even farther, to an imperial courtier family in the sixth century and, with less certainty, to an émigré noble house from the Korean peninsula. But as daimyo preferred warrior ancestors to courtiers, Tadahisa became the official progenitor of the Shimazu line.[7]

This extraordinary genealogy shaped the thinking of Saigō and his cohort. Satsuma samurai could take unique pride in serving the Shimazu, who had ruled the same territory uninterruptedly for more than six centuries. The Shimazu, in fact, proved more durable than the shoguns who invested them: they developed an independent base of power and survived the collapse of the Kamakura shogunate in the 1330s. The second shogunate, known as the Muromachi or Ashikaga shogunate, confirmed Shimazu authority over Satsuma. After the collapse of the Ashikaga regime in the 1400s, Japan deteriorated into pervasive civil war, and the Shimazu, like many daimyo, expended great effort suppressing obstreperous vassals. Unlike many daimyo, however, the Shimazu emerged victorious, and they consolidated and expanded their territories. In the unification struggles of the late 1500s, the Shimazu opposed Japan's preeminent warlords. The Shimazu fought against Toyotomi Hideyoshi in the 1580s and lost their territorial gains in northern Kyūshū. They also opposed the founder of Japan's third shogunate, Tokugawa Ieyasu. In the great Battle of Sekigahara in 1600, the Shimazu and the Tokugawa fought on opposing sides: Tokugawa Ieyasu led the eastern alliance, while the Shimazu fought with the western alliance. The Tokugawa won. Ieyasu's appointment as shogun in 1603 confirmed his supremacy and inaugurated the 265-year reign of the Tokugawa dynasty, Japan's most durable shogunate. To reward his allies and enhance his own holdings, Ieyasu seized millions of acres of land, taking all or part of his enemies' territory. Remarkably, Ieyasu left Shimazu holdings untouched. Although defeated, the Shimazu were still a formidable enemy, and Ieyasu had reason to avoid a fight. Furthermore, because Kagoshima was nearly a thousand miles from the shogun's new capital, Edo, the Shimazu were unlikely to attack the shogunate.[8] The result was a compromise. The Shimazu recognized the supremacy of the shogunate and performed the appropriate acts of obeisance, such as signing an oath of loyalty in blood. For his part, Ieyasu confirmed Shimazu control over their traditional lands in southwestern Kyūshū.

The Tokugawa settlement of the early 1600s still affected politics two centuries later. Having opposed the Tokugawa in 1600, the Shimazu were labeled *tozama daimyō,* or "outside" lords. *Tozama* lords were barred from holding posts in the shogun's administration and excluded from decisions in national politics. Most of the great lords of the southwest were tozama lords, as were most of the daimyo with large holdings. Daimyo who had won Ieyasu's trust before 1600 were commonly enfiefed as *fudai daimyō,* or vassal lords. This distinction between fudai and tozama lords became a cornerstone of daimyo politics: even in Saigō's day, key shogunal offices were reserved for fudai.[9] The fact that daimyo with important shogunal posts were far more invested in the strength of the shogunate than were tozama lords shaped Japan's response to imperialism in the 1850s and 1860s. Many tozama lords pushed for a power-sharing arrangement that would give them a voice in international affairs. Fudai lords were far more wedded to traditional power structures and supported the shogun's exclusive authority over diplomatic matters. The Shimazu were arguably the quintessential tozama lords. They did not openly challenge the shogunate until the 1860s, but they were remarkably independent in civil and diplomatic affairs. The Shimazu thought of themselves less as warlord vassals of the Tokugawa than as Tokugawa equals who had lost a key battle. During the last years of the Tokugawa shogunate, the Shimazu grew particularly brazen, sending an independent delegation to the 1867 International Exhibition in Paris that represented not Japan, but the kingdom of Satsuma and the Ryukyus.

Today the Shimazu no longer rule, but they remain a distinct presence in Kagoshima. The Shimazu descendants are active in tourism, including taxis, hotels, and museums, so any visitor to Kagoshima is likely to meet an employee of the Shimazu. The seal of Kagoshima City is clearly derived from the Shimazu family crest. Nowhere else in Japan are the descendants of feudal warlords as visible in contemporary daily life.

Saigō's homeland, the Shimazu family territories, was a huge domain, encompassing not only the province of Satsuma but also the province of Ōsumi and the southwestern part of the province of Hyūga. With these three provinces, known collectively as Satsuma domain, the Shimazu ruled the entire southern tip of Kyūshū, an area of more than thirty-five hundred square miles. The Shimazu holdings were also among the most populous in early modern Japan: in the 1870s roughly 760,000 people lived in Satsuma domain. Only three domains had larger populations: Kaga, Nagoya, and Hiroshima. The Tokugawa shoguns commonly ranked daimyo by the official rice harvest; by this standard the Shimazu had the second-largest investiture in Japan, smaller only than the Maeda holdings in Kaga.[10]

In the center of Kagoshima City lay Tsurumaru Castle, a strikingly unimpressive fortress built in 1602 as a residence for the daimyo Shimazu Iehisa. Tsurumaru was more a villa than a fortress. The castle had an inner keep *(honmaru)* and outer enceinte *(ni-no-maru),* but nothing in either section was designed to repel a sustained attack. Although the castle originally had steep stone walls and a small moat, it lacked the high, multistory towers common in castles of the late sixteenth and early seventeenth centuries. Shirasagi Castle in Himeiji, for example, now a tourist landmark because of its striking beauty, has a towering six-story keep and three small keeps. Moats, turrets, steep walls, and battlements surround the castle. Routes into Shirasagi are circuitous and deceptive: the inner passages form a maze of blind alleys. By contrast, Tsurumaru's fortifications were both minimal and poorly maintained. A mid-eighteenth-century report on the castle observed, with some exaggeration, "although diagrams of the keep and enceinte show turrets, walls and moats, these do not actually exist." Access to the castle was surprisingly straightforward: a small bridge led directly from Kagoshima City, across the moat, and into the enceinte.[11]

Why did Iehisa build such a simple and poorly defended castle? Today a plaque in front of the castle ruins tells the visitor that the Shimazu did not need an elaborate castle because "the people are their fortress." This is an appealingly populist explanation, but it is seriously misleading. Kagoshima was defended, against both invaders and its own peasants, by a dense network of castles: in Saigō's day more than a hundred small fortresses, called *tojō,* dotted the landscape. Tsurumaru Castle had no defenses because they were not needed: with fortresses throughout the domain, a large central castle would have been redundant. The Shimazu system of rural fortresses was technically a violation of Tokugawa policy, which in 1615 had limited each daimyo to one castle. The Shimazu ignored the order, and the Tokugawa chose not to contest their decision. The Shimazu network of castles meant

Shōkō shūseikan, Kagoshima

Tsurumaru Castle (Tsurumarujō)

that the Satsuma countryside was under constant samurai surveillance. In most domains the vast majority of samurai lived in the daimyo's castle town, and peasant villages enjoyed a margin of self-governance. In Satsuma, however, thousands of low-ranking samurai lived in the countryside, and even the lowliest details of village life were part of samurai rule.[12]

Kagoshima was a sizable city, with a nineteenth-century population of roughly seventy thousand. The vast majority of its residents, perhaps 70 percent, were samurai and their families.[13] Like most warrior capitals, the city of Kagoshima was explicitly hierarchical in its layout. At the center was the daimyo's castle, the political and administrative heart of the domain. Nearest the castle were government offices and the residences of the domain's elite retainers. Next were the residences of lower retainers: the government's middle managers and staff. Last were commoners' residences, which banded the city to the north and south. There lived the artisans and merchants whose activities made urban life possible. In classic castle towns, such as the shogun's capital of Edo, the city's hierarchy resembled a series of concentric rings centered on the lord's castle. Kagoshima resembled this model, but was constrained by a topography that bounded the city to the west by Mount Shiroyama and to the east by Kinkō Bay. The mountain and the sea pressed the standard pattern of rings into a series of bands.

Immediately in front of the castle lay a broad avenue known as Sengoku baba, or, in loose but effective translation, "Millionaire Avenue." Sengoku, or one thousand *koku,* referred to the annual income of the residents. A *koku* was just under five bushels, and one thousand *koku* was, by any measure, a lot of rice. Some residents of Sengoku baba had investitures in excess of ten thousand *koku.* Had these men been direct vassals of the shogun, rather than vassals of the Shimazu, they would have ranked as daimyo in their own right and enjoyed direct audiences with the shogun. The residents of Sengoku baba were the daimyo's senior advisers. They had storied ancestries and privileged access to the daimyo. Some were the lord's distant cousins, descendants of the younger brothers of earlier daimyo, whose residences reflected their wealth and power. The typical residence in Sengoku baba was a large compound surrounded by stone or stucco walls. This housed not only the retainer and his families but also his aides and servants. In Satsuma, as in many domains, the samurai elite was virtually a class unto itself. While Saigō's parents struggled to keep clothes on their growing children, the residents of Sengoku baba agonized over the details of castle protocol and the architecture of their carp ponds.[14]

Just south of this inner district, along the banks of the Kōtsuki River, lay the residences of middle and lower retainers. These were the men who staffed the daimyo's government, drafting correspondence, compiling government edicts, tallying tax receipts, and implementing the policies formulated by their superiors. Lower and middling retainers lived in one of four wards: Arata-machi, Kōrei-machi, Uenosono-machi, and Kajiya-machi. Arata, Kōrei, and Uenosono Wards lay southwest of the Kōtsuki River, while Kajiya-machi lay northeast, tucked away in a river bend. Because Kajiya was on the castle side of the river, it was nominally more prestigious than the other three wards. Kajiya was itself subdivided into two districts: Upper Kajiya (Uenokajiya) and Lower Kajiya (Shitanokajiya). "Upper" in this context meant northwest, or nearer the castle. Lower Kajiya, the less distinguished half of an undistinguished district, was a grouping of roughly eighty residences. The district was crosscut by narrow streets and broad avenues. Colorful street names such as "Cat Shit Alley" (Neko no kuso koro) made it clear that Shitanokajiya was not the high-rent district. The homes were small, single-family residences, with compact gardens and bamboo fences. The district was densely populated, with most plots less than five thousand square feet. On one of the side streets was a slightly larger home, just over ten thousand square feet, belonging to Saigō Kichibei, father of Saigō Takamori.[15] Nearby were the homes of a remarkable number of future leaders: Ōkubo Toshimichi, Saigō's childhood friend, political ally, and eventually the principal architect of the modern Japanese state; Ōyama Iwao, Saigō's cousin and a future army chief of staff and lord privy seal; and Tōgō Heihachirō, later chief of the naval general staff and Japan's most respected admiral.

From Saigō's home the dominant sight was Sakurajima, or "Cherry Blossom Island." Sakurajima lay roughly three miles east of Kajiya-machi, across Kinkō Bay. Strictly speaking, Sakurajima is no longer an island. A massive eruption in 1914 poured lava and ash into the bay, creating an isthmus. "Cherry Island" became the tip of a promontory extending into Kinkō Bay from the Ōsumi peninsula. Sakurajima erupts with great regularity—an average of several times a week—and dumps a constant layer of ash on the surrounding area. The volcanic ash makes the soil on Sakurajima especially fertile, and in the 1800s thousands of farmers lived on the island. The island was a major source for one of the region's specialties, mandarin oranges.

Saigō never witnessed the havoc Sakurajima could cause, but in his youth people still remembered the volcano's huge eruption of 1779. The eruption began on the evening of the 9/29, when tremors rocked the island. On 10/1, at 11:00 A.M., the volcano began to seethe, turning the surrounding ocean a brilliant purple. That afternoon Sakurajima exploded, producing a plume of gas and volcanic debris more than seven miles high. The volcano rained ash over the island for five days, devastating nearby villages. A thick blanket of ash buried virtually all of the island's farmland. One hundred thirty people were killed, and more than five hundred homes were destroyed. The eruption wiped out the orange crop: more than twenty-one thousand trees were destroyed. The devastation was so severe that the Shimazu were unable to make their traditional year-end gift of oranges to the shogun.[16]

Saigō's Lineage

Saigō traced his lineage to an illustrious warrior family, the Kikuchi clan of Higo Province in central Kyūshū. The Kikuchi lineage was renowned for its valiant service in defense of the emperor and against foreign invaders. The clan first distinguished itself during the Jürchen invasion of northern Kyūshū in 1019. The family rose to prominence during the Mongol invasion of Japan in 1281, when the heroism of Kikuchi Takefusa (1245–1285) helped drive back the enemy. The family also was active in the Kenmu Restoration (1333–1336), an attempt by the emperor Go-Daigo to reassert imperial authority against the Kamakura shogunate.[†] The conflict between Go-Daigo and the shogunate centered on succession to the imperial throne. Whereas Go-Daigo demanded the authority to name his own heir, the shogunate insisted on maintaining a thirteenth-century compromise whereby the two rival branches of the imperial line would succeed to the throne in turn. Go-Daigo refused to compromise, and in 1331 he launched a coup against the shogunate. Takefusa's grandson Kikuchi Taketoki (?–1333) joined Go-Daigo's cause. The coup failed, Taketoki was killed, and Go-Daigo was sent into internal exile. Ironically, this failure strengthened the imperial cause: Go-Daigo's supporters, galvanized by his poor treatment, reorganized and destroyed the shogunate in 1333. Once in power, however, Go-Daigo showed strikingly little appreciation for his warrior allies. In the name of imperial rule he sought to strengthen central control at the expense of the regional authority of the warrior class. Although many of his edicts were strikingly innovative, he described his policies as a return to the eighth century, an era before the rise of independent warrior power. In a striking miscalculation he named as shogun his own son, crown prince Morinaga, aggressively slighting the generals who had restored him to the throne. This disregard for warrior privilege alienated Go-Daigo's supporters and undermined his government. In 1335 Ashikaga Takauji, one of Go-Daigo's erstwhile allies, drove him from Kyoto and installed as emperor a member of the rival lineage. Three years later Takauji arranged his own appointment as shogun, founding the Ashikaga shogunate, the second of Japan's three shogunal dynasties. The Kikuchi, however, remained loyal to Go-Daigo. Taketoki's son Takemitsu (?–1373) continued to defend Go-Daigo's line, known as the Southern Court, and fought with Go-Daigo's son Kaneyoshi against the Ashikaga shogunate. The imperial succession

---

[†]The English terms "Kenmu Restoration" and "Meiji Restoration" suggest a parallelism that does not exist in Japanese. The original Japanese terms are *Kenmu shinsei* and *Meiji ishin. Shinsei* means new government, whereas *ishin* means a renovation or restoration of something old. The terms are similar but not identical.

dispute was resolved in 1392, but the resolution represented a victory for the Northern Court. The two lines again agreed to alternate succession, but in practice the Northern line never relinquished control. The current Japanese emperor descends from the Northern Court. The Southern Court effectively vanished.[17]

Despite its failure, Go-Daigo's cause became a touchstone for imperial loyalism. Ashikaga's attack on Go-Daigo became a symbol of treachery, and the entire Ashikaga shogunate was tainted by its founder's duplicity. Ironically, the Northern lineage had a better genealogical claim on the throne, and this made the issue politically explosive, most recently in the twentieth centruy. By Saigō's day, however, there was a remarkable consensus on Ashikaga Takauji. Whichever side was legitimate in the court dispute, Takauji had betrayed his master, and not only nativist and Shinto scholars but also Confucian intellectuals deemed Takauji a vile usurper, symbolic of everything treacherous.

The symbolism of the Northern and Southern Court dispute took on new meaning in the last years of the Tokugawa shogunate. For Saigō and his cohort this fourteenth-century conflict seemed immediately relevant to their own struggle. In the 1860s, when the imperial court and the Tokugawa shogun clashed openly over foreign policy, the Ashikaga became a metaphor for shogunal arrogance. In 1863/2/22, for example, imperial loyalists broke into Tōji-in Temple in Kyoto and beheaded the statues of three Ashikaga shoguns: Takauji, Yoshiakira, and Yoshimitsu. The heads turned up days later on a stand by the Kamo River, exposed for public display like the heads of executed criminals. A note on the stand read, "since these three traitors did the worst evil, their vile statues have been visited with the vengeance of heaven." For those utterly opaque to historical reference, the vandals posted a helpful note on a public notice board, warning unspecified persons not to repeat the treachery of the Ashikaga. If these unnamed traitors did not "immediately repent" and "return to the ancient practice of assisting the court," then loyal samurai would "punish them for their crimes." The decapitation of the shogunal statues alarmed the Tokugawa shogunate, since no one could miss the symbolism. The vandals had metaphorically assassinated the shogun and were threatening to move beyond metaphor.[18]

There is no hard evidence to link Saigō to the Kikuchi clan, but Saigō himself believed earnestly in this genealogy. When in exile on Amami

Ōshima he began to use the pseudonym Kikuchi Gengo, explicitly linking himself to the fourteenth-century loyalists. His friends honored this, addressing their letters to "great lord Kikuchi" *(Kikuchi taikun).*[19] Saigō himself explicitly linked his own proimperial activism with the defense of Go-Daigo four centuries earlier. For a man sent into internal exile by his own lord, the legacy of the Kikuchi was particularly comforting. Taketoki and Takemitsu were failures in their own lifetimes but were ultimately redeemed as defenders of justice and honor.[20] Through the Kikuchi genealogy Saigō could blunt the sting of political failure and associate himself with near-legendary heroes. The Kikuchi genealogy also reinforced Saigō's support for the imperial cause and his suspicion of the shogunate. His descent from the Kikuchi made challenging shogunal arrogance a point of family honor.[21]

Saigō's Family

About Saigō's parents we know little. His father, Saigō Kichibei (1807–1852), was a division chief in the domain's office of the exchequer, the agency responsible for taxation. He held the rank of *koshōgumi,* which was eighth in the hierarchy of ten samurai ranks. Men in the two lowest ranks—*yoriki* and *ashigaru*—were generally restricted to menial posts such as guard duty, so Kichibei was, by rank, near the bottom of "white-collar" urban samurai. As a section head he had effectively risen to the top of his station. He had a reputation as hardworking, loyal, and unconcerned with material gain. About Saigō's mother, Masa (?–1852), we know still less. She was the daughter of Shiibara Ken'emon, a local samurai. In later years Saigō remembered her as even-tempered and sympathetic.[22]

Saigō was born on 1827/12/7 as his parents' first child. Following the custom of the day, Saigō changed his given name several times during his lifetime. Names, in premodern Japan, were not absolute markers of one's identity, but relative markers of one's age, status, and position. A samurai's name changed as he aged. An infant, a boy, a married household head, and a retired household head each had different responsibilities, so a change in name was only natural. As an infant Saigō was known as Saigō Kokichi and Saigō Jūroku, but at age seven he took the name Kichinosuke. At adulthood he took the name Takamori. On 1853/2/10, after his father's death, Saigō filed official papers changing his given name to Zenbei, and on 1858/10/8 he changed his name to Sansuke, but in personal correspondence continued to use Kichinosuke, then Zenbei and Kichibei. Saigō also is commonly referred to by a pen name he adopted during his exile, Saigō Nanshū, or Saigō of the South. Like his contemporaries, Saigō could use several names at once: an official name for work, a colloquial name among friends, and a variety of pen names for poems.[23]

Saigō was the eldest of seven children, four sons and three daughters. The youngest child, Kohei (1847–1877), was nearly twenty years Saigō's junior. The Saigō household also included Kichibei's parents, Saigō Ryūzaemon (?–1852) and his wife (1775–1862), and the family of Kichibei's younger brother Kohei, so at its maximum the family totaled sixteen people. Kichibei's income as a tax official never met his family's needs. The family home in Shitanokajiya was a ramshackle affair, in constant disrepair. Because the family was short of bedding, Saigō slept with his siblings crowded under a single blanket *(futon)*. This was especially onerous because the children were so large: Saigō men commonly reached six feet as adults. In 1855 the family moved across the river to Uenosono, but their new home was equally dilapidated. Saigō's sister-in-law Iwayama Toku recalled that "the house in Uenosono was really a decrepit thing. The floor sagged like a duck's nest."[24]

The Saigō family managed to make ends meet by borrowing and farming. In 1847 and 1848, for example, Saigō Takamori and his father borrowed a total of 200 gold ryō from the Itagaki family, who were wealthy landowners in Mizuhiki district, now a part of Kagoshima City. This was an astonishing sum, equal to several years' income for most samurai or craftsmen. The Saigō family had no collateral save their name and were, in fact, unable to make regular payments. Only in 1872, when Saigō was an imperial councilor *(sangi)* of the Meiji government, was the family able to begin repaying the debt.[25]

With borrowed money the family bought land for farming. The records here are spotty, but we know that the family owned at least one parcel in Nishi beppu, now a part of Kagoshima City. Tax records list the land as owner-cultivated and held by Saigō Kichibei, Saigō's father. Iwayama Toku recalls that Kichijirō, Saigō's younger brother, used to go out to Nishi beppu, collect firewood, bring it back to the samurai quarters on a packhorse, and sell it door to door. It is unclear whether Takamori himself ever stood in a paddy field and planted rice, but, as eldest son and heir, he was intimately familiar with the finances of family farming.[26]

Even with this extra income, the Saigō family lived frugally. The women of the house did the menial work of cleaning and washing, and Iwayama later recalled being mistaken for a maidservant by a visitor.[27] These strained circumstances shaped young Takamori's personality and philosophy. His father, Kichibei, was formally a full samurai *(shi* or *jōkashi),* and the family should, in theory, have lived off of his stipend. But in practice the Saigō family lived more like *gōshi:* self-sufficient rural warriors. *Gōshi* were descendants of the bottom of the military class and were relegated to the countryside, where they governed and controlled the peasantry. As urban samurai, the Saigō were legally superior to the *gōshi.* The gap between urban, true samurai and *gōshi* was so great that if a samurai felt that a *gōshi* had impugned his honor, he was legally entitled to strike him dead. Because the conflict involved a defense of honor, it was not murder, and the samurai needed only to convince his superiors of the gravity of the affront. While young Takamori, as a full samurai, was a member of this elite, economically he lived more like a *gōshi.* The clash between nominal and practical status was a daily experience for Saigō.[28]

This tension between formal status and daily life instilled in Takamori a deep sense of honor and humility. Saigō could not revel in the perquisites of elite status, but he could ennoble his poverty with stoicism and dignity. In 1872, when he finally repaid part of his twenty-five-year-old loan from the Itagaki, Saigō offered an apology so extensive it all but exalted insolvency.

> I arrived safely yesterday in the retinue of his majesty so kindly overlook [the haste of my note]. Years ago my late father borrowed from you and and in the years since, my brothers and I, having experienced much hardship, did not come visit you at all, and let our debt sit as is. For this I am at a loss for words. . . . Last year, when I went to the capital, I was burdened with a major government office, and I was overwhelmed. This important appointment, for which I am most unworthy, is a result of your lending my father a large amount of money, which enabled my late father to raise many children and which opened this path for me. This my father told me time and time again. Because I sincerely want to repay you, I have sought many ways, but I simply cannot find a way to repay the debt; furthermore, I can

but pay only one year's interest, and for this, I offer my apologies. I had hoped to make this homecoming an occasion on which to ease my late father's worries, but since we are a landless family with many dependents, even the basic task of repaying all the interest and principal at once is beyond us. I ask your forbearance on this matter.[29]

In some ways the note reveals too well Takamori's attitudes toward money. It is unclear from his letter whether he is repaying the principal, some interest, or both. Only from the Itagaki's response do we know that Saigō enclosed 400 yen: the principal and roughly eight years' interest. The Itagaki, diplomatically, refused to accept the interest and returned 200 yen.[30]

Saigō learned to revel in his privileged but humble circumstances. In later years, when his finances were less strained, he rejected expensive clothes and furnishings. These were not, he argued, things of interest to a samurai. His favorite pastime in adulthood, hunting with his dogs, was something appropriate for a samurai boy of humble means. He would relax by making his own hunting sandals out of straw, or by making his own fishing lures. Saigō's preference for simple, traditional pleasures distinguished him from his colleagues in the Meiji government who used their new wealth and influence to entertain in Western style, hosting, for example, European-style costume balls. For Saigō, such lavish novelties were emblems of a revolution gone bad.[31]

Saigō's Education

Saigō was educated in a two-tiered school system: he attended both a local school and the central domain academy. All samurai boys in the castle town, save a few members of the elite, attended neighborhood schools called *gojū*. The *gojū* were fraternities as much as schools: hazings were a central part of the *gojū* experience, and boys spent much of their time learning the martial arts and preparing for local festivals. Although the *gojū* did provide a solid rudimentary education, the emphasis was on group solidarity and discipline. Boys fourteen and older served as teachers for the younger members, and each *gojū* was expected to function as a military unit in time of war. *Gojū* regulations emphasized honor, courage, honesty, and exclusivity: younger members were not to speak to members of another *gojū*.[32]

The *gojū* had their origins in the 1590s, when the Shimazu, under the orders of the Toyotomi Hideyoshi, mobilized their samurai for the invasion of Korea. After Satsuma dispatched roughly ten thousand men, this left the castle town with thousands of unsupervised samurai boys. To control these rowdy youths, the domain organized the antecedents of the *gojū* system. Boys were assigned to groups based on their neighborhood and directed to uphold standards of good behavior. The domain's edict from 1596 enjoined members from lawbreaking, strong language, and duplicity. Boys were exhorted to be brave and exemplify the way of the warrior.[33]

In the mid-eighteenth century this simple system of social control was adapted to provide a basic education for samurai boys. The castle town was divided into districts called *gojū:* in the early 1800s Kagoshima had eighteen of these districts, but by the 1860s it had more than thirty. *Gojū* were largely self-regulating. Each district had its own leader, its own headquarters, and its own code of conduct. A few districts had special buildings especially for *gojū* activities, but most used private homes. Boys in each district were organized into two main groups: the younger boys, or *chigo,* and the elder boys, or *nise.*[34]

In common practice, boys joined the *gojū* at age five or six, which by Japanese reckoning was around the boy's seventh birthday.[‡] A boy's seventh birthday was the first of several occasions marking the transition from childhood to adulthood. In common practice a samurai father gave his son a *wakizashi,* a short sword without a sword guard, and took him to the *gojū* center for presentation to the leader *(nise gashira).* Although acceptance as a *chigo* was virtually automatic, the leader sternly reminded the boy of the importance of the *gojū.*[35]

New members were ranked as junior *chigo* and maintained a strict schedule with a curfew. They were not to leave their homes before 6:00 A.M. or after 6:00 P.M. At 6:00 A.M. they would hurry to the home of a local teacher, who would help them through a reading of the texts for that day, commonly excerpts from the Confucian classics. These lessons emphasized smooth reading and memorization rather than interpretation, and boys were often drilled to the point of tears. The teachers were commonly older

---

[‡]In Japanese tradition children are considered one, rather than zero, years old at birth, and turn two on New Year's Day of the following year.

boys, often the *nise* leader. This post was Saigō's first position of authority, and as *nise* leader he drilled several future leaders on the Chinese classics. His students included Ōyama Iwao, Tōgō Heihachirō, and his own brother Tsugumichi.[36] After their morning lessons, the *chigo* were briefly free to eat breakfast, to study on their own, or to help with household chores. At 8:00 A.M. they assembled for sports and exercise led by the senior *chigo*. Morning drill encompassed a wide range of activities, from sumo wrestling to horse driving. Some games, such as *Kōsan iwase,* or "Say uncle," focused as much on machismo as physical prowess: the assembled boys would knock over one player and then pile on top of him until the *chigo* leader called them off. From roughly 10:00 A.M. the boys had a second study period, led by the senior *chigo*. At these sessions boys would be grilled not only on their lessons but also on their behavior. After a midday break, the boys reassembled for further study at 2:00 P.M.[37]

The curriculum for *chigo* was distinctly parochial. The three core texts of *chigo* education—the *Rekidai uta, Iroha uta,* and *Toragari monogatari*—all focused on Satsuma and the Shimazu house. The most basic text, the *Iroha uta* (Alphabet Ode), was attributed to Shimazu Tadayoshi, a great warlord of the 1500s.[38] The ode was a set of forty-six homilies organized in the order of the Japanese syllabary. Its moral precepts were unexceptional: the ode exhorted students to study hard, to avoid vendettas, and to act with propriety. But in Satsuma even basic literacy was linked to the Shimazu house.[39] Other texts were similarly parochial. The *Toragari monogatari* (Tale of a Tiger Hunt), told the story of the Japanese invasion of Korea in the 1590s, but from the perspective of Shimazu forces. The *Rekidai uta* (Ode of the Generations), described the lineage of the Shimazu house, beginning with Shimazu Tadahisa in 1185. The ode duly made note of the imperial house and the various shoguns, but it described the Shimazu lords as monarchs in their own right. Of Shimazu Yoshihisa, who reunified Satsuma after the turmoil of the early 1500s, the ode observed that "he treated the people with virtue and they returned to the ways of humanity." In the language of Confucian discourse this meant that Yoshihisa was more a monarch than a mere warlord. By instilling virtue in the populace he had legitimized his military conquests. This implicitly established the independence of the Shimazu house and construed Tokugawa approval as incidental to the legitimacy of Shimazu rule.[40] In their later years, as *nise,* Shimazu boys studied a more varied curriculum, including the interpretation, rather than mere recitation, of the Confucian classics. At the core of *gojū* education, however, were the history and traditions of the Shimazu house.

At 4:00 P.M. the boys assembled outdoors for martial arts training led by the *nise.* Unlike the morning exercises, this session included serious training in swordsmanship. The boys practiced with wooden swords, but learned the techniques and tactics of real combat.[41] Swordsmanship in Satsuma was taught according to two schools: the Jigen school, developed by Tōgō Shigekata, and the Yakumaru school, a syncretic tradition developed by a Jigen disciple. The Jigen tradition was among the most traditional and aggressive of the major sword schools. While most schools in the nineteenth century used bamboo swords wrapped in cloth to minimize injuries, the Jigen school used traditional wooden swords. Most schools emphasized a combination of offensive and defensive tactics, the latter designed to exploit an opponent's mistakes. The Jigen school was relentlessly aggressive and emphasized striking a single, deadly blow.[42] The Yakumaru school was still more belligerent and emphasized the attacker's willingness to die. Not surprisingly, the Yakumaru school produced some of the most terrifying assassins of the 1860s. Some secondhand evidence suggests that Saigō was affiliated with the Yakumaru school.[43]

The boys practiced outdoors despite wind and rain, but on days of severe weather they played card games with historical themes. In *Musha karuta* the cards represented warriors famous for their loyalty, while *Daimyō karuta* taught the names, rank, and investitures of Japan's major warlords. The boys trained or played until 6:00 P.M., when they returned home. They were now under curfew and were not to leave their homes until the following day, at 6 A.M.[44]

Boys were eligible for promotion to senior *chigo* at age nine or ten. This promotion involved a formidable hazing. A common practice was to stuff the new initiate into the chest used for *gojū* records, tie the box shut, and roll it around the *gojū* headquarters. Another ritual was to wait until the *gojū* leader summoned the boy and then to jump on him and crush him. Senior *chigo* boys had new duties and responsibilities. Like junior *chigo,* they rose early for their lessons, but they were now teachers as well as students and supervised the junior *chigo*'s midmorning and afternoon lessons. While the junior *chigo* were on midday break, the senior *chigo* had lectures at the domain academy. After fencing practice the junior *chigo* were sent home, but the senior *chigo* continued their studies, supervised by the *nise.* From about 7:00 P.M. the senior *chigo* were allowed to watch the beginning of the *nise*'s evening conclave. At 8:00 P.M. the *nise* escorted the senior *chigo* home.[45]

At age thirteen or fourteen boys began the formal, public transition to adulthood. This was marked by three major rituals: a *genpuku* ceremony, an audience with the daimyo, and the promotion from *chigo* to *nise*. In a *genpuku* ceremony boys received adult clothing appropriate to their station; chose a new, adult name; and shaved the front of their heads, the forelocks. They grew the rest of their hair long and dressed it in a variety of ponytails, commonly known as topknots. In Saigō's day this hairstyle, originally developed to conform to warrior helmets, was a sign of manhood for both samurai and commoners. A man's hair immediately marked his sexual status. Shaved forelocks marked an adult man who could initiate sexual activity, either with his wife, a concubine, a prostitute, or a young boy. Forelocks, by contrast, marked either asexual youth, or the more passive, junior partner in a homosexual liaison.[46] At roughly the same time as their *genpuku*, boys of appropriate station had their first audience with the daimyo and received their first commissions. These were, in effect, internships during which boys worked from 10:00 A.M. to 2:00 P.M. and received the minimal stipend of four *koku* per annum. We can infer that Saigō graduated to *nise* sometime in the early 1840s: he received his *genpuku* in 1841, at age fourteen, and started work at the county office in 1844.[47]

The *nise* were exempted from curfew but kept a strict schedule. The *nise* leader was busy from sunrise teaching the local *chigo*. Other *nise* went to the domain academy for their morning lessons and then to their offices. From roughly 4:00 P.M. until 8:00 P.M. the *nise* taught or trained the older *chigo*. After escorting the *chigo* home, the *nise* were free for their own study and recreation. *Nise* commonly gathered again for further reading—in the Chinese classics, military chronicles, or local history.[48] The *nise* also grilled each other in a form of cross-examination known as *sengi*. The examiners posed hypothetical questions designed to test both mental agility and moral vigor. In a typical question, boys were asked what they would do if, after searching all Japan for their father's murderer, they at last found him out on the open seas. To complicate matters, the pursuer's boat was sinking, and the murderer represented the only possibility of rescue. The "correct" solution to this moral dilemma was to accept rescue, cordially thank the murderer, and then exact vengeance by striking him dead. Participants were grilled individually in front of the group and badgered until they could produce an adequate answer.[49]

The traditions of the *gojū* system ranged from refined and elegant to brutal and horrific. Samurai boys in Kagoshima, for example, were encouraged to master the *biwa,* a Japanese lute. In most of Japan the biwa was considered an effeminate instrument and was associated with geisha entertainment. In Satsuma, by contrast, the biwa was considered manly and virtuous. This regional difference was due largely to Shimazu Tadayoshi, who, according to legend, was inspired by a local monk's use of biwa music for sutra chanting, and commissioned songs celebrating loyalty, justice, and filial piety. Japanese travelers noted the distinctiveness of the Satsuma tradition. In *Seiyūki,* a popular travelogue written in the 1790s, Tachibana Nankei observed that "all young samurai play the biwa. In the brave and valorous tradition of those provinces, they hike up their trouser skirts, adjust their long swords and night after night stroll and play the biwa. Their playing is correct and their singing is refined. It is utterly unlike the biwa of other regions." It was common for young samurai to spend evenings on the banks of the Kōtsuki River, relaxing to the sounds of the reed flute *(amabuku)* and biwa.[50]

A sharp contrast to the Satsuma tradition of warrior lutists was a terrifying custom known as *hiemontori.* This was a competition for aspiring swordsmen held in the twelfth month of each year. The prize was the right to practice swordsmanship on a human cadaver. Although samurai regularly practiced with wooden swords, they rarely felt a blade cut flesh and bone. The *hiemontori* contest rewarded the bravest samurai with first slice at the body of an executed criminal. In common practice the *nise* would assemble at the domain prison at Seto. The boys waited for the executioner to sever the head of the condemned and then rushed forward to seize the corpse. The first to bite off an ear or finger and show it to his companions was deemed the winner and was awarded the first round of practice on the cadaver. Saigō's loyal compatriot Kirino Toshiaki and future prime minister Yamamoto Gonnohyōe were among the most zealous and successful competitors.[51]

The *gojū* system was an exclusively male institution. Activities celebrated the traditional male virtues of vigor, courage, and solidarity, but contact with women, other than family members, was proscribed. In Saigō's day none of this was unusual, but by the late 1800s Japanese writers were alarmed by the homoerotic overtones of *gojū* culture. Ballads extolling male beauty, and the close ties between *nise* and *chigo,* were suddenly seen as markers of a culture of homosexuality. By the early twentieth century the association of Satsuma with homosexuality was so widespread that male-male eroticism was described as a "Satsuma habit." In 1899 a major newspaper attributed homosexual conduct in the Japanese navy to the nefarious influence of Yamamoto Gonnohyōe, then naval minister. Even the 1873 conflict between Saigō and Ōkubo Toshimichi that almost toppled the Meiji state was attributed to a long-simmering dispute over a young boy that started when both were members of the same *gojū.*[52]

Was *gojū* culture gay? The question is both intriguing and anachronistic. "Homosexual," as a label for people, did not exist in Saigō's day: sex with men was a practice rather than an identity. Like drinking or fishing, one could enjoy homosexuality regularly, occasionally, or never, according to personal preference. Lacking a biblical story of Sodom, Tokugawa-era Japanese had no concept of sodomy, and Tokugawa-era laws did not criminalize homosexual conduct itself. Legal injunctions against male-male sexuality focused largely on the result of "outrageous" or "provocative" sexual conduct. Like consorting with geisha or drinking, male-male intercourse became a vice rather than a diversion only when taken to extremes. When Yonezawa domain issued regulations on homosexual activity in 1775, for example, it mentioned violence rather than perversion. Any conflict among a handsome young samurai, his father, and his lover could easily lead to drawn swords and mayhem. Homosexuality was a problem only because male lovers' quarrels tended to grow violent and threaten the public order. Defenders of homosexual conduct, however, considered male-male eroticism a natural extension of the bond between warriors. In his treatise on samurai conduct, Yamamoto Tsunetomo wrote that to die for one's lover was the highest form of loyalty. The only complication was a potential conflict with one's other obligations. "To lay down one's life for another is the basic principle of homosexuality. . . . However, then you have nothing left to lay down for your master." This contradiction would not arise if one's lover and lord were the same, and homosexual passion was often a part of *junshi,* the tradition of following one's lord into death. In this context of multiple and fluid conceptions of male-male eroticism, homosexuality probably was an incidental and unremarkable part of *gojū* life.[53]

Was Saigō gay? This question is both intriguing and incongruous. Saigō's letters make no reference to male lovers, and no contemporaneous account of his life mentions homosexual activity. Saigō, however, was remarkably reticent about his personal life, and his letters make only passing mention to his three wives. But more pointedly, Saigō's early letters reveal a man strikingly uninterested in sex of any kind. Saigō's attitudes were shaped largely by a tragic first marriage. He entered an arranged marriage in 1852, but his in-laws annulled it two years later, when Saigō was transferred to Edo. Bitter in the aftermath of his divorce, Saigō expressed his frustrations through sexual self-denial. From his new post in Edo he wrote: "Although I have enjoyed the capital, I have kept a monk's vows as regards women. The wife my parents arranged for me was driven away. . . . Although my marital vows are null and void even now I have no desire to marry again." Although Saigō would eventually remarry twice, father five children, and keep the company of a Kyoto geisha, in 1854 he prided himself on avoiding women entirely. He saw abstinence as empowering rather than constraining: he swore, for example, to keep a monk's vow of celibacy if his lord, Shimazu Nariakira, had a healthy male heir.[54] In his youth Saigō saw sex not as pleasurable dissipation or intimacy but as an impediment to happiness and loyalty.

How else did the *gojū* system influence Saigō? Given the popular image of Saigō as a great warrior, it is striking to realize that he served the *gojū* more as a scholar than as a fighter. The turning point for Saigō was a fateful day in 1839 when, returning home from the domain academy, he got into an altercation with another samurai. Swords were drawn, and Saigō suffered a serious injury on his right arm. The injury impeded his martial arts training and forced him to reassess his goals. From that point Saigō abandoned the martial arts and put his energies into scholarship. As a teacher rather than a fighter, Saigō readily distinguished himself: his selection as instructor for the *gojū* reveals the high regard in which he was held by his peers. Saigō's early experiences as a tutor shaped his adult life: even in his darkest moment Saigō took pleasure in teaching children. In 1858, when in internal exile on the remote island of Amami Ōshima, Saigō treated the locals with ill-concealed disdain but was unable to resist the local children. In a heart-wrenching letter to Ōkubo, he wrote of his crushing depression and isolation but reported, "I was implored by three or so island children and have accepted them [as students]."[55] Saigō found his place on the island as a schoolteacher. His despair gradually lifted and he was able to reconcile himself to internal exile. Three years later, on the tiny island of Okinoerabumajima, while under house arrest, Saigō taught local children the Confucian classics. His students included Misao Tankei, the son of the district constable.[56]

The *gojū* system was but a part of Saigō's education. Like most castle town samurai, Saigō received his more advanced education in the domain academy: the Zōshikan. Founded in 1773, the Zōshikan sat on roughly three acres near Tsurumaru Castle. The campus included a lecture hall, a library, a dormitory, and several shrines to the Confucian sages. The school had a staff of more than seventy, including a professor, a headmaster, fifteen assistant professors, thirty lecturers and instructors, fifteen tutors, ten scribes, and two guards. The Zōshikan served a variety of functions. A major service was providing classes for senior *chigo* and *nise,* but the school also was open to rural samurai and to commoners. The Zōshikan commonly had four hundred to eight hundred students. The school also served the domain elite. The daimyo and his senior retainers regularly summoned the Zōshikan staff to give private lectures on Confucian thought.[57]

Unlike the *gojū* curriculum, the Zōshikan program was strictly academic and the curriculum centered on the Confucian classics. Students were trained in the core texts of the East Asian tradition, known as "the Four Books and the Five Classics."[58] These texts were remote and inaccessible to laymen. Written in ancient Chinese in a laconic and epigrammatic style, they required extensive explanation and commentary. Only after extensive study of literary Chinese could Japanese students begin to parse their assignments. But this classical education made Saigō and his fellow students part of a great intellectual tradition. The core texts of the Zōshikan were scarcely different from those of a Confucian academy in China, Korea, or Vietnam. Not only was this corpus classicus constant across countries, it also was constant across time. By Saigō's day, "the Four Books and the Five Classics" had been the cornerstone of a humanistic education for centuries. This education gave Saigō his historical models of loyalty, honor, and courage. It also shaped his understanding of self-expression. For much of his life, Saigō regularly composed poetry in classical Chinese. While their artistry is questionable, Saigō poems are littered with references to classical Chinese texts. For Saigō, ancient Chinese history was not foreign: it was the shared cultural heritage of all civilized men.

While Saigō developed an appreciation for ancient Chinese literature at the Zōshikan, he also looked beyond the school's understanding of the classics. The Zōshikan followed an orthodox interpretation of the Chinese classics

known as Zhu Xi thought, a school of Song (Sung) dynasty Confucianism.
Zhu Xi (1130–1200) outlined a great synthesis of moral and natural philosophy. There was, he argued, no distinction between the laws governing
natural phenomena and the normative or descriptive principles of human
society. Everything was governed by a single set of universal, underlying
principles. Because there was no distinction between moral and natural philosophy, the study of the natural world was essential to ethical cultivation.
Conversely, meditation and ethical cultivation would lead to a better understanding of the natural world. To this end, Zhu Xi advocated a broad-based
curriculum including reading, sitting quietly, ritual practice, physical exercise, calligraphy, arithmetic, and empirical observation. Zhu Xi's synthesis
can be seen as a Confucian response to Buddhism and Taoism. The idea of
a totalizing unity of man and nature was inspired by Taoism, while sitting
quietly was a response to Buddhist meditation. By incorporating these
ideas and practices, Zhu Xi turned Confucianism from a political and ethical philosophy into a complete religious and metaphysical system.[59]

It is difficult to overstate Zhu Xi's influence on East Asian thought. He
helped define the canon of "the Four Books and the Five Classics," and
his commentaries became, for many, as important as the original texts. In
Japan, Zhu Xi learning dominated most government-sponsored academic
institutions by the late 1700s. The original regulations of the Zōshikan prohibited discussion of other doctrines without permission.[60] This ban was
part of a broader trend in Japanese intellectual life: in 1790 the shogunate
prohibited the teaching of other interpretations in its private academy, the
Shōheikō.

Saigō read and mastered Zhu Xi's most famous work, *Reflections on Things
at Hand* (*Kinshiroku* in Japanese), and was familiar with the fundamentals of
Zhu Xi thought. But, like many nineteenth-century Japanese, he felt
that Zhu Xi offered, at best, an incomplete approach to learning. In Saigō's
day Zhu Xi learning had become associated with narrow scholasticism
rather than effective political action. In this context, Saigō began to study
Ōyōmei learning, a critique of Zhu Xi studies based on the teachings of
Wang Yangming, a Ming dynasty philosopher.[61]

Although Yangming and Zhu Xi drew on the same classical texts,
Yangming's philosophy stressed intuition, experience, and action. While
Yangming did not deny the importance of scholarship, he believed that the
knowledge of good and evil was innate in all people. The task was therefore

to reconnect with this innate knowledge. Whereas Zhu Xi emphasized study and self-reflection, hence his dictum "the investigation of things," Yangming stressed enlightenment and an appreciation of one's a priori moral compass. Yangming also criticized Zhu Xi's dualistic approach to thought and action. The goal of understanding virtue, Yangming argued, was to act on it and thereby to bridge the gap between thought and action. Action based on one's innate sense of good was transcendent: "only when I love my father, the father of others, and the fathers of all men, can my humanity really form one body with my father, the father of others and the fathers of all men. . . . Then the clear virtue of filial piety will be made manifest."[62]

Much of the debate between the Yangming and Zhu Xi schools hinged on fine points of metaphysics. But Yangming's emphasis on action rather than scholarship had radical implications for practical politics. In Japan, the most spectacular uprising of the early 1800s was inspired by Wang Yangming: in 1837 Ōshio Heihachirō, a former Osaka police constable, led an abortive coup against the shogunate. Ōshio had long been appalled by the corruption and incompetence of the Osaka City government but had worked within the system to expose graft and improve governance. Yangming learning offered Ōshio a different path. In the Ōyōmei tradition, the knowledge of good and evil mattered only if one acted on it, and this action mattered more than traditional authority. When the shogunate mishandled a severe rice shortage, Ōshio struck out against the government he had once served. Inspired by Yangming, he exhorted his followers to execute rapacious merchants and "those officials who torment and harass those who are lowly." His coup was a fiasco: many of those who followed his call were opportunists more interested in liberating sake than in smiting despots. Ōshio fled to the countryside and died by his own hand in 1837/3, setting fire to the house where he was hiding so that the government would not be able to mutilate his corpse. His rebellion, although nominally a failure, terrified the ruling elite. What could be more disturbing than a former shogunal servant publicly and violently declaring the shogunate's turpitude and ineptitude? As if to confirm the shogunate's fears, the country was rocked by a spate of small-scale insurrections inspired by Ōshio's failed coup. Ōshio's actions were exceptional, but his coup dramatized the radical potential of Yangming thought. Yangming's emphasis on public action gave a revolutionary edge to the Confucian classics.[63]

Saigō was deeply influenced by Yangming learning but was uneasy with its more radical implications. Rather than abandon Zhu Xi learning for Yangming intuitionism, Saigō sought a middle ground. The teachers with whom Saigō studied Yangming learning were all syncretists who sought to harmonize Yangming and Zhu Xi thought. Saigō's greatest single influence was Satō Issai, a prominent Tokugawa thinker. Satō was a masterful syncretic thinker. He was inspired by Yangming's writings but also was headmaster at the shogunal academy. Rather than openly confront the shogunate's ban on Yangming learning, Satō finessed it, arguing that he was exploring the common origins of Zhu Xi thought and Yangming thought. This ruse allowed Satō to keep his influential teaching position while writing extensively on Yangming learning. In acknowledgment of his skillful conceit, he was known to his contemporaries as "Zhu Xi on the outside, Yangming on the inside."[64] Saigō found Satō's ideas so inspiring that he turned them into a personal handbook, carefully transcribing 101 of Satō's sayings and keeping the volume at his side for consultation.[65]

In selecting passages from Satō, Saigō was drawn to the notion of man's intuitive knowledge. He transcribed Satō's observation that to "know without knowing [why]" was the path to sincere, virtuous conduct. By contrast, to think, but still not know, was the path to selfish actions grounded in ambition and passion.[66] Saigō also copied Satō's commentary on man's innate virtue: "man's soul is like the sun, but ambition, pride, malice, and covetousness obscure it like low-hanging clouds and it becomes unclear where this spirit lies. Therefore, cultivating sincerity is the best way to dispel the clouds and greet a clear day. It is essential to base one's studies on such a cornerstone of sincerity."[67] Saigō was especially taken with the notion of virtuous action as a means of transcending death. A man's body is but a room, a temporary bequest from heaven, but his innate nature (Japanese *sei*/Chinese *xing*) is a gift from heaven that transcends life and death. A sage makes his innate nature manifest throughout his daily life. He leaves instructions to his heirs not in a will, but through the example of his words and deeds. Because he is drawing on his innate capacity for virtue, he is a part of heaven, and is unconcerned with the minor distinction between life and death. The wise but not sage man fears death and is ashamed of his fear, but he cannot overcome it. He struggles to shape his legacy through written precepts for his heirs, but has difficulty in getting those heirs to listen. He can understand death, but he cannot be at peace with it. Thus, observed Satō, "the sage is at peace with death, the learned man understands death, and the common man fears death."[68] This sense that virtue can change the meaning of death shaped Saigō's understanding of his fate and his duty.

Saigō's education in Satsuma was both universalistic and parochial. His studies of Zhu Xi and Yangming connected Saigō with a pan-Asian debate on the Confucian classics. At the opposite extreme were his primers, the texts he first memorized and taught his students to memorize. These were odes and stories about Satsuma, with only passing references to the rest of the world. Saigō did read some of the classic works of imperial history, such as Kitabatake Chikafusa's *Jinnō shōtōki*. But his education was remarkably slim on anything resembling Japanese national history. Saigō was educated less as a Japanese subject than as an East Asian gentleman in service to the Shimazu house.[69]

A final component of Saigō's intellectual cultivation was Zen meditation. Saigō learned Zen from Musan (1782–1851), head monk at Fukushōji, the Shimazu family temple. Musan had, intriguingly, studied Ōyōmei learning before becoming a monk in the Sōtō school of Zen.[70] Saigō found Zen intellectually satisfying, but it also fulfilled a deep emotional need. As Ōkubo observed years later, Saigō, who had a quick, fiery temperament, saw Zen as a means of controlling and calming his passions. Meditation, he hoped, would help him detach from worldly concerns. Ōkubo, however, was sharply critical of Zen's effect on Saigō. It did not calm his temperament but perverted it, making him arrogant and overbearing: Ōkubo indirectly blamed his rift with Saigō in 1873 on the pernicious impact of Zen. Ōkubo's assessment of Saigō's Zen experience is uniquely dark, but his description of Saigō as both emotionally effusive and coolly taciturn is incisive. Saigō was nearly six feet tall and built like a wrestler, so his stony silence was thoroughly intimidating. A striking range of witnesses, from his son Kikujirō to the British diplomatic Ernest Satow, have described the terrifying effect of Saigō's taciturn gaze. But Saigō's stoicism cloaked a deep sentimentality. Years later acquaintances would recall Saigō's reaction when, after the restoration, he was taken to the theater by the Mitsui Company. This was a last-minute change of plan, after sumo wrestling had been canceled because of rain. His hosts were astonished to see Saigō, a famous general and elder statesman, crying openly at the sentimental drama.[71]

Saigō at Work

In 1844 Saigō began work as assistant clerk in the county office. His duties included inspecting farm villages, supervising village officials, encouraging agricultural production, and collecting taxes. His post was neither powerful nor demanding, and it certainly was not a position that foreshadowed national political leadership. As a clerk, Saigō had virtually no authority, and much of his work was repetitive and mundane. But Saigō's experience in the county office had a lasting impact on his political views. However tedious his daily routine, Saigō's work made him deeply aware of a systemic problem in Satsuma politics: the domain's crippling tax levies.[72]

Satsuma had one of Japan's most underdeveloped systems of agriculture and was known throughout the country for its oppressive taxation. The domain's levies were so onerous that farmers regularly deserted their fields and fled to neighboring domains rather than struggle to meet their tax obligations.[73] Although generations of reformers wrestled with this problem, it was an all but inherent part of Satsuma's political economy: the domain had too many samurai and not enough farmers. In Saigō's youth, roughly 170,000 of Satsuma's 650,000 people were samurai or their families.[74] Since in theory, samurai ruled rather than farmed, this meant that some 480,000 farmers were supposed to feed 170,000 warriors. This was completely untenable. Even Japan's most productive farmers could not have fed that many extra mouths. Satsuma met this problem by paying its samurai badly; like Saigō, most retainers received stipends inadequate to their basic needs. Even so, the demands of such a large samurai population mandated heavy taxes. Demography meant that Satsuma was compelled to tax its commoners too much and pay its samurai too little.[75]

Satsuma's chronic need for revenue led to a variety of novel undertakings. The domain sought to promote and tax an astonishing range of products, including shiitake mushrooms, leather, sesame, rapeseed, indigo, cotton cloth, silk cloth, coal, sulfur, bonito flakes (katsuo bushi), and pottery. Many of these endeavors failed miserably. The domain commonly forced farmers to sell to government agents, but these agents often paid so little that farmers could not cover their costs. Rather than lose money, the farmers stopped production.[76]

The severity of the Satsuma tax system was dramatized for Saigō during the farm crisis of 1849. Unseasonable weather had resulted in a harvest shortfall, and the director of the tax office, Sakoda Toshinari, began a survey to assess the need for tax relief. To Sakoda's dismay, however, he learned from his superiors that the survey was pointless. The domain was not prepared to order any tax relief despite the poor harvest. Sakoda was outraged and resigned his post rather than participate in such a disingenuous exercise. According to several biographers, Sakoda's principled resignation had a lasting impact on Saigō. This is difficult to substantiate, but Saigō's thinking about agriculture throughout his lifetime was grounded in moral rather than pragmatic concerns.

In 1852 Saigō suffered a series of losses and disappointments. At the behest of his family he married Ijūin Suga, the twenty-three-year-old daughter of a Kagoshima samurai household. The union was essentially a contractual affair. It was arranged by the couple's parents, produced no children, and was later dissolved by Suga's family. Saigō's only reference to the marriage in all his surviving letters is a complaint about the divorce. Soon after his marriage Saigō lost both his parents. When his father died in 1852/9, and his mother two months later, Saigō assumed the family headship, taking on the responsibility for supporting, on a meager stipend, a family of twelve with two unmarried sisters and three small children.[77] The burdens of family headship and the loss of his parents pained Saigō. In later years he reflected that 1852 was the saddest year of his life. He treated his difficulties with mordant humor, however. After seeing his brother Kichijirō sell firewood to help the family make ends meet, Saigō remarked that they might starve, but they would at least all starve together.[78]

Beyond these hardships, Saigō's early years in Satsuma were thoroughly unremarkable. Although generations of biographers have searched for signs of nascent leadership, Saigō did little to distinguish himself before the late 1850s. Saigō was certainly a keen student, and his childhood in Kagoshima was intellectually rich. He read widely in Japanese history and philosophy. He developed a mastery of literary Chinese and studied the ancient classics. He practiced Zen meditation. But Saigō would soon discover huge gaps in his knowledge, and it is striking what he did not study before his departure for Edo in 1854. Little of Saigō's education emphasized the emperor, and nothing in his studies in Kagoshima prepared him for Mito learning, the imperial loyalist movement critical to the Restoration. Saigō understood the ancient origins of the imperial line but could not conceive of a state based solely on imperial sovereignty and legitimacy. Nor did he have more than an inkling of the technological superiority of the West. The Zhu Xi orthodoxy of the Zōshikan discouraged the study of such "novelties." Saigō would learn of Western technology and military strength through his historic meetings with Hashimoto Sanai in Edo. This would be a shocking experience. For the rest of his life Saigō would struggle to integrate his respect for Japanese tradition, his appreciation for Western society and technology, his loyalty to the Shimazu house, and his loyalty to the emperor. At work, Saigō was diligent and sought in earnest to ameliorate conditions for the peasantry. But he had little to say that had not been said before. When he assumed headship of his family in 1852, Saigō was exceptionally well equipped to follow in his father's footsteps as division chief in a tax office. But he was strangely unprepared for where fate would soon take him: to the shogun's capital and the center of a fierce contest for national power.

Chapter 2

"A MAN OF EXCEPTIONAL FIDELITY"

Saigō and National Politics*

A New Daimyo

In early 1854 Saigō was promoted from assistant clerk to lord's attendant *(chū gokoshō)* and was selected to accompany the daimyo, Shimazu Nariakira, on his biennial journey to the shogun's capital of Edo (now Tokyo). Upon the party's arrival in Edo in 1854/3, Nariakira appointed Saigō as his Edo gardener, an innocuous but important post. As gardener Saigō could travel freely around the city, relaying messages from Nariakira to other daimyo without arousing the suspicion of the shogun's spies. Saigō became the daimyo's confidant and adviser, and emerged as a rising figure in national politics.[1]

The process by which Saigō, a minor clerk in the domain tax office, became his lord's most trusted adviser is among the great mysteries of Saigō's life. None of Saigō's many biographers has found any evidence linking Saigō and Nariakira prior to 1854. No papers, no letters, and no contemporaneous accounts connect Saigō to his lord prior to the sudden promotion in

---

*This quote is from a description of Saigō by Nagaoka Kenmotsu, a house elder in Kumamoto domain. See *DSZ* 1:70–72.

1854/1. Saigō, we can assume, did or said something noteworthy, but we have no hard evidence of what act or statement caught Nariakira's attention. What we have, instead, are numerous plausible but unproven theories. But if we cannot reconstruct how Nariakira came to hear of Saigō, we can reconstruct the turbulent environment in which the lord of Kagoshima, ignoring traditional hierarchy, chose as his confidant a tax office clerk.[2]

Shimazu Nariakira became daimyo in 1851 after a fierce and bloody succession dispute. The brutality of this struggle is surprising, since Nariakira was the obvious choice to succeed his father, Shimazu Narioki. Nariakira was his father's eldest son, and had been designated Narioki's heir at age three, in 1812. Nariakira, widely regarded as an exceptionally talented and capable heir, was strong and robust, and excelled at a variety of martial arts including archery, riding, and fencing. He was intelligent and well-read. His mother, Kaneko, was among the best-educated women of her day, and she tutored Nariakira in the Chinese classics from his youth. Nariakira grew up exchanging classical verse with his mother and had a solid knowledge of Chinese history and thought. He also had a deep interest in Western culture, instilled by his great-grandfather Shimazu Shigehide. From early childhood Nariakira was fascinated by Shigehide's collection of Western artifacts, which included clocks, musical instruments, telescopes, microscopes, and weapons. Like Shigehide, Nariakira could write Roman letters; he sometimes used romanized Japanese as a form of code in correspondence and personal records. In 1826 Shigehide introduced Nariakira to Franz von Siebold, the Dutch physician stationed in Nagasaki. Nariakira was thus among a handful of Japanese to have actually met a European. Nariakira's breadth of knowledge, combined with his commanding physical presence, earned him the respect of his contemporaries. It is said that shogunal officials regretted that Nariakira's status as a tozama daimyo barred him from holding shogunal office. Nariakira was, nonetheless, on good terms with important shogunal officials, especially Abe Masahiro, the chairman of the shogun's council of elders *(rōjū shuseki)*.[3]

Although Nariakira's succession as daimyo was seemingly straightforward, it deteriorated into a bloody family squabble shaped by lust, envy, greed, and sibling rivalry. Nariakira had two key enemies: Okada Yura, his father's mistress; and Zusho Hirosato, a powerful domain elder *(karō)*. In contemporary sources Yura is described variously as a shipbuilder's and a carpenter's daughter. Renowned for her great beauty and charm, she had

Shōkō shūseikan, Kagoshima

Shimazu Nariakira, portrait by Kuroda Kiyoteru

great influence over Narioki, especially after the death of his wife, Kaneko, in 1824. Narioki did not remarry, and Yura became his primary female companion. Narioki had three children with Yura, but only the middle child, Hisamitsu, survived infancy. As the son of a mistress Hisamitsu was not initially a member of the Shimazu house, but in 1827 he was adopted by Shimazu Tadakimi, the daimyo of Shigetomi, and returned to the Shimazu line. Yura had great ambitions for her only surviving child, hoping that ultimately he would succeed Narioki. This put her on a collision course with Nariakira, the heir apparent.[4]

Nariakira's succession also worried Zusho Hirosato, one of the domain elders and the mastermind of the domain's financial recovery. Although he had been born at the bottom of the samurai estate, Zusho impressed both Shigehide and Narioki with his financial acumen. In 1830 he was given broad license to reform the domain's finances. Fewer than fifteen years later

Shimazu Hisamitsu, portrait by Harada Najirō

Shōko shūseikan, Kagoshima

he had turned a crushing debt of more than 5 million ryō into a treasury balance. Zusho rescheduled the domain debt and curtailed spending through an austerity program. His most impressive accomplishment, however, lay in the reform of government enterprises. Zusho systematically challenged the most dysfunctional aspects of the domain's tax system. His methods, such as improving construction of rice bales to lose less grain in shipment, were often remarkably simple. Nevertheless, such seemingly obvious reforms had an astonishing impact on the domain's finances. Many resented Zusho as a parvenu, and he was dogged by allegations of corruption, but even his detractors could not deny his accomplishments.[5]

Zusho did not think of Nariakira as a worldly and accomplished leader, but as a spendthrift dilettante. His hostility toward Nariakira stemmed in part from his experiences with Nariakira's great-grandfather Shigehide. In

Zusho's eyes, Shigehide's passion for things Western had led to inordinate and needless expenses. Imported Dutch books, telescopes, and clocks were pricey baubles that did not advance the economic growth of the domain. Shigehide's fondness for Nariakira only intensified Zusho's suspicions. The heir apparent, Zusho feared, was as much a chronic spendthrift as his great-grandfather had been. Zusho made no secret of his antipathy for Nariakira and by 1849 was openly bad-mouthing Nariakira to high-ranking retainers. Several accounts suggest that Zusho urged Narioki to delay his retirement to deny Nariakira power as long as possible.[6]

Zusho and Nariakira also clashed over military reforms. Emboldened by his tremendous financial successes, Zusho had begun to reform the domain's fief system. Because so many retainers had sold their fiefs to new owners who had no intention of fulfilling the traditional obligation to raise troops, formal investitures could no longer be used as a basis for military mobilization. Under Zusho's reforms, however, retainers would again be required to muster troops in proportion to their fiefs. Nariakira would likely have supported Zusho's attempts at military modernization had not Zusho used the reforms to raise substantially the military rank of Nariakira's half brother Hisamitsu. This made Nariakira suspicious of the entire enterprise, and rather than support the reforms, Nariakira criticized them as insufficient.[7]

Amid this simmering tension, Nariakira's allies were gripped by panic, as Nariakira's children kept dying. Nariakira's first child, a boy, had died in infancy in 1829, and his first and second daughters both died before age three. Given the era's high infant and childhood mortality, these deaths were not suspicious. Nariakira was alarmed by the fate of his remaining potential heirs, however. In 1848 his second son died at age two. In 1849 his fourth son died at seven months, and in 1850 his third son died just before reaching age three. Nariakira's allies sent their condolences, but they openly suggested that Nariakira's losses resulted from a conspiracy. After all, if Nariakira lacked an heir, Hisamitsu would be the preferred successor to Narioki. Rumors of sinister forces began to circulate, and it was widely thought that Yura was casting spells to hasten the deaths of Nariakira's children. Nariakira himself seems to have suspected foul play. As early as 1847 he requested detailed reports on Yura's actions, asking specifically if she was requesting any unusual prayers. He was particularly concerned with rumors that Yura was placing curses on dolls. In 1850/2 Nariakira received a report from his loyal aide Yoshii Taiyu that confirmed his worst fears. Yoshii wrote that Yura had asked at least five people to cast spells on Nariakira and his two eldest sons. He reported the appearance of spectral, disembodied faces while one Takagi Ichisuke was praying for Nariakira's misfortune. Yura had also requested imprecations from the ascetic Maki Nakatarō and had asked for suspicious rituals from the head monks at Karinji Temple. What truly disturbed Yoshii was his inability to combat these spells. When he had asked his brother to shoot a magic arrow designed to dispel evil spirits, it had merely bounced off the target.[8]

Frustrated by Zusho's opposition to his succession and anguished over the deaths of his children, Nariakira conspired to seize power. Zusho's power base was the domain capital of Kagoshima, so Nariakira used his political connections in Edo to unseat his rival. In effect, he betrayed a fellow countryman to the shogunate by blowing the whistle on a long-standing aspect of Satsuma-Ryukyuan relations, the open secret that Satsuma had routinely exceeded shogunal limits on trade through the Ryukyus. The shogunate had known of Satsuma's smuggling activities since the 1820s, but Nariakira leaked extensive details of this illegal trade to the shogunate to undermine Zusho. In late 1848/12 Abe Masahiro, chairman of the shogunal elders, summoned Zusho and began grilling him on the details of Satsuma-Ryukyu trade. To shield his lord Narioki from censure, Zusho accepted full responsibility for Satsuma's policies.[9]

Nariakira's strike against Zusho made an ugly situation worse. Nariakira had hoped that Zusho's demise would secure his own succession, but Narioki still gave no indication that he was about to retire. Bitter and frustrated, Nariakira began a plan to force his father's retirement, preparing to use further disclosures about the Ryukyus and internal dissent within Satsuma to embarrass his father and secure his own succession. This dangerous strategy triggered Narioki's deepest anxieties. Narioki himself had come to power through a struggle between his father and grandfather, in a clash that had resulted in the compulsory suicide of thirteen retainers. The death of Zusho and rumors of conspiracy now led Narioki to suspect the worst of his son. Rather than wait for a coup, Narioki struck first.[10]

On 1849/12/3, a rare snowy day in Kagoshima, Narioki began the systematic elimination of Nariakira's supporters, announcing a wide-ranging indictment for disloyalty and conspiracy. Six of Nariakira's allies committed seppuku (suicide) that same day. Among these first casualties were Nariakira's longtime confidant Konoe Ryūzaemon and his allies

Yamada Ichirōzaemon and Takasaki Gorozaemon. These were devastating losses. Yamada had been the Kyoto chargé d'affaires, Takasaki was scribe for the council of elders, and Konoe was chief city magistrate. In one day, Nariakira lost his best-placed and most loyal retainers. Over the following year and a half, Narioki methodically purged the administration of Nariakira's supporters. By the time the dust had settled in 1850/4 more than fifty men had been politically eliminated. Fourteen had committed suicide, seventeen were sent into internal exile, and twenty others were purged or died in jail. Narioki was as brutal as he was thorough. Since Konoe, Yamada, and Takasaki committed seppuku before Narioki could execute them, he vented his fury on their corpses. Yamada and Takasaki were displayed on crosses, while Konoe's body was cut apart with a saw.[11]

In the short term, Narioki's purge crushed Nariakira's plans to succeed as daimyo. But the brutality of the purge ultimately advanced Nariakira's interests. It discredited Narioki in the eyes of other daimyo, some of whom refused to extradite Satsuma samurai for punishment. With most of his domestic allies dead or purged, Nariakira turned to these sympathetic peers for support. In this effort, his stellar reputation among the warrior elite served him well. Nariakira enlisted the help of Kuroda Narihiro, the daimyo of Fukuoka. Kuroda, in turn, secured the support of Date Munenari, the daimyo of Uwajima, who got the support of Nanbu Nobuyuki, the daimyo of Hachinohe. By mid-1850 an informal committee of daimyo and shogunal officers had convinced Abe Masahiro that Narioki had to go; the questions were only protocol and timing. Narioki realized that he had been outmaneuvered and by late 1850 was avoiding meetings with shogunal aides. On 1850/12/3 he relented and accepted a retirement gift from the shogun. On 1851/1/29 he announced his formal retirement to the shogun. The long, bloody succession dispute was over.[12]

Saigō was too young and unimportant to have had a role in this feud, but he watched the crisis with dismay. His friend Ōkubo Toshimichi was deemed a member of Nariakira's faction, dismissed from his post, and placed under domiciliary confinement for six months. Ōkubo's father was dismissed and sent into internal exile for four years, and the Ōkubo house was plunged into poverty.[13] Saigō's father was a close associate of Akayama Yukie, one of the men executed in Narioki's purge. According to an oft-cited but undocumented story, Saigō's father was a witness at Akayama's ritual suicide and brought home Akayama's bloodstained singlet. The shirt, he told his son, showed the price of justice and loyalty. The Akayama story may be mere legend, but Saigō's allegiances undoubtedly lay with Nariakira's faction.[14] Nearly seventeen years after the seppuku of Konoe and Takasaki on a snowy night in Kyoto, Saigō recalled their deaths with two poems. In the first he contrasted their perduring spirit to the evanescence of the snow. In the second he likened the bitter cold to the injustice of their fate:

> No need to speak of winter's cold
> I lament only the cold cruelty of the world
> Looking back upon that night's snow
> It gleams with piercing sadness and undaunted courage[15]

Nariakira had won, but at a high price. Only by involving the shogunate, an outside authority, had Nariakira been able to prevail over his father and half brother. The conflict left deep, long-lasting scars in the Satsuma body politic. For decades men would bristle at the injustice they or their comrades had suffered. Nariakira had to move carefully in asserting his authority, to avoid restarting or inflaming the conflict. Because the dispute had also decimated the ranks of Nariakira's natural allies, many of his most obvious choices for office were dead. For all these reasons, Saigō was, ironically, a strong candidate for rapid promotion. He was, most critically, alive. He was intelligent, capable, and loyal, but was untainted by any direct involvement in the succession dispute. Saigō's lack of prominence was an advantage at this juncture because his promotion would be unlikely to provoke Hisamitsu and Yura, battered but still powerful defenders of Narioki. Saigō, a capable but naive tax official, thus found himself at the center of national politics.

The Road to Edo

On 1854/1/21 Saigō left for Edo as part of Nariakira's retinue. The journey to the shogun's capital was part of a polite system of hostage-taking known as *sankin kōtai,* or alternate attendance. Under this system, daimyo spent alternate years in Edo and in their home domains. Their households, including wives and children, lived in Edo permanently. The system, whose origins lay in medieval tradition, was initially a means by which daimyo showed their fealty. By the mid–1600s, however, it had become formalized into a rigid system of dual residences. Daimyo commonly left their home domain in either the fourth or the eighth month and spent roughly twelve months in Edo before returning home.

The *sankin kōtai* system had created a lasting schism within warlord culture. After the mid-seventeenth century, virtually all daimyo grew up in Edo rather than their "homelands." Most daimyo did not see the domains they would rule until at least their teens. Nariakira himself did not set foot in Kagoshima until 1835, when he was twenty-six. His detractors noted that he never mastered Satsuma dialect and always sounded like an outsider. Indeed, Nariakira was more politically surefooted in Edo than in Kagoshima. His campaign to force Narioki's retirement had turned the corner when he began to rely on his Edo connections and enlisted other daimyō. Nariakira's alienation from his homeland was not unusual. Young lords were often alarmed by the cultural chasm between Edo and their domains. The daimyo Tsugaru Nobumasa, for example, seeing his homeland of Hirosaki for the first time in 1661, was stunned by the crudeness of his retainers. In a brief poem he described them as barely civilized men living at the far reaches of a bleak region.[16] The ruling elite of Japan thus shared a common experience: they were all educated and socialized in the same city, and all were initially strangers in their own domains. This tension between the homeland and Edo cultures extended to elite retainers. Those stationed in Edo developed a distinct view of the realm. Their understanding of politics focused on the shogunate rather than on the details of the homeland's internal affairs. Edo retainers were indirectly aware of the results of domestic policy. They understood, for example, that a poor harvest meant less money for the domain villas in Edo. But they were more acutely aware of their daimyo's position in relation to other lords and the shogun. Saigō, a tax official, had only the dimmest understanding of the rift between Edo and Kagoshima culture. His acclimation to life in the capital was, therefore, a difficult but formative passage.

Although Saigō did not keep a diary, Yamada Tamemasa, an upper-ranking retainer, carefully chronicled the details of the 1854 embassy to Edo. Like many well-situated retainers, Yamada had a taste for fine things. His journal carefully recorded the local delicacies at each stop on the post roads. But his journal is also an indirect chronicle of Saigō's life, through which we know where Saigō was and what he saw day by day.[17] The retinue left Kagoshima under fair skies at roughly 6:00 A.M. on 1854/1/21.

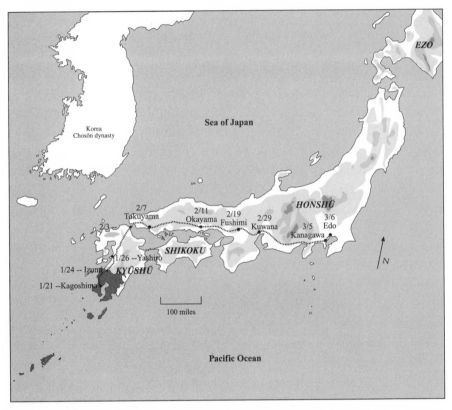

Saigō's journey to Edo, 1854

Nariakira was carried in a palanquin, but the majority of his retainers, and most likely Saigō, walked to Edo, a journey of more than nine hundred miles.[18] The retinue, traveling at about twenty miles per day, arrived on 1/24 at the town of Izumi, at the northern edge of Satsuma domain. The following day, despite snow and unseasonable cold, the retinue left before daybreak and continued northward. Later that morning they crossed into Kumamoto domain, and Saigō was outside Satsuma domain for the first time.[19] Throughout the journey, the embassy received a near-constant stream of envoys and visitors. Local lords and merchants offered gifts of fine food, sweets, and liquor. Messengers arrived nearly every day, bringing news from Satsuma officials in Edo and Kagoshima as well as greetings and news from other lords. Much of this traffic was unexceptional and went largely unnoticed by the embassy. On 2/1, however, the daimyo received the disturbing news that menacing foreign warships were off the coast of Uraga, mere miles from Edo Castle. Two days later the retinue boarded ships at Kokura, crossed Shimonoseki Strait, and arrived on the main island of Honshū: this was the first time Saigō had left his home island. The embassy continued on its way east, stopping at Fushimi on the outskirts of Kyoto on 2/19. Two weeks later, on 3/5, the embassy stopped for a rest in Kanagawa and saw the infamous foreign "black ships" themselves. Looking east to the Pacific, Saigō could see at first hand evidence of the foreign crisis that would help destroy the shogunate.[20]

The "black ships" were part of the fleet of Commodore Matthew Perry, returning to demand that the shogunate conclude a trade treaty with the United States. Perry's mission was the culmination of a long process of American and European encroachment on Japan. For much of the nineteenth century Japan had had minimal direct contact with the Western world. By contrast, in the early 1600s Japan had traded extensively with Spain, Portugal, Holland, and England, as well as its Asian neighbors. At one time Japan's silver exports had comprised more than 30 percent of world silver production, and the country had also been a major exporter of weapons. In the 1630s, however, Japan had begun to restrict its foreign contacts drastically. Japanese overseas traders were ordered to return, and the shogunate prohibited the construction of oceanfaring ships. Trade with Europe contracted dramatically. Alarmed by the missionary activities of the Spanish and Portuguese, the shogunate banned them from Japan. Meanwhile the English were unable to make a profit in the face of Dutch competition and withdrew from Japan for financial reasons. These events gave the Dutch, confined to the artificial island of Dejima in Nagasaki Harbor, a de facto monopoly on European trade.[21]

The early shoguns did not articulate a general policy on trade with Europe. Rather, their actions were guided by the immediate, pragmatic concerns of controlling missionary activity and regulating foreign trade. But later generations would interpret these directives as a rejection of all Western contact save the Dutch concession in Nagasaki. By the 1790s the shogunate was referring to its "ancestral" tradition of limiting Western contact. This new "ancestral" policy would cause the shogunate great distress. As Dutch power in East Asia waned, Japan confronted increasingly aggressive demands from the United States, Russia, and Great Britain. In the 1790s Russian explorers began charting the waters off Hokkaidō, and in

1792 the Russian court formally requested a trade treaty with Japan. The shogunate refused, but the Russians, undeterred, continued to press the shogunate. In 1807 fighting broke out between Russian and Japanese forces. An impending Russian collision with Japan was delayed by the Napoleonic Wars, but the precedent was ominous. British conduct was equally alarming. In 1808 the British frigate *Phaeton* sailed into Nagasaki Harbor under a Dutch flag and then, in prosecution of the Napoleonic Wars, abducted Dutch officials and threatened to set fire to Dutch ships. The incident was resolved without further violence, but shogunal officials were now deeply suspicious of British intentions as well. In 1825, after sailors from a British ship landed in Mito domain in search of provisions, the shogunate issued its "no second thoughts" edict. Local authorities were henceforth to destroy all foreign vessels that came close to Japanese shores, even if it meant the accidental destruction of a Chinese, Korean, or Dutch ship. War was better than trade.[22]

When the shogunate learned of China's defeat in the First Opium War (1839–1842) they rescinded the edict and urged local officials to resupply Western ships in distress. This did little, however, to affect the looming crisis over trade. The Opium War made Japanese officials and intellectuals acutely aware of the horrors of "free trade" imperialism: in defense of its merchants, Britain had forced China to accept the importation of opium, a product illegal in Britain itself. A handful of Japanese thinkers now realized that Japan would need Western technology to repel Western aggression. Britain's defeat of China had convinced them that Japan needed to acquire, through trade, those formidable Western weapons.

Satsuma was exceptionally aware of both the benefits and the dangers of foreign engagement. The domain had profited handsomely from foreign trade via the Ryukyus, but it now had to confront French and British missionaries and treaty demands. These demands threatened to destroy a complex but stable foreign policy arrangement. The Ryukyus were effectively under Japanese control, but China viewed the Ryukyuan kingdom as a separate state and invested the Ryukyuan king as a vassal of the Qing emperor. The Ryukyuan kingdom was, depending on one's perspective, a vassal state of Satsuma, a vassal state of the shogunate, a vassal state of Qing China, or an independent kingdom. This conceit had given Satsuma access to East Asian markets through the Ryukyuan kingdom and had forestalled a territorial conflict between Japan and China. French and British demands on the domain, however, threatened to expose this arrangement. In the context of modern European diplomacy, the Ryukyus could not be simultaneously Chinese, Japanese, and independent.[23]

In the end it was not the British, the French, or the Russians who "opened" Japan to Western trade, but the United States. American interest in Japan was sparked by several forces, including the acquisition of California in 1848 and the decline of Atlantic whaling stocks. American military planners hoped to use Japanese ports and Japan's extensive coal reserves to refuel the navy's growing fleet of steamships. Whalers were interested in hunting in the northern Pacific, and there was general commercial interest in trade with both Japan and China. Japan also fit into broader American ambitions to establish itself as a Pacific power.

The shogunate turned back the first American expedition, led by Commodore James Biddle in 1846, with its standard evasiveness. Biddle had sought to distinguish American policy by taking an overtly pacific tone. When an aggressive samurai knocked him over he remained calm and did not demand compensation. His actions, however, were interpreted by the shogunate as weakness rather than tolerance. In 1849 the United States secured a basic agreement for the repatriation of shipwrecked American sailors, but this did not address any of the broader issues of refueling, resupply, diplomatic recognition, or trade. The failure of these missions shaped the strategy of Commodore Perry, Biddle's successor, who was determined to force the shogunate's hand without resorting to war. On 1853/6/3 (July 8) Perry, in an act of carefully calculated intimidation, led a squadron of four warships into Edo Bay. Perry's command ship, *Susquehanna,* was a state-of-the-art steamship. At more than 2,400 tons, it overmatched at least fifteen Japanese ships put together. *Susquehanna* and *Mississippi* (a 1,692-ton steamship) entered Edo Bay at nearly nine knots, leaving the shogunal navy scrambling in their wake. Shogunal officials were astonished by the ships' armaments. Observing from shore, Kagawa Eizaemon, an aide to the Uraga magistrate, counted about seventy large-caliber cannons. The shogunate had roughly a hundred cannons around Edo Bay, but only eleven of these were of comparable caliber. With four ships Perry had outgunned Japan's supreme warlord. Stunned, shogunal forces were forced to receive President Millard Fillmore's request for a treaty with the United States. Perry had "invaded" Japan without firing a shot.[24]

After delivering Fillmore's letter, Perry left Edo Bay with a promise to return the following year. His visit presented the shogunate with a profound quandary. The shogunate could reject the American request for a treaty, but only at the risk of war. A fight with the American navy was most unappealing, given the formidable armaments of Perry's small fleet. But the alternative was equally unpleasant. How could the shogunate abruptly abandon its "ancestral" policy of seclusion without openly revealing its military weakness? The shogunate faced this dilemma at a particularly difficult moment, because the reigning shogun, Tokugawa Ieyoshi (1793–1853), was dying and was incapable of handling the crisis. The task fell to Abe Masahiro, daimyo of Fukuyama and chairman of the shogun's council of elders. Faced with two equally unpalatable alternatives, Abe sought the advice of the other daimyo. This was sensible: since the burden of mobilizing troops would fall largely on the daimyo, Abe quite reasonably wanted their opinions. Abe also sensed that either choice would draw fierce opposition, and he wanted political cover. Although it was sensible and practical, however, the decision to consult the daimyo was unprecedented. The government of the shogun, who traditionally commanded the daimyo in time of war, was now polling those same men on national security. Worse, the daimyo did not give Abe clear guidance. Of the surviving responses, a majority endorsed the conflicting goals of rejecting a treaty while avoiding an armed conflict. The only consensus was negative, in that the majority of daimyo were unprepared to go to war. In light of this reluctance to fight, Abe resolved to sign the most limited possible treaty when Perry returned.[25]

When Perry returned on 1854/1/16 (February 13), however, he had upped the ante. His fleet was even larger than the year before, with three steamships (*Powhatan, Susquehanna,* and *Mississippi*) and four sailing ships. The shogunate expected Perry to stop at Uraga, the small port at the mouth of Edo Bay where he had dropped anchor in 1853. Perry, however, continued past Uraga toward Edo Castle. The shogunate frantically tried to stop him, but the commodore, as he had in 1853, used nonviolent intimidation. Confident in his fleet's military capabilities, he ignored shogunal requests and dropped anchor near the hamlet of Yokohama. After trying in vain to get Perry to return to Uraga, Japanese officials relented and opened formal negotiations on 1854/2/10 (March 8). Perry's aggressive but nonviolent arrival set the tone for the negotiations. The shogunate had resolved to sign a basic treaty allowing for the resupply of American ships, but it hoped to avoid any commitment to trade. Perry was determined to get trade concessions. In the end the two sides compromised: the shogunate opened the remote ports of Hakodate and Shimoda to American ships and agreed to receive an American consul general for further negotiations, while Perry deferred his demands for full commercial relations. The treaty was signed on March 31 (1854/3/3), two days before Saigō saw Perry's fleet. The shogunate had survived a major crisis. But the damage to the regime was permanent. Japan's supreme warlord had surrendered to the Americans without firing a shot.[26]

Saigō had been remarkably prescient about these events. In a letter dated 1853/5/28, mere days before Perry's initial visit, Saigō wrote that since foreign ships had come to the Ryukyus, others could be expected to follow. He thought it likely that Satsuma would be called on to help defend Edo and Nagasaki.[27] Satsuma's connection to the Ryukyus enhanced Saigō's understanding of the Western threat. After leaving Edo in 1853, Perry had gone only as far as Hong Kong and had stopped for a month in the Ryukyus on his way back to Edo in 1854. Saigō may have learned of international matters through his friend Ōkubo, whose father was closely involved in Ryukyuan affairs. But while Saigō had anticipated Perry's visit, he had not actually seen a Western ship until his arrival in Kanagawa. For Saigō, Perry's fleet was the first physical evidence of an advanced civilization outside Asia. The "black ships" were, in all likelihood, the first large-scale foreign objects Saigō had ever seen. Saigō had envisioned a foreign threat, but now it was tangibly before him.

In the Shogun's Capital

On 3/6 Nariakira's retinue arrived in Edo. The daimyo took up residence in his villa at Takanawa, while the rest of the embassy proceeded to the domain lodge, arriving at about 2:00 P.M. For samurai who regularly accompanied the daimyo this was a welcome end to a long journey; they were "home." As Yamada recorded in his journal: "We offered our congratulations to one and all and then took our leave. We were soon joined by family and, as always, enjoyed wine and good cheer." For Saigō, however, the experience was strikingly different. Not only was Edo not "home"; it was also the largest and most cosmopolitan city in Japan.[28]

The scale of the shogunal capital was likely beyond anything Saigō had imagined. By 1731 the population of Edo had already reached more than 1 million, more than the entire population of Satsuma domain and roughly fifteen times that of Kagoshima.[29] Roughly half of these people were merchants and artisans, and this made Edo an unparalleled center for consumer culture. By the eighteenth century the city imported annually nearly 800,000 casks of sake, more than 100,000 casks of soy sauce, and in excess of 18 million bundles of firewood; by the early 1800s Edo boasted dozens of theaters, more than 600 book lenders, and more than 6,000 restaurants.[30] The city was a center of both high culture and utter decadence, where fashions in prose, poetry, theater, food, and clothing originated before spreading to the countryside. Edo was not, of course, the only Japanese metropolis, or even Japan's only capital. The emperor lived in Kyoto, which remained a center of traditional culture. Economically, Edo was rivaled by Osaka, commonly known as the "kitchen of the realm" *(tenka no daidokoro)* because of its importance in the grain trade. But although Osaka was a major business and financial center, it was of little political importance. Kyoto, although important in imperial politics and high culture, was a secondary site for commerce. Edo, by contrast, was important in almost everything: it was a center for culture, trade, politics, and ideas.

Edo's political, economic, and cultural roles were interconnected. To pay for their expenses in Edo, daimyo and their retainers required the services of merchant wholesalers. These merchants received shipments of commodities, most commonly rice, from the domain and sold them in the market centers of Edo, Kyoto, and Osaka. After deducting a percentage for their services, they sent the proceeds, in gold or silver, to the domain's officers in Edo. This simple function was critical to the *sankin kōtai* system, since daimyo could not provide for their needs in Edo without cash. In fact, the merchant wholesalers soon took on the role of bankers. They would advance funds to a domain with interest, treating the following year's harvest as collateral. Because of the *sankin kōtai* system, Edo rapidly grew to rival Osaka as a center for commerce and finance.

The regular presence in the shogunal capital of Japan's warrior elite produced a dazzling culture of consumption. In the culture of Edo, which has been tellingly compared to the courtier culture of Versailles, daimyo poured inordinate effort and resources into politically motivated entertainment. By the eighteenth century, gatherings in Edo were means of conspicuously displaying breeding, culture, and refinement. Daimyo competed to secure the services of the most esteemed tea masters, landscape architects, balladeers *(jōruri)*, poets, and actors. There was also a thriving interest in things foreign. In about 1824, for example, Shimazu Nariakira's great-grandfather Shigehide sought to impress the head of the shogun's academy with a lavish Chinese banquet. This feast had no fewer than thirteen courses, with more than fifty individual dishes.[31]

Saigō was seemingly overwhelmed by this exciting and intimidating city. In his first surviving letter from Edo, an 1854/7/29 letter to his maternal uncles, Saigō stressed the fine character of his new friends, and he took pains to assure his family that he was not falling prey to the temptations of big city life. He was associating, he wrote, with good people. In something of a contradiction, he also announced that, unlike the other new arrivals to Edo, he was not visiting the brothels in the Shinagawa district.[32] Saigō's closest new friends were men of similar rank and circumstance: Ōyama Tsunayoshi, Kabayama San'en, and Kaeda Nobuyoshi. These three had all come to Edo in 1852 as tea servers, although their actual duties had little to do with tea. Much like Saigō, they were primarily Nariakira's personal aides, men whose low rank allowed them private meetings with the daimyo without the protocol of a formal audience.

Through Kabayama, Saigō entered the turbulent intellectual environment of Edo. Although Saigō had read and studied almost everything available in Kagoshima, Edo was another world entirely. Within months Saigō was swept away by what was, for him, a new ideology: Mito learning. Saigō's exposure to Mito learning in 1854 and 1855 would change his worldview forever.

Mito learning was a form of imperial loyalism developed by scholars in Mito domain, a branch domain of the Tokugawa house. The lords of Mito were descendants of Tokugawa Ieyasu but through his eleventh son, Yorifusa, rather than through his principal heir, Hidetada.[33] This meant that Mito could, during a succession crisis, provide a legitimate heir to the shogunal line and that the Mito house held special status among the daimyo. Paradoxically, given their close ties to the shogunal house, Mito scholars celebrated the importance of the imperial institution, describing the emperor as the mystic and symbolic embodiment of Japanese civilization.[34] From a modern perspective this was an utterly self-destructive project, since Mito scholars promoted the sovereignty of the emperor, which in 1868 was invoked to overthrow the shogunate and which in the 1870s was used to justify the elimination of all domains, including Mito. But Mito learning was completely reasonable within the context of early modern thought and politics in Japan. Mito scholars assumed that the emperor would "reign rather than rule." Nothing in Mito learning provided for rule by the emperor instead of the shogun. Rather, the philosophy promoted rule by warriors for the emperor. This assumption was well grounded in historical precedent: the imperial house had not wielded power effectively since the 800s. The Tokugawa shoguns were nominally imperial servants, but in practice they gave orders to the imperial house.

In emphasizing the shogun's role as an imperial servant, Mito scholars sought to reinforce, not undermine, the shogun's legitimacy. Their program relied on the religious aura of the emperor. According to Mito scholars, the Japanese dynastic line stretched back unbroken to the dawn of time. The emperor was a direct descendant of the sun goddess, Amaterasu, and his authority was divine and transcendent. Building on this divine ancestry, Mito scholars envisioned a Japanese polity revitalized by reverence for the emperor. The shogun was legitimate not merely because he had defeated all rivals, but also because he was an imperial servant. Daimyo were, similarly, legitimate as servants of an imperial servant. The sun goddess herself obliged commoners to obey their daimyo.[35]

Based on their belief in the sanctity of the emperor, Mito scholars favored minimal contact with the West and argued for strict enforcement of the shogunate's ban on trade. Their hostility to Western trade stemmed from a fear of spiritual contamination. Nothing could more effectively undermine the realm than a foreign religion, and everything Western was tainted by Christianity. The leading Mito scholar of the 1850s, Fujita Tōko, believed that all Western books had a covert Christian message. Mito scholars consistently emphasized spiritual over material concerns. In the wake of Perry's first visit Tokugawa Nariaki, the daimyo of Mito, argued that the shogunate should fear peace more than war. An open conflict, he wrote, would galvanize the samurai class and "increase tenfold the morale of the country." So motivated, Japan would be able to drive off the foreigners. Nariakira recognized the superiority of Western weapons, but he and Tōko thought morale and tactics, rather than technology, would decide the conflict. Men inspired to fight for principle could stand up to Western forces, and what Japan lacked in technology it could make up in strategy. Western ships were unquestionably superior, but the foreigners would need to land in order to attack Japan. Once ashore their advantage would vanish, as brave samurai wiped them out with sword and spear. Mito thinkers did not reject Western technology, but they doubted that technology was worth the risk of extensive foreign contact.[36]

From a modern perspective much of Mito learning was naive and xenophobic. Mito thinkers used an imaginary past to confront a chaotic and threatening present. But Saigō, like many of his contemporaries, found Mito learning empowering and enthralling. Mito learning's emphasis on the existing class order made it familiar and comforting, but it invoked the sun goddess to give this conservative agenda a radical energy and vibrancy. For several years Saigō's social and intellectual life in Edo revolved around Mito learning, and through his studies he met with retainers from throughout Japan. Saigō took part in a regular study group that included samurai from the northeastern domains of Echizen and Mito and the southwestern domains of Kumamoto and Yanagawa, all of them, in Saigō's words, "Mito partisans."[37] Saigō also formed a deep personal connection with two important Mito intellectuals, Fujita Tōko and Toda Chūdayū. In a frequently quoted letter he described listening to Fujita Tōko as a near-transcendent experience. It is, he wrote, like "bathing in the pure spring water: all unrest and confusion disappear and my heart and mind become quiet and pure." Saigō was equally impressed with Fujita's lord, the Mito daimyo Tokugawa Nariaki. "I am such an ardent follower of Nariaki," he wrote with conscious hyperbole, "that if his lordship were to crack his whip and lead the way against the foreigners, I would rush in without hesitation."[38] These early letters reveal the goals and attitudes that would shape Saigō's life. He sought a transcendent clarity that he associated with separation from quotidian, practical concerns. At moments of true clarity, thought Saigō, instinct was a better guide than reason. Although few of Saigō's early letters survive, his meeting with Tōko stands out nonetheless as a turning point. Before meeting Tōko, Saigō did not write of the emperor, or of Japan as the "imperial land." After their meeting Saigō routinely referred to the imperial institution to frame his thought and actions.

Saigō's lord, Nariakira, was generally untroubled by Saigō's involvement with another domain. Although all domains were potential political rivals, Nariaki and Nariakira had forged a working alliance. Like Nariaki, Nariakira favored an increased emphasis on the emperor in Japanese politics. The two differed on questions of trade, as Nariakira was far more impressed by Western technology than was the lord of Mito. But Nariakira shared Nariaki's suspicion of Western treaty demands. Nariakira wanted access to Western technology without a demeaning trade treaty. This led to a strategic alliance of Satsuma with Mito, and in 1853 Nariakira nominated Nariaki as a special shogunal adviser on national defense.[39]

Saigō's intellectual connection with Mito learning did not weaken his dedication to his own lord. An eager partisan in domain politics, he actively sought to subvert Nariakira's political enemies.[40] His letters reveal an intense, almost frenzied devotion to Nariakira. In 1854/8, for example, he declared himself willing to die to avenge his lord. The occasion was another mysterious family tragedy: the previous month Nariakira and his son Torajūmaru had fallen severely ill with dysentery. Although Nariakira slowly recovered, Torajūmaru did not. Nariakira's only surviving son died on 1854/i7/24 at age five. Saigō was overwrought with grief. "I cannot dwell on the details," he wrote his friend Fukushimaya Zōda, "because my tears reach the page before my brush." Like many of Nariakira's allies, Saigō suspected foul play. Because Torajūmaru was Nariakira's last surviving son, his death raised the possibility that Hisamitsu or Hisamitsu's son might succeed Nariakira. Given these political ramifications, Saigō concluded that the illnesses were the work of Yura. He was furious: "In my heart I regret life itself and I am ablaze with rage." He declared that he would gladly die if he could destroy Yura and "remove the calamities that plague the state." Saigō's vow reveals the influence of Ōyōmei learning. By striking down Yura, Saigō hoped to "achieve the great peace of death and leap to the heavens."[41] The idea that Saigō could achieve transcendent peace through an act of pure virtue draws heavily on the Ōyōmei tradition. But Saigō's passionate devotion was not limited to his lord's troubles. When Nariakira's mistress became pregnant in 1856 Saigō prayed devoutly for the birth of a healthy son. He swore to keep a monk's vow of celibacy if a potential heir were born. In a letter to his uncles, he revealed the lugubrious loyalty that would shape his life: "So long as I am breathing, I will keep this vow with utter sincerity, and although I believe I have but two or three years more to live I wish to see the birth of my lord's child before I die."[42]

Despite the consensus between Nariaki and Nariakira, Saigō eventually fell into a politically awkward position in the wake of a crisis of succession in the shogunal house. The succession dispute was prompted by the deteriorating health of Tokugawa Iesada (1824–1858), the thirteenth Tokugawa shogun. Iesada had succeeded as shogun in 1853, mere days after Perry's departure. Iesada was only twenty-nine when he became shogun, but he was seriously infirm, unable to speak clearly or to sit up straight for even half an hour. Modern analysis suggests that he suffered from epilepsy. Equally serious, he was childless and seemed unlikely to father a son. His designation of an heir was thus a pressing concern. Under normal circumstances the succession would have been straightforward. Although Iesada did not have a son, he did have a cousin, Tokugawa Iemochi, son of the daimyo of Kii. But while Iemochi had the right bloodlines, he did not, at age eight, inspire confidence as Japan's supreme warlord. Choosing Iemochi as heir would have meant in practice giving full authority to the shogunal administration. Iemochi would be assigned a regent, and real power would fall to those well-placed *fudai* daimyo on the shogun's council of elders. There was historical precedent for such an arrangement, and Iemochi had widespread backing from shogunal supporters. For many samurai, however, the looming foreign crisis demanded a new approach. Japan needed a leader who could hold his own in meetings with foreign emissaries. Nor could leadership by committee push through the reforms Japan needed to respond to the foreign threat. Motivated by these concerns, the dissenting daimyo proposed an alternate candidate: Hitotsubashi Keiki, seventh son of Tokugawa Nariaki, the daimyo of Mito.

Keiki was a healthy, mature, intelligent adult, and these traits became code words for his candidacy. Keiki's advocates promoted his succession with calls for a "mature," "intelligent," and "popular" shogun.[43] This image appealed to many daimyo. But Keiki's allies were a diverse group and disagreed on major issues. One of Keiki's major advocates was his father, Nariaki. He saw Keiki's candidacy as a means of promoting his own views on foreign policy, which were based on the principle of maximum possible isolation. But Keiki was also supported by daimyo with more moderate views on foreign trade, such as Shimazu Nariakira, Yamauchi Yōdō of Tosa, and Nabeshima Narimasa of Saga.[44] What these lords had in common was their *tozama* status, which excluded them from shogunal office. They favored Keiki because they associated him with inclusive government and radical reform. Japan's pressing problems, they argued, required a new level of national unity. The shogunate could not mobilize Japan against imperialism while keeping its most powerful warlords at arm's length because they were *tozama* daimyo. Keiki's *tozama* allies envisioned what might anachronistically be called a national unity government, in which old divisions would be ignored while everyone struggled toward a common goal. Powerful lords like Shimazu Nariakira and Nabeshima Narimasa would get senior positions in the shogun's cabinet, and the new administration would revitalize Japan's military and renegotiate treaties with the Western powers.[45]

Key reformers within the shogunate also were inclined toward Keiki. Abe Masahirō, head of the shogun's council of elders, felt that Japan had to make treaty concessions to the Western powers to avoid a disastrous war. He saw

Scheepvaartmuseum, Amsterdam

Hitotsubashi Keiki

Keiki's candidacy as a way to gain political cover for an unpopular decision. Thus, despite his *fudai* status, Abe backed Keiki. But Abe's desire to get support for the treaties put him at odds with Tokugawa Nariaki, Keiki's isolationist father. In short, although most of Keiki's allies supported him because of his image as a vital leader open to outside advice and radical reform, they disagreed among themselves on pressing questions of foreign policy. The result was an alliance of convenience and an often incoherent campaign to reform the shogunate.[46]

Saigō experienced firsthand this tangle of conflicting interests. Initially he became involved in the succession dispute in 1856, through his friends from Mito domain. Sensing Saigō's influence over his lord, they implored him to arrange Nariakira's support for Keiki. Saigō was apprehensive, but he agreed. He viewed the task as a way to honor his Mito mentors, Fujita Tōko and Toda Chūdayū. Both had died in 1855/10 in an earthquake, and Saigō wanted to repay their intellectual guidance by advancing their cause. Saigō seems not to have realized the implications of his promise. He had committed himself to lobbying his lord on behalf of a "foreign" power.[47]

On 1856/4/12 Nariakira summoned Saigō for an audience. Saigō was thrilled by the honor, but he braced himself for a difficult encounter. Pressing his lord to support the agenda of Mito domain could easily be understood as arrogance, if not treason. When Saigō first broached the subject, Nariakira was noncommittal. This increased Saigō's anxiety. In a letter the following month to Ōyama he recalled being torn between deference to his lord and his obligations to his Mito friends. "What," he wrote, "if I remonstrated two or three times and his lordship decided otherwise? I would have no face before [my comrades in] Mito." Saigō was so anguished that he felt a weight on his chest and his voice trembled. Then Nariakira revealed that he himself was one of Keiki's earliest supporters. Nariakira had been working with Matsudaira Shungaku to advance Keiki's cause, but had not apprised Nariaki. Because Shungaku and Nariakira had been working independently of Keiki's own father, Saigō had been caught in the middle as an unnecessary "intermediary."[48]

Saigō's crisis of loyalties was thus resolved more easily than he had dared to hope. But his anxiety and his trembling voice reflected a deep inner conflict. How could Saigō serve both his lord and Mito? Saigō's dilemma reflected a contradiction at the heart of the samurai sense of loyalty. Part of samurai loyalty was personal, in the sense that as vassals they were loyal to a specific man. This tradition was reflected in the medieval tradition of *junshi,* or following one's lord into death. Rather than serve another lord, samurai would commit suicide after their master's death. Even in the medieval era, *junshi* commonly required a lord's prior approval, and the practice was outlawed by the Tokugawa shogunate in 1663, but it remained a model for individual loyalty. Saigō himself, according to legend, considered suicide after Nariakira's death in 1858.[49] The other aspect of samurai loyalty was institutional, in the sense that a samurai was loyal not to his lord, but to his lord's "state." Institutional loyalty meant that a samurai could oppose his lord's decisions without being disloyal. The vassal had a higher purpose: to serve the lord's polity or "state" and the broader principles of propriety. This face of samurai loyalty drew on the traditions of warrior inheritance. While *junshi* demonstrated a vassal's loyalty to his lord, a dead vassal could not serve his lord's heir. A vassal loyal to the lord's house needed to think of future generations rather than one individual, and to value the lord's posterity as much as his person. This shift in loyalty from a man to an institution meant that vassals could challenge their lord if his decisions seemed to threaten the future of his domain. A vassal was obliged to stop his lord from squandering his inheritance. Institutional loyalty also drew on the Chinese Confucian tradition of service to the emperor. An imperial servant was obliged to remonstrate with his lord, to explain to him the error of his ways. A servant showed his loyalty not by agreeing with his lord's errors, but by dissenting and risking death. The exemplars of such conduct, Boyi and Shuqi of ancient China, were known to every samurai. Appalled by the conduct of their emperor, they voiced their dissent. The emperor ignored their protest, but in recognition of their righteousness dismissed them without punishment. Boyi and Shuqi were unmollified. Unwilling to betray their lord, they did not challenge his authority. Unwilling to eat the grain of an unjust ruler, they starved themselves to death. It was this complicated sense of duty that had made Saigō's voice tremble.[50]

Saigō relied on his abstract loyalty to a cause rather than his immediate loyalty to a man when he braced himself for a conflict with Nariakira. But Saigō's cause was an institution greater than the Shimazu house and a principle nobler than Confucian propriety. Mito learning had led Saigō to the radical concept of Japan as the land of the gods. By serving the emperor and the emperor's realm, Saigō could disagree with Nariakira without being disloyal. That Nariakira himself had turned out to be a Keiki supporter was, for Saigō, further evidence of the legitimacy of the imperial principle. "Even difficult matters of our state [Satsuma] are easy when one acts for the realm," he wrote to Ōyama. Keiki's candidacy, he explained to Ōyama, was the best way "to promote the reform of the shogunate and be a servant to the land of the gods." Saigō's audience with Nariakira was thus the first time he had acted as a Japanese subject rather than as a Shimazu retainer.[51]

In 1856 it was easy for Saigō to serve both the "realm" and the "state." Saigō's "state" was Satsuma, and his "realm" was Japan. The imperial realm had as yet no army, no navy, no treasury, no courts, and no currency. The "land of the gods" was a compelling abstraction, not a political entity. Saigō thought of the imperial realm as something that could unite the shogunate and the domains, not as an independent government. This view of the emperor was the supreme accomplishment of Mito learning, but it was, ultimately, an unstable political principle. The emperor could inspire shogunal reform precisely because the imperial court was too weak to serve as an alternate government. As the imperial court gained power, this utopian understanding of imperial authority collapsed. Within a decade, Saigō himself would advocate the destruction of the shogunate in the name of the emperor.[52]

His Lord's Confidant

Starting in the spring of 1856, Saigō entered Nariakira's inner circle of retainers, those men involved in the most important issues of domain affairs. His rank and stipend remained modest, but he met regularly with his daimyo and became a major figure in domain politics. In 1857 Nagaoka Kenmotsu, a senior retainer in Kumamoto domain, observed that Saigō, "although an official of menial rank, has audiences with his lord" and was privy to Nariakira's private thoughts on national politics. Kenmotsu also found Saigō exceptionally loyal, focused, and disinclined to idle talk.[53] In 1857/4 Saigō accompanied Nariakira to Kagoshima, but in 1857/10 Nariakira, wanting a reliable agent in Edo, sent him back to the capital. Saigō was now expected to execute the wishes of a lord who was nearly a thousand miles away. If Saigō had a question, he would have to wait weeks for a response. Satsuma's Edo-based retainers had dealt with this time lag for centuries, but Saigō's situation was markedly more difficult. Because Nariakira was challenging the established order, Saigō could not rely on traditional solutions. Instead, he would need to guess his lord's responses to unprecedented situations. Saigō rose to the challenge, but he found the situation extremely trying, as he explained in an 1858/1/29 letter to his uncles: "These past days have been difficult. I have been repeatedly attacked by others concerned for acting unilaterally." Upon learning from a letter that his actions were true to Nariakira's plans, Saigō was so relieved that he "wept for several hours."[54]

Once back in Edo, Saigō undertook the politically sensitive task of trying to influence the shogun's choice of heir through two avenues: the shogunal women's quarters and the imperial court. In Kyoto, Saigō's key ally in promoting Keiki was Hashimoto Sanai, a retainer of Matsudaira Shungaku. Saigō and Hashimoto had met in 1855, but their close collaboration began only in 1857/12 at the behest of their daimyo. Nariakira essentially assigned Saigō to work with Hashimoto. He wrote Matsudaira Shungaku that, for purposes of advancing Keiki's candidacy, he should consider Saigō his own vassal.[55] This arguably put Saigō under the authority of Hashimoto, a man six years his junior. At first Saigō was carefully deferential to Hashimoto. On 1857/12/14, for example, he asked Hashimoto to draft a description of Keiki, a set of "talking points" they could use in lobbying the shogunate and court.[56] But the two men readily became trusted partners. In later years Saigō described Hashimoto as a close equal: "I served Fujita Tōko as my master but I supported Hashimoto as my comrade."[57] When Saigō died twenty years later on the hills on Shiroyama he had with him a letter from Sanai.[58]

Hashimoto offered Saigō a bold new vision of Japan. Although Nariakira, like Hashimoto, had a deep appreciation of Western technology, he publicly opposed United States demands for a trade treaty. Hashimoto, by contrast, argued that Japan needed such treaties to gain access to Western technology. By combining the Japanese virtues of benevolence, righteousness, loyalty, and filial piety with foreign "machinery and techniques" Japan could become an international power. Like Saigō, Hashimoto considered himself a disciple of Fujita Tōko, but he rejected the xenophobia of Mito learning. Japan could freely learn from the West as long as it maintained its own cultural traditions.[59] This confident and optimistic vision of Japan's future shaped Saigō's own views. In later years he told his students that the study of foreign customs would help Japan as long as it was combined with a reverence for Japanese tradition.[60]

In Edo Saigō's attempts to promote Keiki hinged on Nariakira's adopted daughter Atsuhime, the shogun's third wife. Atsuhime's marriage to the shogun was a triumph for Nariakira, the fruit of years of political machinations. The idea that Iesada might marry a Shimazu daughter had first surfaced in 1850 after the death of the shogun's second wife, but the plan ran into numerous delays and widespread opposition. Nariakira's ally Tokugawa Nariaki, for example, found it disgraceful that the shogun would choose a bride from "Satsuma, enemies of Ieyasu," rather than someone from an allied warrior house.[61] The foreign treaty crisis and the 1855 Edo earthquake also delayed the marriage. Finally, on 1856/12/18, Iesada and Atsuhime were married. Nariakira had long planned to use the marriage to advance his political interests, and the succession dispute seemed like an ideal opportunity to use his new connections. One of Keiki's staunchest opponents was Iesada's mother, but now Keiki's advocates had allies in the shogunal women's quarters as well.[62]

Influencing the shogunate through the women's quarters seemed promising at first. Atsuhime was politically adroit and she had the help of Ikushima, a lady-in-waiting known for her political savvy. Ikushima, it was said, spent money like water but could discern almost anyone's secret intentions. But the shogun's mother, Honjūin, was equally formidable. Although she had supported Iesada's marriage to a Shimazu bride, Honjūin bitterly opposed outside interference in the shogunal succession dispute. In 1858/2 Ikushima reported that when Atsuhime raised the subject of succession, Honjūin rebuffed her. Iesada was too young to worry about an heir and Keiki was too old to be an adopted son, she declared, and the matter was, in any case, no concern of the Shimazu. Atsuhime persisted and broached the subject with Iesada himself in 1858/4. The shogun seemed willing to consider adopting Keiki, but Honjūin ended such talk by threatening suicide. It was now clear that Satsuma could not sway the succession through the women's quarters.[63]

As the prospects for influencing the succession through Atsuhime dimmed, Saigō focused his efforts on the imperial court. This was unprecedented. Never before had the imperial court intervened in a Tokugawa succession dispute. Nevertheless, the shogunate itself was changing the traditions of Tokugawa rule. In 1857/12 the shogunate made an unprecedented request for imperial support in foreign affairs by involving it in treaty negotiations. The 1858 Harris treaty, named after the American consul Townsend Harris, required Japan to accept extraterritoriality and open several treaty ports to the United States. Without broader support the chairman of the shogun's council of elders, Hotta Masayoshi, was unwilling to sign the treaty, which he regarded as politically lethal. Hotta envisioned imperial sanction largely as a formality, in view of the fact that the imperial court had not opposed the shogunate in more than two hundred years. In 1857/12 Hotta dispatched an emissary to Kyoto to get imperial approval. Since the shogun recognized the emperor as a scholar, not an administrator, Hotta sent the head of the shogunal academy. The emissary was rebuffed. Hotta was stunned, and in 1858/2 he went to Kyoto himself.[64] Unwittingly, Hotta had thus set a precedent for imperial intervention in diplomacy, traditionally a shogunal affair. Now Keiki's advocates sought to have the imperial court influence the shogunal succession itself.

Hashimoto left Edo for Kyoto in 1858/2 and began meeting with imperial courtiers to cultivate support for Keiki. Saigō, politically surefooted in Edo but ignorant of Kyoto politics, was inclined to follow Hashimoto's lead. Hashimoto's general strategy was to link imperial support for the Harris treaty with Keiki's succession. The argument ran as follows: If Japan merely signed the Harris treaty, it would amount to political capitulation to barbarians. A young and vital shogun such as Keiki, however, could take advantage of the opportunities provided by the treaty and could mobilize Japan against future concessions. Saigō arrived in Kyoto a few weeks after Hashimoto and began developing his own network of contacts. Satsuma's principal ally at the imperial court was Konoe Tadahiro, a high-ranking courtier who was related by marriage to the Shimazu house. Konoe, who held the lofty title of "minister of the left," was widely respected at court. To communicate discreetly with Konoe, Saigō worked through Gesshō, a monk whose temple was affiliated with the Konoe house. Gesshō was an unlikely political activist. He was well-known as the head of the Jōjuin, an abbey at Kiyomizu Temple, and was an accomplished poet, but he was not an outspoken imperial loyalist. This lack of political experience made him the perfect courier for sensitive correspondence, however, because he had plausible, apolitical reasons for meeting both Konoe and Saigō. Gesshō maintained a residence in Sokushūin Abbey at Tōfukuji Temple, which housed the graves of many Satsuma retainers. Saigō and Gesshō could meet innocuously in a hermitage behind the graveyard. Then Gesshō could meet with Konoe at Kiyomizu Temple, which housed the Konoe family graves.[65]

Hashimoto made steady progress in generating support for Keiki, and on 1858/3/20 Saigō left Kyoto for Edo confident that the court would soon mandate Keiki's succession. Unbeknownst to Saigō, however, a fierce countermovement was developing. Shogunal conservatives, alarmed by the deterioration of shogunal authority, moved to block imperial intervention. Their leader was Ii Naosuke, the daimyo of Hikone. Ii was an unlikely fig-ure to lead a restoration of shogunal power. The prestigious Ii house had served the Tokugawa shoguns since the 1500s, but the Ii had not played a major role in shogunal politics since the early 1600s.[66] Naosuke himself was the fourteenth son of Ii Naonaka, and had succeeded as daimyo only because many of his elder brothers had been adopted by other families. Although few would have forecast Ii's rapid rise to power, he capitalized on the power vacuum resulting from the treaty crisis. Hotta had taken impe-rial approval for the Harris treaty for granted, but was then unable to secure an imperial edict. Ii quickly eclipsed Hotta in Edo: from 1858/4 until his death on 1860/3/3, Ii was the most powerful figure in Japan.[67]

Using his own contacts at the imperial court, Ii managed to derail Keiki's succession. The court was prepared to issue an edict directing the shogun to name a "mature," "intelligent," and "popular" heir. These code words would have signaled imperial support for Keiki. The actual 3/22 edict, however, merely ordered the shogunate to designate an heir quickly. Ii had engi-neered the eleventh-hour deletion of a key passage and thereby stripped the edict of meaning.[68]

Ii took advantage of the confusion of Keiki's dumbfounded supporters to assert his authority. On 1858/4/23 he took office as great councilor *(tairō)* in the shogunate and began to consolidate his power. By 1858/6 he was ready to challenge his opponents openly, and on 6/19, despite the lack of imperial approval, he ordered approval of the Harris treaty. The Keiki faction was outraged. On 6/24 Tokugawa Nariaki, Matsudaira Shungaku, and Tokugawa Yoshikatsu of Owari went unsummoned to Edo Castle to berate Ii over both the shogunal succession and the treaty. Ii ignored them, and the following day the shogunate definitively rejected Keiki by designating Iemochi as Iesada's heir. Ten days later, for good measure, Ii placed all three daimyo under house arrest and forced Shungaku and Yoshikatsu into retirement. The shogunate, Ii declared, was not a consultative body and Ii would not suffer unsolicited advice from upstart nobles. The shogun was Japan's supreme warlord. Ii, as the shogun's regent, would brook no dissent.[69]

Sensing an impending crisis, Saigō left Edo on 5/17 to see Nariakira back in Kagoshima. As soon as he arrived on 6/7, he met with Nariakira to inform him of the radical changes in Edo and Kyoto. Nariakira was outraged by Ii's actions and, according to legend, considered sending troops to Kyoto to "defend" the court against the shogunate. On 6/18 Saigō left Kagoshima with a letter for Shungaku and instructions to garner support from key daimyo. Saigō arrived in Kyoto on 7/10 and began meeting with friends and associates to assess the political landscape. But the situation had changed radically even since his meeting with Nariakira the previous month, and before Saigō could act, he was confronted by devastating news: his lord was dead.[70]

Nariakira had fallen ill suddenly on 1858/7/9. By 7/11 he was bedridden, with fever, chills, and diarrhea. On the evening of 7/15 Nariakira realized that he was dying and scheduled a last meeting with the domain elders. His condition worsened that night, and at 3:00 A.M. on 7/16 he urgently summoned the head of the lord's privy purse, Yamada Shōemon. Prostrate and exhausted, Nariakira hastily described a plan for succession. Nariakira recognized that his sole surviving son, two-year-old Tetsumaru, was too young to succeed. He authorized his father, the retired daimyo Narioki, to choose one of two possible successors: either Nariakira's half brother Hisamitsu or Hisamitsu's son Tadayoshi. Nariakira asked only that the new daimyo promise to adopt Tetsumaru and to marry Nariakira's daughter, eight-year-old Teruhime. This, he hoped, would provide political stability while allowing Tetsumaru to succeed in the future. Having formulated a succession plan, Nariakira died in the early morning.[71]

Nariakira's sudden death shocked the realm, and it was widely believed that he had been poisoned. Even Pompe van Meerdervoort, a physician with the Dutch navy in Nagasaki, suspected foul play. Nariakira, he wrote, was "possibly the most important person in the country; because of his influence on the emperor and his government, and also because of his own power and his erudition, he was regarded as the reformer of Japan . . . it is not improbable that he was poisoned."[72] For Saigō, Nariakira's death was an emotional and political catastrophe. Nariakira had taken Saigō from obscurity to the center of national politics, and Saigō's personal devotion to Nariakira was boundless. Saigō had declared himself ready to die for his lord's sake. Now that Nariakira was dead, possibly murdered, Saigō felt alone and powerless. Nariakira's trust in Saigō had made him a major figure in national politics. He was, as Nagaoka Kenmotsu had observed, a man who "knew his lord's thoughts on all matters of the realm."[73] Saigō was widely respected for his sincerity and dedication, but his political clout was dependent on his relationship with Nariakira. Without Nariakira, Saigō was morally upstanding but politically unremarkable. His future within Satsuma looked bleak. Saigō had been openly partisan in the rivalry between Hisamitsu and Nariakira, conspiring against Hisamitsu's allies and swearing vengeance against Hisamitsu's mother. Now he would have to serve under Hisamitsu or Hisamitsu's son.

According to legend, Saigō considered returning to Satsuma and committing ritual suicide (junshi) at the grave of Nariakira. Gesshō dissuaded him, arguing that Saigō could better manifest his loyalty to Nariakira by pushing forward with his political plans. On 8/2 Saigō left Kyoto for Edo with a secret communication from Konoe to Tokugawa Nariaki and Tokugawa Yoshikatsu of Owari, but with both men under house arrest he could not make contact. Saigō was distraught and described his feeling in a plaintive letter to Gesshō. "I feel," he wrote, "like a man who has lost his ship and is stranded on an island." Saigō felt that he had failed both Konoe and Gesshō.[74] Saigō returned to Kyoto in late 1858/8 and began meeting with proimperial activists, hoping to raise support for the idea of military intervention.[75]

Responding in part to this threat, the shogunate began a crackdown on antishogunal activity. Known to historians as the Ansei purge, the crackdown began on 9/7 with the arrest of Umeda Unpin, a former samurai from Obama domain in Wakasa.[76] Over the following year Ii systematically targeted the leading figures in the imperial loyalists' movement. The famous Chōshū loyalist Yoshida Shōin, for example, was imprisoned in 1858/12 and executed ten months later. Hashimoto Sanai was arrested in 1858/10 and executed in 1859/10.[77] Sensing impending danger, Konoe Tadahiro asked Saigō to protect Gesshō. Saigō agreed, and on the night of 9/9 Saigō and Gesshō quietly left Kyoto for Osaka. Saigō continued to make his case for a show of force in Kyoto, but the political climate had changed. The shogunate, which had silenced the realm's most outspoken daimyo, could now prosecute ordinary samurai at will. By late 1858/9 Saigō felt he could no longer guarantee Gesshō's safety anywhere near shogunal territory. On 9/24 Saigō, his friend Kaeda Nobuyoshi, and Gesshō fled Osaka for Kagoshima.[78]

Traveling by ship, they arrived in Shimonoseki on 10/1, and Saigō went ahead to secure refuge for Gesshō. The shogunate had issued a warrant for Saigō's arrest, and when he arrived in Kagoshima, the domain ordered him to change his name from Takamori to Sansuke. In deference to his loyalty and reputation, the domain protected Saigō, denying knowledge of his whereabouts to the shogunate. To Saigō's dismay, however, the domain would not commit to protecting Gesshō. In accordance with Nariakira's will, Narioki had named Tadayoshi the next daimyo. The effective ruler of the domain was now Hisamitsu, Tadayoshi's father. Hisamitsu was too politically savvy to betray Saigō to the shogunate, since to do so would ignite another round of internecine strife. But Hisamitsu was unwilling to risk a confrontation with the shogunate over a nonnative monk. Gesshō's primary claim to refuge was his friendship with Saigō, and for Hisamitsu this was scarcely reason enough to invite trouble.[79] Gesshō arrived in Kagoshima City on 11/8, accompanied by his manservant Jūsuke and by Hirano Kuniomi, an imperial loyalist from Fukuoka. Their welcome was ominous. Gesshō found temporary lodging in a temple, but the resident monk, concerned about harboring a wanted man, contacted the domain. Officials appeared immediately and hurried Gesshō and Hirano to a domain lodge, where they were kept from all visitors.[80]

The story of Saigō's flight with Gesshō, the domain's response, and their subsequent actions has become enmeshed with the Saigō legend, and many biographies repeat accounts that are not substantiated by contemporary documents. Remarkably, historians have neglected an intriguing memoir, the recollections of Shigeno Yasutsugu, Japan's first modern historian.

Shigeno did not publish his memoir until 1896, but it was based on conversations held with Saigō in early 1859. Although Shigeno's account was undoubtedly colored by nostalgia, it is unlikely that Shigeno indulged in mythmaking. As a professional historian, Shigeno made his mark on the field by insisting on the difference between history and legend. He became known for his "deletion thesis" (massatsuron) when he argued that several well-known medieval figures, such as Kojima Takanori, were actually no more than legends. Unlike some memoirs, Shigeno's account lacks any major factual errors, and when combined with surviving primary sources, provides a basis for understanding Saigō's thoughts and actions in late 1858.[81]

According to Shigeno the domain was willing neither to protect Gesshō nor to hand him over to the shogunate, and on 11/15 it announced an ingenious compromise. Saigō would convey Gesshō to a small region in easternmost Hyūga Province, near the border with Sadowara domain. This region lay within the domain, but outside the domain's border checkpoints. Because Sadowara was ruled by a branch of the Shimazu house, this unusual boundary arrangement was not a security concern. Placing Gesshō in this border zone satisfied two needs. The domain was honoring the late Nariakira by offering refuge to a monk who had taken up his cause. By moving Gesshō to the border, however, the domain was also preparing to abandon him. If the shogunate found Gesshō, the domain could deny all knowledge of his case. Gesshō, they could declare, had crossed the border and left the domain. For Saigō, the import of the 11/15 order was clear. Satsuma would not cooperate with the shogunate, but it would not protect Gesshō either.[82]

Saigō was crushed. The 11/15 order marked the collapse of his political influence. Mere months earlier, he had been at the center of national politics. Trusted by the most powerful daimyo in the realm and respected by his peers, Saigō had been part of a burgeoning political movement. Now he was powerless, hiding under an assumed name and unable to help a trusted comrade. His friends were being hunted by shogunal agents, and his lord and mentor was dead. His inability to help Gesshō was especially devastating. Saigō felt that he had not only betrayed his promise to Konoe, he also had failed to advance Nariakira's dream. Surveying his world, Saigō saw only failure, isolation, and loss.

On the evening of 11/15 Saigō told Gesshō of the domain's orders. Gesshō declared that he would run no farther. He was a wanted man and had come to Satsuma hoping for asylum. The domain's decision had dashed those hopes. Rather than fall into the hands of the shogunate, Gesshō would go to "another place." Saigō shared Gesshō's bleak assessment of the situation. Recognizing that Gesshō's "other place" was not on earth, he agreed to accompany his friend. Saigō would plan their departure.

Hyūga Province lay on the other side of Kagoshima Bay, and Saigō prepared a boat, food, and sake for the trip across. Late on 11/15, under a full moon, Saigō and Gesshō left Kagoshima City in a simple skiff, accompanied by Hirano, Jūsuke, and a domain-appointed escort named Sakaguchi. The boat was designed for speed, and the party made quick progress across the bay. About three miles into their trip, Saigō called Gesshō to the bow and pointed to Shingakuji, a famous temple on the eastern shore of the bay. The temple, he explained, was a memorial to Shimazu Toshihisa, a younger brother of Shimazu Yoshihisa, head of the Shimazu house in the 1590s. During Hideyoshi's invasion of Kyūshū, Yoshihisa had elected to bow to superior force. He surrendered territory in northern Kyūshū in exchange for Hideyoshi's confirmation of the Shimazu's traditional holdings. Shimazu Toshihisa objected to his elder brother's decision and declared that he would fight on. Hideyoshi, outraged, ordered Toshihisa's death. Toshihisa committed ritual suicide on the site of the temple. Many of his retainers committed *junshi* to follow him into death. More than 250 years later, explained Saigō, Shimazu retainers still visited Shingakuji to pray for the repose of Toshihisa's spirit. Would Gesshō like to see the temple? Saigō asked. Gesshō declared that he would. Saigō and Gesshō faced the temple and prayed. Then Saigō wrapped his arms around the monk and pulled him close. Locked in an embrace and facing a symbol of doomed but principled defiance, Saigō and Gesshō threw themselves into the cold, dark waters of Kagoshima Bay. Looking forward to death, Saigō inhaled water and lost consciousness.[83]

Chapter 3

"BONES IN THE EARTH"

Exile and Ignominy*

Death, Resurrection, and Exile

Hearing a loud splash, the crew rushed to the bow of the boat and realized that Saigō and Gesshō had thrown themselves into the sea. Desperate to stop the skiff, Sakaguchi slashed apart its sails and the men rowed back to where they thought Saigō and Gesshō had jumped. Hirano, Sakaguchi, and Jūsuke all dove into the water and found Saigō and Gesshō still locked in a tight embrace, their bodies too stiff from hypothermia to be pulled apart. The crew rowed quickly to the nearest land, pulled the bodies ashore, and built a fire to warm them. Both men began coughing up water, and Saigō eventually started breathing, weakly but steadily. Gesshō did not revive. The crew loaded Saigō, semiconscious from hypothermia, and Gesshō's corpse back into the skiff and rowed back to Kagoshima.[1]

Saigō spent the morning of 11/16 in a small hut on the shore of Kagoshima Bay before his family sent a palanquin to bring him back home.

---

*Quote is from *STZ* 1: 131–132.

He was delirious for three days and repeatedly cried out for his dead companion. His hearing and mobility were impaired for nearly a month. When Saigō regained consciousness his first words were of lamentation. Out of respect for Gesshō's status as a monk, he had not drawn his sword, but instead agreed to drown himself. Now he was an utter failure. Not only was he still alive, but he had attempted suicide "like a woman." Resolved to keep his vow to Gesshō, Saigō asked for his sword. His family restrained him and asked the question that would shape the rest of Saigō's life: Was his survival mere chance? No, they insisted. Saigō was alive because that was heaven's will. Saigō had not yet fulfilled his duties as a samurai; his task was not yet done. These arguments stayed Saigō's hand, but left him to ponder a momentous question. What was his unfulfilled mission?[2]

Saigō's failed suicide lent increased weight to his quest for a grand gesture of loyalty. He had spoken for years of his willingness to die for a righteous cause. If his survival was not an accident, then a still more noble cause remained. Saigō's search for this greater cause would shape Japanese history. In 1858, however, Saigō also faced the more immediate problem of being a wanted man. Shogunal police had followed him to Kagoshima and were searching for him and for Gesshō. They questioned Hirano and Jūsuke, and took Jūsuke into custody. As before, the domain was reluctant to defend Saigō, but unwilling to betray him. Domain officials declared that both Saigō and Gesshō had drowned. They produced Gesshō's body as evidence and declared that Saigō's corpse had not been recovered. The shogunal inspectors were suspicious but eventually relented.[3]

To sustain their deception, domain officials decided to send Saigō into internal exile on Amami Ōshima, a small island roughly 250 miles southwest of Kagoshima City. Because Saigō was not a criminal he would retain his stipend, but he could not return to Kagoshima without authorization. To conceal his survival, Saigō was ordered to change his name; formally he changed it to Saigō Sansuke, but unofficially he adopted the name Kikuchi Gengo in honor of his imperial loyalist ancestor. Saigō was physically alive but officially dead. The domain was so concerned with concealing his survival that it ordered the preparation of a criminal's cadaver to be presented as Saigō's corpse should the shogunal police return.[4]

After recovering from hypothermia, Saigō left Kagoshima in late 1858/12. His ship stopped in Yamakawa, at the mouth of Kagoshima Bay, before leaving for Amami Ōshima in early 1859/1. On 1859/1/11 Saigō

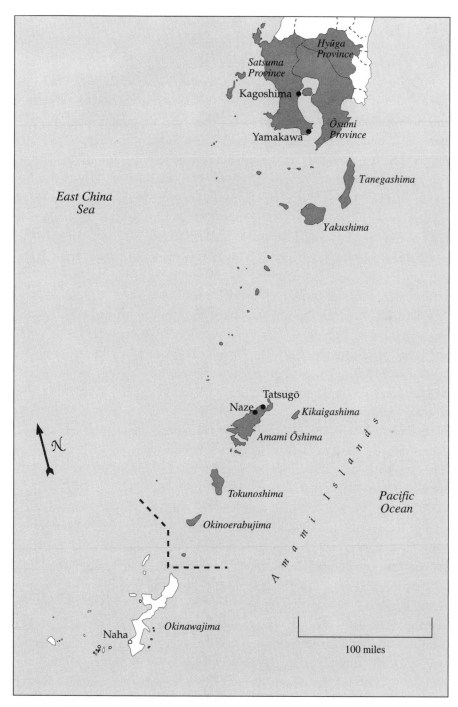

Satsuma and the Amami Islands

arrived in Naze, the main town on Amami Ōshima. After a brief consultation with the local intendant he was transferred to the village of Tatsugō,
where he would spend the next three years.

Although Amami Ōshima was only two hundred miles from Satsuma
proper, it was a different world. Because of ocean currents from the south,
the Amami Islands were markedly warmer than Satsuma proper. Winters
were frost-free and tropical plants such as bananas and aloe grew in abun-
dance. The topography of the island was striking, with high, densely
forested mountains and deep, scenic bays. The coastline of Tatsugō Bay, like
much of the Amami coast, was jagged and twisting; in places the coast
turned so sharply that it was difficult to distinguish islands from peninsulas.
Tatsugō Bay was covered with dense forest that gave way abruptly to rocky
coast and small patches of beach. This terrain made for hardscrabble farming but for fabulous hunting.[5] Saigō wrote fondly of remote spots in the
mountains where he could gaze at the clouds.[6]

Politically Amami Ōshima lay near the southernmost edge of the
Japanese Empire. The islands had been autonomous before the 1500s, when
the Ryukyuan kingdom (now the Japanese prefecture of Okinawa) invaded
and conquered the archipelago. Satsuma seized the Amami Islands in 1609
as part of its conquest of the Ryukyus. After taking the Ryukyuan king
hostage, Satsuma restored much of the kingdom's autonomy. Ryukyuan
independence, or at least the appearance of independence, helped facilitate
trade with China. The Amami Islands, however, won no such autonomy.
They became part of Satsuma territory and were ordered to pay taxes into
the domain treasury.[7]

Although politically part of Satsuma, the Amami Islands were culturally
part of the Ryukyus. The islands shared many religious and social practices
with the Okinawa archipelago, and conquest by Satsuma did little to change
Amami culture. Beyond collecting taxes, the domain government had little
interest in the islands and dispatched only a handful of officials to administer civil affairs.[8] Natives handled most of the island's governance, and the
domain made little effort to change social and religious practices. Shintoism
and Buddhism, the major religious traditions on the Japanese main islands,
were virtually unknown on the Amami Islands before the twentieth century. Thus, although the islands were technically part of Japan, many of their
religious practices were shocking to main-islands Japanese. The Amami
Islanders buried their dead, but commonly exhumed them three years later,

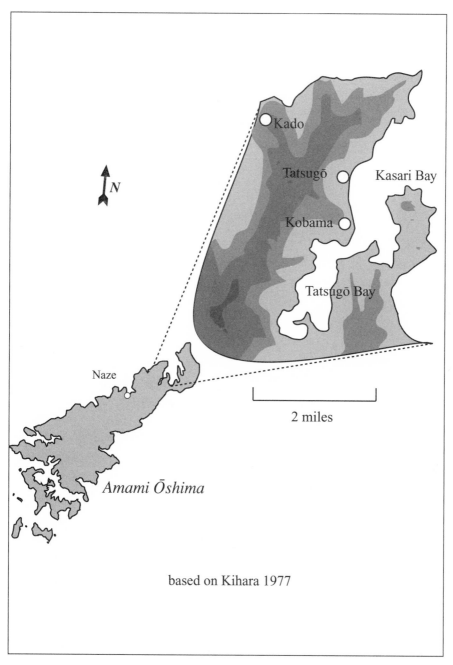

Kado

Tatsugō

Kasari Bay

Kobama

Tatsugō Bay

N

Naze

2 miles

Amami Ōshima

based on Kihara 1977

Amami Ōshima and Tatsugō

cleaned the remains, and deposited the bones in communal caves. Similar reburial practices were common in Neolithic Japan, but had disappeared on the main islands centuries ago. The dominant religious figures on the Amami Islands were *noro,* official village priestesses. As in Okinawa, *noro* had strictly demarcated territories and received land grants to support their religious services, which commonly focused on local deities. The families of important *noro* priestesses formed a hereditary elite: the most powerful men on the island were usually their sons, brothers, or nephews.[9]

Many customs considered refined in Amami were repulsive to people from Satsuma. Island women decorated their hands with elaborate tattoos whose quality was considered a marker of social status. Women tattooed their right hands at twelve or thirteen, when they came of age, and tattooed their left hands when they married. The first tattoo marked chastity. Without a decorated right hand, a woman was unfit for marriage. A tattoo on the left hand, by contrast, represented a woman's obedience to her husband. This symbolism was lost on main islanders, for whom tattoos were associated with criminal behavior and vulgarity. Saigō found the tattoos repulsive, and he derided island customs in a letter to Ōkubo and Saisho Atsushi: "The young women on the island are great beauties," he wrote sarcastically, but unlike the women of Kyoto and Osaka they used a thick layer of filthy ash as makeup and painted the backs of their hands.[10]

Beyond these cultural differences, Saigō was most affected by the island's crushing poverty and despotic rule. "It is painful to see the extent of tyranny here," he wrote in his first letter from the island. "The daily life of the islanders seems honestly unendurable. It is worse than the treatment of the Ainu in Ezo. I am astonished by the bitterness of their lives: I did not think there could be such hardship."[11] Saigō was not the first visitor to be stunned by the island's poverty. In 1777 Tokunō Tsushō, a Satsuma official dispatched to encourage farming, reported the bleakest conditions: "There isn't a home on the island where I would want to even sit and wash my feet. The people worry about their next meal day and night and they eat broken bits of seaweed from the beach. It's hard for them even to wet their throats. . . . Today I suddenly understood the depths of human anguish. My heart was so heavy that it was difficult to even walk."[12] So savage was Satsuma rule on Amami Ōshima that islanders still spoke of it in the 1950s.[13]

The oppressive poverty of Amami Ōshima had one principal cause: sugarcane. Introduced to Amami Ōshima in 1690, this crop was initially grown for local consumption and eaten as fruit rather than refined into sugar. Only in 1746 did Satsuma realize the tremendous economic potential of sugar—a realization that transformed the importance of the island. For rice production, the Amami Islands were almost worthless. Their rice was deemed of poor quality and fetched a low price in the Osaka market. But sugar was a different matter. The islands, by virtue of climate, were ideal for cane cultivation, and sugar was in high demand in Osaka. To increase revenue, the domain began to reverse its agricultural policy, discouraging the cultivation of rice in favor of sugarcane. In 1746 the domain began collecting all taxes in sugar. In 1777 it established a state monopoly on sugar, making private sales punishable by death. This emphasis on sugarcane led to the most brutal aspect of the island economy: widespread slavery and indentured servitude. Slavery had disappeared centuries ago on the main islands. Rice farming was well suited to small, independent farmers, and daimyo realized that such farmers were reliable and productive taxpayers. Sugarcane was different. Cane cultivation was labor-intensive, dangerous, and exhausting, and the most productive farmers were plantation owners who could mobilize scores of unfree workers. By the 1800s the island elite, the district chiefs and local officials, were all slaveholders. By the mid-1800s nearly a third of the populace were *yanchu,* the island term for a chattel slave.[14]

Saigō was touched by the poverty of the islanders and was angry that his own domain could act so brutally. His sympathy for the islanders coexisted uneasily with his own sense of loss. Saigō had been sent to the ends of the earth, and the simple sight of the islanders reminded him of the magnitude of his fall. In 1859/6/7 he poured out his heart to his comrades: "As you know, for five or six years I was close to [the realm's great imperial] partisans, so it is difficult to mingle with these hairy Chinese *(ketōjin).* The feeling is utterly awful and I have even come to regret having survived."[15] Depressed and desperate to deny the immensity of his loss, Saigō kept to himself. According to island legend, he was offered servants but rejected them, preferring solitude. He lived alone, gathering his own firewood and doing his own cooking. He would emerge from his small house periodically for exercise and sword practice. Physically huge, taciturn, and angry, he cut a terrifying figure.[16]

Unwilling to accept exile, Saigō sought desperately to win a pardon and to be repatriated. If Saigō wished to deny the full impact of his exile, his friends gave him ample opportunity to do so. His colleagues asked his opinion on important political matters and even included him, in absentia, in their correspondence with the daimyo's father, Hisamitsu. Although isolated on a remote island, Saigō was consulted and informed about the details of loyalist politics. No other Satsuma retainer was as knowledgeable about national politics or as well connected and widely respected. Although officially dead, Saigō continued to exert a powerful influence over Satsuma's imperial loyalists.[17]

The burning issue for imperial loyalists from the summer of 1858 to 1860/3 was stopping Ii Naosuke, whose Ansei purge had devastated imperial advocates. Not only had Ii imprisoned or executed the movement's most forceful spokesmen and most skilled strategists, he also had cultivated allies in the imperial court and won imperial approval for the Harris treaty. This bold, sudden, and successful reassertion of shogunal power alarmed even moderate samurai. Saigō, in his last days in Osaka and Kyoto, had sought support for a show of military force in Kyoto. In his absence talk turned still more radical. Satsuma retainers began to speak of assassinating Ii, forcing his allies in the imperial court from office, and demanding thorough reform of the shogunate. Ōkubo, who had emerged as the leader of the Satsuma loyalists in Saigō's absence, was concerned about such radical plans and sought Saigō's counsel. In an 1858/12/29 letter delivered to Saigō during his brief stop in Yamakawa, en route to Amami Ōshima, Ōkubo asked Saigō how the loyalists might proceed. How carefully should they coordinate strategy with other domains? What if key members were arrested or executed?[18] Despite his posthumous reputation as a brash hothead, Saigō advised caution. He praised the loyalty of Ōkubo and his compatriots, but urged him not to act rashly and squander his forces by striking without an alliance with samurai from other domains. To die serving the emperor was glorious, but serving the emperor now required caution, forethought, and careful strategy.[19]

Saigō's advice proved sound and served to advance the agenda of both Ōkubo and the loyalists. Rather than strike out with a small, disorganized force, Ōkubo now aimed to sway Hisamitsu and Tadayoshi toward supporting the imperial house. Ōkubo's quiet diplomacy was rewarded. In 1859/11 Tadayoshi, after consulting his father, took the unprecedented step of directly addressing Ōkubo and his group of loyalists directly. In a letter sealed with his *kao,* a lord's formal signature, Tadayoshi urged caution and restraint, but praised the retainers for their spirit. He urged them to become "stone pillars"

Leiden University

Ōkubo Toshimichi

of the state and to defend the imperial court. The letter was addressed to the *seichūshi,* or "loyal retainers," and the recipients adopted this phrase as their name, calling themselves the Seichūgumi, or "band of loyal retainers." The loyalists responded to Tadayoshi with a blood oath. They agreed not to act rashly but urged the lord to strengthen the domain's defenses; to defend the imperial house; to form an alliance with Kumamoto, Mito, and Fukui; and to repatriate Saigō. Saigō was hundreds of miles away, but the Seichūgumi placed his name, Kikuchi Gengo, at the top of their roster, and Ōkubo Toshimichi assured him that they were acting with his ideas in mind.[20]

Tadayoshi's recognition of the Seichūgumi was part of his father Hisamitsu's broader shift in his attitudes toward domain politics. Like his half brother Nariakira, Hisamitsu was embittered by their succession dispute and inclined to distrust his rival's allies. He also recognized, however, the importance of domain unity and of promoting talented reformers from his half brother's faction. In late 1859 Hisamitsu gave several indications that he was ready to embrace Nariakira's supporters. He dismissed as domain elder Shimazu Bungo, a long-standing target of the Nariakira faction, and appointed Shimazu Shimōsa, a Nariakira partisan, as head of the domain elders. This was accompanied by similar changes at lower ranks. Hisamitsu also gradually warmed to Nariakira's stance in national affairs and began to move slowly toward open support of the emperor. Writing of these events in 1859/12, Ōkubo told Saigō he might be repatriated as early as the coming spring.[21] Saigō responded with delight. Hisamitsu, he declared, was like the duke of Zhou (Chou), the ancient Chinese noble celebrated by Confucius for his faithful service to his brother King Wu. Saigō regretted only that he was still in exile, unable to serve his domain and the imperial cause.[22]

The following year brought still better news. On 1860/3/3 a band of samurai assassins attacked Ii Naosuke's cortege, shot him, and cut off his head. Most of the samurai were from Mito, but the sole participant from Satsuma, Arimura Jizaemon, was the younger brother of Saigō's old friend Kaeda Nobuyoshi.[23] Although fatally wounded, Arimura distinguished himself by fleeing with Ii's severed head. Shogunal agents eventually recovered the head, but Ii's assassination stunned the shogunal administration. The leader of the shogunate had been murdered in broad daylight on a busy street in the capital. For months the shogunate refused to acknowledge that Ii was dead. While it was not unusual for samurai houses to delay the public announcement of a leader's death until all matters of succession had been arranged, Ii's case posed special problems. In response to repeated queries from Western diplomats, the shogunate reported that Ii had been wounded and his condition was unchanged. Since Ii had been killed in public, diplomats greeted this subterfuge with barely concealed mirth.[24] More seriously, Ii's murder created a power vacuum. He had single-handedly engineered the resurgence of shogunal authority. In the wake of his death no one was willing to insist on shogunal supremacy, especially in the face of violent imperial loyalism. Battered and confused, the shogunate groped its way toward compromise.[25]

The weakening of the shogunate and Hisamitsu's change of heart seemed to augur well for Saigō's return. Saigō waited expectantly for news, hoping that a letter of pardon would come. "I learn of the state of the world," he wrote to Ōkubo and Ijichi Sadaka on 1860/11/7, "by waiting for fast ships, but I am delighted to learn that things are gradually moving toward justice. " Saigō remained concerned about the specter of imperialism: "If there is not some radical change, we will soon be subjugated and trampled like Qing (Ch'ing) China," he declared. But the reversal of the Ansei purge suggested that the country was moving in the right direction.[26]

Saigō's dream of amnesty went unrealized: no pardon came. His own domain was content to let him languish in isolation and obscurity. In the last months of 1860 his hope slowly faded, and in 1861/1 he began his third year in exile. Facing a seemingly endless exile, Saigō began to wonder where his home was. On 1861/3/4 he drafted a heartfelt letter to his friends. He thanked them for their valiant and persistent attempts to win him a pardon. He was, he wrote, unworthy of their efforts. It was time, however, to admit defeat. He would not be returning to the home islands soon. With a heavy heart he declared that he had "become an islander." Saigō also stunned his friends with a bit of news. "I have done something unseemly in the wilderness," he wrote. ". . . [M]y son was born on 1861/1/2."[27] Saigō's friends in Kagoshima were undoubtedly shocked: Saigō had written nothing about either a wife or a pregnancy. His letters to Kagoshima gave no indication that he had a life on Amami Ōshima beyond simple survival. With this letter Saigō revealed that he had been living a secret life. While furiously lobbying to get back to the main islands, he had become deeply involved in island affairs. He had married a local woman, Aigana, the daughter of powerful local family, and had established a household. He had become concerned with island politics and forged lasting friendships with Toku Fujinaga, a local official, and Koba Dennai, a Satsuma samurai serving as censor *(metsuke)* on the island. He had started a family and become a major figure in community life.

The details of Saigō's life on Amami Ōshima remain a mystery. Saigō wrote little about his time in exile to his friends from Kagoshima, and there are no surviving letters of any sort between 1861/3/4 and 1862/3/27. There are no letters of any sort to Aigana, who was, from all indications, illiterate. Saigō corresponded actively with Toku and Koba, but their correspondence began only after Saigō left Amami Ōshima. There are numerous stories about Saigō in exile, but most were recorded years after his death and have been shaped by decades of retelling and reinterpretation. Saigō, according to island legend, was a tireless defender of the weak and the poor against the tyranny of wicked officials. He turned corrupt and heartless administrators into virtuous leaders and liberated the downtrodden. Always good-humored and gracious, he was generous and kind to all. Selfless and principled, he single-handedly improved daily life on the island. These island legends, like many legendary accounts of Saigō, suggest real virtues magnified beyond all plausibility by Saigō's later fame.[28]

Although reliable sources are limited, we can piece together a rudimentary account of Saigō's life in exile. Although initially repelled by the "hairy Chinese" islanders, Saigō was gradually drawn into village life. His initial connection was with some village children, who asked him to be their teacher. Saigō struggled to remain aloof, but he was too charmed to refuse. In recruiting Saigō as a teacher, the children exposed a hidden face of his persona. Saigō was not only a physically imposing swordsman, he also was a warmhearted and dedicated schoolteacher. Under his fierce facade, he was gracious and modest. Through his interactions with local children, Saigō lost, perhaps unwittingly, his armor of angry stoicism.[29]

As a neighbor, rather than as a bitter and taciturn exile, Saigō was an immensely appealing figure. While perhaps not the hero of island legend, Saigō was too moral and too passionate a man to remain unmoved by the poverty and oppressive governance of the island. From his first months on the island, while he was still complaining that the islanders were as vile as poisonous snakes, Saigō was giving away his personal supplies. He argued with island officials over every aspect of his stipend, including buckets, cooking oil, and spices. He was uncharacteristically petty over his own rations because he was giving away much of his income.[30]

As Saigō's depression lifted, the local elite began to look at him as an attractive potential son-in-law. As a main-islands samurai, Saigō held elite status on Amami Ōshima. He was an exile but not a criminal, and he continued to receive a stipend from the domain treasury. Marriage to a main-islands samurai could enhance the status and wealth of an Amami Ōshima family. There were, however, strict limitations on such marriages. The domain recognized the marriage only for the duration of the samurai's stay on the island; once the samurai returned to the main islands, he could remarry without a divorce. The "island wife," moreover, had no right to leave the island. Her status as an island commoner was unchanged. If the marriage produced children, they claimed descent from the father's line and were therefore main islanders. When the children, either boys or girls, were old enough to leave their mother, they could be taken to the main islands to be raised by the father's family. A woman's prospects in such a marriage were therefore remarkably grim: matrimony often meant senescence in isolation and loneliness. But Japanese marriages were decided by families, not individuals, and the advantages to a wife's family were enormous.[31]

Saigō, according to oral tradition, was reluctant to take an "island wife" but was swayed by the arguments of friends on the island. In 1859/11 he was formally engaged to Otoma Kane, better known by her nickname Aigana. Saigō's bride came from a branch of the Ryū family, a prominent local clan. The Ryū claimed descent from Minamoto Tametomo, a twelfth-century court noble and a distant relative of Japan's first shogun. This is an extravagant and somewhat implausible genealogy, but whatever their ancestry, the Ryū were wealthy and powerful. The main Ryū compound in Tatsugō had more than seventy servants and slaves. Aigana herself, however, grew up in much humbler circumstances. Born in 1837, she lost her father at age five, and leadership of the household passed to her uncle. Although far from poor, Aigana, according to local legend, grew up weaving cloth from plantain fibers to help her family's finances. How Saigō and Aigana met is subject to competing legends. In some accounts their first meeting was arranged, but in others they met by happenstance on the outskirts of Tatsugō. Aigana was, by most accounts, quite beautiful, with jet-black hair and sparkling eyes. But she was unquestionably a product of island culture, illiterate and with heavily tattooed hands. Under any circumstances other than exile, she would have been an inappropriate wife for Saigō.[32]

Saigō's relationship with Aigana is the subject of much legend and speculation. Saigō himself was remarkably reticent about his island "wife." He wrote nothing of her to his friends on the main islands. Aigana was, in many ways, an embarrassment, since although reportedly beautiful and demure, she was nevertheless an islander. Saigō had married, in his own words, a "hairy Chinese." Even at the peak of his political power, Saigō made no effort to bring Aigana to the main islands. She was an overseas indiscretion not suitable for the metropole. Ironically and tragically, Saigō enjoyed life with Aigana and their children. His family, he later wrote, was a source of great happiness. In a letter to Koba in 1862 he regretted focusing on

Satsuma politics while on the island. It had made him foul-tempered when he could have lived in peace.[33]

If Saigō was conflicted about his wife, he faced no such conflict over his island friends Koba and Toku, who were trusted comrades. Koba was a Kagoshima native and a childhood acquaintance of Saigō and Ōkubo. He excelled as a scholar and opened an academy in Kagoshima before receiving a post at the domain compound in Osaka. When Saigō was exiled to Amami Ōshima, Ōkubo and other friends arranged to have Koba posted to the island as a *metsuke,* a censor for government malfeasance. As an inspector, Koba had influence over local officials and thus was able to ensure Saigō's physical well-being. According to oral tradition, Saigō and Koba were tireless crusaders against oppressive government, particularly that of the island intendant, Sagara Kakuhei. Whatever their initial connection, Koba became one of Saigō's most trusted friends, to whom he expressed sentiments he kept hidden from his closest main-islands friends: his happiness while in exile and his disgust with domain politics.[34]

Toku Fujinaga was an Amami Ōshima native, from the hamlet of Kado near Tatsugō. He served as constable for Tatsugō district and was, by marriage, a distant relative of Aigana. Toku and Saigō were kindred spirits. According to local lore, Toku was known for his probity and strength of character and, although his position allowed endless opportunities for graft, he lived simply and dedicated himself to local affairs. In later life he was appointed to the Uken district in southern Amami Ōshima, where his crowning achievement was the construction of a wooden bridge that crossed a small stream dividing the villages of Taken and Yuwan. Like Saigō, Toku was incorruptible because he lacked an interest in material things: Toku and Saigō together enjoyed the simple pleasure of fishing. As with Koba, Saigō's early relationship with Toku is undocumented, but Toku also earned Saigō's deepest trust. After his return to the main islands, Saigō relied on Toku to watch over his wife and children. Saigō felt comfortable revealing both his public and private faces to Toku. In one letter, for example, he advised Toku on which island officials could be trusted, expressed how desperately he missed his children, and shared gossip about an island romance. Saigō confided to Toku the formative conflict of his life: he wanted both to be a great and loyal servant of the realm and to lead a quiet life fishing with his friends.[35]

In Tatsugō today there is a reconstruction of the home Saigō built for his family. According to Ryū Masako, the house owner and one of Aigana's descendants, it has the same footprint as the original and uses some of the original posts. Saigō's letters make no mention of his house, but the oral tradition of Amami Ōshima runs as follows. By late 1861, although Saigō had a family, students, and close friends on Amami Ōshima and the island had begun to feel like home, his house did not reflect this. In his desire for seclusion, Saigō had originally chosen a house on the outskirts of Tatsugō, technically in the neighboring hamlet of Kobama. In 1859 this was an ideal location for an angry bachelor exile. By 1861, however, Saigō had come to reconsider his choice of home. Since he was a family man, a home in the village seemed more appropriate for his wife and child. In late 1861, with help from the Ryū family, Saigō began work on a new home, in the heart of Tatsugō. The home was, by island standards, substantial: a high thatched roof over two rooms with a total of roughly four hundred square feet. On 1861/11/20 the house was completed and Saigō planted a commemorative cherry tree in the garden. In the evening the village gathered at his home to celebrate his move.[36] The tone of Saigō's sole letter from 1861 supports this story. In that letter, Saigō thanked Ōkubo for trying to win him a

Saigō's home in Tatsugō

pardon, but urged Ōkubo to accept failure. Saigō was not only reconciled to exile, he also had begun to show a glint of pride in local culture. He included a sample of Amami-style cured pork with his letter and asked Ōkubo for his opinion. Saigō, in this letter, seems very much a man ready to build a new house for his new family.[37]

In early 1862 Saigō received the astonishing news that he was being recalled to Kagoshima. This was what he had hoped for, but it came after he had given up hope. There are no contemporaneous records of Saigō's feelings, but it is clear from later documents that he left Amami Ōshima with mixed emotions. Saigō had been banished to the ends of the earth, but there he had found community, friends, and family. The happiness Saigō felt on Amami Ōshima was not something he could readily explain to main-islands friends, to whom Amami Ōshima was little better than a penal colony. He disclosed these feelings to his island friends, however, later writing to Toku that he would "never forget the kindness with which the islanders treated me and the warmth with which I was accepted."[38] Saigō was true to his word. While he could not explain his experiences to his friends on the main islands, he wore his exile with pride. After returning to Kagoshima he changed his name to reflect his exile. He now signed his letters Ōshima San'emon: *ōshima* for the island, *san* (three) for his years in exile, and *emon,* a standard suffix in male names.[39] Nor did Saigō forget the plight of his neighbors. In 1864 he petitioned the domain government to reform the sugar monopoly system. In 1873 he drafted another proposal, for the finance minister of the new Meiji government.[40] Even at the apex of his political career, Saigō reflected fondly on his years in exile. In 1869 he wrote to Toku that he was considering resigning and returning to the islands to retire.[41]

Saigō's life on Amami Ōshima points to a central dilemma in his life. He was driven by an immense sense of duty and by the conviction that he was destined to accomplish great things. Saigō openly aspired to change Japan, but he found surprisingly little joy in political power or in the perquisites of power, and he found his greatest joy in simple pleasures. Some of his happiest moments, both in Kagoshima and in exile, came while he was wearing homemade sandals and hunting and fishing with friends. These contradictory passions made Saigō an intensely compelling leader: he wielded power with amazingly little self-interest. But this same conflict also made his life immensely difficult. There was no place for him to find peace.

Into the Breach

On 1862/2/13 Saigō was thrust back into the center of Japanese politics. Within days of his arrival in Kagoshima he met with key domain activists and then with Shimazu Hisamitsu, the daimyo's father and the effective ruler of the domain. This was the return to power for which Saigō had openly hoped, but it proved an utter debacle. Saigō so antagonized Hisamitsu that on 4/6 he was charged with willful disobedience. On 6/10 he was sent again into exile, this time to the remote island of Tokunoshima. What happened? How did Saigō rise and then fall again so quickly?

Saigō's repatriation was prompted by Hisamitsu's political ambitions. Beginning in late 1861, Hisamitsu had began to consider a show of armed force to coerce shogunal reform. Hisamitsu did not wish to topple the shogunate or radically change the social order, but merely to expand Shimazu influence within the existing political framework. His plan, based loosely on Nariakira's proposed embassy in 1858, was to visit Kyoto with a large contingent of warriors and secure an imperial rescript ordering key shogunal reforms. Hisamitsu wanted Hitotsubashi Keiki to be appointed as guardian (kōken) for the young shogun, and Matsudaira Shungaku appointed as a special political adviser. He wanted the imperial court to choose a group of daimyo to help represent the emperor before the shogun. He wanted the shogun to visit Kyoto to settle questions of foreign policy. Once supported by an imperial rescript, these reforms could be portrayed as the will of the imperial house, rather than merely an expansion of daimyo power at the expense of the shogunate.[42]

Radical imperial loyalists were a pivotal part of Hisamitsu's plan. His embassy was prompted in part by loyalists within Satsuma who were demanding concrete action in defense of the emperor. Hisamitsu also understood how the threat of terrorist violence could motivate the shogunate. In his correspondence with the imperial court he observed that an uprising of loyal samurai would be a messy but effective way of changing shogunal policy. But Hisamitsu had no interest in the imperial loyalists' agenda. He wanted the expansion of Satsuma's influence within the existing political framework, not a return to direct imperial rule. Nor did he want to promote unrealistic expectations for foreign policy. Imperial radicals called for the immediate, violent expulsion of foreigners but had no practical responsibilities for national affairs and no understanding of realpolitik. Hisamitsu, as a potential member of a new ruling clique, had no patience for such dangerous and impractical ideas. He did not want anarchic terrorist outbursts, which might disrupt sensitive negotiations. At the same time, however, Hisamitsu could not afford to alienate radical loyalists. He needed their fury to put pressure on the shogunate. At heart, Hisamitsu's strategy required skillful obfuscation. Although he was using the imperial court to advance Shimazu's interests, he needed to look like an imperial loyalist.[43]

In this context Ōkubo argued persuasively for Saigō's return. No other Satsuma retainer had such widespread credibility among imperial loyalists. Saigō was respected not only by men from Satsuma but also by loyalist radicals throughout Japan. Further, he had experience in Kyoto and was well-known in the imperial court. Saigō, Ōkubo argued, could unify the domain and keep radical samurai in check.[44]

Ōkubo's arguments won Saigō a reprieve from exile, but he was faced, from the moment he arrived in Kagoshima, with a formidable task. He needed to keep imperial loyalists under control, even though Hisamitsu's plan did not advance their agenda. He also needed to regain his footing in national politics after three years in exile. Things were rocky from the outset. On 2/13, when Saigō met with key domain leaders to discuss the upcoming embassy, he lambasted them for poor preparations. What, he asked, would they do if the imperial court did not respond to Hisamitsu's request? Would they sit in Kyoto for a year or two waiting for an answer? What would they do if the shogunate allied with the foreigners and dispatched warships? Ōkubo and the assembled samurai had no answer. They had not planned for a determined shogunal response. Saigō was appalled. The domain, he later wrote, was being run by well-intentioned but unruly children drunk with power.[45]

Saigō was equally blunt when he met with Hisamitsu two days later. Hisamitsu was, Saigō observed, following Nariakira's vision, but unlike his half brother, he had not won the support of the other daimyo. Saigō urged Hisamitsu to feign illness and delay the embassy. Saigō was particularly concerned that radicals would see the embassy as a call to revolution. What would happen if trouble erupted in Satsuma while Hisamitsu was away? What if there were rioting in Kyoto?[46]

Saigō's observations were both prescient and anachronistic. Saigō's fear that the shogunate might enlist foreign support anticipated by several years the shogunate's reliance on French military advisers. His fears about bloodshed in Kyoto foreshadowed the chronic violence of 1863 and 1864. And his observation that Hisamitsu's embassy could spark trouble in Satsuma was astute. In 1864 radical imperial loyalism did indeed prompt the outbreak of civil war in two major domains, Mito and Chōshū. At the same time, however, Saigō had seriously misunderstood the extent of the shogunate's decline. Having experienced the power and fury of Ii's purge, he thought of the shogunate as formidable, albeit loathsome. After Ii's assassination, however, no shogunal officer was willing or able to carry on his mission. Saigō had celebrated Ii's death while in exile, but he did not realize how precipitously shogunal power had declined after Ii's assassination.

While Saigō may have misapprehended the shogunate's timidity, Hisamitsu had not. He was pointedly aware of how susceptible the shogunate had become to bullying. Although he listened to Saigō's arguments, he remained unmoved, agreeing only to postpone his departure from 2/25 until 3/15. Disappointed and exhausted, Saigō retired to the hot springs at Ibusuki, some twenty-five miles south of Kagoshima, to cure his sore feet. He considered himself relieved of duty.[47]

Ōkubo remained convinced that Saigō was essential to Hisamitsu's embassy, despite their tense meeting on 2/13. In early 1862/3 Ōkubo visited Saigō at Ibusuki and implored him to travel through Kyūshū, surveying samurai sentiment. He was then to wait in Shimonoseki for Hisamitsu and to accompany the lord on the trip to Kyoto. Saigō agreed, and after receiving official orders left Kagoshima on 3/13.[48]

Saigō arrived in Shimonoseki on 3/22 and was overwhelmed by his reception. He met with samurai from throughout Japan who treated him with a respect bordering on reverence. Kogawa Kazutoshi, a samurai from Oka domain in northern Kyūshū, waxed rhapsodic about his meeting with Saigō. This was the Saigō, he wrote, who threw himself into the sea with Gesshō but survived. He was without parallel in courage and accomplished great things, but he was modest in taking leadership. It was inspiring, Kogawa wrote, to be in the presence of someone so stalwart. The assembled radicals implored Saigō to lead them, and Saigō was all but intoxicated by the respect with which they treated him. After his awkward audience with Hisamitsu, Saigō was elated to be respected and appreciated.[49] The samurai planned to go to Kyoto and use Hisamitsu's embassy as the rallying point for an insurrection against the shogunate. Saigō's duty as a Satsuma retainer obliged him to restrain them, however, lest his lord's mission be derailed by street fighting. Without waiting for Hisamitsu and without receiving authorization to leave Shimonoseki, he sailed to Osaka and then traveled overland to Kyoto.

Saigō arrived in Osaka on 3/27 and began meeting with samurai and *rōnin* (masterless samurai) from across Japan. He was captivated by their sincerity and passion. They were, he later wrote, the sort of people "with whom I would like to die in battle." They were all soldiers on a "deadly ground" *(shichi),* men who had left their lands of birth and their families to serve Hisamitsu in his great mission. Saigō felt that he could not help these men without joining them.[50]

Having lambasted Ōkubo on 2/13 for poor strategy, Saigō was unlikely to have been impressed by the radicals' plans. The only sure thing about their strategy was that many good men would die. But Saigō was moved by their selfless and single-minded devotion to a cause. To strategize and strategize badly was a failing, but to reject strategy in the name of pure motives was, for Saigō, sublime. Saigō's reference to "deadly ground" was both macabre and transcendent. As the famous Chinese strategist Sunzi (Sun Tzu) observed, on "deadly ground" one can survive only by facing death.[51] Seduced by the notion of a noble, hopeless cause, Saigō was unable to resist the radicals' request that he lead them. In this way, his thoughts and actions in 1862/3 eerily foreshadow his death on the hills of Shiroyama fifteen years later. In both 1862 and 1877 he was captivated by the loyalty, sincerity, and passion of men whose plans were spectacular, self-destructive, and naive.

Since Saigō had left Shimonoseki without authorization, his actions were inherently suspect. Had he been able to explain his actions to Hisamitsu, he might have been able to allay the lord's concerns. Unfortunately, when Hisamitsu arrived in Kyoto on 4/6 he learned of Saigō's actions at second and third hand, namely from Hirano Kuniomi, Kaeda Nobuyoshi, and Ijichi Sadaka. Kaeda had been sent to Kyoto to survey the situation in anticipation of Hisamitsu's visit. He did not meet with Saigō, but heard of his actions from Hirano Kuniomi, the Fukuoka retainer who had helped pull Saigō out of Kagoshima Bay. Hirano was an outspoken antishogunal radical: he advocated military assaults on shogunal strongholds in Kyoto, Osaka, and Hikone, and then a final assault on Edo. Hirano, who had traveled with Saigō from Shimonoseki to Kyoto, was convinced that Saigō shared his views and relayed this to Kaeda, who then reported it to Hisamitsu. For Hisamitsu this was unsettling news. Saigō needed to win the radicals' trust to keep them under control, but Kaeda's report made Hisamitsu wonder whether Saigō was using the radicals or whether the radicals were using Saigō. Hisamitsu then heard from Ijichi Sadaka, a Satsuma retainer working as Hisamitsu's liaison in Edo, that Saigō was working with loyalist radicals. Saigō had criticized Ijichi on 4/5 for his foreign policy stance. Ijichi favored a moderate approach on Japan's foreign treaties, believing that since Japan could not expel the foreigners soon, a more prudent course was to strengthen and unify the country in preparation for treaty renegotiation. Saigō, disagreeing, had excoriated Ijichi for his "craven" stance. To accede to the treaties, which the court had approved only under duress, was tantamount to deceiving the court and supporting the shogunate. When Ijichi relayed this conversation to Hisamitsu, the lord became furious. Hisamitsu himself considered expulsion impossible, so Saigō had indirectly equated Hisamitsu's own position with anti-imperial cowardice. More seriously, Saigō's conversation with Ijichi was a private matter and could not be dismissed as mere posturing to keep loyalist hotheads in check. Hisamitsu's worst suspicions were now confirmed: Saigō was dangerous and unreliable, and Hisamitsu ordered his arrest.[52]

Ōkubo and Saigō were stunned by Hisamitsu's reaction. Ōkubo was humiliated. He had won his friend's repatriation, but also laid the groundwork for his downfall. Ōkubo tried to argue Saigō's case with Hisamitsu, but the lord would have none of it. In frustration and despair, Ōkubo proposed a double suicide with Saigō. Saigō declined, invoking the same logic that had stayed his hand three years earlier: samurai exist to serve, and dead men serve no one. Ōkubo needed to survive to carry out the great mission of imperial loyalism. Ōkubo, having proved his honor by offering to die, accepted Saigō's argument. Saigō would face Hisamitsu's fury alone.[53]

Although Hisamitsu had ordered Saigō's arrest, domain officers were unwilling to lay hands on a man of Saigō's reputation and stature. Exasperated, Hisamitsu had Saigō sent under guard from Osaka to the port of Yamakawa in Satsuma. There, Saigō waited for nearly two months before Hisamitsu decided on charges and a sentence. In the end, Saigō was charged with four counts of misconduct: conspiring with *rōnin,* inciting retainers, opposing Hisamitsu's embassy, and leaving Shimonoseki without authorization. As punishment, on 6/6 he was again ordered into exile, this time to

Tokunoshima, a small island just south of Amami Ōshima. Saigō left Yamakawa on 6/11, but his ship was forced to return and then make several stops because of unfavorable winds. Finally, on 1862/7/5, Saigō arrived at the village of Waniya, on the northern end of Tokunoshima.[54]

In exile again, Saigō was overwhelmed by despair and a profound sense of betrayal. He poured out his feelings in a series of letters to his friend Koba on Amami Ōshima. "Even men whom I thought of as family branded me a criminal without so much as asking for the truth. My friends have all been killed. Where am I to turn?" Saigō's claim that all his friends were dead was hyperbolic. Following Saigō's arrest, Hisamitsu had begun a crackdown on loyalist radicals, and on 4/24 Satsuma samurai raided a meeting of loyalists at a lodge in Fushimi, near Kyoto. Swords were drawn, and several Satsuma loyalists were killed. Saigō was shocked by this tragedy, but the dead men were Saigō's acquaintances, not close friends. Hisamitsu had sent Saigō's good friend Murata Shinpachi into exile on the nearby island of Kikaigashima, but Murata did not die until 1877, together with Saigō at Shiroyama. But Saigō's exaggerated claim that his "friends have all been killed" accurately reflected his mood. He could see nothing but perfidy, villainy, and doom. Saigō was not suicidal, however. It would be wrong, he explained to Koba, for him to kill himself out of anger and frustration. Instead, he had reconciled himself to whatever fate was before him. But Saigō had little expectation of ever seeing the main islands again. If all fell to ruin and war broke out, he mused, he might be summoned back in a few years. More likely, thought Saigō, he would live out his life on the islands. This would not be hard, he declared, since he was disgusted with national politics.[55]

Saigō's family was on Amami Ōshima nearby, and in late 1862/7 Aigana brought their son Kikujirō and newborn daughter Kikuko to Tokunoshima. Saigō was ambivalent about their visit. The following month he wrote to Koba that while it was a delight seeing Kikuko, he did not want his family to come again. Saigō's exact reasoning is unclear, but he referred to Aigana as "the woman who serves me" *(tsukaioki sōrō onna),* and it seems he was concerned with her material well-being more than marital intimacy. As long as he knew that his wife and children were safe, Saigō was not especially interested in seeing them. Saigō was primarily concerned that there be someone trustworthy on Amami Ōshima to look after his family. Toku and Koba had looked after Aigana while Saigō was in Kyoto, and now that

Koba's term on Amami Ōshima was drawing to a close, Saigō turned to another friend, Katsura Hisatake. Katsura had been posted to the island in late 1861 with the unusual dual mission of copper mine development and coastal defense, but his family and Saigō's had been close for generations. Soon after his arrival in 1862, Katsura began helping Saigō's wife and children by purchasing, for example, bolts of fabric for Aigana. "Tell [Aigana]," Saigō wrote to Koba, "to relax, since she has nothing to fear as long as Katsura is on the island." Only if Katsura left did Saigō see a need to be near his own family. Saigō reportedly expected to spend years alone on Tokunoshima, and began assembling farm tools to grow his own food.[56]

In 1862/8, however, constables came from Kagoshima with new sentencing orders. Saigō was to be placed in the ship's brig and transferred to Okinoerabujima, another island in the Amami chain. Although just south of Tokunoshima, Okinoerabujima was a starkly different place. Unlike Amami Ōshima or Tokunoshima, Okinoerabujima was for serious offenders, men who had barely dodged a death sentence.[57] The island was a bleak place. In the words of one biographer, "the soil is sterile and the whole land is full of miasma. . . . [I]t is an unpleasant place with strong winds and the sea running high."[58] Even today, Okinoerabujima feels dreary and remote. Despite attempts to promote tourism, most visitors to the island are government agricultural officials. Saigō's transfer to Okinoerabujima was made all the more ominous by the threatening demeanor of the constable sent from Kagoshima. Nakahara Manbei, an eyewitness, later recalled that the constable's glare made him suspect that Saigō would be killed before he reached Okinoerabujima.[59]

Now that he was forcibly separated from his family, Saigō openly lamented not having seen them more. In his first letter from Okinoerabujima, Saigō mourned how he and Kikujirō had parted "like strangers, without getting to know each other." Separation from his children made his second exile all the more painful. "This time around," he wrote to Toku, "whether because of the weight of exile or because I have aged, I have become somewhat weak-mettled. I keep remembering my children and it is hard on me. I ask you to try to imagine [how I feel]. It is strange, because I had thought of myself as naturally strong in body and spirit."[60] This was not a loss Saigō would forget. The cruelty of his exile to Okinoerabujima shaped his thinking about crime and punishment. Years later, in one of his rare endorsements of a Western political institution, Saigō lauded Western prisons as enlightened and benevolent. Unlike Japanese jails, they did not simply punish, but sought to rehabilitate the prisoner. They did not separate him from friends and family, but took pity on his isolation. It was the Western penal system, not the Japanese, he observed, that embodied the Confucian ideals of humanity.[61]

The Ends of the Earth

Saigō was held on Okinoerabujima from 1862/i8 to 1864/2, but there are virtually no records of his first six months on the island. There is, however, detailed folk history of Saigō's life that is part of Okinoerabujima tradition. According to the best-known version, Saigō arrived at the small port of Inobe on 1862/i8/14 and traveled overland to the village of Wadomari. There the island intendant, Tsuzurabara Motosuke, received his orders for Saigō's confinement. Tsuzurabara was perplexed. There were numerous exiles on Okinoerabujima, but they were free to move about the island. Saigō, the orders specified, was to be kept in an "enclosure" at all times. Tsuzurabara was unsure what "enclosure" meant, but the intent was clearly punitive. Since Saigō had come to Okinoerabujima in a ship's brig, Tsuzurabara ordered construction of a similar structure. Workers quickly built a cage for Saigō. The structure was simple, with bamboo bars and a thatched roof. It was, according to legend, about nine feet square, with a fire pit in one corner and a toilet in the opposite corner. As many biographers have noted, it resembled a large animal pen.[62]

Saigō spent two nights in the brig while workers finished his cell. Then he was transferred to his new prison. The roof afforded some protection from the sun, but the cell was by the sea; the sides gave no shelter from heat, wind, or rain; and mosquitoes and other vermin plagued him. Since Saigō was not allowed to leave confinement, he could not bathe or groom himself; his hair grew filthy, matted, and began to reek. The food was awful, and the cell was too small for Saigō to stretch or exercise. With each passing day Saigō visibly deteriorated. A huge, vibrant man, he was slowly succumbing to exposure, malnutrition, and disease.

Saigō, according to oral tradition, met his fate with stoic resolve, quietly practicing Zen meditation and waiting to die. One of his guards, Tsuchimochi Masateru, took pity on him and offered to smuggle him better food. Saigō refused with mordant humor: if you eat an austere diet, he observed, your body doesn't change as much after you die. Tsuchimochi, according to legend, was mesmerized by Saigō's quiet resolve and grew unwilling to watch Saigō slowly die. He appealed to Tsuzurabara to reconsider his interpretation of Hisamitsu's orders. Enclosure, Tsuchimochi argued, need not mean an outdoor cell: it could mean any small, rustic structure, even a teahouse. Tsuzurabara agreed: the orders were to confine Saigō, not to kill him. Tsuchimochi immediately began work on a simple house, and in late 1862/10, after roughly two months in a cell, Saigō was moved to house arrest.[63]

There are no documents to substantiate these stories, whose level of detail suggests generations of embellishment. There is, however, nothing obviously false in these accounts. Rather, they reinforce what is reliably known about Saigō's exile. Nakahara had feared for Saigō's life before his departure, and Saigō later wrote about being transferred from an "enclosure" to a "room."[64] The legend of the outdoor cage plausibly connects these more reliable accounts. We also know from later letters and poems that Saigō and Tsuchimochi formed a deep and lasting connection. Tsuchimochi treated Saigō with a respect bordering on reverence, embracing Saigō's most impractical ideas. In 1863/7, for example, Saigō, although still legally confined to a room, decided to build a ship and sail to Satsuma. English warships had attacked Kagoshima earlier that month in retaliation for an attack on four British subjects by Satsuma samurai, and Saigō was determined to fight for his domain. Tsuchimochi, who embraced Saigō's ambition wholeheartedly, sold a slave and used personal assets to begin building a ship for Saigō. This impracticable plan never came to fruition, however. The battle, known in Japanese as the "Satsuma-English War," was over in one day. Although large sections of Kagoshima burned to the ground, Satsuma forces managed to seriously damage *Euryalus,* one of the seven British ships, and the two parties quietly negotiated a settlement.[65]

Saigō viewed Tsuchimochi as the epitome of loyalty and courage. He called Tsuchimochi a "man of justice" (*gimin*) and declared that if foreign warships came to Okinoerabujima, he and Tsuchimochi would fight to the bitter end. In a poem he declared that Tsuchimochi was so abstemious in his habits and determined in his loyalty that he transcended the boundary between life and death. It is a joy, he wrote to his uncles, to have such a friend.[66] Saigō and Tsuchimochi's bond extended past Saigō's imprisonment on the island. Tsuchimochi dedicated himself to one of Saigō's ideas for local development: a combination reserve granary and compulsory savings program. In 1863 Saigō proposed that islanders be compelled to put a portion of their harvest into a reserve granary. These mandatory contributions would earn interest at 20 percent per annum. Farmers could withdraw the interest only during a crisis, such as a harvest failure or medical emergency, but they could use the principal as they wished five years after starting the account. The plan reflected Saigō's quixotic syncretism. Saigō's term for the granary, *shasō,* was an ancient Chinese expression, and the plan was rooted in Confucian ideas of benevolent despotism. But the high interest rate shows Saigō's other face: an awareness of market forces and self-interest. A decade later Tsuchimochi, who eventually became mayor of Wadomari, attempted to realize Saigō's plan. This proved difficult: the *shasō* was capital-intensive, and the island was capital-poor. But Saigō intervened to help his old friend, lobbying both the finance minister and the governor of Kagoshima to forgive islanders back taxes and debts. With Saigō's help, Tsuchimochi managed to make the *shasō* a solvent, if not thriving, financial institution.[67] The bond Saigō had with Tsuchimochi was emblematic of his relations with his followers. Saigō evoked passionate, sometimes blind loyalty because he treated his followers with honor and respect.

Whether or not Saigō ever sat in an outdoor cage, the legend is so powerful that islanders have turned it into concrete and bronze. In a small park in downtown Wadomari, just behind the main shopping street, there is a model of Saigō in his cage. The enclosure is built to the specifications of island tradition, and Saigō sits inside, robust, calm, and poised. The statue is a striking example of the power of Saigō's fame. When one is in Wadomari it seems absurd to question whether Saigō ever sat in a cage, since there he sits, a physically tangible model of samurai resolve. There also is a shrine nearby commemorating Saigō's contributions to island culture. These monuments on Okinoerabujima give an insight into how daunting Saigō's reputation was, not only for Saigō's rivals, but also for Saigō himself. Saigō was larger than life within his own lifetime, and he was aware of the reverence with which he was regarded. As early as 1863 he saw his fame as both inspiring and ridiculous.[68]

In his first letter from Okinoerabujima, Saigō made a brief mention of an "enclosure" and then described with pride his intellectual growth. "I am undisturbed by daily affairs so I can devote myself without distraction to

Saigō's cage on Okinoerabujima

learning," he wrote, "and it seems as though, at this rate, I will become a scholar."[69] Saigō turned his confinement into an opportunity to study, practice his calligraphy, and teach. He made efforts to improve his calligraphy and developed a more mature style: his writing became more fluid, with bolder, thicker strokes.[70] Saigō read extensively in Chinese and Japanese philosophy. With Kawaguchi Seppō, a fellow exile, he transcribed all six volumes of Hosoi Heishū's collected essays.[71] Saigō read extensively in the Chinese classics, especially, poetry.[72]

Saigō also became an avid poet.[73] Although he wrote in several poetic forms, his great love was formal classical Chinese. "Reflections Whilst in Prison," one of his best-known poems, is a *risshi,* a Chinese form with strict rules on word count and parallelism. For Saigō these rules were empowering rather than constraining. Through classical Chinese poetry Saigō found

Saigō's cage on Okinoerabujima

that he could connect his experience with universal norms and historical truths:

> By day, a man enjoys his lord's favor, but at night, he is crushed and
>   entombed, like a victim of Qin Shi Huang's purge
> Like the cycle of day and night are the vicissitudes of man's fate
> A sunflower turns toward the sun as though the light were unchanged
> So will I remain loyal, even if my fortunes are unchanged
> My dear comrades in the capital are all ghosts
> Prisoner on a southern island, I alone have survived
> Life and death are, beyond doubt, bequests of heaven
> I ask only that my heart and soul might remain on earth to protect his
>   majesty

Here Saigō links his loyalty and determination with both nature and with human history. Come what may, he will turn his face toward the emperor as doggedly as the sunflower faces the sun. He likens himself, as well, to a victim of the founding emperor of the Qin (Ch'in) dynasty, who, according to legend, sought to crush dissent in 213 B.C.E. by burying scholars alive and burning all books except texts on medicine, agriculture, and divination.[74]

Saigō's choice of poetic form was an implicit political statement. Many passionate imperial loyalists viewed Chinese thought and language as contaminants and as a corruption of indigenous Japanese values. It was common for loyalists to write poetry solely in Japanese. Some even sought to avoid Chinese characters, a central part of the Japanese writing system. But Saigō, although an ardent Japanese chauvinist, enjoyed poetry in Chinese. His understanding of the world was deeply rooted in the shared East Asian canon of the Chinese classics. Saigō's love for Chinese learning did not engender respect for modern China. He had, of course, described the impoverished Amami Islanders as "hairy Chinese" to express his contempt. In this he was like his contemporaries in England who could revel in classical Greek learning but mock nineteenth-century Greeks as "wogs."

Despite his confinement, Saigō became an active and beloved teacher. He was holding regular classes as early as 1863/4, mere months after he was allegedly moved indoors. His students were largely sons of island administrators, including Misao Tankei, son of the local district constable Misao Tansai. Despite his status as a prisoner and the relative brevity of his stay, Saigō had a lasting impact on Okinoerabujima. It is an article of faith among islanders that their children are exceptionally scholarly for such a poor and remote island, and that their accomplishments in education are a legacy of Saigō's impact.[75]

Saigō's letters do not discuss his lessons, but some transcripts of his individual teachings to Misao Tankei survive. Saigō guided Misao through the easier texts in the Chinese classics: the Greater Learning and the writings of Mencius (Mengzi). His approach was conventional, following Zhu Xi's interpretation of the Greater Learning and using Song-era terms in his discussion of Mencius. But there is no missing Saigō's distinctive voice even in Tankei's notes on Mencius. He was concerned with transcending the line between life and death. The key to a life of integrity, he argued, was to recognize that death was inevitable, unpredictable, and therefore unimportant. Only once we ignore the "mental distinction" (shiryo bunbetsu) between life and death can we understand our heavenly nature, heaven's principle, and heaven's mandate. There is, strikingly, no mention of death in the original passage from Mencius, and the text can be read as an example of Mencius' optimistic insistence that human beings are innately moral and good. Saigō shared this optimism, but with a morbid twist: only when we no longer fear death can we live in harmony with heaven.[76]

In early 1864 Saigō wrote a lighthearted New Year's letter to his uncles in Kagoshima. "I am," he declared, "thriving on this tiny island." Saigō had about twenty students. During the day he taught basic reading and in the evening he explained the texts. Thanks to his imprisonment, he joked, he was becoming quite a learned man. Saigō made no mention of returning to Kagoshima and complained of nothing. He had not merely dodged a death sentence; he had come to enjoy the bleakest of exiles. As on Amami Ōshima, Saigō had proven himself able to thrive in seemingly hopeless circumstances. In a jail cell on a remote island "full of miasma" he had built a community of devoted students and loyal friends. His contentment and happiness would be brief.[77]

Chapter 4

"TO SHOULDER THE BURDENS
OF THE REALM"

The Destruction of the Shogunate*

From Exile to Capital

On 1864/2/20 the people of Okinoerabujima confronted the rare sight of
the steamboat *Kochōmaru,* one of Japan's few steamships, coming into the
port of Wadomari. The ship was carrying three unexpected visitors for Saigō:
his friend Yoshii Tomozane, his younger brother Tsugumichi, and the Satsuma
retainer Fukuyama Seizō. They brought the astonishing news that Saigō had
been pardoned and was to return to service. This was beyond Saigō's dreams.
He had never questioned his friends' loyalty and devotion. Even in his darkest moments he worried about Ōkubo's safety, not his fidelity. But Saigō had
given up all hope that his friends would win his freedom.[1]

Saigō did not have long to ponder his unexpected good fortune, because
his lord's order was to return posthaste. Saigō would honor his friendship
with Tsuchimochi for the rest of his life, but in the moment he poured out
his heart in a poem:

---

*The quote is from Katsu Kaishū's reflections on Saigō. See *STZ* 6:88.

Parting seems like a dream, like a cloud
The desire to leave, the longing to return, my tears fall like rain
The kindness you bestowed on me in jail is beyond words of thanks
Braving the distant waves, I think ceaselessly of our lord[2]

There was no time for long good-byes; *Kochōmaru* left early the following morning.

Yoshii and company had orders to return to Yamakawa, but Saigō insisted that they stop at Amami Ōshima. At about noon on 1864/2/23 the ship steamed into Kasari Bay on Amami Ōshima and docked near Tatsugō. Saigō disembarked and went to greet the family he had not seen in two years. He spent four days on the island, visiting friends and reconnecting with his wife and children. Kikujirō was four, and Saigō was now able to play with a boy rather than an infant. His daughter Kikusō was no longer a newborn. As always, Saigō was reticent about his feelings, but he confided his emotions to Tsuchimochi: to see his wife, children, and friends was so joyous that "I felt as though I were brought back from the dead."[3] Saigō also noted that Aigana, whom he described as his "mistress" *(mekake)*, was delighted to see him. Despite his elation, Saigō was still a man of duty and ambition. He had come to Amami Ōshima to visit, but his life was in service to his lord. On the morning of 2/26 he left Tatsugō for the second and last time. His children would eventually come to Kagoshima, but he would never see Aigana again.

En route to Kagoshima, Saigō and his companions stopped to pick up Murata Shinpachi from the nearby island of Kikaigashima. Hisamitsu had sent Murata into exile along with Saigō back in 1862. Saigō's rescue party had no specific instructions to retrieve Murata, but according to legend, Saigō was unwilling to leave a loyal friend in exile. On 2/28 *Kochōmaru* arrived in Kagoshima. Saigō was met by a palanquin and taken immediately to his residence in Uenosono. The next day he visited Nariakira's grave and paid his respects. A week later he and Murata left for Kyoto on *Ankōmaru*, arriving on 3/14. On 3/18 Saigō had an audience with Hisamitsu, who formally restored his stipend and appointed him commander of Satsuma's troops in Kyoto. In less than a month Saigō had traveled more than twelve hundred miles. He had been plucked from exile and disgrace and had been entrusted with one of the most powerful posts in the domain government. The entire experience left Saigō disoriented, but he gradually began to understand what had led to his pardon and promotion. National politics had taken an ugly turn, and Satsuma desperately needed a new voice in the imperial capital.[4]

When Saigō arrived in Kyoto in 1864/3/14 he was dismayed by the deteriorating political scene. The situation, he wrote in 1864/4, was dismal. The imperial court had no coherent policy, but merely reacted to daily events. The major daimyo were squabbling among themselves and seemed to have become dupes of the shogunate. Hitotsubashi Keiki was not to be trusted; he seemed dangerously ambitious. It seems, Saigō wrote, as though "there is nothing to do but wait for the outbreak of trouble."[5] This was not the outcome most had expected two years earlier, when Saigō had been sent into exile. The talk then had been of a new era of national unity governments. Hisamitsu's 1862 mission to Kyoto and Edo had seemingly changed the political landscape. Hisamitsu had demanded a new power-sharing structure, known in Japanese as *kōbu gattai* (literally, the "union of imperial court and warriors"), in which the shogunate would remain a powerful force but would include major daimyo in key decisions. This new framework would be authorized and legitimized by the imperial court. Back in 1862 Saigō had worried that Hisamitsu was being too aggressive in pushing the *kōbu gattai* agenda. The goal was noble, but Saigō feared a shogunal backlash. Saigō had been completely mistaken, however. Hisamitsu's timing was perfect.

Rather than accept sole responsibility for unpopular treaties, the shogunate had elected to share power, hoping to share responsibility as well. In response to Hisamitsu's demands, the shogun had agreed to visit Kyoto and confirm the authority of the emperor over shogunal decisions. In 1862/8 the shogunate had appointed Hitotsubashi Keiki, the loser in the 1858 shogunal succession dispute, as guardian of the young and sickly shogun Iemochi. Matsudaira Shungaku, who had been under nominal house arrest since 1858, was named shogunal political director *(seiji sōsai)*, a newly created position comparable to Ii's post of great councilor *(tairō)*. The shogunate even complied with Hisamitsu's recommendation to revise the alternate attendance system, drastically cutting the time daimyo were required to spent in Edo.[6]

In 1862 these changes seemed to augur well for a new era of Japanese government. Yet by 1864 few still believed that *kōbu gattai* could solve Japan's problems. For all the optimistic talk of a union of the imperial court, the shogunate, and the major daimyo, *kōbu gattai* proved an utter failure. This was, in part, a failure of the participants themselves. The daimyo elite proved themselves utterly incapable of forging extensive alliances across domain lines. The major daimyo, including Shimazu Hisamitsu, Yamauchi Yōdō of Tosa, Matsudaira Shungaku of Fukui, and Matsudaira Katamori of Aizu, were a distinctly chauvinistic and parochial group of leaders, as poorly suited to building a modern state as a group of Holy Roman electors. An unexpected problem for the *kōbu gattai* formula was the shogun's guardian Hitotsubashi Keiki, who soon became Hisamitsu's archrival. Keiki proved every bit as capable as his proponents had hoped in 1858, but he used his political skills to secure his own power base. By 1864 Keiki and Hisamitsu, erstwhile allies, had become bitter enemies, and the deterioration of their relationship poisoned the entire *kōbu gattai* project. Saigō, for his part, developed a visceral hatred for Keiki. He began voicing concerns about Keiki's loyalties as early as 1864, and by 1868 he expressly wanted Keiki dead.[7]

The *kōbu gattai* formula also foundered on problems within the imperial court. In theory, reverence for the imperial court would unite rival daimyo. But the court was manifestly unsuited for the tumultuous political decisions of the 1860s. By the terms of the seventeenth-century Tokugawa settlement, imperial courtiers were expected to be concerned with poetry composition, calligraphy, tea ceremony, and other refined activities. The imperial court had not administered an army for roughly a millennium. As early as 1858 Hashimoto Sanai had expressed frustration at how poorly courtiers understood pressing political questions, and even a decade later key courtiers still clung to the notion that the "barbarians" could somehow easily be driven from Japan.[8] Under the *kōbu gattai* formula warriors were to uphold the court, but the court was an anachronistic, weak, and deeply divided institution. The court's incompetence prompted an increasingly ugly and open struggle for its control. By 1864 powerful domains were vying not so much to honor the court as to manipulate its decisions.

The battle over the imperial court was exacerbated by the ideologies of radical imperial loyalism. A significant and growing number of samurai and commoners throughout Japan were enthralled by the notion that devotion to the emperor could solve the nation's political problems. Central to radical loyalism was the belief that foreigners in Japan constituted a pollution of

the "land of the gods." Only by expelling the foreigners could imperial subjects prove their loyalty; anything less was not just cowardice, but also a disgrace to the emperor and the gods. The principal tenets of radical imperial
loyalism could be summarized in one sentence: "Revere the emperor
(sonnō) and expel the barbarians (jōi)." The emotional force of sonnō jōi
thought was enormous. Like radical Islamic fundamentalism in our day, it
seemed to answer deep-seated grievances and humiliations with a vision-
ary, if vague, promise of purity and vengeance. The irrationality of sonnō jōi
rhetoric was part of its appeal. Reflecting on his youth, Itō Hirobumi, one
of the Meiji state's most cosmopolitan leaders, observed that "if one
speaks logically of the things [that happened then], they are impossible to
understand . . . but emotionally, it had to be that way."[9] Saigō could sympa-
thize with the passion of the expulsionists. In 1854 he himself had been
deeply moved by Fujita Tōko's vision of a pure Japan, united by imperial
loyalism and free of foreign contamination. But by 1864 Saigō knew that
"expelling the barbarians" was a long-term project. More seriously, Saigō
had a deep respect for order and could not countenance the anarchic violence of sonnō jōi radicals. They were, as he put it in 1864, little more than
"hooligans."[10]

Driven by their passionate sense of righteousness and their utter oblivious-
ness to hard facts, sonnō jōi radicals brought chaos and mayhem to Japanese
politics. In Mito the result was a military insurrection known as the Tengu
rebellion. In 1864/3 a band of disgruntled samurai, Shinto priests, and
peasants climbed Mount Tsukuba in Mito and declared their intention to
travel to Nikkō, the site of the mausoleum of Tokugawa Ieyasu, the founder
of the shogunate. There they planned to honor Mito daimyo Tokugawa
Nariaki, who had died in 1860, proclaim their loyalty to both Ieyasu and
the imperial house, and move on to Yokohama to drive away the barbarians
by closing the port. Initially the shogunate managed to defuse the crisis, but
by 1864/7 the rebels were recruiting hundreds of followers, and the conflict soon escalated into a civil war within Mito domain.[11]

For the shogunate, the Tengu insurrection was a crisis on several fronts.
The shogun's armies were badly trained and poorly motivated, so despite
their superior manpower and weaponry they were repeatedly routed by
small rebel bands. The eruption of open warfare demonstrated the terrible

fragility of the existing political order. And the success of the rebels in recruiting both samurai and commoner supporters dramatized the vitality of the *sonnō jōi* cause. For months the shogun's armies chased the rebels across Japan, before finally driving them to surrender in 1864/12.

Beyond the threat of the Tengu rebellion, the shogunate also faced the terrorism of small bands of loyalist radicals. By 1864 no one was safe from the terrorists' fury. Foreigners were an obvious target, and the loyalists attacked both military officers and unarmed civilians. The radicals also turned their rage on those Japanese they deemed insufficiently loyal. *Sonnō jōi* radicals were especially outraged by Matsudaira Shungaku, the daimyo of Fukui. They considered him a shogunal collaborator and planned on several occasions to kidnap or assassinate him. The radicals never reached Shungaku, but did manage to set fire to his Kyoto residence. Not even the imperial court was immune from terrorist attacks, as—despite their reverence for the emperor—loyalists grew increasingly willing to attack imperial courtiers. In 1863/1, for example, Sanjō Saneai, a senior court noble, found the severed ears of Ikeuchi Daigaku in his Kyoto residence. Lest Sanjō miss the meaning of the severed ears, the assassins included a note explaining that Ikeuchi, a Confucian scholar, had once loyally served the emperor but had become an ally of the shogunate and thus a villainous traitor. Sanjō, the note helpfully suggested, should resign his position. Iwakura Tomomi, a senior court noble and later a leader of the Meiji state, met similar treatment: he found a severed hand in his residence.[12]

In the background of all these clashes was an emerging rivalry between two of Japan's most powerful domains, Satsuma and Chōshū. Like Satsuma, Chōshū had opposed the Tokugawa in 1600, and the domain had long nursed a grudge against the shogunate. Unlike Satsuma, the domain lacked strong daimyo leadership. In the 1860s Chōshū was effectively ruled by two competing factions, conservatives and radical imperial loyalists. By late 1862 *sonnō jōi* radicals had taken control of the domain and had begun to promote an aggressive foreign policy. These loyalists had little patience for Hisamitsu's pragmatism, which they viewed as an opportunistic defense of the shogunate. Their passionate embrace of loyalism thrilled the more radical members of the imperial court, and by early 1863 the most powerful courtiers were Chōshū allies who pushed the court into an increasingly xenophobic and untenable position. On 1863/2/14 the court ordered the expulsion of all foreigners from Japan, beginning in two months. This was a hopelessly impractical demand, but calmer voices were silenced by a devastating combination of terrorist violence and imperial majesty. Even the shogunate, which had signed treaties guaranteeing the safety of foreign residents, abandoned its sworn responsibility and agreed to expulsion.[13]

Satsuma was infuriated by Chōshū's control over the imperial court. The new policy of expulsion was a direct repudiation of Hisamitsu's pragmatic assessment of the foreign threat. Furthermore, Chōshū was using its new influence at court to exclude Satsuma from imperial politics: on 1863/5/29 Satsuma samurai were forbidden to enter the court. Such a slight could not go unanswered. For Satsuma, the court had been hijacked by a dangerous rival, and the domain's prestige had been called into question. Hisamitsu arranged an alliance of convenience with Aizu, a proshogunal domain in the northeast. With the secret approval of moderate courtiers they organized a coup. At dawn on 1863/8/18 troops from Aizu and Satsuma stormed the imperial palace and seized control of the gates. Their allies in the court held an emergency conference and gave their blessing to the coup, meaning that Satsuma forces were now the emperor's official guardians. Satsuma had routed Chōshū in a stroke.[14]

Chōshū's leadership was stunned. Overnight they had lost the centerpiece of their political strategy, control over the imperial court. The hubris with which Chōshū radicals had excluded their rivals now came back to haunt them. When emissaries from Chōshū sought to petition the court, they were pointedly refused access. On 1863/9/13 the shogunal commander in Kyoto barred a Chōshū delegation from entering Kyoto. In 1863/12 a second delegation was forced to wait while the court deliberated whether to hear their appeal. In the end, they were refused access and returned to Chōshū with the distressing news that the domain had lost all its influence in the imperial capital.[15]

The Satsuma-Aizu coup seemed, briefly, to revitalize the moribund *kōbu gattai* coalition. Having routed the xenophobic radicals, the thinking went, perhaps the moderates could govern after all. In 1863/12, in response to pressure from Shimazu Hisamitsu, the imperial court established a new special council of advisory lords *(chōgi sanyo)*. The members included some of the most powerful lords in the land: Shimazu Hisamitsu; Matsudaira Shungaku of Fukui; Yamauchi Yōdō of Tosa; Date Munenari of Uwajima; Matsudaira Katamori of Aizu; and Hitotsubashi Keiki, who represented the shogunate. This unprecedented union of warrior and courtier power seemed to presage substantial governmental reform. In 1864/2 the shogunate followed the court's example and opened shogunal counsels to "outside" *(tozama)* lords. Externally this looked like great progress toward the realization of *kōbu gattai,* since powerful regional warlords such as Shimazu Hisamitsu now had a voice in both the shogunate and the imperial court. In reality old tensions had only grown worse, and *kōbu gattai* remained as unworkable as before. Many of the shogun's long-standing retainers, the vassal *(fudai)* daimyo, bitterly resented the inclusion of the Shimazu and other "outside" lords in shogunal councils. Similar problems arose in the imperial court. Many courtiers were angered by the appointment of daimyo as imperial councilors: in their mind, warriors were supposed to execute the emperor's orders. What could weapon-toting parvenus, glorified hired guns, bring to the policy deliberations of the august imperial court?

The most destructive tension, however, lay between Hitotsubashi Keiki and Shimazu Hisamitsu. Keiki was deeply suspicious of Satsuma's influence in Kyoto and sought to undermine Hisamitsu by blocking his foreign-policy initiatives. Hisamitsu had proposed a pragmatic approach to the treaty ports based on Ōkubo's advice. Since Japan needed Western technology to fight the West, it would have to open the ports before it could close them. In Ōkubo's words, "opening the ports is the real way to control the barbarians successfully." This approach was radical, but Hisamitsu had won the quiet backing of the imperial court. Keiki, however, was infuriated by the prospect of losing control over foreign policy to Hisamitsu and in particular insisted that a shogunal envoy to Europe could negotiate closing the port of Yokohama to foreigners. When Hisamitsu objected, Keiki showered him with abuse. This angry personal rift was a death knell for the new imperial council. On 1864/3/8 the member lords, disillusioned and angry, dissolved the council and began to leave Kyoto for their homelands. Six days later Saigō arrived in Kyoto.[16]

A Peaceful Warrior

Saigō was stunned by the depth of this political morass. Hisamitsu had dutifully followed Nariakira's *kōbu gattai* ideal, but the imperial council of lords had accomplished nothing. Hisamitsu's efforts had, in fact, made matters worse. *Jōi* radicals, who interpreted his moderate foreign policy as traitorous, now began to target Satsuma's allies in the imperial court. Saigō's immediate connection with this problem was through Nakagawanomiya Asahiko, a collateral imperial prince and one of Saigō's contacts at court. Nakagawa had long been associated with Satsuma and became a target of terrorism soon after the collapse of the imperial daimyo council. In 1864/4 assassins attacked one of Nakagawa's aides, but managed only to kill only the man's mother and his child. Nakagawa's remaining attendants were terrified, and by 1864/6 Nakagawa himself was ready to quit politics and told Saigō that he wanted to retire. On 1864/7/9 Saigō wrote that Nakagawa was so thoroughly terrified and exhausted that he had suffered a complete mental collapse.[17]

Saigō also was troubled by the problem of Chōshū. Now that Chōshū had been expelled from Kyoto there was talk, both in Kyoto and Edo, of a military expedition to punish the domain for its previous actions. As a loyal Satsuma retainer, Saigō relished the way that one of his domain's most arrogant rivals had been brought low.[18] But Saigō also was deeply suspicious of plans to attack Chōshū, and he wondered whether some of the tension between Satsuma and Chōshū wasn't part of a shogunal stratagem.[19] In addition, Saigō was suspicious of Aizu domain, Satsuma's erstwhile ally. On 6/25 Saigō described the punishment of Chōshū as a "private" struggle between Chōshū and Aizu that need not involve Satsuma. Saigō was especially uncomfortable attacking Chōshū while the domain was facing a foreign threat.[20] The Western powers were assembling a fleet to attack Chōshū in retaliation for its actions the previous year, in which Chōshū, acting unilaterally on the imperial court's order to expel the "barbarians," had shelled Western ships in the Strait of Shimonoseki.[21]

Saigō, uncomfortable with ambiguity, wanted a clear answer: was Chōshū good or evil? In 1864/4 he proposed a dramatic means of learning Chōshū's true intentions. He would travel to Chōshū and demand an appropriate admission of guilt for actions in 1862. Saigō fully expected to be killed, but this would be fine, because it would dramatize Chōshū's wickedness: "If I am killed then Chōshū will lose popular support." Alternatively, Chōshū might confess, and then talk of punitive action could be put aside: "If they are reasonable then we will thoroughly [pursue peace]." Either way, Saigō concluded, "I will not return empty-handed." Saigō asked the domain for permission but was told to wait. He would need Hisamitsu's approval for such an important mission. Having learned from his rashness in 1862, Saigō followed orders this time and waited. While biding his time he drafted a Chinese poem:

> With no heed for myself, I vow to go to Chōshū
> Fearing only the fate of the Imperial land, I will speak of peace and amity
> If they take my head, may my blood be as loyal as Yan Zhenqing's
> Frightening traitors for years hence[22]

In choosing Yan Zhenqing (709–785) as his model for loyalty, Saigō revealed the complexity of his vision of heroism. Yan was not a soldier, but a Chinese scholar-administrator best known for two achievements: his unflinching loyalty to the Tang (T'ang) dynasty during the Wang An-shih rebellion, and his distinctive calligraphic style. It was this combination of cultural refinement and loyalty unto death that fired Saigō's imagination.[23]

While Saigō waited in Kyoto, the radicals in Chōshū grew impatient. The failure of Chōshū moderates to regain access to the imperial court had strengthened the hand of *sonnō jōi* partisans. The court, they argued passionately, had been hijacked by Satsuma and Aizu, who were now issuing a flurry of false edicts in the emperor's name. (This, of course, was the reverse of Saigō's perspective.) The only way to rectify the situation was an armed assault on the imperial gates to drive off the usurpers. By 1864/6 Chōshū was openly mobilizing for war.[24] When Saigō received word of Chōshū's mobilization, he placed Satsuma's troops at the imperial palace on heightened alert and waited for war. He did not have long to wait.[25]

On the morning of 1864/7/19 Chōshū troops began moving from the outskirts of Kyoto toward the imperial palace. The palace was defended by troops from many domains, including Tokugawa collateral domains such as Hitotsubashi, Mito, and Kii, but the critical fortifications were manned by Aizu and Satsuma. Saigō and his troops were waiting at Inui Gate, at the northwestern corner of the palace grounds. They met Chōshū's forces coming in from the west at Karasuma Avenue, a major north–south roadway running along at the western edge of the palace grounds. They exchanged withering rounds of cannon fire. Saigō, his younger brother Kōhei, and Saigō's good friend Saisho Atsushi were all injured in the fray. Saigō then called in reinforcements and drove Chōshū into retreat. At the southwest corner of the palace grounds, forces from Chōshū briefly overwhelmed defenders from Aizu and broke through Hamaguri Gate, but before Chōshū could gain access to the palace itself, reinforcements from Aizu and Satsuma arrived. Chōshū was routed and forced to retreat. The battle lasted just hours and involved only a few thousand troops, but it caused extensive damage. War-related fires destroyed thousands of homes in central Kyoto, many of them residences of imperial court nobles. Chōshū's countercoup had failed disastrously: its armies were in retreat, and the imperial court itself was outraged at Chōshū's lawlessness.[26]

The battle, commonly known in English as the Forbidden Gate incident, dispelled Saigō's doubts about Chōshū. The domain was now, in Saigō's mind, an irredeemable villain. In a letter to Ōkubo on 1864/7/20, the day after the battle, Saigō explained how Chōshū had pointed its cannons at the imperial palace and thereby committed high treason. They would now receive "heaven's punishment."[27] Four days after the battle, on 1864/7/23, the imperial court ordered the shogunate to punish Chōshū, and on 7/24 the shogunate ordered twenty-one domains to begin mobilizing troops. This was the clear signal Saigō needed, and he immediately became a passionate supporter of the punitive expedition. On 7/28 he drafted a letter with Komatsu Tatewaki, a Satsuma domain elder, asking Fukui domain to support the expedition. Chōshū, they argued, had conspired to abduct the emperor under the cover of a chaotic battle. In light of this crime, "it is the will of the people of the realm" that Chōshū be punished. Would Fukui fail, they asked in courteous but pointed Japanese, to uphold the authority of the imperial court?[28] Saigō's contempt for Chōshū was almost intractable. Only a few months earlier he had been uncomfortable with the thought of attacking Chōshū while it was facing a threat from the West. But when the Westerners attacked on 1864/8/5, Saigō was unmoved. A four-nation alliance (Britain, the United States, Holland, and France) shelled Shimonoseki, destroyed Chōshū's naval fortifications, and forced Chōshū to surrender, but Saigō's only regret was that Satsuma had not struck before the foreigners.[29]

Had the shogunate moved swiftly to attack Chōshū, there is no doubt that Saigō would have pressed for stiff sanctions against the domain. This would have changed the course of Japanese history, since it was the alliance between Chōshū and Satsuma that eventually toppled the shogunate. But the shogunate was distracted by other concerns. The Tengu insurrection consumed its military resources, and it was desperately trying to secure imperial support for Western treaty demands. Eager to please the imperial court, the shogunate agreed to lead the expedition, but it had trouble finding a suitable commander. In short, the entire Chōshū question became mired in the internal problems of the shogunate. On 1864/8/7 the shogunate finally appointed Tokugawa Yoshikatsu, the daimyo of Owari, as commander of the expedition, but it still was unable to commit sufficient troops. Not until 1864/11/1 did Yoshikatsu leave Osaka for the front in Hiroshima.[30]

Saigō was frustrated by these delays, which had profound consequences.[31] While the shogunate dithered and stalled, Saigō had a meeting that would change his thinking about the future of Japan. On 1864/9/11, at the urging of two acquaintances, Saigō met with Katsu Kaishū, commander of the shogunal navy. Katsu was of humble origins, near the bottom of the samurai estate, and had risen through the ranks by dint of his intelligence and ambition. He had studied Western science and technology at the shogunal naval academy in Nagasaki and in 1864 had been appointed *gunkan bugyō,* commander of the shogunal navy. But despite his rank Katsu was deeply critical of the shogunate. He wanted to lead a national navy, not a shogunal navy, so he had high hopes for *kōbu gattai.* Katsu was furious when Hitotsubashi Keiki scuttled the daimyo council with his impossible promise to close Yokohama. Arrogant, ambitious, and well informed, Katsu was a dangerous malcontent.[32]

Saigō had only the lowest expectations for his meeting with Katsu, but he came away from the meeting awed by Katsu's candor and political acumen. "I first went intending to set him straight but I wound up bowing my head. It seems to me that he is smarter than anyone I know." Saigō compared Katsu to Sakuma Shōzan, one of the pioneers of Western military technology in Japan: "[Katsu] has the ethos of a hero and he is more capable by a good measure than Sakuma Shōzan. In scholarship and discernment Sakuma is in a league by himself, but looking at the present situation, I am utterly enthralled by Katsu." Katsu, for his part, was impressed with Saigō: "Later, when I met Saigō, I thought that I clearly had rather superior opinions and arguments, but I was secretly daunted by the thought, 'perhaps Saigō is the one to shoulder what people call the great burden of the realm.'"[33]

What dazzled Saigō was Katsu's penetrating, critical appraisal of the shogunate. Saigō, like most samurai, had assumed that the shogunate would be a major part of any future political order. However much he distrusted the shogunate, Saigō had not considered Japan without it. Katsu thought otherwise. The shogunate, he told Saigō, was beyond help. It was not a question of replacing one or two weak-willed officials; the entire regime was too feeble to act decisively, and it had lost all credibility with the Western powers through its incompetence and indecisiveness. The only way for Japan to make headway in foreign relations was to speak with a new voice: an alliance of great daimyo. It was time, Katsu declared, to reject the untenable strategy of expulsion and to accept the opening of Nagasaki and Yokohama. But a new government based on an alliance of lords could stand firm on the question of future ports, especially Hyōgo (Kobe).[34]

Katsu's arguments had a catalytic effect on Saigō's thinking. His lingering doubts about the shogunate now crystallized into a coherent political program, which Saigō called "cooperative government" (*kyōwa seiji*). This resembled *kōbu gattai* but with one critical difference: Saigō's political vision no longer included the shogunate. By breaking with the shogunate, Saigō believed, the new regime would have credibility with the foreigners, would be able to renegotiate the treaties, and would restore the honor of the imperial land. Saigō had gone to meet Katsu with the clear negative agenda of stopping Chōshū's rise in national politics. His meeting with Katsu gave him a positive agenda: a plan for a new regime that could defend Japan.[35]

It is important to note the limits of Saigō's change of heart. He remained committed to a military expedition against Chōshū and to the punishment of the domain's leadership. This was scarcely a dovish policy. Many daimyo and samurai, both publicly and privately, were advocating a much more lenient policy, some out of fear of civil war and some in support of Chōshū's expulsionist polices. Saigō, by contrast, still pressed for the execution of the men responsible for Chōshū's attack on Kyoto. But Saigō no longer thought that Chōshū's loss was Satsuma's gain. The primary task was to form an alliance of great lords and rally Japan against the foreign menace. A protracted campaign against Chōshū could not possibly advance this cause. Saigō now wanted the Chōshū affair to be handled fairly and expeditiously so that the country could move on.

Saigō was the leader of one of Japan's largest armies, and the shogunate recognized this by appointing him chief of staff (*sanbō*) of the Chōshū expedition. On 1864/10/24 Saigō met with Tokugawa Yoshikatsu, the expedition commander, to plan strategy. Saigō explained his new thinking on Chōshū. The expedition army needed to confront Chōshū with over-whelming force, but it also had to present reasonable demands. The sho-gunate's demands, which included the public humiliation of the Chōshū daimyo, Mōri Takachika, would merely push Chōshū onto "deadly ground" and stiffen their resolve. By contrast, if the expedition moderated its demands and exploited divisions within Chōshū, it could readily force an apology and surrender. Yoshikatsu agreed. He was already inclined toward a brief campaign, since several important daimyo were critical of the expedi-tion. But Saigō's new attitude was decisive. Satsuma had been one of the key proponents of a punitive campaign, and its military support was critical to the expedition. Saigō's change of heart thus had a "Nixon goes to China" effect: having pressed for the destruction of Chōshū, Saigō could argue for leniency without appearing soft. A quick campaign against Chōshū could no longer be called timid.[36]

Having secured Yoshikatsu support, Saigō headed immediately for Iwakuni, a branch domain of Chōshū. There he met with Kitsukawa Kenmotsu, the daimyo of Iwakuni and a known conservative, whose help Saigō hoped to enlist against the Chōshū radicals. Saigō explained the expe-dition's basic demands. First, Chōshū would send for inspection the severed heads of the three domain elders who had advocated the 7/19 attack. Second, the domain would execute four staff officers involved in the attack. Finally, it would turn over five dissident court nobles who had fled to Chōshū in 1863.[37] These were the core demands. Satsuma wanted to pun-ish evildoers, not destroy Chōshū. To dramatize his point, Saigō released into Kitsukawa's custody ten Chōshū soldiers whom Satsuma had captured in the Forbidden Gate battle. The prisoners, he explained in a subsequent let-ter, were low-ranking vassals and did not realize the political implications of their actions. Since they were innocent of any crime, Satsuma had released them to Kitsukawa, and Saigō hoped that Kitsukawa would do his utmost to ensure that they were not punished, but rather returned to their homes.[38] This was a tangible demonstration of Saigō's intent: he wanted a conditional surrender, not the indiscriminate destruction of Chōshū. Kitsukawa's aides responded as Saigō had hoped, thanking him for his "great mercy" and promising to take his advice on handling the prisoners.[39]

Kitsukawa pressed Chōshū to accept the expedition's terms. On 11/11 the domain government complied, sending the severed heads of the domain elders to Hiroshima and executing the four staff officers at Hagi Prison. On

11/14 Tokugawa Yoshikatsu arrived at the front and inspected the heads. The two most critical aspects of Chōshū's surrender were complete, leaving only the third condition to be met.[40]

The Chōshū expedition seemed headed for a swift and bloodless conclusion when it hit a formidable snag, in the form of the outbreak of civil war in Chōshū. Saigō's decision to exploit the divisions within Chōshū had succeeded all too well. Loyalist radicals and irregulars objected to the proposed surrender, and the domain government sent troops to quiet their dissent. By 1864/12 loyalist battalions and government troops were engaged in sustained combat, and in 1865/1 the domain declared martial law. This threatened the key remaining term of surrender: the disposition of the five dissident court nobles. The Chōshū government, which had been ready to hand over the nobles, could not deliver them after all. On 11/15 irregular loyalist battalions had helped the nobles escape to the branch domain of Chōfu.[41]

Even as the civil war was gathering momentum, Saigō had realized that it could scuttle the agreement and had begun meeting to forge a compromise. In late 1864/11 he discussed the five nobles problem with key figures, including Nakaoka Shintarō. Nakaoka was from Tosa, but had trained with the Chōshū irregulars and could serve as an honest broker between Saigō and the loyalists.[42] With Nakaoka's help, Saigō arranged a meeting with the Chōshū partisans, and on 12/11, accompanied by his friends Yoshii Tomozane and Saishō Atsushi, he traveled to Shimonoseki in rebel territory. The meeting was a dangerous move, but Saigō was determined to win the loyalists' trust. After heated discussions that ran late into the night, the men had reached a compromise. The five nobles would be transferred to a neutral site, Fukuoka domain in northern Kyūshū, and would be guarded by soldiers from five domains. This artful solution allowed Chōshū to surrender the nobles, but not to the shogunate. In Saigō's eyes, this resolved the last major issue with Chōshū and the expedition could disband.[43]

Saigō's trip to Shimonoseki and the agreement on the five nobles changed the political landscape. The Chōshū rebel commanders at Shimonoseki had negotiated peacefully with a man they had every reason to kill: Saigō had foiled their national political aspirations, grabbed the imperial court from their hands, and forced their domain into civil war. To bargain with him took an enormous leap of faith. But the rebels could not miss the point that Saigō did not wish their destruction. With a massive army at his disposal, Saigō nevertheless was not eager to attack Chōshū. The rebels thus kept their promise to Saigō, and on 1865/1/14 the nobles were transferred to Fukuoka. But the rebels had not made peace with their own government. As soon as Saigō left Shimonoskei, they renewed their attacks. By early 1865 the domain was embroiled in a full-scale civil war.[44]

By this point, however, the expedition army had disbanded, in accordance with Saigō's forceful lobbying. Violent dissent in Chōshū, he had argued, was unfortunate, but it was unrelated to the army's mission. The surrender terms had been fulfilled, and it was time to go home. Saigō took maximum advantage of the shogunate's internal divisions and its distance from the front. The expedition's armies, he insisted, could not wait in the field while messengers ran to Edo and waited for definitive terms from the shogunate. Yoshikatsu, who was himself still inclined toward a swift conclusion to the expedition, embraced Saigō's proposal. On 1864/12/27 he disbanded the expedition army, and the Chōshū expedition was over.[45]

The conclusion of the Chōshū expedition was an enormous success for Saigō. He had managed to square a circle. Satsuma had honored the wishes of the imperial court, fulfilled its obligations to the shogunate, and confirmed its position as a political and military power. At the same time, Satsuma had initiated détente with Chōshū: while the two domains remained far short of an alliance, an overture had been made. Satsuma had declined an opportunity to crush Chōshū, and even the Chōshū rebels sensed that something had changed. Saigō's triumph was so enormous that even Hisamitsu responded with accolades. On 1865/1/15 Saigō had an audience with Hisamitsu and Tadayoshi in Kagoshima. They rewarded his efforts with a personal letter of gratitude and an heirloom sword. In 1865/5 Saigō was awarded the post of ōbangashira, the fourth-highest position in Satsuma, and given a stipend of 180 koku. This was the beginning of a series of promotions. In 1866/9 Saigō was formally admitted to the domain council of elders, the daimyo's supreme advisory council. The son of a clerk had become a member of the domain elite.[46]

Saigō was now a figure of national prominence. He had long been known as Nariakira's aide and as an imperial loyalist, but now he was respected even by his social superiors. The brother of the daimyo of Kumamoto, for example, wrote: "I had heard of Saigō from so many people . . . that I was delighted to meet him face to face. He truly is a most impressive person." Hitotsubashi Keiki himself noted Saigō's political prowess, albeit in a backhanded way: although he found Saigō unimpressive, Tokugawa Yoshikatsu seemed drunk with his abilities. That wine they brew from sweet potatoes in Satsuma, Keiki observed, must be very strong stuff.[47]

For Saigō the events of late 1864 marked another life passage. Although he had declared in early 1864 that he was content with his life in exile, by late 1864 he was again eager to represent his domain in national politics. One striking marker of Saigō's change of heart was his choice of names in correspondence. After his attempted suicide in 1858, Saigō had used the name Kikuchi Gengo. After 1862 he had used the name Ōshima San'emon to commemorate his exile on Amami Ōshima. During the Chōshū expedition, however, he began again to sign his name Saigō Kichinosuke.[48] He no longer considered himself an exile; he was now a man of the realm and could again use his father's name. Saigō also decided to marry a woman appropriate to his new station. On 1865/1/28 he wed Iwayama Ito, the daughter of Iwayama Hachirōta Naoatsu, a secretary to the domain elders. This was a prestigious match for someone as lowly born as Saigō, and the wedding was another indication of his rise in the world. The union was, like Saigō's first marriage, one of families rather than individuals. Saigō's marriage to Itō was biologically productive (a son and two daughters), relatively harmonious, and apparently devoid of intimacy.[49]

Like most men of his day, Saigō found passion outside his marriage. Although Saigō himself was extremely tight-lipped about his intimate life, we know of his mistress from the observations of friends. One contemporary, Okatani Shigemi, recalled seeing Saigō as a dapper geisha patron. Saigō would return at day's end to his Kyoto lodgings, shave, change clothes, and then set out, handsome and gallant, to visit his geisha.[50] We know the nickname of Saigō's mistress from the memoirs of Katsu Kaishū. According to Katsu, after Saigō returned from exile he fell in love with a Kyoto geisha so enormously fat that she was known as "Princess Pig" (Butahime), and she was equally ardent for Saigō. Saigō's relationship with "Princess Pig" was apparently well-known in elite circles. When Saigō met with the daimyo of Uwajima in 1873/3 the lord asked him if there was a woman he loved in Kyoto. Saying said that there was indeed, he returned the conversation to politics. Despite her unflattering nickname, "Princess Pig" apparently was a good match for Saigō: at nearly six feet and more than 240 pounds, Saigō delighted in the roundest geisha in Kyoto. Despite his new wealth and power, Saigō's tastes remained simple. From the beauties of the imperial capital he chose a woman his friends found comically round.[51]

A Web of Alliances

The resolution of the Chōshū expedition marked a major turning point in Japanese politics. Satsuma and Chōshū had met in battle in 1863, but by 1865 the domains were steadily moving toward an antishogunal alliance. This was a slow, tentative, and anxious process. Given their fierce rivalry, it was easy for critics on either side to dismiss cooperation as collaboration with the enemy. As Kido Kōin, a key figure from Chōshū, reflected years later, it seemed easier to be crushed by the shogunate than to ask for help from Satsuma.[52] The progress of Satsuma and Chōshū from sworn enemies to nascent allies was based largely on their shared enmity with the shogunate. Satsuma opposed the shogunate because Keiki had scuttled *kōbu gattai*. Chōshū opposed the shogunate because of the Chōshū expedition. The two domains did not trust each other, but both trusted the shogunate less.

The shogunate made itself an inviting target. Between the fall of 1864 and the summer of 1866 the regime was a whirlwind of self-destructive fury. Riven by severe internal tensions, the shogunate was alternately belligerent and conciliatory, and simultaneously aggressive and indecisive. By the end of 1866, men from Satsuma and Chōshū looked on the shogunate with a combination of outrage and disgust. Saigō's own hostility was catalyzed by the shogunate's brutal handling of the Tengu insurrection's aftermath. After forcing the surrender of the rebels in 1864/12, the shogunate executed hundreds of foot soldiers. The shogunate also asked Satsuma to take custody of some thirty-five low-ranking soldiers and to place them in exile on Amami Islands. Saigō was outraged. It was long-standing Japanese tradition, he wrote, that defeated commanders face death after surrender, but foot soldiers should be pardoned. The shogunate's actions were unprecedented in their cruelty, and it would be immoral, he insisted, for Satsuma to accept the prisoners. Ōkubo, like Saigō, was appalled by the shogunate's actions and noted in his diary that the regime's cruelty was a harbinger of its collapse. But Saigō's outrage was personal, since he himself had suffered on Amami Ōshima. Moreover, during the Chōshū expedition, Saigō had pardoned low-ranking Chōshū prisoners as a gesture of sincerity, even while demanding the execution of their commanders. This was how men of honor behaved. How, Saigō wondered, could the shogunate itself fail to understand such a basic principle of samurai integrity?[53]

Saigō's worst suspicions about the shogunate were confirmed by its increasingly belligerent policy toward Chōshū. Tokugawa Yoshikatsu had concluded the first Chōshū expedition without direct approval from Edo, and the shogunate now sought to impose stricter terms as part of a final settlement. Moderates on the shogun's senior council *(rōjū)* wanted the daimyo of Chōshū, Mōri Takachika, to retire in favor of his son and to reduce the domain by 100,000 *koku*. Hard-liners, such as Hitotsubashi Keiki, wanted the domain reduced by at least 150,000 *koku* and thought that both Takachika and his son Motonori should retire.[54]

Chōshū, however, had no interest in making further concessions. Over the winter of 1864–1865 rebel forces had made systematic gains, and by the spring of 1865 the domain was again in the hands of imperial loyalists. The civil war eliminated traditional conservatives from Chōshū politics. The men who had counseled caution in national affairs were dead or permanently discredited. The leaders of the new Chōshū government could not reverse their domain's surrender in 1864, but they would not countenance any further concessions. They refused the shogunate the most basic face-saving gestures, such as a formal statement of contrition that might justify shogunal leniency.[55]

Saigō watched these developments with a combination of amusement and horror. The shogunate, he noted, was run by a "band of fools" divorced from reality. They were pressing Chōshū for concessions using the threat of war, but it was widely known that they were unprepared to fight.[56] "This is a truly bizarre course of events," he wrote to Ōkubo on 1865/8/13, since "even if they lose the negotiations at the outset, they cannot go to war."[57] Watching the shogunate's bizarre approach to Chōshū, Saigō began to suspect that the regime would destroy itself. In 1865/8/28, for example, Saigō predicted that the regime would collapse from internal dissent. The shogun had planned to visit Zeze domain but had changed his itinerary because of rumors of an assassination plot. From this Saigō concluded that the conspirators were shogunal retainers planning to kill their own lord. He also argued that shogunal retainers were behind a suspicious fire at Edo Castle.[58] But even as he awaited the shogunate's collapse, Saigō remained concerned that the regime could cause trouble, especially by isolating Chōshū.[59] Saigō did not see Chōshū as an ally, but he was unwilling to let the shogunate destroy it.

Satsuma and Chōshū had a shared distrust of the shogunate, but still they could not negotiate without the help of neutral outsiders. At this critical juncture two samurai from Tosa, Sakamoto Ryōma and Nakaoka Shintarō, came forward. Both men were from the bottom of the samurai estate. Sakamoto's ancestors, for example, were merchants who had earned samurai status in the eighteenth century by reclaiming land. Both men were passionate imperial loyalists, and both were frustrated by the official policy of Tosa domain. The lord of Tosa, Yamauchi Yōdō, was a member of the daimyo imperial council *(sanyo kaigi)*, but he was far less inclined than Hisamitsu to challenge Tokugawa supremacy. The pretext for this policy was a centuries-old debt to the shogunal house: the Tokugawa had rewarded the Yamauchi for their support at the Battle of Sekigahara with a large investiture. More practically, Yōdō thought that Tosa's interests were best served by a moderate course of pressing for shogunal reform while defending shogunal legitimacy. He had therefore moved to suppress Tosa's radical loyalists, and by 1865 both Nakaoka and Sakamoto were persona non grata in their own domain. Nakaoka found asylum in Chōshū, while Sakamoto took refuge at the Satsuma compound in Osaka. As loyalist fugitives in these two key domains, the men were uniquely qualified to facilitate a Satsuma-Chōshū alliance.[60]

In the summer of 1865 Sakamoto and Nakaoka began working on concrete cooperation between Satsuma and Chōshū. The first item was gun-running. Chōshū desperately needed weapons, but it had only limited contacts with Western arms merchants and had to evade a shogunal arms embargo. Satsuma, however, had developed a substantial business relationship with Thomas Glover, a Scottish merchant affiliated with the British firm of Jardine Matheson. Glover's arms sales to Satsuma violated shogunal edicts, but the British turned a blind eye toward Glover's activities. Although Britain was publicly neutral, British diplomats in Japan were not averse to quiet support for antishogunal activity. Their diffident response to illegal arms shipments was a first step toward secret support for Satsuma and Chōshū.[61]

Satsuma's relationship with Glover dated from 1864/4, when Satsuma had purchased three thousand minié ball rifles, the deadliest guns of their time, from him. At the suggestion of Sakamoto and Nakaoka, Saigō now agreed to help Chōshū buy weapons from Glover. In 1865/7 Itō Hirobumi and Inoue Kaoru, two Chōshū samurai, arrived in Nagasaki and, while staying at the Satsuma residence, negotiated the purchase of seventy-three hundred rifles as well as a warship, the steamship *Union*. In return for Satsuma's support, Chōshū sent nonmilitary provisions to the Satsuma compound in Kyoto.[62]

Encouraged by these steps, in 1866/1 Saigō and Ōkubo began meeting in Kyoto with Chōshū representatives, including Kido Kōin and Shinagawa Yajirō. Their initial meetings were awkward and difficult. Despite their common interests, the two sides still disagreed on important issues. Saigō had called off the Chōshū expedition, but he nonetheless felt that Chōshū had shown insufficient contrition for the 1864 attacks. Similarly, Ōkubo felt that Chōshū should be punished, but that the shogunate's approach was excessive. On the other side, Chōshū's representatives still bristled at Satsuma's alliance with the shogunate in 1864. According to legend, Shinagawa wrote "Satsuma bandits, Aizu villains" on the bottom of his clogs so he could physically debase their names with every step. Kidō and Shinagawa welcomed Satsuma's support in the imperial cause, but they were unwilling to beg for help in their fight against the shogunate. As a neutral party, Sakamoto helped smooth the negotiations by pressing Satsuma to offer help, but the two principals were still distrustful. The stalemate was broken by shogunal belligerence. On 1866/1/22 the shogunate decided to demand the retirement and confinement of Chōshū daimyo Mōri Takachika, the confinement of his son, and a 100,000-*koku* reduction of Mōri family holdings. This was beyond anything Satsuma could support. With their shared suspicion of the shogunate renewed, the two domains quickly hammered out a six-point pact, the formal beginnings of the Satsuma-Chōshū alliance.

The scope of the pact was extremely limited. Satsuma pledged to use its good offices to secure an imperial pardon for Chōshū. If this failed and the shogunate attacked Chōshū, Satsuma would send two thousand troops to Kyoto, but the purpose of these troops was left ambiguous. Satsuma pledged only to "do its utmost" to help Chōshū, so it was unclear whether the troops would actually attack the shogunate or merely hold their ground and look imposing, thereby tying down shogunal troops. Satsuma pledged to join Chōshū in battle only under one condition: if Kuwana domain, Aizu domain, or Keiki's domain of Hitotsubashi used force of arms to block Satsuma's access to the court, then Satsuma would join Chōshū in a war against the shogunate. In the final clause, the two domains pledged to work together for the sake of the "imperial land" *(kōkoku)* and the glory of the imperial house.[63]

This 1866/1 alliance was limited, unbalanced, and fraught with suspicion. Satsuma had promised to fight for Chōshū, but Chōshū had offered nothing in return. Satsuma, in fact, had a renewed interest in a peaceful settlement of the Chōshū issue: if the shogunate would allow an imperial pardon, then Satsuma could fulfill its promise to Chōshū without recourse to war. Saigō himself feared that Chōshū would be emboldened by the pact and would provoke the shogunate. On 1866/3/4 he wrote from Osaka to Ōkubo in Kyoto, urging him to ensure that no rash actions were taken: "No matter how bad things get, we should avoid intemperate actions, and proceed with reason and composure. If we do so to the last, then the shogunate will certainly face turmoil from within." Elsewhere he warned that Chōshū samurai, even Kido Kōin, might "act out blindly" and fall into a shogunal trap. Men from Chōshū, however, were inclined to interpret such caution as inaction. When Satsuma's attempts to win an imperial pardon for Chōshū stalled, Kidō Kōin asked whether Satsuma was really committed to the 1866/1 agreement. After a series of evasive replies the Satsuma representative, Kuroda Kiyotaka, was forced to admit that Satsuma had been unable to outmaneuver Hitotsubashi Keiki and his allies in court politics.[64]

This distrust might have scuttled the Satsuma-Chōshū alliance, but the shogunate continued to antagonize Saigō and other Satsuma leaders. In 1866/3, for example, the shogunate attempted to abrogate the compromise on the five refugee court nobles, putting pressure on Fukuoka domain to send the men to Osaka. Saigō saw this as treachery, and he was particularly angry, since he had visited the nobles earlier to assure them of his commitment to their safety. Saigō dispatched his trusted agent Kuroda Kiyotsuna to Fukuoka with a small squad of soldiers to block the shogunate's efforts. Kuroda was successful, and on 1866/5/29 Saigō reported his success to Ōkubo: Kuroda had demolished the arguments of the shogunal representatives, and Fukuoka was now again united with Satsuma in support of "justice" *(seiron)*. Kuroda had completely thwarted the shogunate's plan, and "this pressure from the shogunal inspectors may become the start of a Kyūshū alliance [against the shogunate]."[65]

. . .

By the summer of 1866 the shogunate was ensnared in a trap of its own making. Because it had publicly insisted on substantial additional concessions from Chōshū, its legitimacy now rested on Chōshū's compliance. But the shogunate could not force compliance without assembling a military coalition, and the most powerful daimyo opposed a second war against Chōshū. The shogunate attempted to recruit support from Satsuma, but its efforts were more comic than effective. The shogunate ordered Satsuma to send troops in early 1866/4, and on 1866/4/14 Satsuma officially refused. Itakura Katsukiyo, a shogunal elder *(rōjū)*, knew he could not coerce Satsuma's cooperation, but he refused to accept Satsuma's refusal. In Kyoto, Ōkubo went to Itakura's residence and demanded that Itakura explain his refusal to accept Satsuma's letter. Rather than explain his actions, Itakura refused any further meetings with Ōkubo.[66] The shogunate, it seemed, would not take no for an answer. Satsuma's refusal to participate and the ensuing farce emboldened other domains to ignore the shogunate's call to arms. Many vassal daimyo sent troops, but they were unwilling to commit substantial manpower or money. To demonstrate their neutrality, several of Chōshū's neighbors refused to commit forces. The shogunate managed to assemble a considerable army, but it was a feckless force, poorly suited for an unpopular war against a spirited foe. This foreshadowed disaster, but the shogunate could find no alternative. The shogunate, it seemed, was fulfilling Saigō's prediction that it would self-destruct.[67]

On 1866/6/7 the shogunate and its allies invaded Chōshū on four fronts: land attacks from Hiroshima domain in the east, Tsuwano domain in the north, and Kokura domain in the southwest, combined with a naval assault from the Inland Sea in the southeast. On the southeastern front the shogunate quickly seized a small island, but this was the high point of its military fortunes. On the other three fronts the shogunate soon fell into retreat. Its troops would not engage, could not cover their flanks, and would not reinforce advance contingents. The shogunal commander on the Hiroshima front, disgusted with the entire enterprise, negotiated a local truce with Chōshū. This freed Chōshū to make further advances on the northern and southwestern fronts. By late 1866/7 Chōshū had seized vast sections of Hamada and Tsuwano to the north, and in early 1866/8, the defenders of Kokura Castle, across the Strait of Shimonoseki, set their castle ablaze rather than surrender to Chōshū. This was a disaster of spectacular proportions. Rather than punishing Chōshū, the shogunate had punished its allies by precipitating Chōshū's invasion of their territory. The shogunate was now fighting desperately to avoid a complete public humiliation.[68]

Amid this debacle, rumors began to circulate that the shogun was dead. Iemochi had, in fact, died in Osaka on 1866/7/20, but his death was unexpected, and the shogunate had not arranged for an heir. Until succession was settled, the regime needed to keep the shogun's death a secret. Iemochi was only twenty and had no sons, so the obvious choice was his regent, Hitotsubashi Keiki, but Keiki showed no enthusiasm for the post. His diffidence was understandable. The shogunate was clearly in collapse, and the title of shogun was arguably more a burden than a blessing. The only way to save the shogunate was radical reform, but Keiki, as an outsider, had little clout with the shogunal administration in Edo. Many historians think that Keiki's diffidence was strategic. If he accepted at the outset, he would appear ambitious and would further alienate the Edo administration. If he accepted after repeated entreaties, he might finally gain the clout he needed to push through reforms.[69]

Keiki's true motivations puzzled his contemporaries and continue to intrigue historians. But his indifference, whether calculated or sincere, exacerbated the succession crisis. The regime's army had been routed and the shogun was dead, but the shogunate could not even announce Iemochi's death until succession had been arranged. On 7/27, after entreaties from key shogunal figures, Keiki finally agreed to become head of the Tokugawa house, but he cagily refused to accept the title of shogun, insisting that he would decline even an invitation from the emperor. As the head of the Tokugawa house, Keiki was now in charge of the Tokugawa troops and began preparations for a renewed assault on Chōshū. This was a controversial decision: hawks such as Matsudaira Katamori still believed Chōshū could be defeated, but most shogunal allies wanted the affair over as soon as possible. On 8/7 shogunal officials in Osaka received word of Chōshū's victory at Kokura; the enemy now controlled both sides of the Strait of Shimonoseki. This tipped the balance in favor of a truce. On 1866/8/20 the shogunate formally acknowledged Iemochi's death, transferred leadership of the Tokugawa house to Keiki, and declared a truce in accordance with official mourning.[70]

Saigō was elated by the shogunate's travails: "I am delighted with this ludicrous turn of events."[71] But he watched the shogunate's self-destruction from Satsuma. Saigō had left Kyoto to take a ship home on 1866/2/30 and did not return to the capital until 1866/10/25. This was his first extended stay in his homeland since his return from exile in 1864. While in Kagoshima, Saigō oversaw the reorganization of the Satsuma army. The domain had already purchased large numbers of Enfield (muzzle-loading) and Snyder (breech-loading) rifles, but now it also reorganized its forces into British-style infantry regiments as part of a broad program of state-led technological innovation. The domain built a large factory complex that included a pharmaceuticals factory, a distillery, a smelting works, and a foundry. At the center of the complex was the Shūseikan, a steam-powered munitions plant. The Shūseikan produced cannons and munitions and repaired steam engines and warships.[72] The Satsuma program was widely admired. Yokoi Shōnan, an influential author and adviser to Matsudaira Shungaku, was impressed by Satsuma's plan to "enrich the country and strengthen the military." Satsuma, he observed, was ignoring shogunal orders against foreign trade and foreign residents, so they could easily import Western technology. Thus their military was growing powerful and their castle town was vital and bustling with foreign merchants.[73]

While Saigō was developing Satsuma's military he also was forging new alliances. In 1866/6 he helped receive Harry Parkes, the British ambassador, whose visit to Satsuma was a pointed insult to the shogunate and an open attempt to nurture Satsuma as a British ally. Parkes arrived in Kagoshima on 1866/6/16 and had a formal meeting with Shimazu Hisamitsu and Shimazu Tadayoshi aboard his ship, *Princess Royal*. The following day Parkes met with Saigō, who was accompanied by Terajima Munenori and Niiro Gyōbu. Britain had long been hinting at its support for antishogunal forces, so Saigō had high expectations of Parkes's visit.[74] Parkes, however, began their meeting with a reiteration of Britain's official policy. Saigō was taken aback, but Parkes was merely feeling Saigō out and tacitly demanding that Saigō be the one to broach the subject of challenging the shogunate. Saigō, however, was concerned that Parkes might leak Satsuma's intentions to the shogunate. With both men reluctant to conspire openly, Saigō took a leap of faith and divulged his plans to Parkes. Satsuma, he explained, hoped the court would take control of Japanese diplomacy and entrust it to a council of five or six great daimyo. These daimyo would forward the revenue from foreign trade to the court and renegotiate the terms of the treaties. This humiliation would force Keiki to resign, and the shogunate would become a minor force in Japanese politics. Parkes commended Saigō on his plan. He warned him, however, that treaty revision would be a slow process and reminded him that Japan needed fundamental political reform. Japan's decentralized government, Parkes declared, was, from an international perspective, fundamentally flawed. Until Japan created a government with "a single national sovereign . . . Japanese would have no honor [literally, 'face'] before foreigners." Saigō silently agreed.[75]

Saigō's meeting with Parkes cemented Saigō's animosity toward the shogunate. Not only had the shogunate failed to uphold Japanese traditions of honor, it also was an impediment to Japan's international reputation. Saigō was determined, now, to overthrow the regime. But he did not yet envision a war. Rather, he thought that pressure from the imperial court and the major daimyo could force the shogunate into collapse. This thinking proved completely wrong, but not for another year would Saigō realize his mistake.

The Road to War

Tokugawa Iemochi's death seemed briefly to revive the fortunes of *kōbu gattai*. Matsudaira Shungaku insisted that Keiki call a meeting of daimyo to determine the course of Japanese politics. The shogunate, he argued, should surrender its authority over foreign affairs to the imperial court and let a daimyo council determine the nature of shogunal rule. Keiki seemed to agree, but he had a very different agenda. Keiki was beginning to recognize the need to reconstitute the shogunate as a national government, rather than a regional government with national obligations. Like Saigō and Ōkubo he envisioned a new Japanese regime, with enhanced political legitimacy and greater military might. For Keiki, however, the shogunate should be a central rather than a peripheral part of this new regime. Further, his refusal to succeed as shogun had actually strengthened his position. By 1866/9 Keiki could expect to real wield real power as shogun, and he now found the prospect of succession to be appealing. Keiki thus wanted a daimyo council, but for different reasons than Shungaku. He wanted the council to confirm his position as shogun rather than examine and redefine it. On 1866/9/7 the imperial court, at Keiki's request, issued a summons for twenty-four major daimyo to come to Kyoto. No one, however, knew quite what the council would do or who would attend. Writing to Saigō from Kyoto, Ōkubo tried to explain this complex situation. The imperial court was chaotic and confused, Keiki was shrewdly manipulating the scene, and Ōkubo suspected that the entire council might come to naught. Still, Ōkubo was excited about Shungaku's plan to strip the shogunate of its powers, restore imperial prestige, and create a new plan for the future of Japan *(kyōwa no taisaku)*. He doubted that this plan would succeed, but Satsuma could not afford to sit by idly.[76]

By late 1866/9, however, the prospects for a substantive daimyo conference were collapsing. Keiki, a master of backroom politics, had convinced the imperial court to again endorse the status quo. Matsudaira Shungaku, angry and unwilling to participate in what he saw as a sham council, left Kyoto for Fukui on 10/1. Most other daimyo voiced their displeasure by their absence. Yamauchi Yōdō, for example, discovered that he was ill. The daimyo of Fukuoka, Kumamoto, Hiroshima, Tokushima, and Uwajima all found reasons to avoid the conference. Finally, on 10/27, Hisamitsu, en route to Kyoto, formally asked the court permission to "delay" his attendance.[77]

Amid this deteriorating situation Saigō and Komatsu hurried to Kyoto. En route, Saigō wrote a brief poem:

On this autumn day I again cast myself into the fray
The steamship billows black smoke as it speeds me south to north
The court wields its authority not, and iniquitous designs hold sway
Oh, to be an autumn maple leaf and fall by the imperial palace[78]

The poem encapsulates Saigō's burgeoning hatred of the shogunate. Only two years earlier he had thought of the shogunate as an essential part of any future Japanese polity. Now he saw every triumph by Keiki as an affront to the imperial house.

Saigō arrived in Kyoto on 10/25, and now he watched firsthand as Keiki eked out another victory. On 11/7 and 11/8 the imperially convened daimyo council recommended Keiki's succession as shogun. Only seven daimyo attended, but the council nevertheless had the aura of imperial authority. Keiki had adopted Shungaku's plan and adapted it to support his own ends. One month later, on 1866/12/5, Emperor Kōmei formally appointed Keiki as the fifteenth Tokugawa shogun.[79] For Saigō and Ōkubo this was dispiriting news. Not only had Keiki triumphed, but also his victory undermined Saigō and Ōkubo's assumption that a daimyo council with imperial support could challenge the shogunate.

The collapse of Shungaku's plan left Saigō and Ōkubo at loose ends. They still opposed the shogunate, but they had little idea of what to do. Ōkubo's diary is strikingly blank for the last months of 1866, and only a handful of letters from Saigō survive for the same period. While watching Keiki and waiting for an opening, Satsuma's most powerful leaders were uncommonly free to play. On 1866/11/11 Saigō invited Ōkubo to join him on a pleasure trip to Saga in the northwestern corner of Kyoto, and on 12/11 Saigō asked Ōkubo to join him and Komatsu on a hunting trip in the mountains.[80] But Saigō was not idle. Although Kyoto politics were at a momentary impasse, Saigō found a bit of hope on the international front. On 1866/12/8 he met with Ernest Satow and came away excited about foreign frustration with the shogunate. This meeting, like Saigō's meeting with Parkes six months earlier, began awkwardly because each party wanted the other to broach the subject of antishogunal action. Years later, in his memoirs, Satow recalled his discomfort: "After exchanging the usual compliments, I began to feel rather at a loss, the man looked so stolid, and would not make conversation. But he had an eye that sparkled like a big black diamond, and his smile when he spoke was so friendly." This was Saigō's intention: "I gave the impression of some hesitancy," he wrote the next day, "so as to sound out Satow's true intentions." Despite their mutual suspicions, the two men were able to have a substantive conversation. Satow prodded Satsuma to take action against the shogunate. Britain, Satow declared, wanted a Japanese government that could fulfill its treaty obligations, and the shogunate was clearly incapable of doing so. Britain could help the daimyo create such a polity, but direct foreign intervention would be improper. Saigō responded truthfully but carefully. Satsuma had tried to support the "imperial land," but the shogunate had gained control of the court. This was frustrating, but since any action by Satsuma might be portrayed as imperial treason, Satsuma had no choice but to wait for two or three years. Satow was astonished. Two or three years was too long, he insisted. Satsuma needed to press the shogunate before the opening of the port of Hyōgo, scheduled for late the following year. Saigō now realized the depth of British interest in Japan. If Hyōgo were opened to foreign trade while under shogunal rule, the shogunate could use trade to reward French support and punish British opposition. Saigō's understanding of European politics was rather shallow, but he grasped this key point and was excited that Satsuma and Britain had a shared interest in opposing the shogunate and France.[81]

While Saigō was pondering his meeting with Satow, startling news rocked the capital. On 12/25, fewer than three weeks after appointing Keiki as shogun, Emperor Kōmei fell dead. His sudden death was suspicious. Kōmei was only thirty-five years old, and he had been vital and active. He had fallen ill with smallpox on about 12/10, but apparently had recovered, when his condition suddenly worsened. The capital was swept by a flood of conspiracy theories, and the emperor's death was widely attributed to poison. Suspects, over the years, have included anonymous shogunal agents, Ōkubo Toshimichi, and the court noble Iwakura Tomomi. Kōmei's symptoms are fully consistent with a smallpox relapse, but this was lost on panicked and suspicious observers.[82]

Kōmei's death changed the political landscape once again. Kōmei had been one of Hitotsubashi Keiki's strongest supporters, and had staunchly opposed the presence of foreigners in Japan. As Satow put it to Saigō, the court seemed to view foreigners as a contamination. Kōmei's xenophobia was similar to the program of *sonnō jōi* radicals, who also favored purifying Japan of foreign invaders. But Kōmei also had opposed radical changes in the political status quo, and he was hostile toward Chōshū expulsionists, especially after the Forbidden Gate incident. The emperor thus had routinely demanded the impossible: both the expulsion of the foreigners and strict maintenance of the existing political order. Keiki had deftly turned this impossible agenda into a mandate. When Satsuma argued that open ports were inevitable, he called them traitors to the imperial will. When Chōshū radicals pressed for immediate expulsion, he labeled them dangerous extremists. Keiki styled himself as Japan's sole voice of reason, steadfast to the imperial will but pragmatic during a dangerous foreign crisis. For Saigō this was utter villainy, but Keiki had managed to fulfill Japan's treaty obligations while maintaining the support of the court. In the process he had not only sustained but also strengthened the shogunate.[83]

With Kōmei gone, Keiki's prospects were far less certain. On 1867/1/9 the late emperor was succeeded by his second son, fifteen-year-old Mutsuhito, better known by his posthumous title, the Meiji emperor.[†] Mutsuhito's regent, the courtier Nijō Nariyuki, was a careful moderate who had long sought to hold together the *kōbu gattai* coalition. Nijō was cautious, but Saigō and Ōkubo both thought that this was a pivotal opportunity. The *kōbu gattai* program, which had seemed moribund a month before, now seemed like their best chance to challenge the shogunate. Saigō flew into action. He left Kyoto for Kagoshima on 1867/1/22 and arrived on 1867/2/1. Upon arrival he needed several days to recover his strength. Saigō was by now chronically ill, often from edema due to filariasis, a parasitic infection. After resting, Saigō began pressing the Satsuma administration to send Hisamitsu to Kyoto for another daimyo conference. Given the miserable results of the 1864 conference and the aborted conference plans of 1866, Saigō expected stiff resistance from the domain elite. To his surprise and delight, the administration was supportive of his plan and endorsed the idea of an embassy to Kyoto. Saigō had a formal audience with Hisamitsu, who formally approved the plan, and then on 2/13 left for Tosa to get support from Yamauchi Yōdō. The daimyo of Tosa was supportive as well and promised to leave for Kyoto the following month. Saigō's only disappointment was his visit to Date Munenari, the daimyo of Uwajima. Munenari was "extraordinarily indecisive" and sought to change the subject of conversation from politics to Saigō's mistress in Kyoto. Saigō refused to discuss his private life, and Munenari refused to give Saigō a firm commitment.[84]

Saigō returned to Kagoshima to report to Hisamitsu and prepare for their embassy to Kyoto. Saigō assembled and drilled roughly seven hundred crack troops, enough to demonstrate Satsuma's resolve but not enough to provoke a war. On 3/25 Saigō, Hisamitsu, and Tadayoshi left Kagoshima with their military retinue on *Sanhōmaru,* arriving in Kyoto on 4/12.[85] All the signs in the imperial capital were good. The court began an amnesty

---

[†]The term Meiji comes from the *nengō,* or era name, declared on 1868/9/8. Previously, imperial courts had declared a new era based on astrological and political events. Thus the arrival of Perry in 1853 prompted the declaration of a new era, and there were five short eras between 1853 and 1868. Beginning with the Meiji era, however, the court established a new tradition: one era name per reign. Thus the Meiji era continued until the Meiji emperor's death in 1912. Mutsuhito was known during his lifetime as the "reigning emperor" *(kinjō heika)* and posthumously as the Meiji emperor.

program, and on 1867/3/29 they allowed Iwakura Tomomi, an influential noble who had been banished from Kyoto since 1862, to return to the capital. All the major daimyo were cooperating. Date Munenari had, in the end, elected to come to Kyoto, arriving on 4/15. Matsudaira Shungaku arrived the next day, and Yamauchi Yōdō on 5/1. All seemed ready for a confrontation with Keiki, and Saigō and Ōkubo now threw themselves into the details of Kyoto politics.[86]

Saigō and Ōkubo were quite explicit about their ultimate goal of destroying the shogunate. As Saigō wrote to Hisamitsu, shogunal authority should be restored to the imperial court, and the shogun's status should ultimately be reduced to that of an ordinary daimyo.[87] But this was a long-term project, and the daimyo conference was just one step along the way. In his memorials to Hisamitsu, Saigō emphasized not the eventual destruction of the shogunate but two other, more pressing issues: the pardon of the daimyo of Chōshū, and the port of Hyōgo. Chōshū had acted intemperately in the past, but now, Saigō insisted, it was critical to treat Chōshū leniently. Saigō gave Hisamitsu a number of carefully coded reasons why the shogunate needed to pardon Chōshū: it would "calm the minds of the people";[88] it would show respect for the court; and it would unify domestic opinion so that Japan could vigorously engage the foreign crisis. The real reasons for the pardon were rather different. In Saigō's thinking, it would fulfill Satsuma's obligation to Chōshū, cement the alliance between the domains, and publicly discredit the shogunate by repudiating its campaign against Chōshū. On the issue of Hyōgo, Saigo insisted that authority over the port be restored to the imperial court. But policy on Hyōgo would depend on the shogunate's handling of the Chōshū pardon, so it was essential to take up the Chōshū issue first.[89]

Saigō and Ōkubo were confident that Hyōgo was the cudgel with which they could beat the shogunate. The court was deeply opposed to foreign trade at Hyōgo, since it would bring "barbarians" perilously close to the imperial capital. But the shogunate was committed by treaty to open the port. According to the Harris treaty (formally the American Commercial Treaty of 1858), Hyōgo should have been opened in 1863, but the shogunate had managed, after lengthy negotiations, to reschedule the opening for 1867/12/7 (January 1, 1868). In 1865, however, the Western powers sought to move up the opening of Hyōgo, demanding the port as an indemnity for Chōshū's attack on Western ships. The "negotiations" were an ugly exercise in gunboat diplomacy, as the Western powers sent a flotilla of gunboats into the harbor in an unsubtle effort to influence the shogunate. This crisis forced the shogunate to ask the imperial court for permission to open Hyōgo. The result was an imperial edict that prolonged rather than resolved the problem. The court assented to "the treaties," thus implicitly endorsing the opening of Hyōgo in 1868, but the court also noted that certain stipulations in the treaties did not "conform to the Emperor's wishes" and insisted that "with regard to Hyōgo no action is to be taken." This response was so evasive that the British representative initially refused to accept it, but the French ambassador, Léon Roches, finessed a compromise.[90]

Keiki had skillfully handled the Hyōgo crisis in 1865, but now Saigō and Ōkubo felt that they had him cornered. If Keiki opened Hyōgo he would be violating an imperial edict, and if he failed to open Hyōgo he would be violating a treaty. While Keiki might have been able to placate Emperor Kōmei, he did not have the same influence over Mutsuhito. Thus Saigo and Ōkubo felt they could force Keiki's hand, compelling him to concede fault over Chōshū in his desperation to get imperial approval for the opening of Hyōgo. This devious strategy required that Satsuma, which had long advocated a pragmatic policy on trade, suddenly oppose the opening of Hyōgo to pressure Keiki. This was overt hypocrisy, but neither Saigō nor Ōkubo was deeply concerned about using duplicity to undermine Keiki, whom they saw as a loathsome schemer.

The daimyo and Keiki began meeting in earnest on 5/14, and Hisamitsu, following his retainers' advice, insisted that the pardon of Chōshū take precedence over all other matters. Keiki quickly discerned Hisamitsu's strategy and counterargued that since the Chōshū war was over, the opening of Hyōgo was more important. Hisamitsu responded by insisting on the precedence of the Chōshū question. Because of Satsuma's promise to work for Chōshū's pardon, this simple question of sequence had become a paramount issue. The survival of the shogunate hinged on the order of debate. The conference dragged out over weeks, deadlocked on this narrow issue. But time favored Keiki: in a war of wits he had deeper forces than any daimyo. After two weeks of stalemate Keiki succeeded in evading Hisamitsu's trap, scheduling a grand meeting of daimyo and shogunal representatives, for the afternoon of 5/23. Saigō sensed trouble in the fact that the court was holding a major council without fixing the precedence of the Chōshū question over the Hyōgo question. On the day of the council Saigō wrote a desperate note to Ōkubo asking for advice, but Ōkubo was equally frustrated. The court, he wrote in his diary, had fallen into the hand of the shogunate. Faced with this debacle, Hisamitsu refused to attend on principle, and Yōdō claimed illness. Ōkubo and Komatsu frantically pressed Shungaku and Munenari to boycott the council, but to little effect. When the imperial court sent a direct summons to Shungaku, he relented and hurried to the palace. Munenari arrived a few hours later, at about midnight on 5/23.

When the council convened, Keiki negotiated with masterful determination, just as Saigō and Ōkubo had feared. Keiki had discerned Satsuma's strategy and refused to yield on the Chōshū question, sensing correctly that this was a battle he could not afford to lose. As the meeting continued into the morning and later on the following day, the weakness of the courtiers' position came to the fore. Although they enjoyed abusing Keiki for failing to repel the barbarians, they were secretly terrified of radical change. The courtier Takatsukasa Sukemasa voiced this fear directly to the emperor's regent, Nijō: If the shogun resigned and the realm fell into turmoil, would the imperial court survive? By the evening of 5/24 Keiki had worn down his opponents, and at roughly 10:00 P.M. Nijō conceded and agreed to provide imperial assent for the opening of Hyōgo. The order included a vague exhortation to treat Chōshū with leniency, but this meant nothing, since it left the definition of "leniency" up to the shogun. Keiki, a master politician, had won again.[91]

Keiki's victory would prove costly, however. He had publicly humiliated the three daimyo, and they knew it. As Hirosawa Sanomi, a Chōshū samurai, observed in a letter to a friend, Keiki was an "evil genius" whose superior resourcefulness had overwhelmed the lesser ability of the three lords. Keiki's manipulation of the court seemed gratuitous. As Date Munenari observed, his "contempt for the imperial court is extreme beyond words." The idea of *kōbu gattai* lay in ashes. The debacle even discredited the imperial court, which despite having a new emperor and regent, had caved in to Keiki. Both the court and the daimyo had failed to lead, and Saigō and Ōkubo abandoned all hope of a peaceful reform. They were not quite ready for a full-scale war, but they no longer imagined that Keiki could be defeated through a peaceful council. They now engaged in a series of secret pacts and alliances designed to put military pressure on the shogunate.[92]

The most pressing matter was Chōshū. Satsuma had pledged in 1866/1 to work for Chōshū's pardon and now, fourteen months later, had nothing to show for its efforts. Chōshū's representatives in Kyoto, Yamagata Aritomo and Shinagawa Yajirō, knew of Satsuma's effort from informal meetings with Saigō, Ōkubo, and Komatsu, but the failure of the four-lords conference still was a crushing blow. If the alliance was to endure, Satsuma needed to demonstrate its good faith. On 1867/6/15 Saigō visited Yamagata to propose an audience for Yamagata and Shinagawa with Shimazu Hisamitsu, father of the daimyo of Satsuma. This was an unprecedented proposal. Yamagata, like Saigō, was by birth a middling samurai, too base to expect a daimyo audience. Hisamitsu, moreover, was an enemy lord, or had been until the previous year. The two Chōshū samurai demurred, but Saigō insisted, and the following day Yamagata and Shinagawa met Hisamitsu at the Satsuma villa in Kyoto. The meeting was short on detail and long on symbolism. Hisamitsu pledged to do his utmost for Chōshū's pardon and gave each man a six-shooter as a gift. He promised to send Saigō to Chōshū in the near future with detailed instructions. That evening Yamagata and Shinagawa went to Komatsu's residence, where they met with Komatsu, Saigō, Ōkubo, and Ijichi Sadaka. The Satsuma representatives now spoke more candidly and passionately about a Satsuma-Chōshū alliance. When pressed for details, Komatsu spoke of taking control of the court and securing an imperial edict against the shogunate. Further details would have to wait for Saigō's visit, however.[93]

While Satsuma and Chōshū were forging a renewed alliance, imperial loyalists from Tosa were coming under enormous pressure. Their lord had left Kyoto in a huff, and they had lost face with their comrades from Satsuma. Satsuma samurai in Kyoto openly mocked Yōdō's departure with doggerel, punning *kashiwa*, "oak tree" (the Yamauchi family crest was three oak leaves), with *kashiwa*, "chicken." Many Tosa samurai shared this anger and frustration at Yōdō. One of Yōdō's key military advisers, Itagaki Taisuke, spoke of raising troops and attacking the shogunate whether Yōdō approved or not. Tosa loyalists also feared for their domain's position in national politics. If Satsuma and Chōshū staged an antishogunal coup, Tosa might be left on the margins. Driven by both principle and pragmatism, Sakamoto Ryōma and Gotō Shōjirō, the head of Tosa's industrial development agency, drafted a proposal for a Satsuma-Tosa alliance. The draft centered on the restoration of imperial power, the elimination of the shogunate, and the establishment of a legislative body. The draft would form the core of the Satsuma–Tosa alliance.[94]

On 6/22 senior representatives from both Tosa and Satsuma met at Sanbongi, a Kyoto restaurant, and hammered out critical details of the agreement. Saigō, Ōkubo, and Komatsu spoke for Satsuma, while Tosa was represented by Gotō Shōjirō and three others (Fukuoka Kōtei, Teramura Sazen, and Manabe Eisaburō). Sakamoto Ryōma and Nakaoka Shintarō also attended, but as observers only, as they were too low-ranking and too radical to speak for Tosa. The pact voiced a broad political vision. The preamble explicitly declared that "it is a violation of the natural order that political matters should be entrusted to the office of shogun." "There cannot be two rulers in one land," it continued, "or two heads in a house, and it is most reasonable to return administration and justice to one ruler." Unlike the Satsuma–Chōshū alliance, the Satsuma–Tosa pact was explicit and detailed. The body of the text called for the abolition of the shogunate and establishment of a bicameral legislature, with daimyo in the upper house and "retainers and even commoners" in the lower house. The shogun would "return to the ranks of the daimyo," but political power would be returned to the imperial court. Informally, both sides agreed that Keiki would not step down unless faced with military force, so Gotō promised to return to Kyoto with troops. On 7/1 the Satsuma representatives in Kyoto gave their formal approval of the agreement, and two days later Gotō left for Tosa to secure his domain's approval.[95]

Saigō was delighted with the pact. In an 1867/7/7 letter to Shinagawa and Yamagata in Chōshū he described Tosa's proposal as an unexpected windfall. Gotō, he explained, was disappointed and angry with Yōdō's actions and had approached Satsuma with a grand plan. Gotō was earnest, and the Satsuma representatives in Kyoto were supportive, so Saigō felt that he should "leap at the opportunity." To allay any suspicions in Chōshū, Saigō attached a copy of the agreement and sent the letter via his trusted friend Murata Shinpachi. "If you have any objections, kindly tell Murata. Further, if there is any opposition within Chōshū, I beg you to let me know." Unfortunately, Saigō reported, the pact would delay his trip to Chōshū, because he needed to wait in Kyoto for Gotō's return. Saigō apologized for the change of plan but asked Yamagata and Shinagawa's indulgence. "I was most eager to go, but I absolutely cannot get out of some messy miscellaneous duties."[96]

The Satsuma-Tosa pact did not address all of Saigō and Ōkubo's goals, but it was an important first step. Saigō viewed the destruction of the shogunate as a long-term, complex process, and Tosa's proposal meant that another major domain was committed to Keiki's ouster. Tosa also had tried to enlist Hiroshima domain, and Hiroshima had quietly indicated that they would join any proposal backed by Satsuma and Tosa. Saigō had every reason to be delighted and optimistic, but to his chagrin this broad coalition of anti-shogunal forces was fragile and short-lived. Initially all seemed well. Gotō arrived back in Tosa on 1867/7/8 and met with Yōdō the following day. Gotō convinced his lord that the Satsuma-Tosa pact was a moderate proposal, preferable to the talk of war circulating among Satsuma and Tosa radicals. Yōdō agreed to the proposal, and Gotō sent word to Saigō that all was well. Before Gotō could return to Kyoto, however, Tosa was consumed by a foreign-policy crisis. On 1867/7/8 two British sailors were murdered in Nagasaki, and Harry Parkes was convinced, based on circumstantial evidence, that the culprits were Tosa samurai. The British sent warships to Tosa, and it seemed in mid-1867/7 as if Tosa, like Satsuma and Chōshū, would fight a small-scale war with Britain. A careful investigation cleared Tosa and the conflict was resolved peacefully, but the negotiations consumed the energies of Gotō and other advocates of the Satsuma-Tosa alliance. In the interim, Tosa conservatives lobbied to undermine the pact, and by 1867/8 Yōdō was no longer willing to press for the shogun's resignation. When Gotō returned to Kyoto in early 1867/9 he had a tepid memorial drafted by Matsuoka Kiken, one of Yōdō's Confucian scholars. It called for a deliberative assembly and a new army and navy, but made no mention of Keiki's resignation or the abolition of the shogunate. Gotō had no troops and nothing to show for his efforts.[97]

Saigō suspected nothing of the trouble in Tosa. In 1867/8/4 he wrote to Katsura Hisatake in Kagoshima that Tosa had "returned fully to [the course of] justice" and that the domain was therefore coming under shogunal suspicion. He was worried that the shogunate was pushing Britain to attack Tosa and wondered if he should somehow intervene on Tosa's behalf.[98] But while Saigō was waiting for Tosa's response, Chōshū was growing concerned about Satsuma. Yamagata had hoped that Satsuma was ready for a massive military assault, but the Tosa pact suggested something quite different.[99] To clarify the details of their vague alliance, Chōshū sent Shinagawa back to Kyoto with Saigō's aide Murata on 7/18, but Shinagawa learned little. Increasingly uneasy, Chōshū send a second set of envoys, Kashiwamura Makoto and Mihori Kōsuke, who finally met with Saigō, Ōkubo, and Komatsu on 8/14. At that meeting Satsuma secretly but formally asked Chōshū for military aid against the shogunate. The following day Kashiwamura met privately with Saigō and pressed for further details. Saigō, for the first time, disclosed his plans. Satsuma had about a thousand troops in Kyoto and would send a third of them to storm the imperial palace and install courtiers committed to "justice." Another third would attack Aizu domain's troops. The final third would set fire to the shogunal barracks in the Horikawa district. In Osaka, three thousand additional troops would besiege Osaka Castle, while in Edo, Satsuma troops and *rōnin* would try to cut off shogunal reinforcements. As for Tosa, Saigō praised Gotō's plan demanding the resignation of the shogun as an excellent idea, but he was certain that Keiki would refuse. At that juncture, Satsuma would step in and break the shogunate's grasp on the court. Saigō emphasized the secrecy of the plan. Only the daimyo and a few others in Satsuma knew of the plan; Kashiwamura would tell only his daimyo and two or three others. The domain elite in Satsuma were not ready to support an attack on the shogunate, so Saigō's hope was to stage a coup and then secure an imperial edict authorizing the attack.[100]

The Chōshū delegation was delighted with Satsuma's plans, but the meetings were fraught with irony. Three years earlier, Saigō and Mihori had met in battle on the streets of Kyoto, when Chōshū had attempted to seize the imperial palace. On that day, Saigō had been an ally of Aizu and the shogunate while Chōshū, as the loser, was blamed for the ensuing fires. Now Saigō was asking for Chōshū's help against the shogunate and Aizu, and Kashiwamura was reminding him to take adequate precautions against fire.

In his conversation with Kashiwamura, Saigō described the Tosa proposal as praiseworthy but doomed. Keiki would not agree, and his refusal would give Satsuma and Chōshū a pretext to attack. But Saigō also would have been pleased with the other alternative. If Keiki did resign as shogun it would be a major step toward the establishment of a new imperial polity. What Saigō did not foresee is what actually occurred: the proposal from Tosa had been eviscerated. When Gotō finally returned to Kyoto in early 1867/9, he and Saigō regarded each other with mutual alarm. Saigō found Gotō's revised memorial intolerably weak, and was appalled that Tosa would not use force to compel Keiki's resignation. For his part Gotō was dismayed that Satsuma was preparing for war, and he asked Saigō to delay his plans for a coup until Tosa had submitted its memorial. Saigō refused. He would not block Gotō's plans, but neither would he alter his own.[101] Tosa and Satsuma were no longer allies, but rivals. Rather than allow Keiki to escape, Saigō began preparing for war.

In the following days, Satsuma and Chōshū began developing a detailed strategy for battle, and on 9/15 Ōkubo left for Chōshū to meet with the daimyo and domain leaders. In Yamaguchi he met with the daimyo Mōri Takachika and his son and forged concrete plans for the deployment of troops. Satsuma would send warships to the Chōshū port of Mitajiri. There they would collect troops from Chōshū and Hiroshima and travel to Osaka. Ōkubo promised that the fleet, would arrive by 9/26 and, thinking his work was done, returned to Kyoto. But conservatives in Satsuma, fearful of a confrontation with the shogunate, delayed the fleet, and radical loyalists in Chōshū began to suspect a double cross. The troops finally arrived on 10/6 and 10/9, proving Satsuma's good intentions, but Chōshū leaders felt that an opening had been lost, and they insisted on revising their military plans.[102]

Meanwhile, in Kyoto, Saigō, Ōkubo, and Komatsu were pressing the imperial court for support. On 1867/10/8 they sent a secret memorial to three courtiers, including the emperor's uncle. Keiki's conduct, they argued, had endangered the imperial land, and they could no longer sit by while the realm fell to ruin. They wanted imperial permission to "punish the crimes [of the shogunate], drive out the wicked schemers, and undertake the great mission of restoring the imperial house to its former state."[103] Six days later, Satsuma received a secret edict to "annihilate the traitor Keiki."[104] The edict, while it bore the emperor's name, had been drafted without his assent. Unable to secure the emperor's backing, Satsuma's allies in the imperial court had forged an imperial decree. This duplicity aside, Satsuma and Chōshū now had their casus belli and could begin final preparations for a coup. Keiki, however, smelled troubled and acted the same day. Seizing on the watered-down Tosa proposal, he apologized for his failings and surrendered his "administration" *(seiken)* to the emperor.[105]

This was a brilliant preemptive strike. Keiki's tactical surrender undermined Satsuma's justification for a coup. But since Keiki's declaration did not mention the office of shogun, it was unclear what authority Keiki was giving up. The imperial court accepted his resignation on 10/15, but it immediately asked him to serve in his traditional capacity while the court called all major daimyo to Kyoto to discuss political reform. Given his skillful handling of the four-daimyo council five months earlier, Keiki had every reason to welcome a general meeting of lords. Satsuma allies in the court, however, were stymied. They were unwilling to support a coup against Keiki now that he had resigned, even if they could not fathom the meaning of his resignation. Keiki, it seemed, had escaped again.[106]

Saigō and Ōkubo were unmoved. Keiki's dodge merely cemented their conviction that radical change would require force. The Tosa plan, which had once seemed like a means of pressuring Keiki, was now a shogunal escape route. Rather than slow their plans for war, Saigō and Ōkubo plowed ahead. Saigō now realized that peace and order favored Keiki and gave a minor order with major repercussions. In mid-1867/10 he ordered Sagara Sōzō, a Satsuma retainer, to gather *rōnin* and to foment general chaos in Edo. Using Satsuma's villa in the Mita district as their headquarters, Sagara and his men ransacked merchant warehouses, set fire to shogunal property, and attacked Edo police officers. If Keiki had the upper hand in the imperial court, Saigō would draw him into the street.[107]

Meanwhile, the leaders of Satsuma and Chōshū returned home to make final plans. On 10/19 Ōkubo, Saigō, and Komatsu boarded a Hiroshima ship from Osaka. That these three powerful men left Kyoto together hinted at the momentous events to come. They traveled first to Chōshū, accompanied by Hirosawa Saneomi, and arrived at Mitajiri on the evening of 10/21. The following day they traveled to the Chōshū capital of Yamaguchi and met with Mōri Takachika and his son. There they reaffirmed Satsuma's determination to fight with Chōshū to topple the shogunate. On 10/26 they arrived in Kagoshima and went immediately to the castle to report to Hisamitsu and Tadayoshi. The following day they had a lengthy meeting with the domain elite: Saigō and Ōkubo were resolved to topple the shogunate, but they wanted the daimyo himself to lead troops into Kyoto. Despite deep reservations, the domain elders assented, and on 10/29 the domain formally decided to send Tadayoshi to Kyoto at the head of a small army.[108]

By mid-1867/11 antishogunal forces began to move on Kyoto. Saigō and Shimazu Tadaoyshi left Kagoshima on 11/13 at the head of three thousand crack troops. They stopped at Mitajiri to regroup and to provide transport for Chōshū forces. The Satsuma contingent arrived in Osaka on 11/20 and entered Kyoto three days later, where they joined some two thousand troops already in the capital. Chōshū forces, led by Mōri Motonori, arrived in Osaka on 11/20 but did not enter Kyoto. Chōshū was still under imperial sanction, so they dared not enter the imperial city. Asano Mochikoto, son of the daimyo of Hiroshima, arrived with three hundred men. The thin pretext for this convergence of daimyo was the imperial court's summons of 1867/10/15 to discuss Keiki's resignation. Ostensibly the troops were justified by the need to defend the imperial court.[109]

Backed by armed force, Satsuma now pressed the imperial court for a decree against Keiki. On 12/8 Saigō, with Ōkubo and a domain elder, drafted a letter to Iwakura. A great and formidable task was at hand, they declared, and the future of the realm hung in the balance. The "minds of the people" were polluted by more than two hundred years of Tokugawa rule, and restoring imperial rule would be a dangerous affair. While it was tempting to compromise with the Tokugawa in the name of "magnanimity," this would actually endanger the court. Nothing less than a reduction in Keiki's land and rank to that of an ordinary daimyo would satisfy the imperial will. Talk of peace was thus talk of treason: "Those who say one should not be fond of war are [the same] as those who say we should not act in accordance with great principles *(daijōri)*."[110]

On that same day the imperial court convened an assembly to determine the fate of the shogunate. The assembly quickly resolved several preliminary issues. They pardoned several loyalist nobles, including Sanjō Sanetomi (one of the five refugee nobles), and completed the pardon of Iwakura Tomomi so he could again appear before the emperor. That evening they granted a full pardon and restoration of court rank to Chōshū daimyo Mōri Takachika and his son. Satsuma had at last fulfilled its primary obligation under the 1866/1 pact. But the most contentious issue, an imperial order dismantling the shogunate, remained. Negotiations dragged on through the night and into the early morning.[111]

Early in the morning on 12/9 the conference broke for recess, and the imperial regent Nijō returned home. Iwakura strode into action. He called in troops, primarily from Satsuma, to defend the gates of the imperial palace. Then he summoned the daimyo and key retainers from Satsuma, Hiroshima, Tosa, Fukui, and Owari to the imperial palace for a formal ceremony. While the assembly waited, the boy emperor Mutsuhito called collateral princes

Arisugawanomiya and Yamashinomiya to his library (gakumonjo) and reported the "imperial will." He then went before the assembled daimyo and, seated behind a bamboo screen on a high platform, read a "grand edict" (daigōrei) dissolving Japan's political structure. The shogunate was abolished. This command encompassed the office of shogun as well as Matsudaira Katamori's office of Kyoto protector (Kyōto shugo) and the post of Kyoto deputy (Kyōto shoshidai). Key offices of the imperial court were eliminated. Nijō's post of imperial regent (sesshō), a center of power since the seventh century, was no more. In place of the shogunate and the traditional imperial court, the emperor declared a new political structure. Prince Arisuga-wanomiya would be president (sōsai); major daimyo and high-ranking courtiers would be senators (gijō); samurai and lower courtiers would be councilors (sanyo). This was the swift, bloodless coup Saigō and Ōkubo had planned for months, but deference and decorum required that they remain inconspicuous. Ōkubo sat discreetly at the back of the assembly room. Saigō stood outside, at the gates of the palace, commanding Satsuma's troops.[112]

The presence of thousands of Satsuma troops in the capital had helped forge a broad but ephemeral antishogunal alliance. Yamauchi Yōdō and Matsudaira Shungaku, scarcely Satsuma allies, both supported the decree rather than be excluded from the new political order. They were appropriately rewarded with the rank of senator in the new imperial council. Hitotsubashi Keiki and Matsudaira Katamori, by contrast, refused to attend the meetings, not wishing to legitimize by their presence an antishogunal putsch. Thus the imperial decree precipitated a tense stalemate rather than a clear victory. To avoid a potentially explosive confrontation, Keiki left Kyoto for Osaka on 12/12. Keiki complied with the edict without quite acknowledging its legitimacy. He accepted, for example, Matsudaira Katamori's resignation as Kyoto protector, but cited illness rather than imperial edict as the cause. Meanwhile Keiki's defenders, including Yōdō and Shungaku, desperately tried to parse the edict to Keiki's advantage. The imperial order dissolved the office of shogun, but it did not strip Keiki of his imperial office of lord keeper of the privy seal (naidaijin). Perhaps then he could retain his landholdings as an imperial officer. From Osaka, Keiki agreed to resign as shogun and to surrender lands, provided that all daimyo also surrender land to the imperial house to defray its expenses. This was an intriguing idea, and even Iwakura began to waver. Time again seemed on Keiki's side.[113]

On 12/28 Saigō wrote a distressed letter to Minoda Denbei in Kagoshima. Keiki's retreat to Osaka, Saigō feared, was less a sign of submission than a means of consolidating his forces. Although the import of the imperial edict was clear enough, Tokugawa Yoshikatsu and Matsudaira Shungaku were working to help Keiki keep his land and even be named a senator in the new government. If the court immediately issued a decree to attack Keiki, then even collateral daimyo (shinpan) such as Yoshikatsu would abandon the shogunate. Instead, the situation had settled into a standoff. Things were not entirely bleak, however. Several important domains were disassociating themselves from the shogunate and, in Tosa politics, Itagaki and his loyalists seemed to be edging out Gotō and his "sinister schemes." But the situation was unsettled, and both Saigō and Ōkubo were frantically busy trying to keep the antishogunal alliance together.[114]

The stalemate was broken on 12/28 when Keiki received news from Edo. Five days earlier, after weeks of rumors that Satsuma agents were planning to attack Edo Castle, a suspicious fire had broken out and destroyed the castle women's quarters. That same evening someone had shot at the Edo villa of Shōnai domain, a close shogunal ally. When men from Shōnai gave chase, the assailants had fled through the city to the Satsuma villa. These events came on the heels of weeks of brigandage attributed to Satsuma-led rōnin. Edo officials were outraged, indignant, and ready to fight. On 12/25 they attacked and burned the Shimazu villa, killing several men. In Edo, if not in Kyoto, war had broken out.[115]

The crisis in Edo was Saigō's handiwork, the result of his orders to Sagara Sōzō, and the plan had finally pushed Keiki into a corner. Keiki was willing, if not eager, to step down as shogun and to surrender responsibility for the quagmire of foreign affairs. But the attack on Edo Castle and the Shōnai villa challenged Keiki's dignity as a warrior. He could not ignore such an affront and still command the respect of his men. Keiki had consistently outwitted Saigō and Ōkubo in negotiations, so Saigō had brought talking to an end. Now, to retain his authority, Keiki would have to fight. With his honor hanging in the balance, Keiki responded to Saigō's challenge. On New Year's Day (January 25 by the Gregorian calendar) Keiki stated his grievances to the imperial court. The traitorous Shimazu Hisamitsu, Keiki declared, had been acting contrary to imperial wishes and deceiving the young emperor. Satsuma's forces had not only seized control of the imperial palace in Kyoto and forced the emperor's regent to resign, they also had "pillaged and bullied about the city [of Edo], firing upon the personnel and residence of Sakai [Shōnai]." There had been violence and banditry in Edo, "and Hisamitsu's vassals have fostered it in order to speed an alliance of east and west and confound the imperial land." Keiki would now take matters into his own hands. If the court did not order the arrest of these traitors, "it is unavoidable that the death penalty be imposed on them."[116]

The Tokugawa and their allies now began deploying their forces. The battle lines formed at the village of Toba and the town of Fushimi, both south of Kyoto along the Toba highway. At Toba the Tokugawa massed roughly 2,500 men against a Satsuma force of 900. At Fushimi the Tokugawa, with Aizu and allied domains, assembled 3,000 troops against 500 men from Satsuma, 725 from Chōshū, and roughly 200 from Tosa. These were daunting odds, and the new government was ready for the worst: if Kyoto fell, they would create a diversion by moving the imperial palanquin to Mount Hiei, in northeastern Kyoto, while troops from Satsuma and Chōshū evacuated the emperor to Hiroshima.[117] On 1868/1/3 Saigō dashed off several letters to Ōkubo. Saigō doubted that Aizu would attack without explicit imperial orders, but nonetheless he wanted immediate reinforcements for the Fushimi front.[118] He had reviewed battle plans with Inoue Kaoru, a Chōshū commander, and Ijichi Masaharu, the Satsuma commander at Toba. All was well, but Saigō was pragmatic about the daunting size of the enemy forces and made detailed recommendations for the emperor's escape route.[119] At dusk that same day, Satsuma cannons at Toba opened fire on the Tokugawa. Saigō left for the front to watch his outnumbered troops attack the most powerful government Japan had ever known.[120]

Chapter 5

"TO TEAR ASUNDER THE CLOUDS"

Saigō and the Meiji State*

The End of the Tokugawa Regime

Beginning on the evening of 1868/1/3 Satsuma, Chōshū, and their allies pounded the shogunal military to pieces in three days of fierce fighting. Saigō was elated but astonished by his own victory. Writing to Katsura Hisatake on 1868/1/10, Saigō boasted that his forces had routed an enemy five times their size. The same day, writing to Kawaguchi Seppō, he claimed a ratio of ten to one. Saigō's estimates were inflated, colored by euphoria and the fog of war, but his troops were indeed outnumbered. Large parts of the Tokugawa army existed only on paper, but at Fushimi-Toba shogunal forces still outnumbered the imperial army by at least two to one.[1]

The shogunal forces were not only large, they also included some of the best troops in Japan, such as the shogunate's French-trained infantry. Many troops on the shogunal side also fought with great courage. The battalions from Aizu showed how dangerous the traditional weapons of the samurai

---

*Saigō to Katsura Hisatake (1869/7/8) at *STZ* 3:41–42.

could be. On at least two occasions the troops rushed Satsuma and Chōshū riflemen with swords and pikes, sending them fleeing before they could reload. The shogunate had manpower and matériel, but it was undermined by feckless leadership and chronic disunity. The shogunate's troop deployments lacked any coherent strategy and, with troops consistently in the wrong place at the wrong time, they were unable to take advantage of their numerical superiority. The army also was racked by poor morale and disobedience. Even after victories their troops did not advance, giving the imperial army time to regroup. Reinforcements did not deploy as ordered, leaving attacking forces with their flanks exposed. As the stench of defeat spread, the shogunate's allies began to hedge their bets. Inaba Masakuni, the daimyo of Yōdō, was nominally allied with the shogunate, but he refused to allow shogunate troops to seek shelter in his castle. The final blow came on 1/6 when, during a critical engagement, artillery forces from Tsu domain switched sides and began shelling Aizu forces rather than advancing imperial troops. Battered from without and hollowed from within, the armies of the shogunate imploded.[2]

On the evening of 1868/1/6 Keiki learned of Tsu's defection and decided to abandon Osaka and head east. It was unclear whether he was preparing to surrender or attempting to regroup his forces in Edo for a defensive stand. His statements and actions were contradictory, leaving his allies demoralized, his enemies anxious, and historians confused. But the outcome of Fushimi-Toba was unmistakable: shogunal forces had ceded the western half of the country to an alliance of southwestern daimyo. The war was far from over, but momentum was with the imperial rebels.[3]

Saigō was revitalized by the thrill of battle. As a senior commander he was not supposed to go to the front lines, but he could not resist the temptation. Late on 1/3 he wrote to Ōkubo, "Today, when I got news of the battle, I could not contain myself and although I expect to be scolded by our lord, I went out to Fushimi and I have just now returned."[4] Tadayoshi did indeed reprimand Saigō for his recklessness, but Saigō furtively visited the front again on the night of 1/5. Saigō was fighting beside his relatives and took pride in their courage. His cousin Ōyama Iwao, a future army general and army minister, took a bullet wound on the ear, but continued fighting without pause. Saigō's younger brother Tsugumichi received a long wound from his ear to his neck but, Saigō declared with pride, he would be ready for battle if needed.[5] Saigō also was heartened by signs of popular support. When Satsuma troops passed by, commoners rushed into the streets, clasped their hands together, and bowed, chanting, "Thank you, thank you, thank you." I never realized, Saigō wrote, how much the populace hated the shogunate. Saigō was savvy enough to understand that apolitical forces also were at work. The commoners, he noted, might be celebrating the end of fighting and the corresponding fall in rice prices, rather than the arrival of the imperial army. Still, he took joy in seeing commoners pour into the streets to fete his troops with food and drink.[6]

The defeat of the shogunate was a personal triumph for Saigō, but it provoked deeply conflicted emotions. Saigō reveled in his military victory and the stalwartness of his men. But he also was troubled by feelings of sorrow, inadequacy, and his own mortality. He was deeply saddened that he was enjoined from fighting at the front, and took this as a sign of weakness. On the first day of 1868 Saigō had, by traditional reckoning, turned forty, and this seems to have made him acutely aware of his age. He confided his feelings to Kawaguchi Seppō, his companion from Okinoerabujima who was now caring for Saigō's family in Kagoshima:

> I regret that I've joined the ranks of old men, so I can no longer fight, but just depend on others. I have already decided that when the fighting dies down I will ask for my leave and retire. To tell the truth, I can no longer serve like a man [*ningen*], and I am so timid and self-conscious that it's unbearable.[7]

Saigō swung between bravado and tenderness. He urged his younger relatives into battle, threatening to disown them if they fought without courage and came back uninjured. But he was humiliated that he himself could not enter the fray. Then he confided to Kawaguchi, "I'm truly delighted that they fought well and were injured, and I now think I won't disinherit them, but will treasure them like keepsakes [*hizō*]."[8] As the fighting died down, his thoughts turned to his infant son, Toratarō, back in Kagoshima. Toratarō had fallen ill and, in an uncharacteristically personal passage, Saigō asked Kawaguchi not to let the child eat too much while still recuperating.[9] At a moment of unparalleled military triumph Saigō was unnerved by his own physical failings and by thoughts of his new son hundreds of miles away.

It was more than a year before Saigō could clearly articulate the roots of his anomie, but in the interim he was troubled by a nagging lack of purpose. After his suicide attempt in 1862, he had found the will to live in his sense of duty. Heaven had not let him die in Kinkō Bay because his duty on earth was not yet complete. Saigō's duty to Nariakira, his one true lord, clearly encompassed the destruction of the shogunate. But now, with the shogunate in collapse, Saigō began to wonder if his mission was complete. Could he retire, or did his duty also include the establishment of a new, imperial state? The destruction of the shogunate had consumed Saigō's energies, but as the shogun's armies retreated, Saigō was left to wonder what his loyalty to Nariakira now entailed. This was an especially painful question since Nariakira's vision for Japan, a *kōbu gattai* council, now lay in ashes. Not only had daimyo councils failed to challenge the shogunate, but also conservatives such as Matsudaira Shungaku and Yamauchi Yōdō were using the conciliatory language of *kōbu gattai* to defend Keiki. Saigō was beginning dimly to sense that a new imperial state might require the destruction of the traditional polity, including daimyo sovereignty. In other words, the spirit of Nariakira's vision was in complete conflict with the details of Nariakira's political program. This was a conflict Saigō could never quite face, much less reconcile. This unspoken and unresolved tension became a latent crisis for both Saigō and for the Meiji state: one of the founders of the modern Japanese state was deeply ambivalent about his own creation.[10]

Saigō revealed his ambivalence toward the nascent Meiji state in the early months of 1868, complaining openly about the imperial army. The new state required a new military command for its operations against the shogunate. Although the "imperial" army was just a loose amalgam of domainal armies, in 1868/2 the government created four military divisions: the Tōkaidō, Tōsandō, San'indō, and Hokurikudō, each named for a major highway. Overseeing these four armies was a new high command: the Eastern Expeditionary High Command (Tōsei daisōtokufu). The nominal head of the high command was collateral prince Arisugawanomiya, and the two senior staff officers were court nobles. This connected the assembly of domainal forces with the imperial court, the only national institution in a still unformed nation-state. Saigō was one of two junior staff officers, the highest-ranking samurai in the army.[11] Saigō, however, soon was grousing that he had been saddled with a prestigious but odious desk job. He found staff meetings unbearable and longed for a real command. In 1868/3/5 he sent off an impassioned plea to Yoshii Tomozane, a fellow Satsuma samurai, begging to be replaced. His letter included a macabre quip: Saigō asked to be relieved of his high office so he could die in battle and "wait for you [Yoshii] in hell."[12]

Despite his bitter protests, Saigō remained in office and supervised the imperial army's eastward progress. Their forces met little resistance between Osaka and Odawara, a castle town roughly fifty miles southwest of Edo. Then the army fell back to Sunpu (present-day Shizuoka), established a command center, and began plans for an attack on Edo. On 3/6 the expeditionary high command met in Sunpu to debate possible terms of surrender. They decided to demand the execution of major Tokugawa officials and the surrender of all castles, warships, and war matériel. If their demands were not met, they would attack Edo on 3/15. Saigō embraced these strict terms. Nothing less than Keiki's death would cool his ire, and he was incensed that some courtiers were leaning toward a pardon. Letting Keiki retire, he wrote Ōkubo, was typical of the court's destructive vacillation.[13]

Keiki, however, had shrewdly withdrawn himself from the scene. On 2/11 he had voluntarily gone into domiciliary confinement and had placed Katsu Kaishū in charge of the Tokugawa armed forces. Katsu was a surprising but clever choice. In 1864 Katsu had undermined the shogunate by opposing an attack on Chōshū, but his opposition was principled: the shogunate was pursuing a narrow vendetta rather than the national interest. This same standard now motivated Katsu to defend the shogunate. A needless war against the Tokugawa, he believed, was as bad as a needless war against Chōshū. Katsu was arrogant and self-serving, but he was not without his principles.[14] On 3/6 Katsu contacted Saigō in Sunpu via an emissary, Yamaoka Tesshū. Katsu knew better than to appeal directly for "mercy" or "leniency." Saigō, after all, hated Keiki in part for his cynical approach toward "leniency" for Chōshū. Katsu appealed instead to Saigō's understanding of loyalty. Imperial loyalism, he reminded Saigō, was nonpartisan and was not a basis for petty squabbles. Japan faced danger from within and without: "The current situation in the imperial land is different from the past in that, although brother is pitted against brother, they also know that it is time to avoid such a disgrace." Katsu further appealed to Saigō's sense of honor: "To exhaust one's strength suppressing lowly vassals is not a worthy path *(michi)* but merely a decision to die a fruitless, angry death under a hail of bullets."[15]

As in 1864, Saigō was won over by Katsu's argument, and he agreed to meet with Katsu to negotiate more moderate terms of surrender. On 3/13 and 3/14 they met in Edo, and Katsu again spoke to the shared interests of the opposing sides. Keiki, he argued, was a respectful imperial servant; that was why he had withdrawn from the Kinai and resigned as shogun. Keiki was prepared to surrender vast portions of his holdings as well as the city of Edo, and he had no interest in more fighting: "My lord is not one who, grieving for the fate of his own house, goes to war and kills his own countrymen (kokumin)." Katsu warned ominously that a civil war could lead to social turmoil, with widespread samurai and commoner insurrections. Would Saigō, out of petty vengeance, deny Keiki a reasonable share of his ancestral holdings and risk domestic chaos? By contrast, if Saigō would embrace a more moderate settlement, then "there will be no disgrace before heaven, the authority of the court will rise, and, seeing the nurturing justice of the imperial land, the entire country will instantly echo this, and when foreign countries hear of it, their faith in our country will be restored, and harmonious relations will be cemented." Katsu's argument resonated with Saigō's longing for a sense of grand purpose and his long-standing concern with honor. His argument also captured Saigō's fascination with transcendent acts of virtue. Treating the Tokugawa with justice, Katsu argued, would instantly spread virtue across the realm. For Saigō, this was a deeply moving argument. He promised to postpone the planned attack and to make Katsu's arguments to the high command. Saigō insisted that he could not speak for the government without consultation, but Katsu was confident that Saigō's voice would be decisive. Saigō presented Katsu's terms to Arisugawanomiya at Sunpu and then left for Kyoto to secure imperial government approval.[16]

After weeks of negotiations, the final terms of surrender were announced at Edo Castle on 4/4 by an official imperial embassy, including two imperial courtiers, representatives of the military high command (including Saigō), and roughly sixty attendants. Keiki was spared death and was allowed to retire to Mito domain, despite having "deceived the imperial court" and committed capital crimes. He was later granted a full pardon, and he died quietly in 1913, having outlived almost all of his rivals. Keiki's defenders, despite their "grave crimes," were granted imperial clemency and allowed to retire from public life. Edo Castle was to be surrendered to the lord of Owari, a collateral Tokugawa house. The Tokugawa promised to surrender all war matériel, but the imperial government promised to return a "suitable portion" at a later date. These terms were a negotiating triumph for Katsu and a stark departure from the Saigō's earlier demand for Keiki's ritual suicide. Saigō's enmity toward the Tokugawa had been dispelled by Katsu's arguments, and he was swayed by the "extreme obedience" of

Tokugawa officials. In a letter to Ōkubo the following day Saigō even found kind words for Ōkubo Ichiō, a Tokugawa official who had helped negotiate the surrender. Saigō was amused, however, by his new authority and he thought it was funny that he could now stride, still wearing a sword, to the inner recesses of Edo Castle.[17]

The surrender of Edo Castle concluded the first phase of what Japanese historians call the Boshin War: *bo* (earth) and *shin* (dragon) were the Chinese zodiac signs for the year 1868. The formal rituals of surrender went smoothly, and on 4/11 Owari domain, acting as a representative of the imperial government, took possession of Edo Castle. Ordinary Tokugawa retainers, however, were less willing to surrender than Tokugawa leaders, and the subsequent stages of the surrender went awry. Kumamoto domain, acting as an imperial representative, was supposed to take custody of more than 2,000 Tokugawa soldiers and all Tokugawa firearms. In the event, they received only 722 Japanese-made rifles and a handful of men. The best weapons and troops had vanished. By mid-1868/4 dissenting Tokugawa troops had formed guerrilla bands in the Kantō and were attacking the imperial army. Katsu did his best to ensure compliance with the surrender agreement, but he could not quiet the widespread discontent within the Tokugawa alliance. In both Edo and the northeast there was talk of continued war against the "wicked traitors."[18]

Saigō faced this looming crisis firsthand in Edo. The city was patrolled by the Shōgitai, or "League to Demonstrate Righteousness," a newly formed brigade of former shogunal soldiers. These troops had helped keep peace and order during the surrender of Edo Castle, but now they bristled at the thought of abandoning the shogun's capital to Satsuma forces. From their base at Kan'eiji Temple at the top of Ueno Hill they mocked imperial troops, and by 1868/i4 they had begun attacking imperial patrols. Katsu attempted to restrain them, but to no effect. Saigō, although concerned, was reluctant to rush a confrontation. With so many imperial troops in the northeast and rural Kantō, imperial forces in Edo were actually outnumbered. At a command meeting on 5/1 Saigō argued against attacking until reinforcements arrived, but the Chōshū commander, Ōmura Masujirō, disagreed. The imperial government had plans to make Edo its new capital, and shogunal forces would therefore have to be eliminated. Saigō still had his reservations, but when the Shōgitai escalated its attacks on Satsuma forces, he relented. The final assault was set for 5/15. At dawn that day imperial forces attacked the Shōgitai. Satsuma's forces rushed the gates of Kan'eiji head-on and met fierce resistance. After a frustrating delay, Chōshū forces launched an attack on the rear of the temple compound, but not before Satsuma had suffered heavy losses. Despite the poor coordination and the Shōgitai's superior numbers, by evening the Shōgitai was defeated. The shogunal capital was now an imperial capital. Two months later the city was renamed Tokyo, or "Eastern Capital."

Saigō had every reason to be disgruntled with the Ueno campaign. Ōmura, a Chōshū officer and technically only a military adviser, had seized the initiative on military command and designed the attack strategy. His plan had led to heavy Satsuma casualties, in part because Chōshū reinforcements failed to support Satsuma at a critical moment. Saigō, leading his troops on the ground, had witnessed this at close range, while Ōmura watched from a command tower miles away. Yet Saigō was too energized by the thrill of battle to complain: "With our ample preparations we made short work of [the enemy] and this is an exceptional and extreme delight." Rather than resent Ōmura for seizing command, Saigō seemed to appreciate the chance to lose himself in the fog of war. Despite his overall dysphoria, Saigō found courage in the fray of combat, and this renewed his fame. The court noble Sanjō Sanetomi reported, in a letter to Iwakura Tomomi, that "as for Saigō's troops, the fierce engagement at the Black Gate (Kuromon) was truly a spectacular fight and they have won the admiration of all." Etō Shinpei echoed these sentiments: "I am overwhelmed with admiration for Saigō's courage and for Ōmura as a master military strategist."[19]

With Edo secure, Saigō turned his attention to the widening conflict in the northeast. The imperial government had expected strong resistance from Aizu and Shōnai domains, both of them stalwart defenders of the shogunate. The northeast, however, not only resisted but also showed powerful regional solidarity. In 1868/i4 domain elders from Sendai and Yonezawa, two large northeastern domains, solicited support for a petition calling for clemency for Aizu and Shōnai. The petition won backing in neighboring domains, and the joint appeal quickly became the basis for a broader regional alliance. By 1868/5 the imperial government faced a confederation of seventeen northeastern domains, sworn to work jointly for the just treatment of Aizu. The Alliance of Northeastern Domains (Ōuetsu reppan dōmei) was not eager for a military conflict with the imperial government. On the contrary, many members of the alliance thought that they could avert war by negotiating lenient surrender terms for Aizu and Shōnai. But the imperial government was nonetheless appalled by this implicit threat to its sovereignty: the confederation had challenged the new government's authority over the northeastern fifth of the country. In the words of Sera Shūzō, an imperial staff officer, the "vulgar domains" of the alliance were "making light of the imperial court" and there was no choice but to "view the entire northeast [ōu] as the enemy."[20]

Saigō returned to Kagoshima to raise additional troops for the campaign against the alliance. Soon after his return on 6/14, however, he was incapacitated by poor health and retired to the countryside for a hot-spring cure. Saigō finally left Kagoshima with three platoons on 8/6 and arrived at the northeastern port of Kashiwazaki four days later. His participation in the northeastern campaign was preceded by tragedy. His brother Kichijirō was badly wounded in battle on 8/2 and died on 8/14, only four days after Saigō's arrival. Saigō respected the dignity of dying in battle but felt that he, as the eldest, should have died first. Because of illness Saigō had missed much of the war, and by the time he arrived, the tide had already turned in favor of the imperial government. Saigō led his troops in the siege of Shōnai and proved himself a capable commander, but he was already deeply nostalgic. In one of his few surviving letters from the northeastern campaign, he steeled one of his officers for battle with the admonition that "if you do not show the righteous indignation of olden days, then you will be unable to show your face to anyone."[21] Saigō's most important action in the northeast was showing graciousness in victory. Because men from Shōnai had burned the Edo Satsuma villa in 1867, they now braced themselves for retaliation. Saigō, however, commanded an orderly occupation and withdrew his troops as soon as the surrender of the Shōnai castle town was complete. This unexpected gesture of goodwill won Saigō great fame in the northeast. He was now celebrated as an emblem of samurai virtue even by his enemies.[22]

Saigō and Domain Reform

By late 1868/9 the northeastern campaign was effectively over, and Saigō left for Edo and then home. Once in Satsuma, he headed for Hinatayama, an unremarkable but pleasant hot-spring town near the northeastern corner of Kinkō Bay. Saigō was drawn to Hinatayama largely by the waters, which soothed his chronic aches and pains. Today the waters are recommended for neuralgia, muscular pain, joint pain, painful and stiff shoulders, chronic digestive disorders, and general exhaustion, but even those who question the efficacy of this liquid panacea can enjoy beautiful scenery while soaking in the mildly alkaline waters. Hinatayama also was ideal for two of Saigō's great loves, hunting and fishing. The Amorigawa River, which runs through Hinatayama, was known for *ayu,* a delicious freshwater fish. The surrounding hills were ideal for hunting rabbit, deer, and wild boar.[23]

Whether Saigō intended to retire from public life or hoped merely to rest is unclear, and he probably was unsure of his own plans. In 1869/1 he received a request from the imperial government to return to the capital, but he politely declined. Then, in 1869/2/25, Saigō was startled by the unexpected appearance of an illustrious guest. The daimyo of Satsuma, Shimazu Tadayoshi, personally visited Saigō in Hinatayama and implored him to return to government service. Saigō was not especially enthusiastic about the proposition, but he could not refuse his lord. Tadayoshi's request appealed to both Saigō's sense of duty and his sense of pride. Saigō relented and agreed to become a counselor *(sanyo)* in the domain government.

Tadayoshi needed Saigō to defuse a potentially explosive issue, the nettlesome matter of Satsuma domain reform. The imperial restoration had brought to the fore long-simmering tensions within the samurai class. The soldiers who returned victorious to Satsuma in late 1868 were from the bottom of the samurai estate and had chaffed for years under traditional restrictions on rank and office. Having chosen the winning side in a decisive political struggle, they felt entitled to demand radical reform, and they returned from battle with little patience for an elite they now considered coddled, weak-willed, and cowardly. The domain elite, known as the *mon-batsu,* was, by contrast, thoroughly discredited. Deeply invested in the status quo, they had opposed an attack on the Tokugawa until the last months of 1867. The frustration of the lower samurai quickly spilled into public conflict, and by early 1869/1 Satsuma samurai were staging public demonstrations demanding that important government positions be opened to low-ranking but capable retainers.[24]

These demands for radical reform were difficult to dismiss because they seemed in harmony with the decrees of the central government. In a major policy declaration, the Charter Oath of 1868/3, the emperor had vowed before his illustrious ancestors to reshape the Japanese polity. Japan would now seek knowledge throughout the world, important questions of national policy would be decided by "public discussion," and "all classes, high and low" would now "unite in vigorously carrying out the adminis-tration of affairs of state." What precisely this meant was unclear. Radicals would later argue that "all classes" included commoners and that "public discussion" meant a parliament. But even the most conservative interpreta-tion of the central government's directives was bad news for the *monbatsu*. The Meiji state would not help a small clique of families maintain their monopoly on political power. At the same time, the Meiji state had dodged the question of whether the reform of hereditary privilege meant the end of daimyo rule. In 1869/1, under intense pressure from reformist samurai, the daimyo of Satsuma, Chōshū, Tosa, and Saga, in a carefully orchestrated gesture, surrendered their investitures to the imperial government. The emperor promptly reappointed these men to their old holdings as domain governors *(han chiji)*. Shimazu Tadayoshi was now the imperially appointed domain governor of Satsuma, but it was unclear how this differed from his previous post of daimyo. Had the daimyo institution been strengthened by imperial approval, or weakened by imperial control?[25]

Shimazu Hisamitsu outlined this confusing situation in a remarkably direct missive to Saigō. Writing in 1869/2, the lord observed that "in the current situation, it is obvious that government appointments should be made irrespective of rank" and that some retainers had, accordingly, peti-tioned for the abolition of the *monbatsu*. This struck Hisamitsu as "a reason-able argument" but upon "careful reflection" he became concerned. The *monbatsu* were descendants of men who had rendered "meritorious service" to the Shimazu house, so it seemed wrong to strip them of their rights. Most seriously, "to leave my own hereditary privileges unchanged while abolish-ing completely the hereditary privileges of those below me is utterly con-trary to duty and human kindness and will be judged harshly by history." Hisamitsu thus struck at a central question for the new state: was the Meiji Restoration a revolutionary attack on hereditary privilege or restoration of traditional rights and duties? Could the new government conduct a limited assault on privilege? In this fluid and uncertain situation, Hisamitsu again sought the help of Saigō, a man he distrusted and disliked. More precisely, Hisamitsu needed Saigō's reputation to contain a volatile and dangerous sit-uation. Practically, Saigō did not need to do anything. He merely needed to

be affiliated with the domain government and thereby, through his reputation, tame a seemingly uncontrollable demand for radical reform.[26]

On 1869/2/25 Saigō formally became one of several councilors *(sansei)*
in the domain government and presided over the reform of Satsuma's social
and political institutions. Saigō paid little attention to the particulars of
reform. He found the minutiae of government administration crushingly
dull and spent many days in retreat at Hinatayama. Saigō's major role was
symbolic. His presence in the domain government assured lower samurai
that their interests would be heard. Saigō's friend Katsura Hisatake played a
similar function for a different constituency. Katsura, the younger brother of
Shimazu Shimōsa, a domain elder, was the token representative of the traditional domain elite. Saigō and Katsura had enjoyed a long relationship.
Katsura had been dispatched to Amami Ōshima to organize military
defenses in 1862, just as Saigō was recalled from his first exile. Katsura had
looked after Aigana and her children, and Saigō owed him a debt of gratitude. Serving together in the domain government deepened their friendship, and Saigō began to confide his most intimate feelings to Katsura.
Because of Katsura's lofty status Saigō's letters are appropriately formal, but
they are, nonetheless, remarkably direct.[27]

Over the next two years the domain implemented sweeping changes in
all major areas of government. The most striking change came in the distri-
bution of samurai income. The Satsuma government ordered the *monbatsu* to
surrender their private holdings to the domain, and used revenue from this
land to effect radical income redistribution. Prior to reform, roughly a hundred elite *monbatsu* families enjoyed more than 200,000 *koku* in rice income:
the top 0.2 percent of the samurai population controlled about 43 percent
of samurai income as their own autonomous investitures. After reform the
monbatsu received about 7 percent of total income, paid as ordinary stipends.
The reforms slashed *monbatsu* income by more than 87 percent and simultaneously increased the stipends of common samurai by an average of 21
percent. By sacrificing the domain elite, Satsuma was able to raise living
standards for most samurai while still spending less on total stipends. The
domain also restructured its army, incorporating thousands of low-ranking
retainers into a modern, British-style military system. The domain reorganized administration, dissolving traditional institutions such as the council of
domain elders and replacing them with a cabinetlike system of departments
and bureaus. Appointment to the new offices would be based on talent

rather than rank; the domain abolished all major status distinctions among its samurai. The government conducted a new land survey and simplified its system of tax collection. It continued, with renewed energy, the promotion of modern industry, especially textiles and shipbuilding.[28]

These reforms had a transformative impact on the domain. By 1872 Satsuma had confronted the major inadequacies of traditional governance. The domain had a modern military instead of a decentralized feudal army. Its civil administration was limited to samurai but was based on ability rather than birthright. The domain had abolished the autonomous authority of *monbatsu* families, asserted new control over rural villages, and created a rationalized, central administration. Astonishingly, despite the cost of restoration war, Satsuma was increasingly solvent. While retaining core elements of samurai privilege, reformers had created a stable, modern, bureaucratic regime. This was a stunning accomplishment, for which Hisamitsu was commended by the emperor. But the Satsuma reforms also posed a latent threat to the Meiji state. The radical reform of domain governance created an implicit alternative to a powerful, centralized nation-state. If Satsuma could create a modern state within the boundaries of a traditional domain, then perhaps local autonomy was a viable alternative to initiatives from Tokyo.[29]

Saigō approved of the reforms, but he longed for military action. Then, in the spring of 1869, the central government began operations against the last stronghold of military opposition, Enomoto Takeaki's self-declared "republic" in Hokkaidō. Enomoto, a former shogunal naval officer, had absconded with eight warships in 1868/8 and joined the northeastern alliance. After the defeat of the Ōuetsu reppan dōmei, he had fled farther north, to Hokkaidō, where he occupied the city of Hakodate. In 1869/5/11, after the spring thaw had begun in the far north, the government began an attack on his forces. Saigō gathered troops and headed north to take part in the campaign, but Enomoto surrendered after only seven days, and Saigō arrived after the war was over. Humiliated and exhausted, he returned to Kagoshima. The news was not all bad: on 1869/6/2 the government granted him a stipend of 2,000 *koku,* the most financially generous of a series of awards honoring his service to the imperial court. Nothing, however, could quite dispel his sense of failure from having missed the action at Hokkaidō. Saigō's career as a soldier for the Meiji state ended with a whimper, not a bang.

Saigō returned to Kagoshima and headed north to escape the heat and relax at a hot spring in the mountains of Miyazaki. There he received a letter from his friend Katsura Hisatake describing his plans to retire from the domain government. This wrenching news cut to the heart of Saigō's own ambivalence about public service. Saigō rebuked Katsura in a polite but pointed letter dated 1869/7/8. Saigō appreciated that Katsura was ill, but this was not a reason to resign. Saigō himself was ailing, and after five days at the hot spring he had begun to suffer from a high fever and stomach pain. Then he had developed severe diarrhea and broken out in boils and scabies. "I have loose bowels twenty-four or twenty-five times a day, sometimes with blood, but my mood is entirely unchanged." Saigō insisted that he was in high spirits because his symptoms merely showed that the hot spring was purging his body of the illness. Having confessed his physical frailty, Saigō then voiced his deep inner conflict and his anguished longing for Nariakira:

> I was once labeled a disloyal vassal and even thrown into prison, [but] it would have been inexcusable toward his late lordship [Nariakira] if I had rotted there. I thought that if I could have one chance to participate in the great affairs of state and clear myself of allegations of disloyalty, I would humbly report to Nariakira in the nether world, shut my mouth, and say no more. This was my sole preoccupation, and with this thought alone I served my lord Hisamitsu. However, there is no reason to assume that a lord and vassal will share both feelings of tenderness and duty [*jōgi*] toward each other, and I have been serving [my present lord Hisamitsu] based on the single word "duty." Would it be utterly unreasonable if you took pity on me [in such a predicament]?

Having bared his soul to Katsura, Saigō implored him to postpone his resignation for two years and to retire later with Saigō. "You know that your resignation due to illness will have a great effect on public feelings in the realm [*kokujū*], and irrespective of that trouble, it would be heartless of you to leave me behind."[30] Saigō literally begged Katsura not to retire. Saigō found the details of administrative reform impossibly tedious, and the prospect of serving the domain government without the company of a trusted friend was more than he could bear.

At the heart of Saigō's anguish was his understanding of samurai service.

Having enjoyed such a close connection with Nariakira, Saigō wanted nothing less than the ideal lord-vassal relationship: a bond cemented by both deep personal affinity and a mutual commitment to duty, what Saigō called *jōgi*. Most samurai lived and died without having ever enjoyed a private conversation with their daimyo, so Saigō was uniquely privileged. Still, having enjoyed the samurai ideal, he was saddened by anything less. Saigō's samurai ideal has no direct parallel in contemporary American culture, but one aspect of his crisis is remarkably accessible. Saigō yearned for passion. He brought to government service the same dual, possibly contradictory, expectations that Anglo-American society now brings to marriage: love and duty. In our modern marital ideal, couples are united by both a deep emotional affinity and by legal norms. A marriage held together solely by legal sanction is generally seen as sad and hollow. Saigō brought a parallel set of expectations to government service. He did not want to serve solely out of fealty. He wanted to serve because of deep passion. Strikingly, Saigō had no such concerns about marriage. Like a good samurai, he married for decorum and status. Saigō never thought to complain that he did not love his wife. Wives were supposed to be dutiful, and Saigō was satisfied with Ito's execution of her duties. Saigō found passion in his relationship with "Princess Pig," and he freely confessed his love for his geisha, although the relationship had no public standing. In politics, however, Saigō wanted both duty and passion. He thus wrote of government service after 1869 with the quiet but simmering anguish of a spouse trapped in a loveless marriage.[31]

With Katsura's support, Saigō weathered his emotional crisis. Katsura agreed to remain in the domain government and, in fact, died together with Saigō on the hills of Shiroyama eight years later. Saigō continued to serve the domain, although he remained fixated on death and redemption. His passionate outburst to Katura seems to have been cathartic, and Saigō's subsequent letters show greater equanimity. As Saigō explained to Ōkubo in a letter on 1870/8/3, "now I am resolved either to dispel Hisamitsu's doubts [about me] or to die," and this dual resolve was making his life much easier. Rather than worrying about the future, he was now living each day as though it were his last. He had found that "because I am paying a great deal of attention to one thing at a time, I am finding it easy to serve."[32] This was a morbid path to a quiet mind, but it gave Saigō a sense of peace.

On 1870/11/16 Saigō commemorated a traumatic event, the thirteenth anniversary of Gesshō's death. Saigō had long been troubled by his own survival, and the anniversary must have given new immediacy to old anxieties. Saigō recorded his thoughts in a commemorative poem:

> We swore to throw ourselves together into the depths
> Alas, who could have known my fate was to be reborn upon the waves
> Thinking back, these ten-odd years seem like a dream
> Across the divide between the living and the dead, I weep in vain over
> your grave[33]

The poem gave voice to Saigō's grief, but more striking is Saigō's equanimity. There is no urgency to the poem, and no onerous sense of duty. Saigō lamented the loss of his friend and ally, but he did not turn Gesshō's death into an inspiration for acts of loyalty, courage, or martyrdom. Saigō's description of his life as being "like a dream" matches the mood of his letters from the same period. Saigō wondered why he was alive, but this question no longer drove him to political engagement. He had, albeit temporarily, set aside his quest for grand purpose and transcendence, and he was content to grieve quietly.[34]

Saigō had thus struck a balance between withdrawal and engagement. He was an adviser to the Satsuma domain government and was thereby fulfilling his obligations to his lord. But he was, by his own description, living day to day, with no grand purpose other than to assuage Hisamitsu's doubts. He would soon find this tenuous balance impossible to maintain.

A Reluctant Statesman

On 1870/12/18 a grand embassy from Tokyo arrived in Kagoshima. Iwakura Tomomi, Ōkubo, Yamagata Aritomo, and Kawamura Sumiyoshi had come to persuade Saigō and Shimazu Hisamitsu to join the central government. This visit was prompted by a growing sense that domain autonomy, especially the autonomy of Satsuma, was a threat to the Meiji state. The central government's vulnerability had been dramatically revealed three months earlier, when Satsuma had withdrawn its troops from the imperial palace guard as part of a regular troop rotation but failed to send replacements. This was widely interpreted as preparation for a coup. The central government was effectively paralyzed by this threat because it did not have an army. Its military was an amalgam of troops volunteered by different domains. So serious was the perceived threat that it became front-page news in the *New York Times:*

> The Daimios are acting independently of the Mikado, and Prince SATSUMA seems ready at any moment to break into open rebellion. Foreigners are generally apprehensive of a renewal of civil war during the coming Summer. SATUSMA has withdrawn all his troops from Yeddo and already public feeling is becoming alienated generally from the Mikado.

Things were scarcely better in Chōshū, where disgruntled samurai had staged a major insurrection in 1870/2. The general situation was, as Kido noted in his diary, "simply deplorable," and in 1870/11 Kido and Ōkubo resolved to return to their respective domains and address the problem firsthand.[35]

Ōkubo's mission was thus to win Saigō's support for a stronger central government, and to this end he met daily with Saigō from 1870/12/19 to 1870/12/22. Ōkubo was initially concerned about Saigō's support, but on 12/22 he noted, with a sense of relief, that they were in "complete agreement." This was something of an overstatement. In fact, Ōkubo and Saigō had sharply different plans for the future of Japan. Ōkubo was determined to create a modern, centralized bureaucracy, while Saigō questioned the very need for intrusive government. Saigō's opposition to a central bureaucracy was rooted in a Confucian understanding of power: governments should rule, he thought, through broad precepts and moral example rather than extensive regulation. But Saigō and Ōkubo agreed on the pressing need for a national military, independent of any domain. Saigō promised to accompany Ōkubo back to Tokyo, where he would help turn the imperial guard *(shinpei)* into a national army.[36]

Saigō threw himself into this project with great energy. He traveled from Kagoshima to Chōshū, where he met with Kido, and then to Tosa, where he met with Yamauchi Yōdō and Itagaki. On 1871/2/2 Saigō arrived in Tokyo for more meetings, and on 2/8 he and representatives from Chōshū and Tosa reached an agreement on a new national force. A week later Saigō returned to Kagoshima to collect troops from Satsuma. On 4/21 he returned to Tokyo with four battalions of troops led by the daimyo Shimazu Tadayoshi, Satsuma's contribution to the imperial guard.[37]

The reorganization of the imperial guard calmed the anxious situation in the capital. The *New York Times,* which had warned of civil war two months earlier, now described a new level of national unity. "The adhesion of the Satsuma to the Mikado," it reported, "has given a sense of security to Jeddo [Tokyo] not hitherto felt."[38] Sanjō Sanetomi, writing to Ōkubo on 1871/2/18, expressed a similar sense that the government now had a secure base from which to pursue further reforms, and he singled out Saigō for his "exceptional efforts."[39] Saigō himself took great satisfaction in his accomplishment. He celebrated the imperial guard with a poem:

> The enervation of the imperial house has startled the people
> Grieving and angry, one hundred thousand soldiers have offered their lives
> Resolute in their loyalty, their spirits are like iron
> As cornerstones and pillars, they build an impregnable fortress[40]

On the narrow issue of reforming the imperial guard, Saigō was in complete harmony with the rest of the Meiji oligarchy. He, Ōkubo, Kido, Itagaki, Iwakura, and Sanjō Sanetomi all agreed that Japan needed a national military. Beneath this consensus, however, lay serious disagreements on the future of Japan.[41]

The turmoil of 1870 had convinced Kido and Ōkubo that Japan needed radical political centralization. Without the destruction of daimyo power the imperial government would be unable to pursue radical reform and unable to meet the daunting challenge of Western imperialism. The Tokyo government had used the return of the daimyo investitures *(hanseki hōkan)* in 1869 to consolidate many small and fragmented domains and replace them with prefectures under central government control. It also had turned former shogunal holdings into prefectures. But the government had moved only tentatively against the authority of the major daimyo. Kido and Ōkubo were now prepared to challenge their own domains. Unless the domains of Satsuma, Chōshū, and Tosa were abolished, they argued, the authority of the Tokyo government would never be secure. As Kido wrote in his diary on 1871/6/11, "we must now strive toward the second step, giving reality to the return of the investitures, and unifying the nation."[42]

Ōkubo had discussed the abolition of the domains with Saigō in late 1870, but Saigō had been noncommittal.[43] Once Saigō returned to Tokyo in 1871/4, however, Kido and Ōkubo began pressing forcefully for his support. Because of Saigō's influence among Satsuma samurai, his agreement was critical. If Saigō embraced the replacement of domains with prefectural governments *(haihan chiken)*, then even disapproving samurai would feel compelled to show restraint. Also, Saigō was commander of the imperial guard, which might be needed to face down recalcitrant daimyo. Kido was initially frustrated with Saigō's evasiveness and wrote in his diary that Saigō was avoiding a discussion of "the fundamental matter of the foundation on which the government rests." On 1871/6/27, however, Kido and Saigō spoke for several hours, and "in the end, I [Kido] felt that he had rather suddenly accepted my view. Saigō's unselfishness touched my heart, and I admired him for it." "This man," Kido continued, "is filled with sincerity" and "for the sake of the country, I jump for joy."[44]

With Saigō having agreed to the dissolution of the domains, his primary concern was to move quickly and decisively. To speed negotiations, he favored limiting debate to one representative each from Satsuma, Tosa, and Chōshū. The other oligarchs agreed to a slightly modified version of this plan. On 1871/6/25 all seven standing imperial councilors *(sangi)*, including Ōkubo, resigned and were replaced by two men: Kido and Saigō. On 1871/7/14, two other councilors were added: Itagaki from Tosa, and Ōkuma Shigenobu, a samurai from Saga. This framework, with one councilor from each of the four major domains, would hold until early 1873. Although Ōkubo stepped down to make way for Saigō, Ōkubo was promptly appointed head of the finance ministry and remained at the center of political power. Ōkubo replaced Date Munenari, the daimyo of Uwajima, and this was the first step in a long process of political reform: the replacement of daimyo and court nobles ("dummies of high birth," as Satow called them) with powerful and capable administrators. Overall the governmental reorganizations of 1871 concentrated political power in the hands of a few lowly born samurai from four southwestern domains.[45]

On 7/12 Saigō, Kido, and Ōkubo met in secret to discuss the details of the abolition of the daimyo class. Only once they had reached an agreement did they inform Itagaki, Ōkuma, or the imperial court. The daimyo themselves were neither consulted nor given prior notice. At 10:00 A.M. on 1871/7/14, Shimazu Tadayoshi, Mōri Motonori of Chōshū, Nabeshima Naohiro of Saga, and Itagaki Taisuke, representing Yamanouchi Yōdō, were summoned for an imperial audience and informed that their domains had been abolished. Four hours later, the emperor appeared before an assembly of fifty-six former daimyo, now domain governors, and announced that to protect the Japanese people and achieve parity with the nations of the world, the domains were being dissolved. Hereditary rule over domains, the emperor declared, had undermined reforms, and it was now the imperial will to "do away with the dangers of divergent government orders." The audience, stunned, did not at first fully comprehend that they had been effectively stripped of all authority.[46]

Over the following months the central government systematically redrew local boundaries and appointed prefectural governors to replace the former daimyo. These governors were representatives of the Tokyo government and they, not descendants of local warlords, would implement national standards in taxation, civil administration, law, and education. Remarkably, the daimyo class yielded with minimal dissent. Many daimyo, especially those with small domains, were daunted by the prospect of turning their principalities into modern states and greeted the abolition of the domains with relief. Some daimyo, such as Uesugi Mochinori of Yonezawa, thought that the reforms violated centuries of Japanese tradition but were unwilling to oppose the imperial government and its troops. Others appreciated the genuine need for radical centralizing reform. Mōri Motonori of Mito, for example, openly supported the abolition of the domains and even advocated more radical challenges to hereditary privilege. Finally, many daimyo were swayed by the government's generous financial settlement. Former domain governors were given lifetime stipends equivalent to 10 percent of their domain's tax income and also were granted elite status within a newly created national peerage. The sole outspoken opponent of *haihan chiken* was Shimazu Hisamitsu. Convinced that the abolition of the domains was nothing less than treason, Hisamitsu alternated between ominous sulking and furious tirades against Saigō and Ōkubo. Hisamitsu had lost much of his power to challenge the central government, but he remained fully capable of tormenting Saigō.[47]

Saigō was proud of the smooth transition and understood that without his support, *haihan chiken* might have been a protracted and violent affair. But he was painfully ambivalent about the abolition of the daimyo class. *Haihan chiken* forced Saigō to confront a painful conflict of loyalties. He appreciated Kido and Ōkubo's arguments that the abolition of the daimyo class was necessary to secure the foundations of the Japanese state, but he felt nonetheless that he was betraying the Shimazu house. Kido sensed some of this tension, and he lauded Saigō's willingness to put the good of Japan above his personal desires. But even Kido was unaware of the depths of Saigō's anguish. In a letter to Katsura, now his closest confidant, Saigō laid bare his inner conflict. "If the four domains that led the realm with the return of the domain investitures had failed to bring this to fruition," he wrote on 1871/7/20, "we would not only have suffered great derision in the realm, but [our failure] would have amounted to deceiving utterly the imperial court." This would have seriously weakened the international reputation of the imperial government and undermined national security. Saigō had therefore supported *haihan chiken,* but he had done so with a heavy heart:

> When the imperial order was given, my personal feelings were diffi-cult to endure [since] I have, along with you, enjoyed the blessings of the Shimazu house for centuries. But this is the general course of the realm and no matter what I say, I cannot defend against it for ten years: I think this movement is something beyond human strength.

Saigō supported the abolition of the domains only because he felt that he had to; that betraying his lord was less awful than undermining the impe-rial house. This was a tortured rationale for supporting the creation of a modern, centralized state. It was an ominous sign that for Saigō, the Meiji state was not a triumph but merely the lesser of two evils.

Although Saigō was from the outset ambivalent about the state he helped create, he concealed this inner discord. Saigō could, as Ōkubo observed, hide his emotions under a stoic facade, and now he struggled to hide his inner turmoil. Mere days after the *haihan chiken* announcement, Saigō was visited by Joseph Hübner, a retired Austrian diplomat enjoying a pleasure trip to Japan. Hübner later published a memoir of his trip, and his depiction of Saigō is telling. Hübner clearly understood Saigō's importance to the Meiji state and explained that "it was necessary to ensure [Saigō's] support before attempting any reforms." He also appreciated Saigō's character and demeanor: "Saigo is of Herculean stature. His eyes are full of intelligence, and features of energy. He has a military air, and his manners are those of a country gentleman." But Hübner discerned no tension, discomfort, or anguish and reported merely on Saigō's lack of engagement: "[T]hey say he is bored to death with the court, and dying to get back to his own property in the country." This disengagement, which Hübner reported as boredom, was how Saigō managed his inner conflict.[48]

The Caretaker Government

The success of *haihan chiken* secured the domestic foundations of the Japanese state. Whatever problems lay ahead, the Meiji oligarchs no longer feared that the state could be toppled by recalcitrant daimyo. With this new sense of domestic security, the oligarchs turned their attention to the long-simmering question of foreign relations. The humiliating unequal treaties had undermined the legitimacy of the shogunate, and Meiji leaders were eager to begin the process of treaty revision. Iwakura had long favored some sort of diplomatic mission, but had delayed his plans because of domestic issues. Ōkubo and Inoue Kaoru, a rising figure in the finance ministry, were especially interested in treaty revision because of the need for tariff reform. Kido was initially ambivalent about an embassy, but was intrigued by the idea of a general study tour of Europe and America. Despite these slightly different agendas, there was a broad consensus that a high-ranking embassy should visit the major Western powers. The most troubling question was membership, and it took several months to sort out who would leave, who would stay, and in what capacities the delegates would serve. By 1871/9 the oligarchs had agreed that Iwakura should lead the mission as ambassador plenipotentiary, accompanied by four vice ambassadors, including most prominently Kido; Ōkubo; and Itō Hirobumi, a former samurai from Chōshū who had visited England in 1863. The embassy also included an enormous staff, more than forty men, who were charged with studying Western institutions.[49]

The departure of so many key officials raised the prospect of administrative chaos, so both the embassy and the caretaker government agreed to restrain their actions. The embassy was charged with exploring and evaluating Western institutions "with the object of adopting them in Japan and establishing them here." They were also authorized to conduct exploratory talks on treaty revision, but they were not given authority to conclude new treaties. In the words of the American ambassador, Charles De Long, "it appears to be an Embassy unauthorized to conclude anything but advised to consult about everything."[50] The caretaker government, for its part, agreed to make no new appointments to high political offices and to inform the embassy regularly of domestic affairs. Since part of the embassy's mission was to research domestic reforms, the caretaker government agreed to defer, wherever possible, major domestic initiatives until the embassy's return. On 1871/11/7 Saigō, Kido, Iwakura, and Sanjō signed a formal pledge to this effect, and on 1871/11/12 the embassy left Yokohama for San Francisco.[51]

Saigō had, at first, strongly objected to the embassy, and he remained skeptical about the project.[52] It seemed odd to him that the caretaker government was being asked to delay domestic reform, although everyone recognized that treaty revision would require precisely that. In a letter to Katsura, Saigō specifically cited the need to give foreigners freedom of residence within Japan and to allow foreigners and Japanese to marry one another. The Iwakura mission would research Western models for these reforms, but Saigō had promised to do nothing until their return. This struck Saigō as a needless delay, and he described himself as an "anguished caretaker" *(nanjū no rusuban)*.[53] The junior members of the caretaker government felt even more strongly than Saigō that reform could not wait, and they actively pressed for radical change. Saigō and Sanjō thus found themselves presiding over a radical reformist government.[54]

Etō Shinpei, the justice minister *(shihōkyō),* put forward one of the most ambitious and progressive proposals for reform. He had been studying European law and was convinced that the wealth of Western nations stemmed from their superior legal systems. In Japan, he argued, the vagaries and inequities of law meant that every loan or sale could result in protracted litigation, and this discouraged both agriculture and industry. In the West, by contrast, laws were strict but clear, so that people could devote themselves to business and, in growing rich, would make their countries rich. Etō thus proposed a new civil code and system of courts that would make Japanese subjects feel secure in their rights. This, he argued, was the key to national prosperity. An equally bold proposal came from Ōki Takato, Etō's protégé and minister of education *(monbukyō)*. Ōki argued for immediate action on a new national school system that would provide elementary education for every child in Japan.[55]

No one could contest the need for legal and educational reforms, but these proposals were extraordinarily ambitious and dauntingly expensive.

The cost of the reforms drew opposition from Inoue Kaoru, the leading figure in the finance ministry, who faced the challenge of establishing Japan's fiscal solvency.[56] The dissolution of the domains had shifted the burden of samurai stipends to the central government, but the Meiji state still did not have a modern tax system. This meant that the central treasury was hemorrhaging cash, and Inoue did not think Japan could fund either the immediate construction of a national court system or Ōki's proposal for fifty thousand elementary schools. Inoue's goal was, in fact, as radical as Etō's: he wanted the government to run a budget surplus and to establish the yen as a convertible currency. In late 1872, Inoue proposed cutting the education budget from ¥2 million (roughly $2 million) to ¥1 million and the justice budget from ¥960,000 to ¥450,000. This drew a predictably furious response from Etō, who threatened to resign. When Saigō and Sanjō sought to appease Etō by reexamining the budget, Inoue threatened to resign in turn.[57]

This domestic battle was complicated by military reform. The military was preparing to conscript commoners and beginning to replace samurai with a modern national army. In light of the cost of conscription and military modernization, the army was given a massive budget, ¥8 million in 1873, but substantial sums disappeared through blatant corruption. In 1872, for example, Yamashiroya Wasuke, a former Chōshū samurai, borrowed $150,000 from the military budget to start a textile company. When his company failed, Yamashiroya borrowed more, running up losses of more than ¥600,000 before eventually fleeing to Europe. A similar scandal erupted the following year when Mitani Sankurō, another Chōshū merchant, embezzled nearly ¥350,000. These scandals pointed to chronic problems in military administration and undermined the authority of the head of the army, Yamagata Aritomo. By 1873 Yamagata was losing control of the imperial guard as non-Chōshū samurai questioned his integrity and ability to lead.[58]

In addition to these struggles within the caretaker government, there were also rising tensions between the caretaker government and the Iwakura mission. Inoue, ever determined to cut government expenditures, proposed to replace samurai stipends with government bonds. Stipends consumed nearly half the government budget, and Inoue hoped to eliminate these payments entirely within six years. Saigō, despite his sentimental attachment to tradition, saw the wisdom of Inoue's plan and supported the program in a letter to Ōkubo. But the plan drew furious opposition from the Iwakura mission. Iwakura argued that the plans were "much too severe," and Kido complained that the samurai were being sacrificed dispropor- tionately. Their opposition was based more on power than principle. Saigō and Kido had discussed the need to abolish stipends, and in fact upon their return the Iwakura mission members made Inoue's proposal the basis for stipend reform. But the mission was unwilling to negotiate the details of stipend reform from halfway around the world.[59]

Saigō managed these rising tensions to the best of his ability, but he was not, by temperament, a skilled administrator. Saigō's great political assets were his integrity and charisma, not his ability to forge bureaucratic con- sensus or to delineate clear administrative boundaries. At heart, Saigō was ideologically opposed to extensive bureaucratic planning. In his under- standing of Confucianism, it was the purpose of the government elite to provide general moral guidance rather than extensive legal regulation. The details of commerce, education, and law were, for Saigō, things that could be left to lower-level functionaries or to the people themselves. As he wrote in 1870, it was essential for the government to have laws, but it was still more important to cultivate virtue so that the people, guided by "loyalty, filial piety, humanity, and love," would have no need for an explicit legal code. For much of 1872 and 1873 Saigō was thus presiding over what he secretly felt were irrelevant discussions.[60]

Saigō's colleagues in the caretaker government viewed his estrangement with considerable frustration. Ōkuma Shigenobu, for example, described in his memoirs how Saigō's lack of interest in politics undermined the work- ings of the government:

> Saigō and Itagaki, when the lunch break came, would hurriedly retreat to the anteroom. Thereafter, they would pass the time engrossing themselves in nonsensical conversation and never return to the cabi- net meeting. Rarely would they show up again, even when someone was sent to call them back for the meeting. What they inevitably con- versed about were stories of battle, which always fascinated both men, or of sumo wrestling, or else of hunting and fishing.

Ōkuma, with some justification, saw Saigō's attitude as profoundly irresponsible.[61]

Saigō's limited ability to manage the caretaker government was further challenged by the incessant tirades of Shimazu Hisamitsu. Despite repeated requests to come to Tokyo and take a ceremonial position in the new government, Hisamitsu refused and remained in Satsuma, where he fulminated against the government and stoked the discontent of local samurai. In late 1871, frustrated by the abolition of the domains, Hisamitsu began demanding that he be appointed prefectural governor. Saigō was shocked and appalled by Hisamitsu's demands. Appointing Hisamitsu as Kagoshima governor, he observed, would undermine the basis of *haihan chiken* and cause serious domestic trouble. Saigō did not want to oppose his lord publicly, but he feared that Hisamitsu's agenda could damage the Meiji state, so he worked quietly with Katsura Hisatake and Sanjō to block Hisamitsu's request. Saigō was disgusted by the entire affair, since he suspected that Hisamitsu's plan was largely a ruse to delay an official visit to Tokyo. Hisamitsu, in Saigō's mind, was making light of imperial orders.[62] Although Hisamitsu finally abandoned his plan to become governor, he continued to rail against the central government's policies. Hisamitsu's objections ranged from grand to commonplace. He was angry that the new government had stripped the daimyo class of power and was abolishing traditional distinctions between samurai and commoners. But he also fulminated against the adoption of Western dress, which failed adequately to distinguish between high- and low-born; against the education of women, which he considered contrary to orthodoxy *(seigaku)*; and against the intermarriage of commoners and samurai, which he deemed scandalous.[63]

Hisamitsu's tirades deepened Saigō's sense of conflict between his obligations to the emperor and his debt to the Shimazu. His predicament was especially acute because he had come to revere the Meiji emperor with the same passion he had once reserved for Nariakira. The emperor, he wrote in an 1871/12/11 letter to his uncle, was robust, diligent, intelligent, and accessible. Saigō was awed that he had been invited to dine and discuss politics with the emperor three times in one month. "[His Majesty] has completely dispelled the arrogant and overbearing ways [of the past], and lord and vassal now enjoy close, personal relations *(suigyō)*."[64] Saigō was, of course, eager to adore the new Japanese monarch, but even Western observers were reasonably impressed with Mutsuhito. William Willis, a British surgeon who met the monarch in 1872, described him as "ugly enough" but "a sensible sort of man."[65] For Saigō, however, the emperor's equanimity and affability were sublime, and he projected onto his relations with the Meiji emperor the idealized lord-vassal relationship he had described to Katsura in 1869.

Saigō's internal conflict grew in 1872/6, during the emperor's tour of the southwest. Saigō was a member of the grand imperial procession, and the emperor's visit to Kagoshima would, under other circumstances, have been a crowning moment in Saigō's career. Instead, Saigō agonized over the simmering tensions between Hisamitsu and the imperial state. On 1872/6/19, three days before their scheduled arrival in Kagoshima, Saigō cracked. The emperor's departure from Kumamoto had been delayed because of a scheduling error and Saigō, standing in the imperial parlor, publicly lambasted Kawamura Sumiyoshi, a future admiral, for his incompetence. Saigō then vented his rage on a watermelon, hurling it into the garden and smashing it to bits. The emperor watched this from nearby and was, according to legend, splattered with melon juice, but he was more amused than alarmed. The incident, a moment of unscripted, passionate loyalty in his otherwise sheltered life, became one of his favorite stories.[66]

The imperial procession's arrival in Kagoshima seemed on the surface to go smoothly. On 6/22 the emperor was greeted with a cannon salute and a military parade, and he had an uneventful meeting with Hisamitsu. Over the next ten days the monarch observed a range of local sites, including a traditional pottery village, a modern textile factory, local folk dancing, and a medical college run by the British surgeon William Willis. The only problem seemed to be inclement weather, which forced some changes in itinerary and delayed the embassy's departure, but they left for Tokyo without incident on 1872/7/2. Unbeknownst to Saigō, however, Hisamitsu had met on 6/28 with the imperial courtier Tokudaiji Sanenori and submitted a bitterly accusatory memorial. The government's policies, Hisamitsu declared, were "insanely arrogant" and were debilitating the imperial state. Left unchecked, these policies would lead Japan to become a colony of the "barbarian nations." To stop this disaster, Hisamitsu recommended a return to tradition. Distinctions between high and low should be honored, dress should be strictly regulated, and traditional educational standards restored. Hisamitsu's memorial was a general attack on the Meiji state, and he was calling, in effect, for a repudiation of the Charter Oath of 1868/3. But Hisamitsu singled out Saigō and Ōkubo for special abuse, demanding that they be dismissed from the Meiji government, and he refused to come to Tokyo unless his demands were met. Since Ōkubo was, at that moment, preparing to leave Boston for England, Saigō was Hisamitsu's prime target.[67]

Saigō, learning of Hisamitsu's outburst upon his return to Tokyo, was appalled by his lord's actions. It was "extremely lamentable," he wrote to Ōkubo on 1872/8/12, that Hisamitsu's discontent had become such a public affair, and while Saigō felt certain that the imperial court would ignore Hisamitsu's demands, he was nonetheless at a loss to contain the problem. He confessed to Ōkubo that he felt overwhelmed by Hisamitsu's tirades.[68] By early 1872/11 Saigō felt obliged to return to Kagoshima to placate Hisamitsu, and upon his arrival he submitted a formal apology for failing to seek a formal audience during the imperial embassy earlier that year. Hisamitsu, however, was in no mood to be mollified, and he took Saigō's visit as an opportunity to berate him for insubordination, disloyalty, and self-aggrandizement. Saigō was "thoroughly disgusted by his lordship's absurd arguments," but he was equally disturbed by the political climate in Satsuma. "The mood of Satsuma," he wrote to Kuroda Kiyotaka on 1872/12/1, "is markedly different and things have deteriorated considerably." People now speak of nothing but their obligations to Satsuma, and this, Saigō predicted, would certainly cause trouble in the future. In light of Hisamitsu's anger and these ominous political signs, Saigō felt obliged to extend his stay.[69]

A month after his letter to Kuroda, Saigō commemorated the end of the traditional Japanese calendar. In 1872/11 the government ordered the adoption of the Gregorian calendar, effective as of 1872/12/3. The reform eliminated nearly four weeks from the end of the year. The date 1872/12/3 became January 1, 1873, and so the traditional Japanese New Year fell on January 28. Despite the strange sensation of "losing" a month, Saigō was in no mood to decry the new calendar. Amid Hisamitsu's endless tirades, Saigō could not indulge in his own love of tradition. Instead he looked to the countryside as a repository of Japanese tradition:

> Since long ago this has been the day to greet the New Year
> How will the solar calendar reach the rough, remote villages?
> The snow announces the coming of a bountiful year and the elderly are each family's treasure
> How joyous are the shouts of the village children[70]

Saigō here voiced the guarded optimism that allowed him to support so many of the Meiji state's radical reforms. Even with a new calendar, Saigō felt certain that the traditions that mattered, such as reverence for the aged, would endure.

The Crisis of 1873

The need to contain Hisamitsu kept Saigō in Satsuma until the spring of 1873. Sometime in 1872/12 or early January 1873 Hisamitsu made an informal promise to come to Tokyo, but this was formalized only in March, after Katsu Kaishū and Nishiyotsutsuji, a court noble, visited Kagoshima bearing gifts and a special entreaty from the emperor.[71] This freed Saigō to return to the capital, but his extended stay in Kagoshima had put enormous stress on Sanjō back in Tokyo. Sanjō's power rested largely on his status as the highest-ranking court noble in the Meiji government, and he was not, by nature, a forceful politician. With Saigō gone, Sanjō was left alone to handle a series of protracted crises. Sanjō detailed his concerns in a letter to Iwakura on January 6, 1873. He was worried about Shimazu Hisamitsu, who continued to rail against the central government. He was deeply troubled by the ongoing feud over the budget, which had now become a general governmental crisis. Rather than yield to Etō's demands, Inoue had refused to compile a budget and had stopped work at the finance ministry. Sanjō was hopeful that Ōkuma might be able to mediate the standoff, but he felt personally unable to manage the crisis. In addition, Sanjō was struggling with two foreign-policy questions: Taiwan and Korea.[72]

The Taiwan crisis was sparked by the shipwreck of some Ryukyuan officials on Taiwan in late 1871. The men were killed by Taiwanese aboriginals, and Japanese expansionists seized on this as a pretext for the seizure of Taiwan. If the Qing government could not control headhunters on Taiwan, they argued, then it could not claim sovereignty over the island. This dangerous situation was further complicated because Tokyo had only recently claimed direct control over the Ryukyus, and China had not recognized this claim. The Tokyo government, Sanjō explained to Iwakura, planned to dispatch Soejima Taneomi, the foreign minister, to negotiate with China, but some sort of armed conflict between Japan and China seemed inevitable.[73]

The Korean crisis was equally complicated, although Sanjō considered it less explosive. The Korean Yi dynasty, keeping strictly to Chinese diplomatic protocol, had refused to recognize the Meiji emperor, because the Korean king recognized only one emperor, the Chinese sovereign. Instead, the Korean court insisted on late Tokugawa-era diplomatic protocol, whereby the shogunate communicated with the Korean court through representatives of the Japanese domain of Tsushima. Korea's refusal to recognize the imperial government was interpreted as a grave insult and sparked talk of a military response. Support for a military expedition was especially strong among samurai and in Satsuma.[74]

In the last lines of his letter to Ōkubo, Sanjō confessed to feeling utterly overwhelmed, and he asked Iwakura to return to Japan as quickly as possible. On January 19, 1873, the government issued orders to this effect, recalling the mission. Sanjō's crisis was not, however, a national crisis, and the order was sent as a letter rather than a cable. Word finally reached the mission in Berlin two months later. By then, however, the mission was as divided as the caretaker government. Trouble had started soon after their arrival in Washington, when Itō Hirobumi and Mori Arinori, the Japanese consul in Washington, persuaded Ōkubo that the time was ripe for treaty revision. Not wanting to miss such an opportunity, Ōkubo returned to Tokyo to seek enhanced diplomatic authority. The caretaker government, however, insisted on the original agreement whereby the mission was entrusted only with preparatory talks. In 1872/6 Ōkubo returned to Washington empty-handed, leaving Kido angry and dismayed. It had been a mistake, he wrote in his diary, to change the purpose of the embassy and to attempt to renegotiate the treaties while in Washington. The United States, he now realized, had never been prepared to yield on any major issue, and by raising the level of negotiations, the embassy had merely humiliated Japan. "I regret no end," he wrote on 1872/6/17, "that after arriving here in haste we brought things to this state." All our efforts, he lamented, "have come to naught."[75]

Frustrated, disappointed, and angry at each other, the members of the mission could not agree on how to interpret the Tokyo government's orders. After several days of debate, the mission members agreed to return separately. Ōkubo decided to leave for home immediately and arrived in Japan on May 26. Kido left after continuing the mission, visiting Russia, Italy, Austria, and Switzerland before finally reaching Tokyo on July 23. Iwakura did not return until September 13, after a leisurely tour that included stops in Sri Lanka, Saigon, Hong Kong, and Shanghai.[76]

Upon his return to Tokyo, Ōkubo found that he had lost control over the government he had helped to create. The struggle between Etō and Inoue had been resolved, but Etō had won the last round. On April 19 Etō, Ōki, and Gotō Shōjirō were appointed as imperial councilors *(sangi)*, and on May 2 Etō engineered an emendation of the power of the imperial council *(sei'in)*. The council now claimed control over budgetary appropriations, minting, and foreign and domestic loans. With his ministry effectively stripped of all power, Inoue resigned on May 7. The clash between Etō and Inoue was Japan's first modern political crisis. Inoue vented his frustrations by publicizing the budget deficit in the Japanese press. The government then released its own budget numbers and slapped Inoue with a fine for disclosing government secrets. In contrast to the secret deliberations of the Tokugawa regime, Meiji government leaders were beginning to battle for public support.[77]

For Ōkubo these events were a crushing defeat. He had resigned as imperial councilor in 1872 but had maintained titular control of the finance ministry. That ministry, however, had now lost control over the budget, so Ōkubo was essentially powerless. The appointment of new imperial councilors and changes in the powers of the imperial council were blatant violations of the pact between the Iwakura mission and the caretaker government. Ōkubo, however, had little basis for complaint, since he himself had asked to abrogate the agreement in order to conclude treaties in Washington. Ōkubo was dismayed, but he lacked the power to challenge his rivals, and rather than fight a battle he could not win, he left the capital to relax at a hot spring and climb Mount Fuji.[78]

Saigō seems not to have understood fully the implications of these changes to the central government. His letters from the period make no mention of Inoue's resignation or the appointment of new imperial councilors. This corresponds with the recollection of Shibusawa Eiichi, a key supporter of Inoue, that Saigō was "politically powerful, but basically uninterested in finance."[79] Saigō's principal concern in April and May remained Hisamitsu. The Shimazu lord finally came to Tokyo on April 23, leading a retinue of some 250 attendants. His retinue carried swords rather than firearms and wore their hair in *chonmage* style, with the forehead shaved and with a topknot, rather than the Western hairstyles the government had promoted since 1872. Hisamitsu's public show of tradition was seen as somewhat absurd, and the *Shinbun zasshi* newspaper reported that his attendants were "wildly proud and self-satisfied with their swords."[80] But Saigō was worried about serious trouble. In a letter to his brother Tsugumichi on April 20 he warned that "his lordship, not to mention those beneath him, fear only the army." In a letter to Katsura on May 17, Saigō was even more concerned, and wrote of rumors of possible attacks against the government and attempts on his life.[81] Saigō's fears were excessive, and Hisamitsu's visit was not disturbed by violence. He was showered with gifts from the imperial house, and he eventually accepted a ceremonial position in the central government. From this perspective the visit was a resounding success. True to form, however, Hisamitsu used his visit to Tokyo to unleash another series of tirades against Saigō and the general trend of reform. By now Saigō was thoroughly exhausted by Hisamitsu's abuse, and he privately ridiculed his lord's "infantile whims." Saigō's feelings were understandable, since this was an emotionally wrenching situation for him. In 1869/7 Saigō still had hoped to honor Nariakira by showing loyalty to his half brother Hisamitsu. Now Saigō had to confront his own open contempt for his late lord's successor.[82]

Saigō's disdain for Hisamitsu was exacerbated by his own increasing respect for the Meiji emperor. In late April, Saigō attended the emperor during military exercises in Chiba. The emperor took part in the exercises and stayed in an ordinary campaign tent. During the night a fierce storm flipped the tent and left the emperor drenched by rain. Saigō hurried to the site and was astonished to find the emperor soaked, but composed and collected.[83] By most standards the emperor's equanimity was unremarkable, but for Saigō it was a stark contrast to Hisamitsu's constant, dyspeptic ranting.

By early May the strain of politics had taken its toll on Saigō's health and he began to suffer from severe angina. His condition worsened, and on June 6 the emperor sent his personal physician, Theodore Hoffman. Hoffman diagnosed arteriosclerosis and explained the problem to Saigō in layman's terms: his blood vessels had narrowed due to fatty deposits and this was causing chest pain. Hoffman thought that Saigō had only narrowly avoided a heart attack or stroke, and he prescribed an intriguing combination of treatments: regular exercise, a low-fat diet, and the nineteenth-century cure-all, powerful laxatives. To follow Hoffman's instructions, Saigō moved from his residence in central Tokyo, where he disliked taking walks, to his brother Tsugumichi's house in Shibuya, now a busy shopping district but then, in Saigō's words, "the real backwoods" *(kyoku inaka)*. Out in the countryside,

Saigō could enjoy walks in the woods and rabbit hunting, and he was soon feeling so robust that he asked Hoffman if he might resume sword practice or sumo to keep active on rainy days. Hoffman politely suggested that Saigō keep, for the time being, to less vigorous exercise.[84]

Saigō's astonishing recovery was as much psychological as physical. Although his angina recurred after he returned to work, his love of the countryside, and a much-needed respite from the demands of government, had restored his spirits. Saigō described his time in Shibuya as a retreat from a chaotic world. His heart was at peace, and he did not wish to lose his composure by reentering the political fray. In a June 29 letter to his uncle, Saigō wrote of "forsaking the way of the world" and avoiding "muddy, turbid water" *(dakusui)* in favor of "pure water" *(shimizu)*. Water was, for Saigō, a deeply resonant metaphor. In *Genshiroku,* the Satō Issai text that Saigō transcribed, "muddy, turbid water" represented a chaotic life, confused by external distractions and petty ambition. "Pure water," by contrast, was a metaphor for moral clarity and the ability to remain true to oneself. By "taming the self" and maintaining ritual propriety, an enlightened man could stay true to himself amid turmoil and, metaphorically, purify muddy water. Saigō, however, felt inadequate to this task and, rather than drink muddy water, he preferred to give up on public life.[85]

While Saigō was in Shibuya, considering a permanent withdrawal from public life, the diplomatic standoff over Korea deteriorated. Korea was resisting Japanese attempts to turn the Tsushima trading post in Pusan, the *waegwan,* into an imperial government consulate, and Korea had broken off trade after realizing that Mitsui company agents had been posing as officials of a Tsushima merchant house. The local prefect, Chŏng Hyŏn-dŏk, ordered his officers to keep strictly to traditional protocol, and declared that the Japanese, by changing their dress and customs, had become a "lawless nation." These were inflammatory remarks and, although there were no threats to Japanese personnel nor any clear and present danger to the *waegwan* staff, the foreign ministry took the issue extremely seriously. In July 1873 the foreign ministry recommended to the imperial council that Japan either repatriate all its subjects or force Korea to sign a treaty.[86]

When the imperial council met to deliberate the matter, there was passionate support for the dispatch of warships. Sanjō was incensed at the insult to Japanese national honor, and Itagaki argued that troops were necessary to secure the safety of Japanese subjects. Saigō argued otherwise. It would be wrong, he argued, to lead with force. Japan should, instead, send a diplomatic delegation to determine Korea's true intentions. Sanjō was inclined to support this idea, but he thought the envoy should be Foreign Minister Soejima, then in Beijing. Saigō insisted that he personally be allowed to go, but the meeting adjourned without resolution.[87] Over the following month Saigō passionately lobbied Sanjō and Itagaki to support his appointment as special envoy to Korea, and on August 17 the council met again, this time to approve Saigō's plan. On August 19 Sanjō informed the emperor of the council's decision, but the monarch asked that the issue be reexamined after the Iwakura mission returned.[88]

Saigō's sudden determination to go to Korea has puzzled generations of historians, and the political crisis sparked by his mission is one of the most intensely debated topics in Japanese history. For many years the most influential explanation was that Saigō expected to provoke a violent clash in Korea and, through his death, provide a rallying point for disaffected samurai. Saigō could thus atone for supporting the abolition of samurai privilege, and thousands of samurai could prove their worth by conquering Korea and then, perhaps, seizing control in Tokyo. This argument links Saigō's mission with later Japanese imperialism on the Korean peninsula and depicts him as a passionate reactionary.[89]

Several of Saigō's letters are bellicose and support this interpretation of his actions. He wrote repeatedly to Itagaki of wanting to die in Korea and of wanting to provoke a war. On July 29 he told Itagaki that he fully expected to be assassinated in Korea. Soejima, he allowed, would be a better ambassador, but since the mission was to die, Saigō felt he was up for the task.[90] In a series of letters in August he worried that the government would fail to use his death as a casus belli but would portray it instead as a consequence of his own rashness. He urged Itagaki to stand firm and ensure that he did not die in vain.[91] Saigō was aware of domestic agitation for a war with Korea and seems to have thought of his mission as a means of stealing this issue from Hisamitsu.[92]

Elsewhere, however, Saigō insisted that he had no intention of provoking a war, but only of strengthening Japanese-Korean relations. In a lengthy statement to the cabinet on October 17, Saigō argued that he had never wanted anything but peaceful negotiations:

> I disagreed completely with the idea of troops, and [said that] if we did
> things in that way it would result in war and that would be contrary

to our original intent. My point was that the proper course was to send an emissary in an open manner, and that it would be a source of regret if we did not make every effort [to negotiate] until the Koreans revealed their true intentions, even if they refused our overtures, broke off relations, and declared war.

It would be disrespectful, Saigō argued, if Japan sent troops without first exhausting diplomatic options.[93]

Viewed in this way, Saigō's explanations were either inchoate or contradictory: he seems not to have known whether he wanted war or peace. Yet this very indeterminacy points to Saigō's true purpose. His quest was moral rather than strategic. In Saigō's mind, the most pressing matter was to determine the Koreans' true intentions and ascertain whether they intended to impugn the Japanese imperial house. Saigō was committed to upholding imperial honor, but how he did so was secondary and dependent on how the Koreans responded to his demands. Saigō's mission to Korea was thus a personal rather than a political quest and, as he explained to Sanjō, "if [you agreed to send me], no matter how much abuse is put upon me, and even if I do respond at all, I will have peace of mind and I will therefore be completely untroubled."[94]

Saigō expressed similar sentiments in a poem composed to commemorate his appointment as ambassador:

Summer's brutal heat has passed and autumn's air is clear and crisp
Seeking a cool breeze I journey to the capital of Silla [Korea]
I must show the constancy of Su Wu through the bleakness of the years
May I leave behind a name as great as Yan Zhenqing
What I wish to tell my descendants, I will teach without words
Although I depart, I cannot forget my vows to my old friends
As the bright autumn leaves wither in that foreign land
I will pay my respects to that high throne with my keen sword by my
  side[95]

The first classical Chinese reference in the poem, to Su Wu (c. 140 B.C.E.–60 B.C.E.), is intriguing. Su Wu was a semilegendary Han dynasty official who was sent as a diplomatic envoy to the Xiongnu, a nomadic people of Central Asia. The Xiongnu took him hostage and pressed him to defect, but he refused. In an attempt to break his will, the Xiongnu subjected him to extreme hardship, and images of Su Wu alone on a Central Asian wasteland stoically herding sheep became a favorite theme of Chinese and Japanese painting. Steadfast in his loyalty, Su Wu not only refused to join the Xiongnu, but also won the admiration of Han officials who had defected. In 81 B.C.E., after holding Su Wu for nearly twenty years, the Xiongnu relented and sent him home. Su Wu had spent the prime of his life in exile, but he was celebrated, both in his old age and posthumously, for his unwavering devotion to principle. If Saigō expected war in Korea, then Su Wu was an extremely strange metaphor. The story of Su Wu, on the contrary, suggests that nonviolent but unwavering dedication to principle is the mark of a truly civilized man.[96]

The second reference, to Yan Zhenqing, recalls one of Saigō's earlier poems on politics. Saigō had compared himself to Yan in 1864, when he was contemplating war with Chōshū. Saigō was then unsure whether Chōshū was treacherous or merely misguided, and he proposed to go to Chōshū and demand an admission of guilt. In doing so he would either provoke a war, and thereby garner concrete evidence of Chōshū's treachery, or win an apology, and thereby secure peace. In point of fact, Saigō's trip to Chōshū became the basis for the Satsuma-Chōshū alliance. But in 1864 as in 1873, Saigō had no clear plan for his antagonist, only a devotion to upholding what he understood as the honor of the imperial house. This sense of moral rather than practical reason is further reinforced by the next line of the poem, where Saigō writes of instructing his heirs with deeds rather than words. This line is a reference to Satō Issai and his distinction between the intelligent man *(kenja)* and the enlightened or sagely man *(seijin)*. The wise man struggles to understand death and, dependent on critical thought, seeks to teach his heirs through an *ikun,* a collection of written precepts. The sage, however, does not write an *ikun* because he has made the words and deeds of his life models for his heirs. The sage, Satō continued, can die peacefully because he appreciates that life and death, like day and night, are but parts of a greater whole. Saigō here declared that his mission to Korea was not practical or rational: his statements were contradictory because he had not considered fully the implications of his actions. This was not, however, a problem because Saigō was seeking to emulate the sage rather than the wise man. His mission was transcendently moral. Once he had declared the integrity of the imperial house, Saigō did not care whether he lived or died.[97]

Saigō evinced a similar attitude in his later letters on Korea. In 1875, after he had left the government, Japan forced the issue of relations with Korea. On September 20 the Japanese ship *Unyō* ventured into Korean territorial waters, ostensibly on a surveying mission. The Japanese successfully provoked fire from Korean shore batteries and then responded with overwhelming force, destroying both the coastal batteries and a fort on Yŏngjong Island. The Japanese government, now led by Ōkubo, used the incident to dispatch warships to Korea and to force treaty negotiations. In the ensuing treaty, Korea recognized the Japanese imperial government, opened key ports to trade, and provided for extraterritoriality for Japanese subjects in Korea. This was, by any practical standard, a triumph of gunboat diplomacy, but Saigō was appalled. The underhanded tactics of the Japanese fleet, he wrote, were a violation of "heaven's principles." There was nothing wrong with Japan and Korea going to war, he argued, but fighting should be based on a real and explicit conflict of principles. By provoking Korea through such a "wicked scheme," the Japan government had failed to uphold principle and shown merely that it "disdains the weak."[98]

The struggle between Saigō and Ōkubo was, at this level, a conflict between profoundly different understandings of politics. Ōkubo was explicitly and emphatically pragmatic, and he understood government as an arena for careful calculation. In his tour of the world, Ōkubo had been most impressed by Bismarck. Nothing, he wrote to Saigō in March 1873, seemed beyond Bismarck's abilities.[99] Ōkubo had long represented the rationalist stream in Japanese tradition, and his thinking was catalyzed by his tour of Europe. In his October opinion paper on the crisis, Ōkubo thus openly acknowledged that Korea's actions were insulting and degrading, but he insisted that the imperial council consider the question coolly and rationally. If a policy is disadvantageous, it should be abandoned "even if this entails shame, and even if we must endure this shame." Applying this logic to Korea, Ōkubo found that while the Koreans had indeed besmirched Japanese honor, the council had not examined whether a war would be in the interests of the state. Ōkubo argued that a war would be disastrous. It would swell an already colossal budget deficit, undermine the progress of domestic reform, damage the economy, and delay treaty revision with England and France. Geopolitically, Japan could not afford a war with Korea because of the greater threat from Russia. Ōkubo did not argue against a war with Korea. He merely argued, pragmatically, that Japan needed to resolve other important domestic and diplomatic issues before it embarked on a war with Korea.[100]

For Ōkubo, Saigō's approach to diplomacy was dangerous and irrational. It was "reckless" for Saigō to go to Korea without first determining the costs and benefits of war. For Saigō, however, Ōkubo's logic was equally flawed. It was impossible to advance the interests of the imperial house without considering the fundamental questions of justice and honor. Ōkubo's explicit statement that Japan must endure "shame" to avoid a budget deficit was, for Saigō, beneath contempt. Saigō derided him as "the biggest coward in Satsuma." Watching this conflict, Sasaki Takayuki, a vice minister of justice (shihō taifu), was sympathetic to Saigō but infuriated by his tactics. Saigō, Sasaki thought, wanted to restore Japan's martial vigor, but he was ignoring the interests of the Japanese polity in favor of his own personal quest.[101]

This conflict over Korea inflamed a basic political problem: How would the mission members, who had been gone almost a year longer than expected, be reintegrated into the government? Who would yield power to make room for the embassy? By October this struggle had embroiled all the major figures in the government. Iwakura supported Ōkubo, and shared his sense that Saigō's scheme was dangerous and rash. Kido was opposed to Saigō's mission, but he was still angry at Ōkubo and was contemplating retirement from public life. Despite his position as an imperial councilor, he gave Ōkubo only indirect support. Soejima, who became an imperial councilor on October 13, supported Saigō. He had returned from Beijing in late July, having secured what he interpreted as a promise of Chinese nonintervention in Korea and Taiwan. This was an enormous victory, and Soejima's support for Saigō strengthened his hand. Etō, Itagaki, and Ōki were all firmly in support of Saigō.[102]

The imperial council officially met to reconsider the Korea question on October 14. Ōkubo had been reappointed to the imperial council on October 12, but he still lacked the votes to press his agenda, and on October 15 the council reconfirmed Saigō's appointment as envoy. Ōkubo and Iwakura were unwilling to yield, and they threatened to resign unless the cabinet delayed the mission. This threat bore heavily on Sanjō, who felt that he could not run the government without Ōkubo. Saigō, however, had warned Sanjō that delaying the embassy would weaken imperial authority and added, ominously, that such a crime could be atoned for only by death.[103] Pressed by Saigō to report the council's decision to the emperor and by Ōkubo and Iwakura to delay, Sanjō collapsed on October 18, the victim of either a nervous breakdown or a mild stroke. In his stead Iwakura became prime minister *(dajō daijin)*, and this gave Ōkubo and Iwakura a dominant voice in the government. Iwakura now controlled access to the emperor. On October 22 he summoned Saigō, Itagaki, Etō, and Soejima to his residence and announced that he would not report the council's confirmation of Saigō's appointment. Etō angrily objected that Iwakura was improperly arrogating power, but Iwakura ignored him. Kirino Toshiaki, an imperial guard officer who had accompanied Saigō, reportedly came close to drawing his sword. Saigō was furious. Ōkubo had outmaneuvered him not through open debate but through subterfuge. But Saigō was not, despite his words to Sanjō, prepared either to kill or to die. Instead, the following day, Saigō submitted his resignation as imperial councilor, army general, and commander of the imperial guard.[104]

Saigō's resignation fractured the government along predictable lines, and on October 24 Soejima, Etō, Itagaki, and Gotō Shōjirō all left the government as well. Their resignations reflected both solidarity with Saigō and the deep antagonism that had developed over the preceding months. Ōkubo had hoped for Etō's resignation, but the trouble now spread to the imperial guard, where officers from Satsuma grumbled about the government's treatment of Saigō. On October 28 the government issued an imperial proclamation ordering men to remain at their posts, but this had limited effect. Within a week forty-six high-ranking military men had resigned, including Shinohara Kunimoto and Kirino Toshiaki, both majors general in the imperial guard. Rather than expose its lack of control, the government downplayed the resignations and placed the officers on inactive duty. Had Saigō been planning a coup, the moment was ripe. Kido observed in his diary that "although many are trying to calm things down, some disorder is likely to develop," and should an insurrection spread it, "the work of many years will come to naught." Even the laconic Ōkubo confessed to being "troubled by the acute confusion in the imperial guard." But Saigō did not lead his men to revolt. He brooded quietly for three days, avoiding his usual haunts. Then, on October 28, he left Yokohama for Kagoshima, never to return.[105]

Ōkubo's victory in 1873 gave him decisive control over Japanese politics. He filled the vacancies in key ministries with his allies and, from 1873 until his death in 1878, he was effectively the most powerful politician in Japan.

Ōkubo's realpolitik became the cornerstone of Japanese foreign policy, and over the following decades Japan amassed a formidable overseas empire, steadily expanding its territory through careful geopolitical and economic planning. Saigō's defeat arguably saved Japan from a protracted and disastrous war, but it is difficult to celebrate his failure as a victory for peace, especially given Japan's eventual colonization of Korea. Saigō, for his part, had little interest in Japan's empire: although a chauvinist who believed firmly that the defense of Japanese honor was worth a war, he was not an imperialist. Nowhere in Saigō's arguments for war did he argue that Japan should seize Korean territory; he thought that war for economic advantage was reprehensible and barbaric. Although Saigō admired much in Western statecraft, he faulted the West on this point. The West was not "civilized," he argued, because it conquered weaker nations and profited from their misery. Truly civilized nations would rule through the force of superior virtue. Saigō did not think that his insistence on war for honor rather than lucre was either traditional or distinctly Japanese. In a complete reverse of Ōkubo's logic, Saigō argued that Prussia's victory over France in 1871 stemmed from Prussia's greater sense of honor and courage, rather than its superior geopolitical strategy.[106] Ironically, Saigō had much in common with the Korean diplomats who refused to recognize the Meiji state. They both clung to the Confucian notion that international relations should be rooted in propriety and justice. It is tempting to indulge in the romantic notion that Saigō might have reached a rapprochement with his Korean counterparts based on their shared Confucian language. One of the great constants in Saigō's life was his willingness to alter radically his politics for the sake of grand principle. Saigō had made peace with Chōshū because honor so demanded and had given up his quest to kill Hitotsubashi Keiki because vengeance was unbecoming a gentleman. What would Saigō have made of Korean insistence on traditional protocol? And what would Korean diplomats have made of Saigō's invocation of Su Wu? But these counterfactual speculations are distractions from the real course of Saigō's life. Saigō did not die in Pusan or Seoul, but in the foothills of Shiroyama.

Chapter 6

"THE BURDEN OF DEATH IS LIGHT"

Saigō and the War of the Southwest*

A Pastoral Statesman

The men who quit the Meiji state in 1873 were unified in their antipathy for Ōkubo and his policies, but they did not share a political agenda. Itagaki was eager to regain political power and turned to the nascent popular rights movement as a vehicle for his political career. Starting with samurai in his native Tosa, Itagaki began a campaign for a popular assembly, using the radical Western idea of representative government to pressure the Meiji state. While Itagaki's commitment to democratic ideals was self-serving, his contribution to Japanese politics was enormous: he created what became Japan's first political party. Etō, Soejima, and Gotō were all signatories on Itagaki's 1874 memorial requesting a deliberative assembly, but only Gotō remained involved in the popular rights movement. Soejima left Japan to travel in China and later rejoined the government as an adviser and privy councilor. Etō returned to Saga and accepted leadership of the Seikantō, a

---

*SSTKS 102; STZ 4:82.

faction of disgruntled samurai committed to war in Korea. The Seikantō promised to fight in Korea even without government approval, and in February 1874 the Tokyo government sent troops to occupy the prefectural capital and prevent trouble. This sparked an attack by several samurai factions, including the Seikantō, and by mid-February Saga was embroiled in civil war. But the rebels were hopelessly outgunned, and the rebellion lasted only two weeks. Etō was hunted down, summarily tried, and executed, his severed head displayed publicly on a pike.[1]

Saigō chose none of these paths. He rejected Etō's request for help in the Saga rebellion and showed no interest in either the popular rights movement or government office. Saigō had written in June 1873 of rejecting "turbid, muddy water" in favor of pure water, and he remained determined to avoid political entanglements. But Saigō's long-standing desire to withdraw from politics was now impossible. He was a legendary figure, whose every action was parsed for its political meaning. The turbulent political environment in Satsuma had heightened the meaning of Saigō's resignation, and he returned to Kagoshima in November 1873 to confront a profound irony. Saigō had supported many of the boldest reforms of the Meiji state, including the replacement of samurai stipends with bonds and the creation of a conscript army. Now Satsuma samurai angry at those reforms looked to Saigō as an exemplar of traditional virtues and a symbol of opposition to the state. As a member of the Tokyo government Saigō had viewed the rising tide of parochialism in Kagoshima with contempt, but now those very forces declared themselves to be his loyal followers.

Because of Saigō's role in the War of the Southwest, historians have scrutinized his words and deeds in search of a plan to challenge the Meiji state. Although Saigō was clearly bitter toward the Meiji government, only the most strained reading of the evidence supports the argument that he spent his years in Kagoshima preparing for rebellion. Instead, Saigō seems to have indulged in his favorite pastimes: hunting, fishing, and playing with children. He seems to have spent much of his time in Hinatayama avoiding direct involvement in politics. Saigō's sister-in-law Iwayama Toku described in her recollections how earnestly Saigō sought to escape political concerns:

Many people came from Kajiki to visit Saigō at Hinatayama. But for some reason Saigō made no effort to meet them and would often leave to avoid them. It was hard for us, since we knew that they had come a long way. I don't suppose that foolish women like we could understand even a bit of what Saigō was feeling. When he was alone in the house, he would smoke his long pipe and lose himself in thought, almost as though he were asleep. Now, when I put it all together, I realize that when he was alone in the house he was quietly thinking about the world. Not that I would presume to know what he was thinking.[2]

According to Iwayama, Saigō enjoyed telling jokes to local children and making the straw sandals he wore when hunting. Saigō's regular adult companion at Hinatayama was Naoyon, a sumo wrestler, who regularly joined him for hunting and fishing.

This surprising image of Saigō is corroborated by other sources, such as the letters of William Willis, the British physician who ran a medical school in Kagoshima. In July 1874 Willis wrote, "I expect today an ex-Commander in Chief to call at my house with his boys (little fellows) and I am about to show them some shadows thrown by a magic lantern which I dare say will amuse them."[3] This is not the behavior of a man preparing a rebel army for battle. Saigō's letters from this period show a similar, willful disengagement from politics. In an April 1875 letter to his cousin Ōyama Iwao, Saigō thanked him for sending a dog collar and then gave a detailed request for four or six more of the same but $3\frac{1}{2}$ inches longer. Saigō then noted in passing that Prussia and France seemed headed for war. Saigō remained keenly aware of domestic and international politics but chose to pay more attention to his hunting dogs.[4]

Saigō's only regular involvement in public affairs was through the Shigakkō, a system of private schools established in 1874. The schools were designed to provide a constructive outlet for the energies of the young soldiers who had resigned with Saigō in 1873. The Shigakkō had two main divisions: infantry, supervised by Shinohara Kunimoto; and artillery, supervised by Murata Shinpachi. The curriculum focused on military training and the Chinese classics. Initially the Shigakkō enrolled fewer than eight hundred students, but over the following two years the schools became a major institution in Satsuma society and politics. In each district the Shigakkō established branch schools, which supplemented the existing school system. The educational program resembled a traditional *gojū*: in the afternoon, after *gojū* had ended, the branch Shigakkō assembled local youth for study and military drill, and in the evening they gathered for debate.[5]

Saigō was widely celebrated as the spiritual leader of the Shigakkō and his statement of principles was posted in each school. But Saigō's extensive involvement was limited to two schools outside the main Shigakkō system: the Shōten gakkō and the Yoshino kaikonsha. The Shōten gakkō, started in Tokyo in 1873 under the name Shūgijuku, was dedicated to soldiers who had fallen in the Boshin War. It received financial support from Satsuma veterans who donated their awards for valorous service to the school; Saigō, for example, contributed 2,000 *koku* annually, Ōyama Tsunayoshi (the Kagoshima prefectural governor) gave 800 *koku,* and Kirino Toshiaki gave 200 *koku.* When Saigō left the government in 1873, the Shūgijuku left with him, relocated in Kagoshima, and took its new name. The educational emphasis at the Shōten gakkō was on military affairs, but the curriculum was syncretic and included the Chinese classics as well as English, French, and German. The school hired foreign instructors and encouraged select students to study in Europe. Saigō was active in determining school policy and in recruiting instructors.[6]

The schools' emphasis on foreign languages and foreign study reflected Saigō's distinctive understanding of the Confucian tradition. Saigō was convinced that key values of Confucianism were universal rather than culturally specific. "The foundation of government," he declared, "is the cultivation of loyalty, filial piety, benevolence, and love," and this is true everywhere, even in the West. While Westerners might not explore the "way" through the Chinese classics, the principles of good government were the same in Japan, China, and Europe. Saigō thus believed that Japan could learn Confucian values through a critical evaluation of Western institutions. Saigō made this notion of Confucian universalism explicit when he praised Western prisons because they epitomized the virtue of compassion and the ideals of the ancient sages better than Japanese jails did. Saigō also faulted the West in Confucian terms for pursuing "profit" in underdeveloped lands rather than benevolently guiding them toward civilization. Saigō's fear was not that Japan would learn from the West, but that Japan would learn the wrong things from the West and import the facade of Western culture rather than the underlying virtues that had led to Western strength. He was concerned that Japan would exhaust its resources on "toys" such as railroads, and thereby inculcate a sprit of "frivolity" in the people. Saigō thus turned to the Confucian classics as a means of preparing students to evaluate the West. Suitably schooled in classical Chinese texts and fortified by love for the Japanese emperor, Satsuma students would learn courage from the Prussians rather than indolence from the French. It was this belief in Confucianism as a common human heritage that allowed Saigō to hope that Japan could maintain its traditions while claiming a place among the world powers.[7]

The Yoshino kaikonsha, or Yoshino Land Reclamation Society, reflected a different but related agenda. The school was named after its location, a small village near Kagoshima City. Students and faculty cleared land at Yoshino and did farm work, growing rice, millet, and yams *(satsumaimo)* during the day. They studied at night, from a curriculum that included military training and the Chinese classics. Saigō was closely involved in the construction and operation of the school, even handling such details as the wages of carpenters, and he spent extended periods living at Yoshino. The school's curriculum appealed to Saigō's vision of the ideal samurai: learned, practical, and self-reliant. The school's program suggests why Saigō did not publicly protest the elimination of samurai stipends in 1876. He hoped to save the samurai class by inculcating frugal self-sufficiency. These samurai would rule through superior virtue rather than mere hereditary privilege. He described his days at Yoshino enthusiastically to Ōyama Iwao in April 1875. "These days I'm a farmer through and through, and I'm studying earnestly. At first it was rather difficult, but now I can till about two plots a day. I've gotten used to [simple food such as] soup with tofu lees *(yuba)* and sweet potato *(imo),* and so, with no sense of privation and unperturbed by anything, I am at peace." For Saigō, working at Yoshino was, like fishing at Hinatayama, a fragment of an ideal world.[8]

Saigō's activities from 1874 to 1876 constituted, at a practical level, a retreat from politics. But Saigō's detachment from political affairs was also a profoundly political statement. Saigō's central objection to the Meiji state was moral. He was not satisfied by the 1875 attack on Korea because it was not rooted in a Confucian sense of honor. Similarly, Saigō was not anti-Western, but he detested the trappings of Western culture. The Tokyo government, it seemed, was eager to adopt such frivolities as ballroom dancing but loath to emulate the probity of Western government officials. Saigō, like any good Confucian official, he was too principled to criticize the state publicly. Instead he hoped that his daily life would serve as an example of a superior mode of political action: pastoral, stalwart, self-reliant, and deeply moral. This vision of a morally grounded retreat from quotidian affairs suffused Saigō's poems and letters. In an 1875 poem celebrating theYoshino kaikonsha, for example, he suggested that only a select few could appreciate the school's mission:

The burden of death is light as I respond to my lord's favor
Laboring ceaselessly, muscle and bone, tilling the fields
Who appreciates how during our respites from farming
We keep with the Ban Bao, the classic of war, free from childish thoughts[9]

A similar theme appears in a poem extolling the virtues of fishing alone at Hinatayama:

I moor my skiff in the creek of flowering reeds
With a fishing pole in hand, I sit on a stepping-stone
Does anyone know of this high-minded man's other world?
With my pole I fish in autumn's creek
    for the bright moon and the cool breeze[10]

These poems, suffused with an air of self-satisfied superiority, shed some light on why Ōkubo thought that Zen mediation had made Saigō impossibly arrogant. But Saigō's smugness was rooted in the sense that his retreat to the countryside was part of a great cultural project. One of his disciples later recalled:

Morning till night, Master Saigō spent his time hunting; urging on his dogs, chasing rabbits, and traversing the mountain valleys. When back at his country house, after a bath, his spirit seemed greatly refreshed and, with an attitude of perfect composure, he declared, "I believe the mind [kokoro] of a gentleman [kunshi] is always thus."[11]

In the Chinese classics the term kunshi refers to a man of virtue, culture, and honor, so by "gentleman" Saigō meant someone of noble spirit rather than noble birth. Saigō thus drew a direct connection between his own sageliness and his retreat from politics.

Saigō's satisfaction with his own virtue is certainly unappealing. But given the reverence with which he was regularly greeted, it is remarkable that Saigō retained any of his affable humility. Iwayama Toku, in her recollections, provided a striking glimpse of Saigō's experiences as a living legend. In 1875 or 1876 Saigō left for Hinatayama with a large party that included his sons Toratarō and Torizō; his wife, Ito; Ito's mother, Ei; and Toku. They had planned to travel from Kagoshima by boat, but en route Ei and Toku became seasick and Saigō noticed their discomfort. "Saigō," Toku related, "was strikingly, exceptionally big, but he was someone who noticed small, minor things." Saigō had the boat put in at Kajiki, a few miles short of their destination, and he suggested that they walk to Hinatayama. As they passed through the town of Kajiki, Toku recalled, all the townspeople came out and bowed, "as though we were the procession of a lord."[12] Saigō experienced such reverential treatment throughout Satsuma and he began, understandably, to think of himself as a Confucian gentleman. He would criticize the government not through his words but through his silence.

The Impending Crisis

Under ordinary circumstances, Saigō's retirement would have posed no threat to the central government. Saigō was critical of the Meiji state but publicly he said nothing to justify violent antigovernment action. Saigō even helped recruit troops for the government's expedition to Taiwan in 1874. The central government and Satsuma were, however, on a collision course, and Saigō's passivity became increasingly untenable.

At the heart of the conflict were two different political agendas: the desire to build a powerful centralized state, and the desire to maintain Satsuma as a distinct polity. This clash of principles appeared early on in matters such a stipend reform. After the central government assumed responsibility for samurai stipends, it attempted to impose national standards and in 1870 ordered the prefectures to eliminate distinctions within the samurai class. Kagoshima ignored this order and maintained several categories of rear vassal, such as *ashigaru* and *fuzoku,* in addition to full samurai. After a second order, in 1872, Kagoshima regrouped its samurai into two categories, but it remained in defiance of the government's original order. Kagoshima restricted some samurai privileges, such as their right to independently administer criminal justice, but the authority of rural samurai over their villages was left largely unchanged. The prefectural government also ignored the national land tax, which broke feudal custom by establishing private ownership of land. The Tokyo government ordered new surveys for the land tax in 1873, and Kagoshima made limited preparations for the new system, but it was introduced only in 1878, after the War of the Southwest. The Meiji policy of opening government service to commoners had little impact on Satsuma, and all important positions, even in rural government, were dominated by samurai.[13] The central government had implicitly allowed some level of Satsuma exceptionalism by appointing a native, Ōyama Tsunayoshi, as prefectural governor. Ōyama, however, openly opposed most of the government's reforms.[14]

These rising tensions between Satsuma and Tokyo were reflected by the Shigakkō, which began in 1875 to prohibit their students from leaving Satsuma. Henceforth students were not allowed to study in Tokyo or overseas without special authorization. Many faculty and students thought these new regulations were absurd, and the change led to impassioned debate. At the Shigakkō in Kajiki, for example, the issue so divided the school that more than seventy teachers and students left in protest. In November 1875 Saigō was summoned to mediate the dispute. Saigō had lamented the rising tide of Satsuma parochialism as early as 1872, and the restrictions ran contrary to his educational philosophy. But Saigō was ominously passive and failed to defend those who opposed the restrictions. His inaction was readily interpreted as an endorsement of the policy.[15]

In 1876 the central government began its most direct assault on samurai privilege. On March 28 the government barred anyone except officers at state ceremonies, soldiers, and police from carrying swords. In August the government ordered the conversion of samurai stipends into thirty-year bonds. This had been optional since 1873, but few had accepted the offer. The bonds paid a yield of 5 to 7 percent interest, but for most samurai this meant a drop in annual income of at least 30 percent. Combined with the ban on swords, stipend reform struck at the heart of samurai identity.[16] In Kagoshima, Governor Ōyama showed no intention of implementing the mandates, and in September Tokyo ordered him to step down, but the entire prefectural government threatened to resign in protest and he remained in office.[17] Elsewhere the response was swift and violent. On October 24 nearly two hundred furious samurai stormed Kumamoto Castle, the army's major military installation in Kyūshū, killing the garrison commander (chindai shichō) and mortally wounding the prefectural governor. The rebels, known as the Shinpūren, or "Divine Wind Party," were culturally and politically reactionary. They launched their rebellion after consulting an oracle, and they refused to use firearms or other weapons of Western origin. Their fierce, mass assault initially overwhelmed the Kumamoto garrison, but imperial forces regrouped, and by the following day the rebellion was effectively over. Three days later a rebellion was narrowly averted in Akitsuki, a castle town near Fukuoka, when the government learned of a planned assault on the Fukuoka garrison. On October 29 several hundred samurai in Chōshū, led by Maebara Issei, took up arms against the central government. Maebara had been a prominent member of the Meiji government, holding the posts of imperial councilor and vice minister of the army, but had quit in 1870. Maebara's insurrection was quickly suppressed, but not before the rebels raided an arsenal and plundered a district treasury.[18]

Saigō watched these rebellions with mixed emotions. He was himself deeply disturbed by the actions of the Tokyo government and was sympathetic to the rebels' cause. He confessed his ambivalence to Katsura, his most trusted friend. Maebara's uprising, he wrote in November 1876, was "remarkably good news." Saigō had learned of the rebellion via telegraph and was certain that "Osaka will soon be in [Maebara's] hands." Saigō's major criticism of Maebara was related to timing. He had not waited until November 3, the emperor's birthday, and thus had missed a symbolic date that would have inspired sympathizers throughout Japan. Had Maebara waited, thought Saigō, "people in Edo would certainly have joined him and . . . I would have enjoyed seeing uprisings in all directions." But Saigō himself would not join the rebellions, and he refused to leave Hinatayama for fear that his appearance in Kagoshima might be interpreted as a sign to rebel. Saigō was both delighted and disturbed by his own influence. He felt unable to leave Hinatayama but thought that "if I once were to rouse myself, it would startle the world."[19]

Saigō did not explain his sympathy for the rebels, but many historians have argued that he supported their defense of samurai privilege. Yet although this was undoubtedly true, for Saigō the central issue was maintaining a government based on virtue. Saigō was concerned with the dissolution of the samurai estate because they were the class that epitomized honor and selfless valor. Within this general vision of virtuous rule, Saigō was equally concerned with how central government initiatives would undermine the moral integrity of commoners. Fragmentary records show that Saigō was deeply concerned about the impact of the land tax and the institution of private property. In two anonymous documents he lamented how private property would "contaminate" Satsuma's *kadowari* system, in which farmers tilled commonly held land. Saigō's view of traditional landholding in Satsuma was overly optimistic: the system was riddled with inequities, and the tax burden was oppressive. But Saigō had a clear understanding of the dangers of introducing market principles into landownership. In hard times, he observed, the poor would be forced to sell their land to the rich, which would exacerbate their poverty and lead them to flee the domain. Saigō was thus eager to reform the *kadowari* system to ensure that all farmers had adequate plots and then maintain the principle of common land. This was the only way to avoid the unseemly spectacle of people "fighting over land, blinded by the prospect of immediate gain." Saigō was unwilling to let commerce corrupt the Satsuma countryside, and he was ready to subvert the will of the central government to protect the virtue of his domain.[20]

While Saigō brooded over the impending spread of commerce, radicals among the Shigakkō spoke openly of a coming war with Tokyo. Even those favoring moderation felt powerless to contain the situation. In the words of Murata Shinpachi, restraining the Shigakkō was like trying to hold together "a rotten barrel full of water with a rotten rope."[21] In January 1877, fearing an inevitable conflict, the Tokyo government dispatched the Mitsubishi ship *Sekiryūmaru* to remove munitions from Satsuma. Word of this plan infuriated radicals in the Shigakkō students, and on the night of January 30 a small group raided the Somuta powderhouse in Kagoshima City. They captured the guards and removed some sixty thousand rounds of ammunition. Local police reported the incident to the leaders of the Shigakkō but took no independent action, and the following night the students attacked again, this time destroying much of the powderhouse. On January 31 they attacked the central government's arsenal and shipyard at Iso, seizing arms and ammunition.[22]

Further adding to the chaos in Kagoshima was the discovery of spies working for the national police department. Beginning in late 1876, the chief of the national police began dispatching Satsuma natives to their home province with orders to infiltrate the Shigakkō and dissuade them from antigovernment action. The nominal leader of these agents, Nakahara Hisao, was enthusiastic but incompetent, and in late January 1877 he reportedly confided his mission to Taniguchi Tōgorō, a loyal member of the

Shigakkō. Taniguchi promptly informed his superiors that Nakahara had assembled a network of men to undermine the Shigakkō and that he was preparing to assassinate Saigō. Nakahara was arrested, tortured, and on February 5 signed a confession confirming Taniguchi's report. Nakahara later repudiated his confession, but he was a shadowy figure and even Kido Kōin was inclined to suspect him of treachery. In Kagoshima, Taniguchi's report and Nakahara's confession were widely accepted as confirmation of the Tokyo government's villainy.[23]

During this turmoil, Saigō was hunting in Konejime, across Kagoshima Bay on the Ōsumi peninsula, and he did not return to Kagoshima until February 3. There are no contemporaneous accounts of Saigō's reaction to the uprising, but according to Saigō lore he was appalled by the actions of the Shigakkō students and exclaimed "Oh, what a mess [*shimatta*]!" Then he declared that although he disapproved of their actions, he was moved by their loyalty and vowed to die with them in battle. This is a moving story, but Saigō's letters from March suggest something quite different. The arrest of Nakahara and his confession changed Saigō's understanding of the Tokyo government. Since 1873 Saigō had suspected Ōkubo of treachery, and Nakahara's confession confirmed his worst fears. Saigō had long sought to defend Satsuma against what he saw as Tokyo's amoral rule, but now the regime had come after him, and such wickedness demanded a response. Saigō still faced a profound ideological dilemma: the Tokyo government was the imperial government, and Saigō was loath to become an imperial rebel. But the government's actions now demanded a response. On February 7 Saigō announced his decision to go to Tokyo and confront the central government.[24]

Under Saigō's leadership, Satsuma now began mobilizing for war. The largest number of troops was from the Shigakkō system, and they formed the nucleus of the rebel army. The Shigakkō had trained its men in modern warfare, and they carried Snider (breech-loading) and Enfield (muzzle-loading) rifles, various carbines, and pistols as well as swords. The two artillery units collected virtually all the field guns in Satsuma, including twenty-eight mountain guns (5.28-pounders), two field guns (15.84-pounders), and thirty assorted mortars. The army totaled nearly twelve thousand men, grouped into seven battalions, and their spirits were high, but the weakness of the Satsuma force was apparent from the outset. Whatever its strengths, the army had no logistical support. Each soldier carried his own provisions, and there was no standing plan for resupply. The army's initial supply of ammunition allowed only a hundred rounds per man. The imperial army, by contrast, was backed by the resources of a national government. The standing army totaled more than forty-five thousand, but their critical advantage was in supplies. The army had more than a hundred artillery pieces, including two Gatling guns, and in excess of sixty-three million rounds of ammunition, more than fourteen times the rebel army's number of rounds. Moreover, by March, the nascent Japanese arms industry was producing nearly half a million rounds of ammunition per day. The longer the war lasted, the greater the Tokyo government's advantage in munitions and supplies.[25]

On February 15, amid unusually deep snow, the first two battalions of the Satsuma army assembled near Tsurumarujō and began marching north, toward Kumamoto. The army had a battle plan, to force the surrender of the Kumamoto garrison, but they had no explicit manifesto. The official purpose of the rebellion was to accompany Saigō to the capital so he could "question" *(jinmon)* the Tokyo government. This word hinted obliquely at Nakahara's purported conspiracy, but it was a thin justification for the mobilization of more than ten thousand men. The rebel soldiers themselves, in their later testimonies as prisoners of war, gave diverse reasons for joining the rebellion. Many of the Shigakkō members cited a vague sense of national crisis, and some cited the alleged plot to assassinate Saigō or hinted at the goal of overseas expansion. Some soldiers responded to a vague sense of coercion: Sakamoto Jun'ichi reported that samurai who did not volunteer were considered as bad as enemy soliders. Many soliders claimed not to have fully understood the implications of enlisting in the rebel army. Nagashi Renjirō, for example, claimed that he was inspired by Saigō's call to selflessly serve the state, but did not initially realize that this meant attacking the central government Most responses, however, revealed a powerful but inchoate sense that the war was a just and glorious cause. For example, Kabayama Sukeami, a forty-three-year-old soldier from Kagoshima City, averred that "although I had doubts about [the plan to] take up arms and go to the capital to interrogate [the government], what with the situation in the prefecture at that time even women and children were rousing themselves and volunteering to go along." It seemed, he continued, as if even the packhorse drivers in the rebel army were honorable. "I thought," he concluded, "that if it was Saigō's doing it just could not be a mistake." Saigō had thus launched a rebellion without a cause.[26]

Hostilities officially began early in the afternoon on February 21, when government troops fired on the advancing Satsuma army near Kawashiri, some three miles south of Kumamoto Castle. The rebels pressed forward, and by the following day were preparing their siege of the Kumamoto garrison. On February 23 and 24 the rebels attacked Kumamoto Castle, storming the walls fearlessly. "Sword in hand," recalled the garrison commander, Ideishi Takehiko, "the enemy often clambered over the stone walls and came into the attack, pressing forward under a hail of fire. It seemed that no sooner had one attack been repulsed than another was pressed."[27] The rebels could not sustain this intensity of combat, however, and by the evening of February 24 their offensive had tapered off. The attack now settled into a long siege. It is something of a romantic cliché to treat the clash between Satsuma and the imperial army as a war between tradition and modernity, but the siege of Kumamoto Castle reflected a more complicated reality. Although the Japanese government had equipped the imperial army with modern weapons, at Kumamoto their greatest asset was the castle itself, one of the great fortresses of the seventeenth century. The castle was massive: the outer wall was more than five miles around with nearly fifty turrets, and the grounds had more than a hundred wells to supply water

Kumamoto Castle, 1871

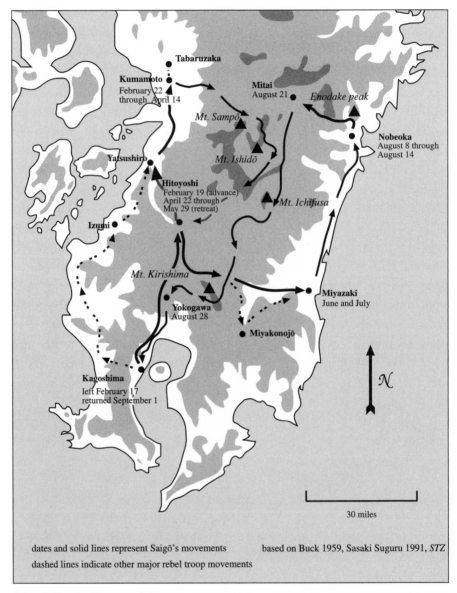

Saigō during the Satsuma rebellion

during a protracted siege. The massive stone walls curved back slightly at the top, a design called *musha gaeshi,* and this made them virtually impossible to scale. To inflict any damage on the castle, the rebels needed to move their field guns into close range, but this exposed them to counterattacks from the castle's defenders. In this case the modern weapons of the rebels were overmatched by the traditional technology of the imperial government. At other times, the situation was reversed. When the rebels breached the castle gates they were decimated by carefully positioned land mines, a scourge of modern warfare. The conflict also was a battle between samurai and commoners, but even this played out in unexpected ways. Among the conscripts in the Kumamoto garrison were vaudevillians who improvised performances for their fellow soldiers during the long siege. Satsuma soldiers heard laughter and the sound of the lute *(shamisen)* drifting out from the castle and could only image that the officers had smuggled in geisha to amuse themselves. This misunderstanding gained widespread currency through a woodblock print *(nishikie)* showing the garrison officers calmly watching geisha in pointed mockery of the rebels nearby.[28]

Meanwhile, beyond the castle town, a remarkable political drama was unfolding. The northward march of the Satsuma army had catalyzed long-simmering discontent throughout Kyūshū. In Kumamoto, the countryside erupted in rebellion as thousands of peasants voiced their grievances against the Meiji government. The commoners were suspicious of the new land tax and angry over new local levies designed to pay for national mandates, such as public education and land surveys. Across the prefecture they both petitioned and physically attacked local officials, demanding delays in the new land tax and reductions in levies. The Satsuma army made no direct appeal to these commoners, but the ambiguity of Saigō's mission was, paradoxically, an asset: villagers could impute to Saigō their own agendas. In the village of Katamata, for example, violence erupted when one Fujii Ihei returned from Kumamoto City on February 25 and reported the arrival of Satsuma troops. If the rebels came to Katamata, he declared, villagers would not have to pay taxes and would be able to choose their own village officials. Local officials managed to contain the situation for a week, but by early March they were confronted by death threats and fled the village. Order was not restored until the rebel army was driven from Kumamoto in the fall.[29]

The rebels also drew support from a range of disaffected samurai groups. In Fukuoka and Nakatsu there were sympathetic uprisings by traditionally minded samurai. In Kumamoto the rebels were joined by the Gakkōtō, a group of conservative dissident samurai. They also were joined by the Kyōdōtai, a samurai brigade formed by members of the Ueki gakkō, a radical school in the town of Ueki. The core curriculum at the Ueki gakkō included translations of Rousseau's *Social Contract,* Mill's *On Liberty,* and Montesquieu's *The Sprit of Laws,* and the school's founder, Miyazaki Hachirō, was an important participant in Itagaki Taisuke's campaign for an elected national assembly. Miyazaki reportedly later declared that he was not joining Saigō so much as using him to destroy the Meiji government, but at the moment this did not matter: the Kyōdōtai provided Saigō with high-spirited local troops ready to gather intelligence for the rebellion.[30]

Saigō's vague goal of "questioning" the Tokyo government did little to unify this diverse group of sympathizers, who lacked any common ideology. Within weeks, however, the popular press had created a slogan for Saigō: *Shinsei kōtoku* (A New Government, Rich in Virtue). The origins of the slogan are unclear, but on March 3 the *Yūbin hōchi shinbun* newspaper reported that Saigō was using the slogan on his battle flags. There were no such flags: Saigō's pennants were simple variations on the Shimazu family crest. The slogan was entirely a creation of woodblock print *(nishikie)* artists, which the newspaper mistakenly construed as fact. The slogan, which appeared in scores of different prints, became a cautious way for artists to show support for Saigō without violating Meiji press law. Artists dutifully described Saigō as a treacherous rebel in prose but then drew him in heroic poses with his valiant slogan. The slogan itself is paradoxical: it looks forward to a new government but harkens back to the notion that the state should be benevolent rather than bureaucratic. Implicit in the slogan was the contradictory but compelling desire for the vitality of a free society combined with the security of a Confucian patriarchy. Saigō, at least in popular fantasy, could embody both.[31]

The Long Defeat

Saigō's strategy assumed widespread popular support, but he seriously overestimated the impact of scattered rebellions. His expectations were excessive but not absurd. Even Yamagata Aritomo, who commanded the imperial army, was terrified by the prospect of widespread public unrest. Saigō, however, did little to encourage or organize popular support. On March 2 Saigō wrote to Ōyama Tsunayoshi, urging him to publicize the confessions of the national police spies as a means of explaining the purpose of the rebellion.

But Saigō never proclaimed his objectives, and the protests and rebellions never grew large enough to turn the tide of battle.[32]

Saigō's battle plan had assumed a quick victory at Kumamoto, and the long siege played into the hands of the imperial army. On March 9 the government landed forces in Kagoshima and seized control of all the war matériel there, including more than four thousand barrels of gunpowder. They took Governor Ōyama into custody and sent him to Osaka for the duration of the war. The imperial army also sent thousands of reinforcements to Kumamoto to break the siege. In response, the rebels sent forces north to Ueki to seize control of the main road out of Kumamoto, and on March 3 the armies met at Tabaruzaka, a small hill some twenty miles from the castle. The highway from Tabaruzaka to Kumamoto was designed as part of the extended defensive structure of Kumamoto Castle. The design of the road, cut into the hillcrest so that it was slightly lower than the surrounding forest, created two forms of defense. Not only was the hill a natural defense against an initial attack, but also the dense, elevated cover allowed defenders to slow approaching troops by attacking from the roadside. For eighteen days the imperial army attempted to dislodge the rebels from the hilltop, and the battle at Tabaruzaka became the decisive engagement of the war. Both sides had mustered some ten thousand men apiece, and the battle was fought with devastating ferocity, with casualties approaching four thousand soldiers on each side. Although the imperial army was not yet at full strength, it still brought to bear massive firepower, expending more than three hundred thousand rounds of small-arms ammunition per day in the assault on the hilltop. The rebels were handicapped by dwindling supplies of ammunition and inclement weather. Driving rain rendered useless their muzzle-loading weapons, and their cotton clothing became waterlogged, but they fought with swords in deep mud and quipped in doggerel that they feared the rain more than cannons. Despite these conditions the rebels held their positions until March 20, when the imperial army broke through on their western flank and seized the hillcrest. The rebels retreated east to the town of Ueki, where they held their ground until April 2. The rebels' valiant efforts slowed the advance of the imperial army from the north, but to little effect. On April 15 the imperial army, advancing from the southwest, defeated the rebels at Kawashiri and broke the siege of Kumamoto Castle. The Kumamoto garrison had suffered nearly 20 percent casualties in the fifty-four-day siege and, with their food supplies dwindling, had made plans for a suicidal breakout mission. Upon the arrival of government troops the soldiers, recalled the commander, wept as though "their children had come back from death."[33]

Saigō had foreseen these defeats a month earlier. On March 2 he was still assuming that sympathizers from Tosa would seize Osaka and that uprisings throughout Japan would affect the war. By March 12, however, his thinking had changed decisively. He had pursued, despite arguments to the contrary, a siege of Kumamoto, and he now realized he had "fallen into their trap and taken the bait of a castle siege." The enemy was approaching from all sides and, he feared, would gradually wear down his forces. Saigō was not without hope, but now he doubted that anyone could turn the tide of battle, even Mengben, the legendary Chinese warrior who could pull the horns off a live bull. But, Saigō claimed, this did not really matter. He was not fighting for victory but for the "chance to die for principle [jōri]."[34] When the siege of Kumamoto was broken, Saigō fell back and reassembled his men at Hitoyoshi. He held camp at Hitoyoshi from mid-April to late May, hoping that sympathizers from Tosa might arrive and bolster his dwindling force. On May 27, however, after three weeks of intermittent combat with the rebels, the imperial army began a general assault on Hitoyoshi, and Saigō ordered a retreat.[35]

With the retreat from Hitoyoshi, the character of the war changed decisively, and the rebel offensive became a protracted retreat. Between May and September 1877 the imperial army chased the shrinking band of rebels across the length and breadth of Kyūshū. The rebels were no longer trying to reach Tokyo but to dodge the imperial army and return home. Lacking ammunition, they largely abandoned their firearms in favor of swords, and they increasingly favored guerrilla engagements over conventional combat. The rebels blunted the enemy's numerical superiority by scattering and regrouping, thus forcing the imperial army to disperse its own forces. The rebels used the terrain to their advantage, cutting through mountains and forests in small groups. The pursuit began in earnest in June after Saigō sent the core of his force south from Hitoyoshi to Miyakonojō on the Ōsumi peninsula, while he himself cut some fifty miles east across Kyūshū to Miyazaki, on the Pacific coast. The imperial army gave chase, defeating the rebels at Miyakonojō on July 24, before turning north to pursue Saigō. Saigō's forces escaped up the eastern coast of Kyūshū to Nobeoka, where they met with a massive government offensive on August 10. Saigō's three thousand remaining troops were outnumbered at least six to one, but they held out for a week against the imperial army before fleeing west into the mountains. The imperial army managed to surround Saigō on the northern slopes of Enodake, a twenty-four-hundred-foot peak just north of Nobeoka. This was expected to be the end of the war. John Capen Hubbard, an American ship captain employed by the Mitsubishi Steamship Company to transport government troops and supplies, was present at Nobeoka and heard on August 18 that "the rebels were entirely surrounded and would be finished that night." The following day, however, he learned that "Saigō and Kirino, with the other leaders . . . had broken out of the magic circle, as they have done so often before." Saigō had escaped by cutting through trackless forest and had again frustrated the imperial army. "To me," continued Hubbard, "the end seems a long way off." The rebels would be defeated, he wrote, "but I fancy it will take some time to find them, and they will probably turn up in some place where they are not expected." Hubbard was right. Fewer than two weeks later, on September 1, Saigō's forces slipped back into Kagoshima, a city occupied by more than seven thousand imperial soldiers. The rebels reassembled at the crest of Shiroyama to make their last stand.[36]

Saigō's exact role in this remarkable retreat remains a mystery. There are no extant letters from the period between May 17 and August 6, 1877, and the few firsthand reports on his activities are contradictory. One oft-cited contemporary journal observed that Saigō was "hiding" at his headquarters and was rarely seen. Other testimony, however, indicated that he liked to lose his bodyguards and go rabbit hunting. But this conflicts with reports that Saigō was so crippled by a parasitic inflammation of the testicles that he was unable to walk.[37] Saigō's thoughts also are a mystery, but it is clear that by early August he had come to terms with his defeat. On August 6, en route to Nobeoka, he issued a circular to his troops. They had fought well for six months now, but "just as we seemed on the verge of victory, our fighting spirit weakened and I lament that [now] at the end we are trapped in desperate straits." Saigō urged his men to continue with courage and "leave no shame for the hereafter." Saigō was still fighting, but he was preparing for death.[38]

Meanwhile, the popular press was preparing for Saigō's demise by sending him to the heavens. An August 10 print by Haneda Tomijirō shows a crowd of commoners praying to a celestial Saigō. Haneda used this image to offer his insightful but coarse commentaries on rapid cultural change. The monk in the print, for example, is expressing gratitude that the Meiji state has abolished traditional Buddhist strictures, allowing him to enjoy women and meat. Unfortunately, people have stopped coming to his temple. "Please," he prays to Saigō, "restore things to the way they were before."[39] This print must have sold well, because Haneda used the same idea again a month later, although now the commoners are so unhappy that they are trying to bring Saigō back to earth by dragging him down with ropes. In this second print a fictitious merchant laments that the abolition of old customs (kyūhei) has caused a drop in his sales of traditional festival merchandise. The boatman complains that the building of bridges and railroads has undermined his livelihood. The geisha in the print likes some changes: she is pleased that she can conceal a large fart in a Western-style drawing room merely by playing her shamisen loudly enough to cover the noise. She complains, however, that her "enlightened" (kaika) clients with their Western haircuts do not even seem to notice whether she is playing well.[40]

While Haneda's vision of Saigō was satiric, others offered a more respectful, albeit still fantastic view of Saigō. A September 10 print by Tsukioka Yonejirō, for example, depicts the government's attempt to shoot down Saigō's star with a military balloon. One onlooker declares that Saigō is so great (erai) that he can become a star while still alive, while another argues that such a change in the heavens is merely a reflection of turmoil down below. A third observer comments that it is not Saigō's rebellion (hōki) that has changed the heavens but his revolution (isshin).[41]

Back on Earth, Saigō and roughly three hundred men dug defensive positions around the crest of Shiroyama. They had little food, little ammunition, and no medicine. Yamagata's forces surrounded their position and began a steady artillery bombardment, but Yamagata remained concerned that Saigō might escape again. According to legend, on September 23 Yamagata sent a letter to Saigō urging him to abandon his struggle. Saigō had proven his honor through his valiant struggle, but there was nothing to be gained from more fighting. Yamagata did not use the word "surrender" and did not offer clemency, but declared that he understood Saigō's true motivation. Saigō did not reply, and at 3:55 A.M. the following morning the imperial army began its final assault on Shiroyama.[42]

Death and Transcendence

Let us return now to the opening question: On September 24, 1877, where was Saigō's head? The most reliable accounts note only that Saigō's head was not with his body, and was recovered later by government troops.[43] According to various Saigō legends, his head was buried by his manservant at the gate of a private home, but there is disagreement on the name of the manservant and the owner of the residence. It also is unclear who found Saigō's head, although the most frequently cited name is that of Maeda Tsunemitsu, an imperial army soldier.[44] Although these details are in dispute, we have a good account of what happened next: Saigō's head was rejoined with his body in a strikingly unceremonious fashion. As witnessed by Captain Hubbard, who described the event in a letter to his wife, the bodies of the rebel leaders were laid in two rows on a hill near the imperial army's barricades. Hubbard quickly recognized Saigō:

> He was a large powerful looking man, his skin almost white. His clothing had been taken off and he lay there naked. It was a few seconds before I realized his head was cut off. Next to Saigo lay Kirino, then Murata. Saigo's was the only headless body, but the others were a fearful sight to look at. Their heads were dreadfully cut up and it was quite evident that they killed each other. No doubt their heads would all have been cut off by their own people had time permitted. While [we were] looking at the bodies, Saigō's head was brought in and placed by his body. It was a remarkable looking head and any one would have said at once that he must have been the leader.[45]

Hubbard's letter suggests the grandeur of Saigō's physical presence, which was obvious even to a Boston-born ship captain working for the Meiji state.

Hubbard's account of Saigō's head is, however, virtually unknown in Japan. It is an eyewitness report, but it is not what the Japanese populace wanted to hear or what history seemed to demand. Saigō's heroic march down the slopes of Shiroyama to face certain death and the valiant effort to conceal his head were part of a familiar narrative, a clear invocation of the traditional tropes of warrior valor. *Nishikie* artists immediately understood

The Presentation of Saigō's Head
Seinan heiteiki in the Reimeikan

how Saigō's story was supposed to end. Beginning in early November, artists began publishing prints showing the formal presentation of Saigō's head (along with the severed heads of Kirino, Murata, and Beppu) to the leaders of the imperial army, Yamagata Aritomo and Arisugawanomiya, the collateral imperial prince and nominal commander in chief. The prints were commonly entitled *kubi jikken* (inspection of heads), an explicit reference to the medieval warrior tradition. The events depicted in these prints had no factual basis, and the imperial army never conducted a formal, ritualized inspection of heads. For the Japanese public, however, this was obviously the correct conclusion to the broad arc of Saigō's life.[46]

Japanese historians faced a different quandary. They, too, were uneasy with the unceremonious disposal of Saigō's head, an event that seemed to rob Saigō's life of narrative closure. The facts of Saigō's death were deeply unsatisfying and singularly lacking in majesty, mystery, and symbolism. A legendary life needed a legendary death, and it was difficult to leave Saigō's head plopped next to his naked corpse near an earthen warren at the base of Shiroyama. But the *nishikie* tale of a formal presentation was obviously false, and Saigō's defenders sought a less glaringly fictitious denouement. The most enduring myth about Saigō's head was developed in 1897 by Kawasaki Saburō. In that account, Maeda, acting more like a samurai than a soldier, delivered Saigō's head to his commander, Yamagata Aritomo, for inspection. Yamagata treated Saigō's head with great deference and decorum. Saigō was a rebel, but he had once been one of the three most powerful men in Japan, a chief councilor of state, and a commander of the imperial guards. Yamagata also recalled how they had fought together to topple the shogunate. His severed head demanded respect. Yamagata washed the head in clear water and held it in both hands. Then he turned to the assembled commanders and spoke of Saigō's glorious death. He called their attention to Saigō's calm countenance, unchanged even in death. Then, holding Saigō's head, Yamagata wept for his fallen comrade.[47] This was a death befitting the last samurai.

This fanciful account of Saigō's death has become a powerful part of the Saigō legend. The conservative cultural critic Etō Jun has interpreted this scene as a transcendent moment in Japanese history. Writing shortly before his death in 1999, Etō described Yamagata's gesture as a reflection of the power of Saigō's ideas. "This was not Ōyōmei learning, or even Saigō's slogan of 'Revere heaven and love the people,' nor was it nationalism [kokusuishugi] or xenophobia [haigaishisō] but rather the ideology of Saigō nanshū [Saigō of the south], which transcends all of these and has, unceasingly, deeply moved the hearts of the Japanese." Nothing, declared Etō, including Marxism, anarchism, modernization theory, and postmodernism, had given the Japanese a more powerful ideology than Saigō. Etō's interpretation of Saigō's death stemmed from his deeply conservative understanding of Japanese history and culture. Japan, he believed, had sacrificed its traditions for second-rate facsimiles of Western "individualism" and "liberty." Etō had long inveighed against the superficiality of postwar Japanese materialism, and in the late 1990s he saw in Saigō's death an antidote to Japan's cultural malaise. Etō explicitly cited Saigō's death with dignity on the hills of Shiroyama as a model for finding meaning in the collapse of the Japanese economy. Japan, he argued, had lost twice, first as a military superpower and now as an economic superpower, but Saigō's death showed how much could be won amid defeat.[48]

Etō's understanding of Saigō's head was part of his own neonationalist vision, but it would be a mistake to see Saigō solely as a symbol for the Japanese right. Etō's account of Yamagata weeping is as fanciful as the 1870s idea of Saigō's ascension into the heavens, but both spring from a desire to transcend the contradictions of modern life. The quest for a world both modern and traditional underlay not only Etō's passionate political rhetoric but also the comic quips in *nishikie,* such as the monk who wanted to enjoy women and meat but not lose the support of a devoted parish. More seriously, both Etō and the *nishikie* artists who employed the phrase "A New Government, Rich in Virtue" saw in Saigō the potential for a life that was practical, modern, and yet deeply moral. Saigō himself failed to reconcile these contradictions. He found authenticity only by withdrawing from public life, but his life was by then too public to allow him privacy. Thus Saigō was a failure, but he failed with such singularity of purpose, self-awareness, and equanimity that, as Etō observed, his failure was as compelling as any victory. Thus his missing head continues to fire the imagination.

Notes

Introduction

1. Ivan Morris (1975, 101) cites the legend of Yoshitsune's head without attribution, but I have traced it to the *Azuma kagami,* chapter 9, 1189 (Bunji 5)/6/13.
2. Ikegami 1995, 100–103. I am concerned here less with the details of medieval practice than with the legends that informed early Meiji images of medieval practice. For some examples of rituals for severed heads in English see translations of *Heike Monogatari* (Tale of the Heike), sections 10:1 and 11:18, and the last section of *Gikeiki* (Yoshitsune).
3. Yui, Fujiwara, and Yoshida 1989, 68. My translation closely follows that in Tsunoda, de Bary, and Keene 1958, 2:197.
4. For the arsenal used against Saigō see Ikai 1992, 180–182, 209–215.
5. *STD* 8:147–148; *STZ* 3:553.
6. Mushakoji 1942, 476–477.
7. My account here draws largely on *Shiroyama hifū yokyō* and *Kajiki jōju Shiroyama rōjō chōsa hikki,* two accounts reprinted in Kokuryūkai 1908–1911, 4:703–704. For a similar account in English see Mushakoji 1942, 478–481. For a modern retelling see Etō 1998a, 226–231. These four accounts do not assert that Saigō actually cut his abdomen. *Nishikie* artists, however, often described or depicted an actual ritual suicide, and these prints worked their way into English-language accounts. See, for example, Morse 1917, 1:269, and Mounsey 1879, 216–217. For *nishikie* see *Saigō shoshō seppuku no zu, Kagoshima nikki: Shiroyama kōgekisen zu,* and *Kagoshima seitō zenkinai.* It is also worth noting here that an acceptable variation on *seppuku* was for the victim to submit to beheading by his second, the version to be found in the four accounts of Saigō's death. There is an extensive collection of Japanese-language accounts of Saigō's death in Kokuryūkai 1908–1911, 4:698–708.
8. For a discussion of Saigō's autopsy see Murakami. See also Yates 1994, 167–168i; Inoue 1970, 2:305–307; *STD* 4:148.
9. *Tokio Times,* September 1, 1877.
10. Quoted in *Tokio Times,* September 1, 1877.
11. Uchimura 1908, 33–34, 36–37.
12. Fukuzawa 1959, 6:529–533, quote from 6:552–553.
13. Ikai 1992, 5–6; Tan'o and Kawada 1996, 5–6; Morris 1975, 226.
14. Ikai 1992, 3–4; *Seinan chinbun.*
15. Shinoda 1947, 69–70.
16. Ikai 1992, 3–4.
17. Morse 1917, 1:269.

18. Kawahara 1971, 27; *Saigō nehanzō*.
19. For a detailed discussion of Sugawara see Borgen 1986. See also Borgen 1995 and Morris 1975, 41–66.

Chapter 1: "Powerfully Sentimental"

1. Ihara Saikaku 1972, 197.
2. For a detailed discussion of *karaimo* and *satsumaimo* see Sakai Kenkichi 1999, 59–64.
3. Smits 1999, 15–46; Haraguchi Izumi et al. 1999, 178–183, 217–220; Hellyer 2001, esp. 35–42.
4. Toby 1984, 45–46, 182–190. Matsumae is discussed at length in Howell 1995 and Walker 2001.
5. See "Kagoshima buri" in Miyamoto, Haraguchi, and Higa 1968, 9:393. I am indebted to Kajiya Sadayuki of Kagoshima University for this reference.
6. For an overview of Japanese foreign policy see Maehira 1991. Japanese castaways were often allowed to return, but trading voyages were prohibited. The exact prohibition on ships was a capacity limit of 500 *koku*. See Totman 1993, 73–77.
7. Takemitsu 1999, 162–165; Haraguchi Izumi 1999, 106–107, 113, 118–119.
8. I refer here to the overland route: Kagoshima is just over 600 air miles from Tokyo.
9. For *tozama* and *fudai* see Totman 1993, 117–120. For an extensive discussion of the role of *fudai* see Bolitho 1974.
10. These population and land figures exclude the Ryukyus, which would push the total population to nearly nine hundred thousand. For some recent examinations of the Satsuma population see Oguchi 1999, 2000. The comparison with the populations of Kaga, Nagoya, and Hiroshima is based on the census data in *Tōkei shūshi* 8 (April 1882):96–107.
11. Kagoshima-shi shi hensan iinkai 1969–1971, 1:319–322; Kagoshima kyōiku iinkai 1983, 1–14.
12. For a careful examination of the history of the castle see Hatanaka Akira 1992.
13. Kagoshima-shi shi hensan iinkai 1969–1971, 1:326–327.
14. For an outline of the domain hierarchy see, in English, Hall 1973, 24–25
15. *Kagoshima ezu,* at Kagoshima kenritsu toshokan, Kagoshima. For discussions of the neighborhood see *KKKyS* 114–116 and Haraguchi Izumi 1990. I also have relied on the carefully researched model of nineteenth-century Kagoshima on display at the Ishin Furusatokan in Kagoshima.
16. Imura 1998, 373–383; Takeuchi 1983, 306–308. For a detailed discussion of the volcano see Hicks 1993, 37–41.
17. *STD* 1:3; Tamamuro 1960, 3. There is limited English-language material on Go-Daigo, the Kenmu Restoration, and Northern and Southern courts. See Morris 1975, 106–142, and Varley 1971. For a critical reevaluation of Go-Daigo and a critique of Varley see Goble 1996.
18. Walthall 1995, esp. 157–158; Huber 1982, 112–113.
19. See, for example, *STZ* 5:29–33.

20. See, for example, Saigō's invocation of Kusunoki Masashige in an 1859/1/2 letter to Ōkubo. *STZ* 1:136–137.
21. Kanbashi 1985, 289–299; *STZ* 6:348; Inoue 1970, 1:11–12.
22. *STZ* 4:426–427, 4:451; *STD* 1:4–5; Inoue 1970, 1:10; Kanbashi 1985, 292. The family name Saigō means "western village," but the name's origins are obscure.
23. A census document *(shūmon aratame)* from 1847/6 records a household of sixteen. See *STZ* 4:407–408. See also *STZ* 4:411, 4:416–417, 4:432, 4:437. For a useful Saigō genealogy see Kanbashi 1985, 290–299.
24. Inoue 1970, 1:12; Tanaka Sōgorō 1958, 1–2, 5–7; Iwayama and Iwayama 1999, 22–23. For the 1855 transaction documents see *STZ* 4:439–440.
25. Tanaka Sōgorō 1958, 3–4; Inoue 1970, 1:14.
26. Iwayama and Iwayama 1999, 22–26. See also *STZ* 4:425–426, 4:530.
27. Iwayama and Iwayama 1999, 31–33.
28 For a succinct description of the Satsuma status system see Robert Sakai 1957.
29. Saigō to Itagaki Yosōji, June 23, 1872, in *STZ* 3:273–275.
30. *STZ* 3:275–278. For Itagaki Yosōji's response and loan calculations see *STZ* 5:476–481.
31. For sandals see Iwayama and Iwayama 1999, 192. For the fishing lures see Nobori [1927] 1977, 199–202. Saigō wrote extensively about the dangers of luxuries. See, for example, his 1870 policy paper in which he described frugality as a cornerstone of good government in *STZ* 3:86.
32. Andō Tamotsu 1999, 2–4; *KKKyS* 96; Inoue 1970, 1:14–15.
33. *KKKyS* 84–86. For an in-depth discussion of the origins of the *gojū* see Andō Tamotsu 1990, 1991
34. *KKKyS* 91–93, 97: Haga 1968, 32.
35. *KKKyS* 92.
36. Haga 1968, 32; Yates 1987, 114; *KKKyS* 92–94, 117; Hall 1973, 38–39.
37. *KKKyS* 92, 94–95; Inoue 1970, 1:14–15; Fujioka 1999, 27; Hall 1973, 39.
38. Andō Tamotsu 1999, 5; *KKKyS* 94.
39. Shimazu Tadayoshi 1993.
40. *Rekidai uta.*
41. *KKKyS* 94–95.
42. Hurst 1998, 62–63.
43. *KKKyS* 112–114. For a brief mention of Saigō's Yakumaru teacher see Yamada Jun [1944] 1997, 7.
44. *KKKyS* 94–95.
45. *KKKyS* 92–95.
46. For same-sex relations see Pflugfelder 1999, esp. 26–96.
47. *KKKyS* 95; *STZ* 6:537.
48. Inoue 1970, 1:15; *KKKyS* 95.
49. Hall 1973, 40–41.
50. *KKKyS* 101–102. For *Seiyūki* see Tachibana [1795] 1974, 2:7–11. The quote is from p. 9. The text is also known as *Saiyūki.*
51. Hall 1973, 42; *KKKyS* 112.

52. Pflugfelder 1999, 207–211; Ujiie 1995, 80–86.

53. Pflugfelder 1999, 23–145; Ikegami 1995, 209–210; Yamamoto 1979, 58–59.

54. See Saigō to Ichiki Shōnojō, 1856/12/1 in *STZ* 1:81–85 and Saigō to Shiibara Kunimoto and Shiibara Gombei, 1854/7/29 in *STZ* 1:31–33.

55. Saigō to Saisho Atsushi and Ōkubo Toshimichi, 1859/2/13 in *STZ* 1:143.

56. For Saigō on Okinoerabumajima see chapter 3 below.

57. *KKKyS* 60–64.

58. The Five Classics were ancient Chinese documents, largely records of the Zhou dynasty (1122 B.C.E. to 771 B.C.E.). They included records of Zhou politics, court ritual, religion, and poetry. Confucians considered the Zhou dynasty the high point of ancient culture, and they treated its practices as a guide to the ideal political order. The Four Books were largely commentaries and reflections on the Five Classics. They were comparatively more recent texts, written between the fifth and first centuries B.C.E., and included the writings of China's greatest ancient philosophers, Confucius and Mencius.

59. The bibliography on Zhu Xi and Song dynasty thought is enormous and beyond the scope of this study. I have relied on de Bary and Bloom 1999, 1:667–840, esp. 697–713, 800–810; Chu Hsi and Gardner 1990, esp. 3–87.

60. Hall 1973, 49–50.

61. Ōyōmei is the Japanese pronunciation of the Chinese name Wang Yangming. According to *STZ* 6:300, Saigō, Ōkubo, and some companions studied Yangming learning with Itō Mōemon (1816–?), a local philosopher, in 1850 and 1851. According to Yamada Jun, however, Saigō began his studies with Itō in about 1846. See Yamada Jun [1944] 1997, 8–9.

62. On Wang Yangming see Ching 1976 and de Bary and Bloom 1999, 1:509–526. The quote is from Ching 1976, 131.

63. Najita 1970, 155–79. For the quote from Ōshio's manifesto see Lu 1997, 280–281.

64. For a discussion of Satō's life and work see Okada 1984, 218, 235, and Sagara, Mizoguchi, and Fukunaga 1980, 709–725.

65. It is unclear when Saigō began reading Satō's writings, but his early studies with Itō would have directed him toward Satō. Satō also was Itō's intellectual grandfather: Itō's own teacher, Arakawa Hideyama, had studied in Edo with Satō. See *STZ* 6:300. Also, Itō, like Satō, pursued an eclectic approach to scholarship, refusing to identify with a single school. See Yamada Jun [1944] 1997, 8–9. For a detailed study of Itō see Ōhira 1993. Another syncretic influence on Saigō was Kasuga Sen'an. See Nakayama 1992, 41.

66. Saigō's transcription of Satō's writings, titled "Shushō genshiroku," is reproduced in Yamada Seisai 1939, 5–70.

67. See *Shushō genshiroku* 85 in Yamada Seisai 1939, 61, and *Genshi tetsuroku* 56 in Sagara, Mizoguchi, and Fukunaga 1980, 176, 276. My translations of the terms *tenshin* and *jinshin* follow Ching 1976, 215–219.

68. "Shushō genshiroku" 88 in Yamada Seisai 1939, 62, and *Genshi tetsuroku* 66 in Sagara, Mizoguchi, and Fukunaga 1980, 177, 277.

69. This discussion draws on Saigō's *Shushō genshiroku* 15, 16, 20, and 21, which correspond, respectively, to *Genshiroku* 132, 133, 137, and 138. See Yamada Seisai 1939, 32–36 and Sagara, Mizoguchi, and Fukunaga 1980, 32–34, 237–238.

70. *KKKyS* 95. For a careful consideration of Saigō's intellectual influences see Nakayama Hiroshi 1992, 39–56. Furukawa Tesshi argues that Saigō's beloved phrase *keiten aijin,* "revere heaven and love man," reveals the influence of Hirose Tansō. I find this idea intriguing but extremely speculative. See Furukawa 1967, 15–16, and Kassel 1996.

70. *STZ* 6:430; *STD* 1:16.

71. *STZ* 6:63–64, 6:430; Okatani Shigemi 1915, 25–26. For Kikujirō's recollections see *STZ* 6:106.

72. *STD* 1:5–6; Inoue 1970, 1:18; Tanaka Sōgorō 1958, 15.

73. Haraguchi Torao 1966, 102–107.

74. These figures draw on Oguchi 2000, 19. Statistics from 1871 present an even more dire situation: 530,000 commoners supporting 230,000 samurai. See also Kanbashi 1993, 4; Inoue 1970, 1:12–13.

75. Haraguchi Torao 1966, 102–107.

76. *STD* 1:5–7; Inoue 1970, 1:19; Tanaka Sōgorō 1958, 15. For Saigō's early thoughts on agriculture see his 1856 opinion paper at *STZ* 1:71–80.

77. Kihara 1999, 111–113. A tax document at *STZ* 4:428–429 lists Saigō's household as twelve: fourteen minus two deaths. Although the records are not specific, it seems the household was reduced from sixteen to twelve by the deaths of Saigō's mother, father, and grandfather, and by the marriage of his sister Koto.

78. Iwayama and Iwayama 1999, 23–24.

Chapter 2: "A Man of Exceptional Fidelity"

1. "Saigō nanshū itsuwa," 4:105–106.

2. More than a century ago Katsuta Magoya remarked that Saigō himself may not have known how he came to Nariakira's attention. The most common explanation is that Nariakira was impressed by an opinion paper *(ikensho)* that Saigō had written. See *STD* 1:28–29, 33–34. One of Saigō's early letters mentions an upcoming audience with Nariakira, but no opinion paper survives. See Saigō to Ichiki Shōnojō (1853/2/10) at *STZ* 1:25

3. Kanbashi 1993, 10–16, 18–19, 22–25; Inoue 1970, 1:28–29; Kanbashi 1980, 155–157.

4. Kanbashi 1993, 15, 50–51.

5. Kanbashi 1993, 7–10. For an overview of Zusho's reforms see Haraguchi Torao 1966, 93–128.

6. Haraguchi Torao 1966, 159–163; Robert Sakai 1970, 222–223; Kanbashi 1993, 44.

7. Kanbashi 1993, 35–48; Haraguchi Torao 1966, 142–149; Robert Sakai 1970, 223–224.

8. Kanbashi 1993, 50–54; Robert Sakai 1970, 226–227.

9. Kanbashi 1993, 35–48; Haraguchi Torao 1966, 142–149, 165–168; Robert Sakai 1970, 223–224; Hellyer 2001, 93–103, 125–134.
10. Kanbashi 1993, 48–50; Robert Sakai 1970, 227–228.
11. Kanbashi 1993, 54–62; Robert Sakai 1970, 227–228.
12. Kanbashi 1993, 64–67; Robert Sakai 1970, 228–233; Iwata 1964, 33.
13. Iwata 1964, 32–33.
14. Inoue 1970, 1:31–32; Tanaka Sōgorō 1958, 19–20.
15. *SSTKS* 62–63; *STZ* 4:59–60.
16. For Tsugaru Nobumasa see Miyazaki 1970, 146.
17. Yamada's journal for 1854 is reproduced in *KKSNKS* 4:920–939. I am thankful to Oguchi Yoshio of the Reimeikan for directing me to this remarkable document.
18. *KKSNKS* 4:920.
19. *KKSNKS* 4:921–922.
20. *KKSNKS* 4:922–939.
21. Maehira 1991, esp. 131–132.
22. For an overview of Japanese foreign relations see Duus 1998, 35–40, 61–69; Wakabayashi and Aizawa 1986, 58–99.
23. For a good summary of the Ryukyuan arrangement in English see Smits 1999 or Robert Sakai 1964.
24. Ishii 1989, 16–21. Kagawa's count was quite accurate: the fleet had 66 large-caliber guns. See Heine [1856] 1990, 12.
25. Ishii 1989, 21–27; Duus 1998, 66–68.
26. Ishii 1989, 25–27 For Perry's account see Perry 1968, 155–165.
27. Saigō to Iwasaki Shōzaemon and Maeda Shiroda at *STZ* 1:26–29.
28. *KKSNKS* 4:939.
29. McClain, Merriman, and Ugawa 1994, 13.
30. Ibid., 218–19, 346–347; Harada 1989, 145.
31. Kanbashi 1980, 42–45. The guest of honor was Hayashi Jussai.
32. Saigō to Shiibara Kunimoto and Shiibara Gonbei (1854/7/29) in *STZ* 1:31–33.
33. For a discussion of Ieyasu's sons see Ōishi Shinzaburō 1990, 20–21.
34. Webb 1960, 135–149.
35. The English-language bibliography on Mito learning is now quite extensive. The best general study is Koschmann 1987. For an excellent analysis and translation of *Shinron,* the most influential Mito text, see Wakabayashi and Aizawa 1986. Dated, but still useful, is Earl 1964.
36. Chang 1970, esp. 92–96. For Nariakira's recommendations see W. G. Beasley 1955, 102–107.
37. Saigō to Kabayama San'en (1855/6/1) at *STZ* 1:43–44, and Saigō to Kabayama (1855/8/20) at 1:50–51 and at Yamada Shōji 1992a, 265.
38. Saigō to Shiibara Kunimoto and Shiibara Gonbei (1854/7/29) at *STZ* 1:31–32.
39. For Nariakira's support of Nariaki see W. G. Beasley 1955, 113.

40. See Saigō to Ichiki Shōnojō (1855/9/29) at *STZ* 1:53. Saigō was particularly concerned with the ouster of Shimazu Bungo, a domain elder. See Saigō to Ōyama Tsunayoshi (1855/6/29) at *STZ* 1:46–48; and Iwata 1964, 35–36.

41. Saigō to Fukushimaya Zōda (1854/8/2) at *STZ* 1:37–40.

42. Saigō to Ichiki Shōnojō (1856/12/1) at *STZ* 1:81–85.

43. Wilson 1970, 241–244; W. G. Beasley 1972, 129–132; Kanbashi 1993, 187–188. Technically, until his succession in 1858 Iemochi was known as Tokugawa Yoshitomi, but I have used his shogunal name anachronistically in the interests of simplicity.

44. Wilson 1970, 241–244. For Yamauchi Yōdō's evolving attitudes toward foreign trade see Jansen 1961, 67–72.

45. W. G. Beasley 1972, 129–132; Wilson 1970, 244–246.

46. Wilson 1970, 241–242; Kanbashi 1993, 187–188.

47. Saigō detailed his commitment to Mito and his meeting with Nariakira in a long letter to Ōyama Tsunayoshi dated 1856/5/4. See *STZ* 1:57–62. See also Inoue 1970, 1:47–50.

48. The origins of Nariakira and Shungaku's alliance are unclear. The memoirs of Shungaku's aide Nakane Yukie suggest that the two first discussed Keiki's candidacy in 1853, but Nariakira's earliest letter mentioning Keiki's candidacy is dated 1856/7/5. This later date would explain why Mito retainers would ask Nariakira to support a policy he was already supporting. For details see Kanbashi 1993, 188–189. Saigō's letter to Ōyama is in *STZ* 1:57–62.

49. For a discussion of *junshi* see Ikegami 1995, 218–220. For Saigō and *junshi* see Inoue 1970, 1:58.

50. I discuss these different aspects of samurai loyalty in Ravina 1999, 16–46. For the story of Boyi (Po Yi) and Shuqi (Shu Ch'i) see Sima Qian's (Ssu-ma Ch'ien), *Records of the Grand Historian* in Ssu-ma Ch'ien 1969, 11–15, and the Analects of Confucius, esp. 5:23, 7:15, and 16:12.

51. Saigō to Ōyama Tsunayoshi (1856/5/4) at *STZ* 1:57–62.

52. My distinction between "state" and "realm" is based on Saigō's usage of the terms *"kokka"* and *"tenka."* For a discussion of this see Inoue 1970, 1:49–50.

53. Kenmotsu to Tamiya Yatarō (1857/11/4) at *DSZ* 1:70–72.

54. Yates 1987, 133; Kanbashi 1993, 199, 203–204. Saigō to Ichiki Shōnojō (1858/1/29) at *STZ* 1:115; *STZ* 6:540–541.

55. *Sakumu kiji* in Nakane 1921, 2:280–281; Kanbashi 1992, 58–62.

56. Saigō to Hashimoto Sanai (1857/12/14) at *STZ* 1:101–102.

57. Inoue 1970, 1:46–47.

58. The letter itself, which is remarkably uninteresting, is the 1857/12/14 cover letter for Sanai's "talking points" *(kyōjōki).* See *STZ* 5:5–6; Kanbashi 1992, 73.

59. Wilson 1970, 237–241.

60. *Nanshū ō ikun* in *STZ* 4:197.

61. For the details of Nariakira's adoption of Atsuhime and her marriage to Iesada see Kanbashi 1993, 187–195, and *Sakumu kiji* in Nakane 1921, 2:285–286.

62. Kanbashi 1993, 187–195.

63. Kanbashi 1993, 199–205; Kanbashi 1992, 73–83; *Sakumu kiji* in Nakane 1921, 2:446–456.

64. These events are detailed in Wilson 1970, 247–250; Kanbashi 1993, 201; W. G. Beasley 1972, 105–116, 133–134.

65. Saigō's relationship with Gesshō is thinly documented, possibly because the two were cooperating on such sensitive issues. Saigō never appears, for example, in Gesshō's journal, although this may be because the most relevant year of the journal (1858) is missing. See Tomomatsu Entai 1961, 140–152.

66. As Conrad Totman has observed, "for two centuries the Ii's family's high office had conveyed no power" (Totman 1967, 164–165). See also Bolitho 1974, 123–124.

67. For an overview of the struggle to influence the imperial court see W. G. Beasley 1972, 133–136.

68. Ishin shiryō hensankai [1939–1941] 1983, 2:421–431; W. G. Beasley 1972, 134–135; Wilson 1970, 254–255.

69. Wilson 1970, 256–257; W. G. Beasley 1972, 136.

70. *STZ* 6:542; Inoue 1970, 1:56–58.

71. Kanbashi 1993, 217–220.

72. Pompe van Meerdervoort 1970, 71.

73. *DSZ* 1:70–72.

74. Saigō to Gesshō (1858/8/11) at *STZ* 1:119–126.

75. Saigō to Kusakabe Isōji and Ijichi Sadaka (1858/9/17) at *STZ* 1:126–131; Inoue 1970, 1:58; *STZ* 6:542.

76. *STZ* 6:307.

77. W. G. Beasley 1972, 136–139; Wilson 1970, 257–258.

78. Saigō to Kusakabe and Ijichi Sadaka (1858/9/17) at *STZ* 1:126–131, 6:307.

79. *STZ* 5:615–617; *STD* 2:134–137.

80. Shigeno, "Saigō nanshū itsuwa," 4:76–77; *STD* 2:137–138; Inoue 1970, 1:62. Gesshō's own account of his attempts to find refuge are at *STZ* 5:22–23.

81. Shigeno's memoir is Shigeno, "Saigō nanshū itsuwa," 4:70–114. Saigō mentioned meeting with Shigeno in a letter to Ōkubo and Saishō (1859/2/13) at *STZ* 1:142–144. For the standard account of Saigō and Gesshō's flight see Yates 1995, 37–39, or *DSZ* 3:183–198.

82. "Saigō nanshū itsuwa," 4:76–77. According to Katsuta, the domain explicitly declared that Gesshō was Saigō's responsibility, not Satsuma's. See *STD* 2:138–139. Sadowara domain was created in 1587 as a reward for Shimazu Iehisa, the youngest brother of Shimazu Yoshihisa, then head of the Shimazu house. Iehisa recognized Hideyoshi's authority before his elder brothers, and Hideyoshi confirmed his holdings as an independent investiture. See Haraguchi Izumi et al. 1999, 162.

83. "Saigō nanshū itsuwa," 4:77–79; *STD* 2:140–141; Inoue 1970, 1:63–65. Saigō's account of Toshihisa's demise was part of local legend, but it does not conform to the historical record. Hideyoshi ordered Toshihisa's death because he was implicated in a conspiracy to undermine Hideyoshi's invasion of Korea. See Haraguchi Izumi et al. 1999, 163, 167.

Chapter 3: "Bones in the Earth"

1. "Saigō nanshū itsuwa," 4:79. This account of Saigō's suicide attempt draws on Shigeno Yasutsugu's remarkable memoir. Hypothermia is my own diagnosis, based on discussions with physicians. The symptoms of delirium, hearing loss, and impaired mobility are all consistent with hypothermia rather than drowning. Indeed, it is likely that hypothermia "saved" Saigō: his metabolism slowed so severely than he did not die, or suffer brain damage, from oxygen deprivation.

2. STD 2:143–144; "Saigō nanshū itsuwa," 4:79–80. For an explicit link between Saigō's suicide attempt and his quest for a grand mission see Saigō to Nagaoka Kenmotsu (1858/12/19) at STZ 1:131–133 and Saigō to Ōkubo, Saisho, Kaeda, and Yoshii Tomozane (1860/2/28) at STZ 1:161–162.

3. STD 2:142–143.

4. STD 2:144–145; Saigō to Nagaoka Kenmotsu (1858/12/19) at STZ 1: 131–134.

5. For the climate and topography of Amami Ōshima see Kaitei Naze-shi shi hensan iinkai 1996, 1:43–58. The bananas are Musa basjoo, or "Japanese banana."

6. Saigō to Saisho and Ōkubo (1859/2/13) at STZ 1:144.

7. Smits 1999, 15–35; Naze-shi shi hensan iinkai 1963, 2:7–9.

8. Naze-shi shi hensan iinkai 1963, 2:13; Sakaguchi [1921] 1977, 231–232; Hellyer 2001, 35–42.

9. Kaitei Naze-shi shi hensan iinkai 1996, 3:50–54, 3:199–210; Döderlein 1880; Naze-shi shi hensan iinkai 1963, 2:10–11.

10. Saigō to Saisho and Ōkubo (1859/2/13) at STZ 1:141; Nobori [1927] 1977, 22–23; Yamashita Fumitake, personal communication. Examples of Amami tattoos can be found in Ehara 1973, 286.

11. Saigō to Saisho and Ōkubo (1859/2/13) at STZ 1:143.

12. Haraguchi Torao 1966, 103–104.

13. Haring 1952, 78.

14. Naze-shi shi hensan iinkai 1963, 2:9–18; Haraguchi Izumi et al. 1999, 215–217.

15. Saigō to Ōkubo, Saisho, Yoshii Tomozane, and Kaeda (1859/6/7) at STZ 1:150. Ketōjin literally means "hairy Tang people," but in the 1800s it could be used as an epithet for any foreigner. Saigō, however, never referred to Europeans or Americans as tōjin or ketōjin, so I have translated the term as "hairy Chinese" rather than "hairy foreigners." "Hairy" had connotations of disgust, and the term was pejorative.

16. Nobori [1927] 1977, 24; Inoue Kiyoshi 1970, 1:4–5. Much of this island lore is supported by Saigō's letters. In an 1859/4 letter to the island intendant (daikan), for example, he complained that he was gathering his own firewood, and his detailed request for cooking oil and spices suggests that he did his own cooking as well. In the same letter he complained that the islanders were treating him like a criminal and a freak, but noted that he had given away his candles. See Saigō to Yoshida Shichirō (1859/4/21) at STZ 1:147–148. I can find

no confirmation that Saigō practiced swordsmanship on Amami Ōshima, but this seems extremely likely, since it was one of his preferred forms of exercise. See, for example, Saigō to Shiibara Kunimoto (June 29, 1873) at *STZ* 3:363–364.

17. For a good sense of Saigō's regular communication with his friends in Kagoshima see Saigō to Ōkubo, Saisho, Yoshii, and Kaeda (1859/6/7) at *STZ* 1:150–152; Saigō to same (1860/2/28) at *STZ* 1:159–163; Saigō to same (1860/3/25) at *STZ* 6:577–579; and Ōkubo to Saigō (1859/12) at *STZ* 5:33–42.

18. Ōkubo to Saigō (1860/2/28) at *STZ* 5:23–28; Iwata 1964, 40–41.

19. Saigō to Ōkubo (1859/1/2) at *STZ* 1:135–141.

20. Ōkubo described these events to Saigō in an 1859/12 letter at *STZ* 5:33–42. Hisamitsu's letter is at *STZ* 5:43. The loyalists' response is at *Ōkubo Toshimichi monjo* 1:34–39. The roster is at *Ōkubo Toshimichi monjo* 1:32–34. See also Iwata 1964, 41–42, and *STZ* 5:42–44.

21. Ōkubo to Saigō (1859/12) at *STZ* 5:33–42, esp. 5:41–42.

22. Saigo to Ōkubo, Saisho, Yoshii, and Kaeda (1860/2/28) at *STZ* 1:159–164.

23. For Saigō's commemoration see Saigō to Ōkubo and Saisho (1861/3/4) at *STZ* 1:171–172.

24. As noted in the main text, it was not unusual that the shogunate initially refused to acknowledge Ii's death. Japanese governments commonly delayed official announcements until succession arrangements had been made; Satsuma, for example, did not publicly disclose Nariakira's death until the domain had resolved all aspects of his succession. The problem with Ii's death was that the shogunate's statements were so patently false: assassins had taken his head in broad daylight in the capital. See Alcock 1863, 1:304–308.

25. Beasley 1972, 173–175.

26. Saigō to Ōkubo and Ijichi Sadaka (1860/11/7) at *STZ* 1:164–166.

27. Saigō to Saisho and Ōkubo (1861/3/4) at *STZ* 1:171–173.

28. The standard account of Saigō in exile is Nobori [1927] 1977. For a discussion of this compilation of island oral history see the bibliographic essay.

29. These general observations about Saigō's character are informed by Iwayama and Iwayama 1999, 31–45, 49–55, 191–192. See also Saigō's letter to Shiibara Kunimoto (June 29, 1873) for Saigō's own description of how much he enjoyed playing with children (*STZ* 3:363–364). His initially cold relations with the islanders are described in Ryū 1968, 6–7.

30. Saigō to Yoshida Shichirō (1859/4/21) at *STZ* 1:147–150; Nobori [1927] 1977, 39.

31. Sakaguchi [1921] 1977, 231–232; Inoue Kiyoshi 1970, 1:81–82.

32. Kihara 1999, 113–119; Kihara 1996, 165–178; Nobori [1927] 1977, 41–42; Inoue Kiyoshi 1970, 1:79–80.

33. Saigō to Koba (c. 1862/7) at *STZ* 1:202–203, and to Tsuchimochi Masateru (1864/3/4) at 1:280–282.

34. *STZ* 6:343–344; Nobori [1927] 1977, 51–56. Saigō's longest and among his most personal letters is to Koba. See *STZ* 1:183–204.

35. Saigō to Toku (1863/3/21) at *STZ* 1:215–218, and to Toku (1869/3/20) at 3:25–26. The story of "Fujinaga Bridge" is at *STZ* 6:391. For the oral tradition see Nobori [1927] 1977.

36. Nobori [1927] 1977, 70–71; Ryū 1968, 8; Inoue 1970, 1:102–103.

37. Saigō to Saisho and Ōkubo (1861/3/4) at *STZ* 1:171–174.

38. Saigō to Toku (1862/6/30) at *STZ* 1:179.

39. Nobori [1927] 1977, 73. The official change-of-name request, dated 1862/2/15, is reproduced in *STZ* 4:467–468.

40. Yates 1995, 60. The petitions are in *STZ* 1:272–280, 4:330–331.

41. Yates 1995, 114; Saigō to Toku (1869/3/20) at *STZ* 3:25–26.

42. Beasley 1972, 178–182.

43. Beasley 1972, 180, 200–201.

44. *STD* 3:18–22.

45. Saigō to Koba (c. 1862/7) at *STZ* 1:183–186; *STZ* 6:544–545.

46. Saigō to Koba (c. 1862/7) at *STZ* 1:187–190; *STZ* 6:545.

47. Yates 1995, 50; Saigō to Koba (c. 1862/7) at *STZ* 1:188–190

48. Saigō to Koba (c. 1862/7) at *STZ* 1:189–190; *STZ* 6:545; Inoue 1970, 1:105; Iwata 1964, 53.

49. *STD* 3:32–34; Saigō to Koba (c. 1862/7) at *STZ* 1:191–192.

50. Saigō to Koba (c. 1862/7) at *STZ* 1:191–193; *STZ* 6:545.

51. The term "deadly ground" *(shichi)* can mean merely a place to die, but in this context it seems like a reference to Sunzi's (Sun Tzu's) famous treatise *The Art of War.* Sunzi defines nine types of situation or ground, including such types as "surrounded ground" and "open ground." For each type of battlefield there is a specific strategy. "Deadly ground" is a unique case where the only response is to show a resolve to die. Ironically, by facing death, a commander can save his forces: "Throw them into a lethal situation and they will survive; drop them onto deadly ground and they will live." See Sunzi 11:58. This passage from Sunzi survives in modern Japanese as an aphorism: *"Shichi ni otoshiire, shikaru nochi ni iku."*

52. Saigō to Koba (c. 1862/7) at *STZ* 1:191–197; *STZ* 6:545; *STD* 3:32–37; Iwata 1964, 57. Ijichi had come to agree with Nagai Uta, a prominent samurai from Chōshū. For Nagai's views see Huber 1981, 101–103, 239–240, and Beasley 1972, 177–178. For Hirano's views see Beasley 1972, 184–185.

53. *STD* 3:37–38; *OTN* 1:118. Ōkubo later claimed that Hisamitsu was about to order Saigō to commit suicide and that he managed to have had Saigō's sentence reduced to exile. See "Saigō nanshū itsuwa," 4:84–87.

54. The details of Saigō's trip from Yamakawa to Waniya are at *STZ* 1:179–180, 6:545–546. I have here related Saigō's understanding of the charges against him. See Saigō to Koba (c. 1862/7) at *STZ* 1:193–194.

55. Saigō to Koba (c. 1862/7) at *STZ* 1:199, 1:202–203; Saigō to Koba (1862/8/20) at 1:208.

56. Saigō to Koba (1862/8/20) at *STZ* 1:209. See also Saigō to Toku (1863/3/21) at *STZ* 1:215–218. For Saigō's faith in Katsura see also Saigō to Toku (1862/6/30) at *STZ* 1:179 and Saigō to Katsura Hisatake (1863/4/12) at

1:222–223. For Katsura and his mission see Kagoshima-ken shiryō kankōkai 1986, 1–4. For his gifts to Saigō's family see Katsura's diary in Kagoshima-ken shiryō kankōkai 1986, 13–14. For Aigana's visit to Tokunoshima see Katsura's diary at 28–29. For some related legends see Nobori [1927] 1977, 137–141.

57. "Saigō nanshū itsuwa," 4:89.

58. Mushakoji 1942, 115.

59. *STD* 3:54–55; *STZ* 6:402.

60. Saigō to Toku (1863/3/21) at *STZ* 1:216.

61. Saigō's *ikun* at Yamada Seisai 1939, 9.

62. Nobori [1927] 1977, 150–156.

63. Nobori [1927] 1977, 156–176; Yamada Shōji 1992b, 17.

64. Saigō to Toku (1863/3/21) at *STZ* 1:215; Saigō to Ryū Teiyōki (1863/6/2) at 1:225; *STD* 3:54–55.

65. "Senzai no haraisage gansho" in *STZ* 1:240–244. For Saigō's poem about Tsuchimochi's efforts see *SSTKS* 14–15 or *STZ* 4:89–90. For the attack on the four British subjects (the Namamugi incident) and the resulting battle see Hashimoto 1987; Beasley 1972, 183, 198–200. I also relied on an official British naval dispatch reprinted in Arikawa et al. 1964.

66. Saigō to Shiibara Kunimoto and Shiibara Gonbei (1864/1/20) at *STZ* 1:261. The poem is at *SSTKS* 16–17 and *STZ* 4:125–126.

67. "Shasō shui sho" at *STZ* 1:269–272. For more detail see Hiratsuka 1937. Tsuchimochi was technically mayor *(kochō)* of Wadomari and seventeen nearby villages.

68. See, for example, Saigō to Ryū Teiyōki (1863/6/2) at *STZ* 1:226.

69. Saigō to Toku (1863/3/21) at *STZ* 1:215–216.

70. Yamada Shōji 1987, 171–172.

71. Yamada Shōji 1987, 164, *STD* 3:60–61.

72. Saigō did not keep a comprehensive reading list, but his letters suggest he had access to a substantial library. In an 1864/1/15 letter to Misao Tankei, for example, Saigō asked to borrow a specific volume of Tang dynasty poetry from the *Wenxuan* (Japanese, *Bunsen*), a sixty-volume anthology. See *STZ* 1:259–260 and 6:427.

73. Saigō's development as a poet is discussed in "Saigō nanshū itsuwa," 4:107–108.

74. *SSTKS* 10–11 and *STZ* 4:103–104.

75. Saigō to Misao Tankei (1863/4/29) at *STZ* 1:224; *STZ* 6:427; Nobori [1927] 1977, 195–196. For a celebration of Saigō's impact on Okinoerabujima see Motobu 1996, esp. 67–106.

76. Misao Tankei's lecture notes at *STZ* 4:151–159. Saigō was commenting on the final sentence of Mencius 7A (Jin Xin):1. In Irene Bloom's translation the full section runs: "One who has fully developed his mind knows his nature. Knowing his nature, he knows Heaven. By preserving one's mind and nourishing one's nature one has the means to serve Heaven. When neither the brevity nor the length of a lifespan engenders doubts, and one cultivates one's person in an attitude of expectancy, one has the means to establish one's destiny" (de Bary and Bloom 1999, 155).

77. Saigō to Shiibara Kunimoto and Shiibara Gonbei (1864/1/20) at *STZ* 1: 260–262.

Chapter 4: "To Shoulder the Burdens of the Realm"

1. *STD* 4:88–89. This source gives the date of arrival as 2/24, but this conflicts with the dates in Saigō's letter to Tsuchimochi of 1864/3/4. See *STZ* 1:280–282 and 6:547.
2. *SSTKS* 59 and *STZ* 4:126–127.
3. Saigō to Tsuchimochi (1864/3/4) at *STZ* 1:280–281.
4. Ikai 1992, 14–15. Saigō described his amazement at this sudden promotion in letters to Toku (1864/3/21) and Tsuchimochi (1864/3/21). See *STZ* 2:33–40, esp. 2:33 and 2:37–38.
5. Saigō to unknown (c. 1864/4/10) at *STZ* 1:284.
6. W. G. Beasley 1972, 178–184; Aoyama 1996, 91–93; Totman 1980, 3–21.
7. For a good summary of these issues see Totman 1975, esp. 393–395. For Saigō's thoughts see Saigō to unknown (c. 1864/4/10) at *STZ* 1:284 and Saigō to Ōkubo (1868/2/2) at 2:406–407.
8. Wilson 1970, 254; Sasaki Suguru 1998, 101.
9. Craig 1961, 198.
10. Saigō referred to the radicals as *bōkaku*. See Saigō to Ōkubo (1864/9/16) at *STZ* 1:397.
11. The Tengu insurrection is also known as the Kantō insurrection, the Tsukuba war, and the Genji disturbance *(Genji no ran)*. The English-language sources on the Tengu rebellion are limited but excellent. For a focus on Mito see Koschmann 1987, esp. 152–176. For the shogunate's efforts to suppress the rebellion see Totman 1980, 108–120.
12. Walthall 1995, 152–154; Craig 1961, 196–197, 205.
13. For a summary of these events see Craig 1961, 167–207.
14. Craig 1961, 204–207; Sasaki Suguru 1998, 56–65.
15. Craig 1961, 211–213.
16. Ikai 1992, 14; Sasaki Suguru 1998, 69–73; Craig 1961, 216–223; W. G. Beasley 1972, 201–204; Totman 1980, 100–104. The Ōkubo quote is from Sasaki Suguru 1998, 70.
17. Saigō to Ōkubo (1864/5/12) at *STZ* 1:287–288; Saigō to Ōkubo (1864/6/2) at 1:296–297; Saigō to Ōkubo (1864/7/9) at 1:352.
18. Saigō to Ōkubo (1864/5/12) at *STZ* 1:290–291.
19. Saigō to unknown (c. 1864/4/10) at *STZ* 1:284–285.
20. Saigō to Ōkubo (1864/625) at *STZ* 1:332–333.
21. W. G. Beasley 1972, 194–196.
22. Saigō to unknown (c. 1864/4/10) at *STZ* 1:284–285.
23. Saigō included the poem in the aforementioned letter. See also *SSTKS* 18. For a discussion of Yan Zhenqing see McNair 1998.
24. Craig 1961, 223–230.
25. Saigō to Ōkubo (1864/6/27) at *STZ* 1:337–339. For a useful overview of the

political context of the Forbidden Gate incident see Haraguchi Kiyoshi 1996b, 49–54.

26. Craig 1961, 230–231; Totman 1980, 101. For Saigō's account of the battle see Saigō to Ōkubo (1864/7/20) at *STZ* 1:359–361.
27. Saigō to Ōkubo (1864/7/20) at *STZ* 1:361.
28. Saigō and Komatsu to Nakane Yukie and Sakai Jūnosuke (1864/7/28) at *STZ* 1:367–369.
29. Saigō to Ōkubo (1864/9/7) at *STZ* 1:382–385.
30. Totman 1980, 122–133; Sasaki Suguru 1998, 77–79.
31. Saigō to Ōkubo (1864/9/7) at *STZ* 1:382–383.
32. Matsuura 1968, 124–133; Steele 1981, 299–316, esp. 300; Totman 1980, 562, 564.
33. Saigō to Ōkubo (1864/9/16) at *STZ* 1:399; Katsu's recollections at *STZ* 6:88.
34. Saigō to Ōkubo (1864/9/16) at *STZ* 1:396–400; Sasaki Suguru 1998, 79–81.
35. *STZ* 1:399–400. *Kyōwa* also can mean "republican," but given Saigō's focus on the emperor as the source of state authority I have translated the term as "cooperative."
36. Saigō to Komatsu Tatewaki (1864/10/25) at *STZ* 1:434–438; Ikai 1992, 18; Totman 1980, 133–134; Yates 1995, 75.
37. Craig 1961, 246–247; Yates 1995, 76.
38. Saigō to Kitsukawa's aides Kagawa Ryō and Yamada Umon (1864/11/8) at *STZ* 1:438–440.
39. Yamada Umon to Saigō (1864/11/10) at *STZ* 5:72–73.
40. Saigō to Kiire Settsu (1864/11/15) at *STZ* 1:442–443; Craig 1961, 247–248.
41. Craig 1961, 248–249.
42. Jansen 1961, 202; Yates 1995, 77; Yamada Shōji 1992b, 24–25.
43. Saigō to Kiire Settsu (1864/12/14) at *STZ* 1:466–473; Saigō to Komatsu Tatewaki (1864/12/30) at *STZ* 1:469–472; Ikai 1992, 19–20; Aoyama 1996, 120–121; Craig 1961, 249. For the details of the negotiations over the five nobles see Aoyama 2000b, 64–71.
44. Craig 1961, 248–249.
45. Totman 1980, 138; Craig 1961, 249–251; field journal of Fukui forces at *STZ* 1:460–463; Saigō to Komatsu Tatewaki (1864/12/30) at *STZ* 1:469–472.
46. Yamada Shōji 1992b, 25–26.
47. Tamamuro Taijō 1960, 61. Satsuma was known for brewing wine *(shōchū)* from sweet potatoes. Even today, *shōchū* outsells sake in southwestern Japan.
48. See, for example, Saigō to Ōkubo (1864/10/8) at *STZ* 1:416.
49. *STZ* 6:345–346. There is no surviving correspondence between Saigō and Itō, and Saigō probably communicated with his family through Kawaguchi Seppō, who helped with Saigō family affairs in Kagoshima while Saigō was in Edo/Tokyo and Kyoto. Yamada Shōji 1987, 165–171.

Saigō's sole surviving reference to Ito is in a poem, where he described her as a good wife *(ryōsai)* who did not complain even when money was tight.

See *SSTKS* 44–45 or *STZ* 4:57. For some interesting anecdotes about Saigō and Ito see Kihara 1999, 115–116.

50. Okatani 1915, 25.
51. Katsu's recollections are in *STZ* 6:90–91.The meeting with Date Munenari, the daimyo of Uwajima, is from an 1867/3/3 diary entry by Nakaoka Shintarō and is noted in *STZ* 2:191–192. See also Inoue 1970, 2:12–13, for speculation about Saigō's mistress.
52. Aoyama 1986, 2. Aoyama notes critically that Kidō's comments were made years later.
53. Memorial by Saigō (c. 1865/3) at *STZ* 2:31–32; *OTN* 1:242 (1865/2/11).
54. Totman 1980, 136, 151–152, 168–171; Aoyama 1986, 3.
55. For the Chōshū civil war see Craig 1961, 251–301. For negotiations see Aoyama 1986, 5.
56. Saigō to Ōkubo (1865/6/11) at *STZ* 2:52–54.
57. Saigō to Ōkubo and Minoda Denbei (1865/8/23) at *STZ* 2:57.
58. Saigō to Ōkubo and Minoda Denbei (1865/8/28) at *STZ* 2:67–68.
59. Saigō to Ōkubo (1865/6/11) at *STZ* 2:52–54.
60. Jansen 1961, esp. 22, 78–79, 182–184, 195–204.
61. Totman 1980, 212–213; Fox 1969, 151–176. The Satsuma-British rapprochement is thoughtfully analyzed in Hashimoto 1987, 83–89. For Glover see Sugiyama 1984, 124–125, 130–131.
62. The *Union* purchase was so complicated that it was unclear who owned the ship. The official buyer was the Kaientai, or "Naval Auxiliary Force," a dummy corporation in Nagasaki run by Sakamoto with Satsuma protection and funds. Initially Satsuma, Chōshū, and Sakamoto all claimed ownership, but Satsuma eventually relinquished control to Chōshū. See Jansen 1961, 214–216; Totman 1980, 212–213; Craig 1961, 315–317; Fox 1969, 172–174, 330–333.
63. These meetings are discussed in Jansen 1961, 219–221, and Craig 1961, 317–319. I follow slightly a different interpretation based on Aoyama 1986, 1–11, and Aoyama 1996, 115–132. The pact was concluded in the utmost secrecy and, perhaps for this reason, Saigō's letters make no direct mention of the agreement.
64. Saigō to Ōkubo (1866/3/4) at *STZ* 2:130–131; Saigō to Ōkubo (1866/5/29) at 2:147–148; Aoyama 1986, 7–9.
65. Saigō to Ōkubo (1866/5/29) at *STZ* 2:143–151, 6:337; Aoyama 1986, 14–16.
66. Sasaki Suguru 1998, 92.
67. Totman 1980, 186–190, 201–203, 231; Aoyama 1996, 145.
68. Totman 1980, 186–190, 227–266; Craig 1961, 329–333; Aoyama 1996, 144–145.
69. Aoyama 1996, 146–147; Totman 1980, 256–257. Iemochi probably died of beriberi, a form of nervous degeneration due to vitamin B_1 deficiency. In severe cases, beriberi can lead to paralysis and heart failure. Beriberi was a disease of wealth and privilege: the vitamin B_1 deficiency resulted from a diet

high in polished white rice. For the details of Iemochi's death see Totman 1980, 516 n.52.
70. Aoyama 1996, 146–147; Totman 1980, 260–266; Sasaki Suguru 1998, 94–96.
71. Saigō to Ōkubo (1866/7/28) at *STZ* 2:174–176.
72. Haraguchi Izumi et al. 1999, 252–255; *STD* 3:63–76.
73. Inoue 1970, 1:193–194. For Yokoi's thought see Harootunian 1970, esp. 354–386. For Yokoi's writings in translation see Miyauchi 1968.
74. *STZ* 2:163–164; McMaster 1992, 153–155; Fox 1969, 179–182; Cortazzi 1994, 10–12.
75. Saigō to Iwashita Masahira (c. 1866/7) at *STZ* 2:157–161; Inoue 1970, 1:194–199.
76. Totman 1980, 269, 271–282; Aoyama 1996, 148. Ōkubo's letter to Saigō (1866/9/8) is at *STZ* 5:287–292.
77. Totman 1980, 276, 289–293; Aoyama 1996, 148–149; Sasaki Suguru 1998, 96; *OTN* (1866/10/27) 1:331.
78. *SSTKS* 19 and *STZ* 4:136–137.
79. Aoyama 1996, 149. *OTN* 1:331 gives Saigō's arrival as 10/26.
80. Saigō to Ōkubo (1866/11/11) at *STZ* 2:177 and Saigō to Ōkubo (1866/12/11) at *STZ* 2:184–185.
81. Saigō described his meeting with Satow in a letter to Komatsu on 1866/12/9. See *STZ* 2:179–183. Satow's account of the meeting is in his memoirs: Satow [1921] 1968, 181–184. There are some intriguing discrepancies between Saigō's letter and Satow's recollections. Satow notes that "Saigō, as I had all along suspected, turned out to be identical with the man introduced to me as Shimadzu Sachiū in November 1865, and he laughed heartily when I reminded him of his alias." See Satow [1921] 1968, 181. Saigō's letter makes no mention of a previous meeting. In Saigō's account, Satow actively prompts Satsuma to challenge the shogunate, but Satow's memoirs are more discreet. Satow's account, however, has a much more extensive discussion of the problem of Hyōgo. For another account of the meeting, based on Satow's diary and Parkes's correspondence, see McMaster 1992, 158–159.
82. Aoyama 1996, 151–152; Jansen 1961, 282; Sasaki Suguru 1998, 97. For an overly credulous summary of these conspiracy theories see Calman 1992, 90–92.
83. Aoyama 1996, 133–136, 139–140, 149–151; W. G. Beasley 1972, 201–202. For Satow's remarks to Saigō see Saigō to Ōkubo (1867/7/27) at *STZ* 2:234.
84. Saigō to Ōkubo (1867/2/30) at *STZ* 2:187–189 and excerpt from Nakaoka Shintarō's diary (1867/3/3) at *STZ* 2:190–192.
85. *STD* 5:113.
86. Aoyama 1996, 168–170; Totman 1980, 310.
87. Memorial to Hisamitsu (c. 1867/5/12) at *STZ* 2:205–206. Saigō wrote four memorials to Hisamitsu in 1867/5, detailing strategy for the daimyo conference. Saigō seems to have coauthored this one (*STZ* 2:203–206) with Ōkubo. For a memorial from Ōkubo see W. G. Beasley 1955, 312–313.

88. Memorial to Hisamitsu (c. 1877/5) at *STZ* 2:208–209.
89. Memorial to Hisamitsu (c. 1877/5) at *STZ* 2:201–202; Memorial to Hisamitsu (c. 1877/5) at 2:208–209. For Satsuma's interpretation of "leniency" toward Chōshū see also Totman 1980, 311–312.
90. W. G. Beasley 1972, 251–252. Many of the relevant treaties can be found in W. G. Beasley 1955, esp. 56–57, 79–83, 183–189, 208–211, 216–217, 304.
91. Saigō to Ōkubo (1867/5/23) at *STZ* 2:211–212; *OTN* (1867/5/18–5/24) 1:361–365; W. G. Beasley 1955, 314–319; Totman 1980, 310–312; Aoyama 1996, 154–162; Kawabata 1967, 324–329. The protest letter by the four lords is in *STZ* 2:213–214 and *OTN* 1:363–364. A subsequent letter, similar in tone, can be found in W. G. Beasley 1955, 319–320. For an overview of the entire conference see Jansen 1961, 286–291. *Zoku saimu kiji* suggest that Ōkubo anticipated how a vague promise of "leniency" for Chōshū would be a victory for Keiki. See *Zoku saimu kiji* 6:286–287. For a detailed description of the conference from Shungaku's perspective see *Zoku saimu kiji* 6:289–305.
92. Sasaki Suguru 1998, 99–101; Aoyama 1996, 162–164; Kawabata 1967, 324; Hirao 1961, 160–162. Yōdō's comments to Shungaku are in *Zoku saimu kiji* 6:241–243. Hirasawa's letter is reproduced in Aoyama 1998, 42–43.
93. Hackett 1971, 44–45. Yamagata and Shinagawa's account of the meeting is at *STZ* 2:224–226.
94. Aoyama 1996, 163–164; Jansen 1961, 293, 297–298; Miyaji 1991, 245–246. The pun is from the memoirs of Sasaki Takayuki: see *Kinnō hisshi* 2:403.
95. The text of the Satsuma–Tosa alliance can be found in *STZ* 2:219–222. My translation closely follows Jansen 1961, 299–301. For the Satsuma–Tosa meetings see *Kinnō hisshi* 2:418–422; Sasaki Suguru 1997, 2–5; Miyaji 1991, 244–246.
96. Saigō to Yamagata and Shinagawa (1867/7/7) at *STZ* 2:217–219.
97. *Kinnō hisshi* 2:403–422, esp. 2:418–422; Sasaki Suguru 1997, 11–16; Jansen 1961, 301–317.
98. Saigō to Katsura Hisatake (1867/8/4) at *STZ* 2:240–241, 246–248. See also Saigō's letter to Yui Inai and Sasaki Takayuki (1867/7/29) at *STZ* 2:237–238.
99. Hackett 1971, 45–46.
100. Aoyama 1998, 43–48; Sasaki Suguru 1997, 8–10. The most important account for these meetings is Kashiwamura's diary, reproduced at *STZ* 2:254–258. Saigō briefly mentioned the meeting in a letter to Ōkubo. See *STZ* 2:251–252.
101. Sasaki Suguru 1997, 12–16; Aoyama 1996, 183.
102. Sasaki Suguru 1997, 17–21, 24; Sasaki Suguru 1998, 103–105; Aoyama 1996, 183–184.
103. Saigō, Ōkubo, and Komatsu to Nakayama Tadayasu, Sanjō Saneai, and Nakamikado Tsuneyuki (1877/10/8) at *STZ* 2:277–278.
104. *STZ* 2:287–288.
105. Aoyama 1996, 185–187; Sasaki Suguru 1998, 105–109. Keiki's resignation can be found in *Tokugawa Yoshinobu kō den: shiryō hen* 3:183–184. Keiki

resigned the title of shogun on 10/24. See *Tokugawa Yoshinobu kō den: shiryō hen* 3:201–202.

106. Sasaki Suguru 1997, 15; Aoyama 1996, 184–189; Totman 1980, 386–388.
107. Ikai 1992, 25–26; Ochiai 1893, 79–80; Steele 1990, 131–132.
108. Sasaki Suguru 1997, 29; Aoyama 1996, 187.
109. Sasaki Suguru 1997, 27–28, 30; Sasaki Suguru 1998, 109–110.
110. Saigō, Ōkubo, and Iwashita Masahira to Iwakura (1867/12/8) at *STZ* 2:309–313.
111. Totman 1980, 398–399; Aoyama 1996, 190; Sasaki Suguru 1998, 112.
112. Sasaki Suguru 1998, 113–114; Totman 1980, 399–400; Aoyama 1996, 190–191; Inoue 1970, 2:50.
113. Aoyama 1996, 189–194; Totman 1980, 397–400, 406; Ikai 1992, 22.
114. Saigō to Minoda (1877/12/28) at *STZ* 2:327–332.
115. Totman 1980, 408–415; Aoyama 1996, 199.
116. Totman 1980, 416–417.
117. *STZ* 2:352–353; Totman 1980, 420–424.
118. Saigō to Ōkubo (1868/1/3) at *STZ* 2:347–349.
119. Saigō to Ōkubo (1868/1/3) at *STZ* 2:351.
120. *OTN* 1:422–423; Saigō to Ōkubo (1868/1/3) at *STZ* 2:355.

Chapter 5: "To Tear Asunder the Clouds"

1. Saigō to Katsura (1868/1/10) at *STZ* 2:366–367; Saigō to Kawaguchi (1868/1/10) at 2:370. For a careful consideration of troops numbers see Totman 1980, 418–424.
2. Totman 1980, 425–429, 435; Sasaki Suguru 1977, 26–27.
3. Totman 1980, 436–439; Sasaki Suguru 1977, 29–31.
4. Saigō to Ōkubo (1868/1/3) at *STZ* 2:355.
5. Saigō to Kawaguchi (1868/1/10) at *STZ* 2:370–371; Saigō to Kawaguchi (1868/1/16) at 2:381.
6. Saigō to Katsura (1868/1/10) at *STZ* 2:367; Saigō to Minoda (1868/1/16) at 2:373–374.
7. Saigō to Kawaguchi (1868/1/16) at *STZ* 3:381.
8. Saigō to Kawaguchi (1868/1/10) at *STZ* 2:370–371.
9. Saigō to Kawaguchi (1868/1/16) at *STZ* 2:380.
10. For some problems with daimyo councils see Ikai 1992, 22–28.
11. Sasaki Suguru 1977, 41–42; Ikai 1992, 30–32.
12. Saigō to Yoshii (1868/3/5) at *STZ* 2:419.
13. Saigō to Ōkubo (1868/2/2) at *STZ* 2:406–407.
14. Steele 1981, 301.
15. Steele 1981, 302–303; Katsu to Saigō (1868/3/5) at *STZ* 2:431–433.
16. Steele 1981, 304; Satow [1921] 1968, 365; Excerpts from Katsu's papers at *STZ* 2:436–440.
17. Saigō to Ōkubo (1868/4/5) at *STZ* 2:444, orders to shogunate at 2:449–450; Steele 1981, 304–305.

18. Sasaki Suguru 1977, 57; Steele 1981, 306–307.
19. Steele 1982; Steele 1981, 311–313; Sasaki Suguru 1977, 62–63. Saigō gave a detailed description of the battle in his 5/20 letter to Ōkubo and Yoshii. See *STZ* 2:492–498. The Sanjō quote is from *STZ* 2:500 and the quote from Etō in Ikai 1992, 41. On renaming the capital see Fujitani 1996, 44–46.
20. Sasaki Suguru 1977, 67–123, esp. 106–107; Hoshi 1995, 2–100, esp. 27–29; Bolitho 1979.
21. *STD* 6:149–155; Ikai Takaaki 1992, 44–45; Bolitho 1979, 265. For Saigō's belief that he should have predeceased Kichijirō see Saigō to Toku (1869/3/5) at *STZ* 3:26. For the admonition see Saigō to Yamashita Ryūemon (1868/8/25) at *STZ* 2:519.
22. *STD* 6:154–155.
23. There is a reconstruction of Saigō's country home in Hinatayama, built on a hillside facing east across the Amorigawa River, but locals insist that the original house was near the river and faced south, toward Sakurajima. The Saigō-don yu (Master Saigō Bathhouse) in Hinatayama claims to have been Saigō's favorite spa. Information about the curative powers of the waters is from the Japanese government certificate posted at the Saigō-don yu.
24. Haraguchi Izumi et al. 1999, 266–268; *KKS* 3:515–524.
25. For thoughtful examinations of *hanseki hōkan* see Katsuta Masaharu 2000, 48–64, and Umegaki 1988, 59–65, 100–104.
26. *KKS* 3:522–530; Shimazu Hisamitsu to Saigō (c. 1869/2) at *STZ* 5:435–436.
27. *STD* 7:2–11; *KKS* 3:524–529. For biographical background to Katsura and his relationship with Saigō see Kagoshima-ken shiryō kankōkai 1986, 1–10. Saigō described his own noninvolvement in reforms in a letter to Ōkubo dated 1870/5/7. See *STZ* 3:64–65. None of his letters from this period discuss the details of domain reform, although he did find time to go hunting.
28. *KKS* 3:531–618.
29. Haraguchi Izumi et al. 1999, 265–268; *KKS* 3:619–642, 670–704, 710–762.
30. Saigō to Katsura (1868/7/8) at *STZ* 3:40–45 and *DSZ* 2:451–457.
31. My thoughts on modern marriage are informed by Giddens 2000, 69–84.
32. Saigō to Ōkubo (1869/8/3) at *STZ* 3:75.
33. *SSTKS* 81; *STZ* 4:98. The editors of *STZ* argue that the poem commemorates the seventeenth anniversary of Gesshō's death, but I favor the dating of Yamada in *SSTKS*. See also *STD* 7:2–3.
34. See, for example, Saigō's 1870/7/23 letter to Yamauchi Jingorō, which is concerned primarily with hunting dogs. *STZ* 3:70–72. See also the observation by Ijichi Masaharu quoted in *STD* 7:3 and Yates 1995, 115.
35. Katsuta Masaharu 2000, 112–115, 133; Umegaki 1988, 66; *Diary of Kido Takayoshi* 1:415 (1870/10/1), 1:438 (1870/11/19), 1:440 (1870/11/25); *New York Times,* March 19, 1871 [1871/1/29].
36. *OTN* (1871/12/22) at 2:145; Ōkubo to Iwakura (1871/12/29) at *Ōkubo Toshimichi monjo* 4:159–160, 170–171; Iwata 1964, 141–142. For Saigō's opinions see *STZ* 3:78–87.

37. *OTN* 2:152–154, 163–164; *STD* 7:43–46; *Diary of Kido Takayoshi* 1:472 (1871/2/12), 1:473–474 (1871/2/15).
38. *New York Times,* May 14, 1871 (1871/3/25).
39. Sanjō Sanetomi to Ōkubo (1871/2/18) in *Ōkubo Toshimichi monjo* 4:211–212.
40. *SSTKS* 73 and *STZ* 4:28.
41. The importance of the 1871 reorganization of the imperial guard, known in Japanese as *sanpan kenpei,* is discussed in Umegaki 1988, 68–71, and Katsuta Masaharu 2000, 115–117, 131–135.
42. *Diary of Kido Takayoshi* 2:48. For the development of Kido and Ōkubo's thought on *haihan chiken* see Umegaki 1988, 65–74. In Japanese see Katsuta Masaharu 2000, 76–77, 140–158. For an overview of the movement toward the abolition of the domains see Beasley 1972, 335–346.
43. Saigō opinion paper at *STZ* 3:78–87. I follow Katsuta Masaharu's argument that Saigō's undated opinion paper was part of his discussions with Ōkubo in 1870/11 (Katsuta Masaharu 2000, 130). There are three copies of this text, one in the collected papers of Ōkuma Shigenobu, one in the papers of Iwakura Tomomi, and a third in the papers of Hayase Mikuma; the three versions relate different opinions on the future of the domains. In the Ōkuma and Iwakura versions Saigō argues that the prefectural system *(gunken)* will not last long, but the in the Hayase version he argues the opposite: that the domain system *(hōken)* will be short-lived. There is a lively historical debate over which version is most reliable, but I am struck by the consistencies in all three versions. In all cases Saigō opposed radical, rapid change, arguing that reform should be based on careful discussion and consensus. For a good discussion of the variant texts see *STZ* 3:87–90; Ikai 1992, 103–106; and Inoue 1970, 2:117–118.
44. *Diary of Kido Takayoshi* 2:55–56 (1871/6/27); Katsuta Masaharu 2000, 146–148.
45. Saigō to Katsura (1871/7/10) at *STZ* 3:108–110; Beasley 1972, 346–347; Satow [1921] 1968, 381.
46. Katsuta Masaharu 2000, 5–7; *Diary of Kido Takayoshi* 2:63–64. For the edict in English see McLaren [1914] 1979, 32; in Japanese see *Ōkubo Toshimichi monjo* 4:339. For Saigō's concern with secrecy see Saigō to Katsura (1871/11/3) at *STZ* 3:174.
47. Katsuta Masaharu 2000, 160–170, 187–188; Beasley 1972, 346–349; Umegaki 1988, 97–108.
48. Hübner 1874, 1:431–432. Hübner met with Saigō on September 6, 1871, or 1871/7/21.
49. Beasley 1972, 366–369; Mayo 1966; Mōri 1979, 4–35; opinion paper by Ōkubo and Inoue (1871/8) at *Ōkubo Toshimichi monjo* 4:361–363. Mōri has the most cynical reading of the mission and argues that Ōkubo usurped Ōkuma's plan.
50. The instructions to the embassy are from Beasley 1972, 367–368. The De Long quote is from Mayo 1966, 358.

51. For the pledge see *STZ* 3:179–186. For analysis see Mayo 1966, 360, and Beasley 1972, 371.
52. For Saigō's objections to the mission see *Diary of Kido Takayoshi* 2:91–92 (1871/9/19) and Mōri 1979, 15–16.
53. Saigō to Katsura (1871/11/3) at *STZ* 3:173–176.
54. Umegaki 1988, 164–168.
55. Mōri 1979, 41–45, 85–90; Mōri 1978, 182–183.
56. Ōkubo retained his title of finance minister, but in his absence, Inoue, the vice minister *(taifu),* was the ranking official.
57. Mōri 1979, 78–79; Umegaki 1988, 168–174; Shibusawa [1894] 1994, 144–147.
58. Mōri 1979, 66–69, 93–95; Umegaki 1988, 172–173; Hackett 1971, 54–67, 71.
59. Umegaki 1988, 169–170; Beasley 1972, 387; *Diary of Kido Takayoshi* 2:106 (1871/10/29), 2:164 (1872/5/8); Saigō to Ōkubo (1872/2/15) at *STZ* 3:228–229.
60. Saigō opinion paper at *STZ* 3:83–84.
61. Umegaki 1988, 166
62. Saigō to Katsura (1872/1/4) at *STZ* 3:203–211; Saigō to Katsura (1872/1/12) at 3:213–214; Saigō to Ōkubo (1872/2/15) at 3:229–233.
63. My account of Hisamitsu's grievances draws on his detailed memorial of June 1873 in *Shimazu Hisamitsu-kō jikki* 3:211–225. For another account of these grievances see Kunaichō rinji teishitsu henshūkyoku 1968–1977, 3:89–90.
64. Saigō to Shiibara Kunimoto (1871/12/11) at *STZ* 3:186–189.
65. Cortazzi 1985, 191.
66. Kunaichō rinji teishitsu henshūkyoku 1968–1977, 2:715. For the context of the imperial visit see Gluck 1985, 74–75.
67. *Shimazu Hisamitsu-kō jikki* 3:199–203, 211–225; Kunaichō rinji teishitsu henshūkyoku 1968–1977, 2:716–726; Saigō's diary at *STZ* 3:268–269; Saigō to Ōkubo (1872/8/12) at 3:294–295.
68. Saigō to Ōkubo (1872/8/12) at *STZ* 3:294–297.
69. Saigō to Shimazu Hisamitsu (1872/11) at *STZ* 3:318–324 and *STZ* 6:588–589.
70. *SSTKS* 149.
71. *Shimazu Hisamitsu-kō jikki* 3:206–207; Sanjō to Iwakura (January 6, 1873) at *Iwakura Tomomi kankei monjo* 5:209–210.
72. Mōri 1979, 76–79.
73. Eskildsen 2002; Kim 1980, 78–88, 171–180, 191–203; Mōri 1979, 80–81.
74. Kim 1980, 15–25, 88–169 passim; Mōri 1979, 81–83; Duus 1995, 29–37. The Korean court sent embassies to Edo until 1811, but thereafter all contact was through the Japanese legation in Pusan, administered by Tsushima. For the development of traditional Japanese-Korean relations see Toby 1984.
75. Mōri 1979, 23–28. For disappointment with the outcome of the mission see

also Nish 1998b. For the fiasco in Washington see Swale 1998, 19–24. The relevant sections from Kido's diary are 2:142–143 (1872/2/18), 2:167–168 (1872/4/17), 2:168–169 (1872/4/20), 2:180 (1872/5/21), 2:186–187 (1872/6/17).

76. Mōri 1978, 9; Nish 1998b, 188–190.

77. Umegaki 1988, 172–174; Huffman 1997, 68–69; Mōri 1978, 182–184.

78. Ikai 1992, 131–132; Iwata 1964, 162–163; Mōri 1978, 9–10; Mōri 1979, 90–93. In an August 15 letter to Murata Shinpachi and Ōyama Iwao, Ōkubo described himself as a powerless spectator (Ōkubo Toshimichi monjō 4:521–522). It is worth noting that this letter makes no mention of the Korea crisis (Mōri 1979, 136–143).

79. Shibusawa [1894] 1994, 145.

80. Mōri 1979, 95.

81. Saigō to Saigō Tsugumichi (April 20, 1873) at STZ 3:327; Saigō to Katsura (May 17, 1873) at STZ 3:343.

82. Saigō to Katsura (May 17, 1873) at STZ 3:344. Saigō mentions Hisamitsu's abuse in the opening of his letter to Terada Heinoshin on May, 4 1873 (STZ 3:337). For some of Hisamitsu's complaints see Kunaichō rinji teishitsu henshūkyoku 1968–1977, 3:89–90.

83. Kunaichō rinji teishitsu henshūkyoku 1968–1977, 3:57–58.

84. Saigō to Shiibara Kunimoto (June 29, 1873) at STZ 3:363–369 and DSZ 2:727–733.

85. Saigō to Shiibara Kunimoto (June 29, 1873) at STZ 3:366. The relevant passage is in Shushō genshiroku 56 (Yamada Seisai 1939, 50) and Genshi banroku 17 (Sagara Tōru, Mizoguchi Yūzō, and Fukunaga Mitsuji 1980, 110, 154). The phrase "taming the self" refers to Analects 12:1. This letter also recalls Saigō's description of Fujita Tōko (STZ 1:31–33).

86. Kim 1980, 177–178; Duus 1995, 37–38; Mayo 1972, 810–811; Ikai 1992, 124–125.

87. The canonical date of the first council meeting on Korea is June 12, and this is repeated in most English-language sources on the subject, including Duus 1995 and Mayo 1972. There is, however, no contemporaneous basis for this date and, as Mōri (1978, 3, 8) and Ikai (1992, 124) observe, the meeting probably occurred in late June or early July. My readings of Saigō's letters suggest that he was not thinking seriously about Korea until after June 29. For the content of the meeting see Mōri 1978, 3–5.

88. Mōri 1978, 5–7; Ikai 1992, 124–128; Sanjō Sanetomi to Saigō (September 1, 1873) at STZ 5:512–514.

89. For this approach in English see Conroy 1960, 17–77; Mayo 1972. The Japanese bibliography is enormous, but Tamamurō 1960 and Inoue 1970 are representative of this thesis. For a critical survey of the bibliographic essay on what is known in Japanese as "Seikanron" (the debate over subjugating Korea) see Mōri 1978, esp. 31–62.

90. Saigō to Itagaki (July 29, 1873) at STZ 3:371–373. Several of Saigō's letters to Itagaki are translated in Tsunoda, de Bary, and Keene 1958, 2:148–150.

91. Saigō to Itagaki (August 14, 1873) at *STZ* 3:383–384; Saigō to Itagaki (August 23, 1873) at 3:390–392.
92. Saigō to Itagaki (August 17, 1873) at 3:385–387. Saigō does not explicitly refer to Hisamitsu, but to the "old government" *(kyūseifu)*. Saigō implicitly declared his intention to die in a September 12 letter to Beppu Shinsuke (*STZ* 3:398–399).
93. "Chōsen haken shisetsu kettei shimatsu" by Saigō (October 17, 1873) at *STZ* 3:414–419.
94. Saigō to Sanjō Sanetomi (August 3, 1873) at *STZ* 3:377.
95. *SSTKS* 24–25; *STZ* 4:53–54.
96. For a brief account of Su Wu see Loewe 2000, 493–495.
97. The relevant passage is no. 16 in Saigō's transcription (Yamada Seisai 1939, 33) and no. 133 in the original *Genshiroku* (Sagara Tōru, Mizoguchi Yūzō, and Fukunaga Mitsuji 1980, 32, 227). The analogy of day/night and life/death is from Wang Yang-ming's "Instructions for Practical Living" (J. Denshūroku), part I, verse 126. For a translation see Chan 1963, 82–83.
98. Saigō to Shinohara Kunimoto (October 8, 1875) at *STZ* 3:479–483; Kim 1980, 226–255; Duus 1995, 43–49.
99. Ōkubo to Saigō (March 21, 1873) at *STZ* 5:508–511.
100. Ōkubo's statement can be found in *Ōkubo Toshimichi monjo* 5:53–64. There are alternative translations of this statement in Conroy 1960, 47–49, and Tsunoda, de Bary, and Keene 1958, 2:151–155. Sasaki Suguru, in his articulate defense of Ōkubo, concedes that Ōkubo was a callous and "cold-hearted, bureaucratic politician" who followed the exigencies of the moment. He argues, merely, that these qualities were essential for the formation of the Meiji state (Sasaki Suguru 1998, 217–220).
101. Diary of Sasaki Takayuki (October 24, 1873) at *Hogohiroi* 5:404–405.
102. Ikai 1992, 132–137; Kim 1980, 173–179; Mayo 1972, 805–811.
103. Saigō to Sanjō Sanetomi (October 11, 1873) at *STZ* 3:412–413.
104. Ikai 1992, 138–144; Mōri 1979, 176–205; Saigō's letter of resignation (October 23, 1873) at *STZ* 3:423–425.
105. Ikai 1992, 146–148; Mōri 1979, 205–207; Haraguchi Izumi et al. 1999, 272; *KKS* 3:864–866; *OTN* (October 28 and November 2, 1873) at 2:208–209; *Diary of Kido Takayoshi* 2:386–387 (October 28, 1873); *STZ* 3:424–425.
106. Saigō's *ikun* at Yamada Seisai 1939, 10–11.

Chapter 6: "The Burden of Death Is Light"

1. Vlastos 1989, 388–391, 402–414.
2. Iwayama and Iwayama, 1999, 56–57, 192.
3. Cortazzi 1985, 175.
4. Saigō to Ōyama Iwao (April 5, 1875) at *STZ* 3:470–471.
5. *KKS* 3:868–870. The name Shigakkō, literally "private school," probably stemmed from their relationship with the "public" *gojū* system.
6. *KKS* 3:869–873; *STZ* 3:47–475, 6:344. Saigō's thoughts on the founding of

the school are in an 1873 document at *STZ* 3:330–331. Although there is some doubt as to whether all sponsors gave their full merit stipends, Saigō, Ōyama, and Kirino did. For a fascinating example of Saigō's involvement in the Shōten gakkō see his undated letter to Shinohara where he promotes the inclusion of French-language lessons (*STZ* 3:462–463).

7. See Saigō's *ikun* at *STZ* 4:197–199, 201–202, 215.

8. *KKS* 3:873–874; Saigō to Ōyama Iwao (April 5, 1875) at *STZ* 3:470–471. Saigō discussed carpenters' wages in an April 26 letter to his younger brother Kohei (*STZ* 3:473). A letter to Ōyama Tsunayoshi dated January 17, 1875, seems to refer to clearing land for the Yoshino kaikonsha (*STZ* 3:468–470).

9. *SSTKS* 102, *STZ* 4:82. The *Ban Bao* is one of the six Zhou dynasty classics of military strategy. For a similarly celebratory poem see *SSTKS* 104–105, *STZ* 4:41–42.

10. *SSTKS* 211, *STZ* 4:139.

11. Saigō's *ikun*, *STZ* 4:213–214.

12. I have here quoted from a 1937 newspaper interview with Toku. She related the same story in slightly different fashion in 1952. Toku's recollection of the exact date of the trip is contradictory. She said that she was twenty-two, which by the traditional Japanese system of ages would mean the trip was in 1877. But she also recalled that the trip took place about two years before the outbreak of war, or early 1875. See Iwayama and Iwayama 1999, 191.

13. Haraguchi Izumi et al. 1999, 268, 275–277; *KKS* 3:729–762. For background on the land tax system and status distinctions see Yamamura 1986 and Jansen 1986.

14. Tamamuro 1966, 13–14, 16.

15. Murano 1985, 121–123.

16. Jansen 1986, 80–81; Beasley 1972, 388–389.

17. Haraguchi Izumi et al. 1999, 273.

18. *Diary of Kido Takayoshi* 3:382–383 (October 29, 1876), 3:385 (November 1, 1876); Vlastos 1989, 391–393; Buck 1959, 106–111.

19. Saigō to Katsura Hisatake (November 1876) at *STZ* 3:506–507.

20. *STZ* 3:513–520. These manuscripts are undated, but internal evidence suggests they were written in 1876.

21. Buck 1959, 115; Buck 1973, 429.

22. *KKS* 3:895–896; Buck 1959, 123–124. The Iso arsenal and shipyard were formerly Nariakira's *Shūseikan*.

23. *Diary of Kido Takayoshi* 3:489–491 (April 24, 1877). The Nakahara story is one of the murkiest aspects of Saigō's life, and the various confessions, testimonies, reports, and memoirs conflict not only on the grand questions of intent and motive but also on such basic details as the date of Nakahara's arrest. For a brief survey of the debate see *KKS* 3:897–924. In English see Buck 1973, 429–430, and Yates 1995, 165–166.

24. *KKS* 3:924–925.

25. Buck 1973, 431–432, 440; Buck 1959, 144n; *KKS* 3:926–929.

26. Sasaki Suguru 1991, esp. 3–4, 7–12, 18–19, 21–23.

27. Buck 1973, 438; Ideishi [1918] 1976, 26–27; Buck 1959, 162–163. The quote is from Ideishi.
28. Ideishi [1918] 1976, 43–44. See also the *nishikie* titled *Zokugun chōrō no zu.*
29. *Jūnen seinan senran no sai jinryoku seshi junnsashō yochō.* The incident is discussed in Mizuno 1978, 234, and Mizuno 2000, 73–76. For the Kumamoto rebellions in general see Mizuno 2000, 69–149, and Mizuno 1978, esp. 226–278.
30. Shindō 1982, 25–26; Vlastos 1989, 399–401; Tamamuro 1966, 138–140; Buck 1959, 175–176. Saigō specifically mentioned his use of the Kyōdōtai as spies in a March 12 letter to Ōyama Tsunayoshi (*STZ* 3:538).
31. Sasaki Suguru 1994b. For an example of Saigō being disparaged in the text and glorified in image see *Saigō Takamori senshi no zu.*
32. Buck 1973, 432–434; Saigō to Ōyama Tsunayoshi (March 2, 1877) at *STZ* 3:530–536.
33. Ideishi [1918] 1976, 49–61; Buck 1973, 435–446; Buck 1959, 163–169, 176–183; Ueki-chō 2001. My understanding of these battles was also informed by the exhibits at the Tabaruzaka shiryōkan and the museum at Kumamoto Castle.
34. Saigō to Ōyama Tsunyoshi (March 2, 1877) at *STZ* 3:530–531, and (March 12, 1877) at 3:537–540.
35. Saigō to Kiyama headquarters (April 23, 1877) at *STZ* 3:542–543, Saigō to Beppu (May 17, 1877) at *STZ* 6:590–592; Buck 1959, 185–191, 196–200. The question of when Saigō arrived in Hitoyoshi is discussed at *STZ* 3:544.
36. Nock 1948, 371–373; Buck 1959, 196–219.
37. Sasaki Suguru 1991, 3–4, 34–40; Kita 2001, 125, 142, 237–240.
38. *STZ* 3:546–548.
39. *Ryūkō boshi no chinsetsu.*
40. *Shūjin negai no ito.*
41. *Seinan Saigō boshi no zu.*
42. Buck 1959, 220–231. The text of this letter is in *KKS* 3:1001–1003. The full "text" of this letter appears in *Seinan kiden,* but I suspect that it was composed after the Battle of Shiroyama, since it first appeared in 1911.
43. See, for example, Kawaguchi [1878] 1988, 2:356–357.
44. See the various accounts in Kokuryūkai 1908–1911, 4:698–708.
45. Nock 1948, 372–375.
46. See, for example, *Kagoshima chintei: kubi jikken no zu, Seinan heiteiki,* and *Zokkai no shukyū jikken no zu.*
47. Kawasaki 1897, 1066–1067. To my eye this is a fairly explicit reference to the Azuma kagami account of the presentation of Yoshitusne's head.
48. Etō 1998a, 232–233; 1998b, 51–63. For a good overview of Etō see Olson 1992, 1–41.

Bibliography

Abbreviations

DSZ   Dai Saigō zenshū henshū iinkai, ed. 1923. *Dai Saigō zenshū*. 3 vols. Tokyo: Heibonsha.

KKKyS   Kagoshima-ken kyōiku iinkai, ed. [1961] 1985. *Kagoshima-ken kyōikushi*. Reprint, Tokyo: Maruyama gakugei tosho.

KKS   Kagoshima-ken, ed. [1939–1967] 1974. *Kagoshima-ken shi*. 7 vols. Reprint, Kagoshima: Kagoshima-ken.

KKSNKS   Kagoshima-ken rekishi shiryō sentā Reimeikan, ed. 1983. *Kagoshima-ken shiryō: Nariakira kō shiryō 4*. Kagoshima: Kagoshima-ken.

OTN   Nihon shiseki kyōka, ed. [1927] 1997. *Ōkubo Toshimichi nikki*. 2 vols. Reprint, Tokyo: Hokusensha.

SSTKS   Yamada Shōji, ed. 2000. *Shinpen Saigō Takamori kanshi shū*. Revised ed. Kagoshima: Saigō nanshū kenshōkai.

STD   Katsuta Magoya. [1894] 1976. *Saigō Takamori den*. 5 vols. Reprint, Tokyo: Shigensha.

STZ   Saigō Takamori zenshū henshū iinkai, ed. 1976–1980. *Saigō Takamori zenshū*. 6 vols. Tokyo: Yamato shobō.

Archival Sources

Jihen nisshi A compilation of Kumamoto government dispatches and records from 1877. Kumamoto kenritsu toshokan.

Jūnen seinan senran no sai jinryoku seshi junsashō yochō An 1877 compilation of Kumamoto constabulary reports. Kumamoto kenritsu toshokan.

Kagoshima chintei: kubi jikken no zu Nishikie print by Tsukioka Yonejuirō, printed November 5, 1873, copy in Kumamoto shiritsu hakubutsukan. Catalog 16–1. Cataloged in *Kumamoto hakubutsukan kanpō* 7 (1995):44.

Kagoshima nikki: Shiroyama kōgekisen zu Nishikie print by Yamazaki Tokusaburō, printed October 1877, copy in Kumamoto shiritsu hakubutsukan. Catalog 14-7. Cataloged in *Kumamoto hakubutsukan kanpō* 7 (1995):40.

Kagoshima seitō zenkinai Nishikie print by Andō Tokubei, printed November 2, 1877, copy in Kumamoto shiritsu hakubutsukan. Catalog 15-7. Cataloged in *Kumamoto hakubutsukan kanpō* 7 (1995):43.

Nanshū ō shoshō gochō Saigō's transcription of passages from the Lesser Learning. National Diet Library (Tokyo), Kensei shiryōshitsu, 242291. Available at the Kensei shiryōshitsu's Web site: http://www.ndl.go.jp/site_nippon/kenseie/

Nagoya Sagenta, *Nantō zatsuwa* Kagoshima Prefectural Library.

Rekidai uta   Anonymous poem describing the accomplishments of the Shimazu house, used in gōjū education. Kagoshima kenritsu toshokan, Kagoshima.

Ryūkō boshi no chinsetsu   Nishikie print by Haneda Tomijirō, printed August 10, 1877, copy in Kumamoto shiritsu hakubutsukan. Catalog 17-3. Cataloged in *Kumamoto hakubutsukan kanpō* 7 (1995):46–47.

Saigō boshi jiraku jinmin no guchi   Nishikie print by Hayase Tokunosuke, printed on October 3, 1877, copy in Kagoshima shiritsu bijutsukan.

Saigō nehanzō   Nishikie print by Nagashima Tatsugorō, printed October 5, 1877, copy in Kagoshima shiristu bijutsukan, Kagoshima.

Saigō shoshō seppuku no zu   Nishikie print by Shōgetsu Hosei and Hayakawa Tokunosuke, printed October 11, 1877, copy in Reimeikan, Kagoshima.

Saigō Takamori senshi no zu   Nishike print by Yōshūai Chikanobu, printed on October 6, 1877, copy in Reimeikan, Kagoshima.

Seinan chinbun   Nishikie print by Takeuchi Yoshihisa, no. 7 in a series by the same title, printed on August 23, 1877, copy in Kagoshima shiristu bijutsukan, Kagoshima.

Seinan heiteiki   Nishikie print by Yamazaki Tokubei, printed on November 30, 1877, copy in Reimeikan and Kumamoto shiritsu hakubutsukan. Catalog 16-2. Cataloged in *Kumamoto hakubutsukan kanpō* 7 (1995):44.

Seinan Saigō boshi no zu   Nishikie print by Tsukioka Yonejirō, printed on September 10, 1877, copy in Kagoshima shiristu bijutsukan, Kagoshima.

Shūjin negai no ito   Nishikie print by Haneda Tomijirō, printed September 3, 1877, copy in Kumamoto shiritsu hakubutsukan. Catalog 17-10. Cataloged in *Kumamoto hakubutsukan kanpō* 7 (1995):48.

Zokkai no shukyū jikken no zu   Nishikie print by Kobayashi Eisei, printed on October 11, 1877, copy in Kumamoto shiritsu hakubutsukan. Catalog 16-3. Cataloged in *Kumamoto hakubutsukan kanpō* 7 (1995):44.

Zokugun chōrō no zu   Nishikie print by Takeuchi Eikyū, printed April 30, 1877, copy in Reimeikan, Kagoshima.

Zokushō Saigō boshi no zu   Nishikie print by Takeuchi Eikyū, printed August 23, 1877, copy in Kagoshima shiristu bijutsukan, Kagoshima.

Selected Published Primary Sources

Diary of Kido Takayoshi   Kido Takayoshi. 1983. *The Diary of Kido Takayoshi*. Translated by Sidney DeVere Brown. 3 vols. Tokyo: University of Tokyo Press.

Hogohiroi   Sasaki Takayuki. 1970–1979. *Hogohiroi: Sasaki Takayuki nikki*. Edited by Tōkyō daigaku shiryō hensanjo. Tokyo: Tōkyō daigaku shuppankai.

Iwakura Tomomi kankei monjo   Nihon shiseki kyōkai, ed. 1931. *Iwakura Tomomi kankei monjo*. 8 vols. Tokyo: Tōkyō daigaku shuppankai.

Kinnō hisshi   Sasaki Takayuki, and Tsuda Shigemaro. [1915] 1980. *Kinnō hishi: Sasaki Rō kō sekijitsudan*. 2 vols. Reprint, Tokyo: Tōkyō daigaku shuppankai.

Ōkubo Toshimichi monjo   Nihon shiseki kyōkai, ed. [1928] 1968. *Ōkubo Toshimichi monjo*. 10 vols. Reprint, Tokyo: Tōkyō daigaku shuppankai.

"Saigō nanshū itsuwa"   Shigeno Yasutsugu. [1896–1897] 1989. "Saigō nanshū itsuwa." In *Zōtei Shigeno hakase shigaku ronbunshū,* edited by Ōkubo Toshiaki. 4 vols. 4:70–114. Tokyo: Meicho fukyūkai. Originally published in Meika dansō.

Shimazu Hisamitsu-kō jikki Nihon shiseki kyōkai. [1910] 2001. 3 vols. Tokyo: Tōkyō daigaku shuppankai.

"Teichu sōran ki" Ijiki Jirō, undated manuscript. Reprinted in *KKS* 3:889–1021.

Tokugawa Yoshinobu kō den: shiryō hen Nihon shiseki kyōka, ed. [1918] 1975. *Tokugawa Yoshinobu kō den: shiryō hen.* 3 vols. Reprint, Tokyo: Tōkyō daigaku shuppankai.

Zoku saimu kiji Nakane Yukie, Murata Ujihisa, and Sasaki Chihiro, eds. [1921] 1974. *Zoku Saimu kiji.* 6 vols. Reprint, Tokyo: Nihon shiseki kyōkai.

General Published Sources

Alcock, Rutherford. 1863. *The Capital of the Tycoon: A Narrative of a Three Years' Residence in Japan.* 2 vols. New York: Bradley.

Andō Hideo. 1976. *Hyōden Saigō Takamori.* Tokyo: Shirakawa shoin.

Andō Tamotsu. 1990. "Gōchū kyōiku no seiritsu katei (jō)." *Kagoshima daigaku kyōiku gakubu kenkyū kiyō: jinbun shakai kagaku hen* 42:199–213.

———. 1991. "Gōchū kyōiku no seiritsu katei (ge)." *Kagoshima daigaku kyōiku gakubu kenkyū kiyō: jinbun shakai kagaku hen* 43:23–49.

———. 1992. "Gōchū kyōiku no kansei (jō)." *Kagoshima daigaku kyōiku gakubu kenkyū kiyō: jinbun shakai kagaku hen* 44:1–17.

———. 1993. "Gōchū kyōiku no kansei (chū)." *Kagoshima daigaku kyōiku gakubu kenkyū kiyō: jinbun shakai kagaku hen* 45:51–67.

———. 1999. "Bakumatsu ishin-ki Satsuma-han no gojū kyōiku." *Nihon rekishi* 613:1–18.

Aoyama Tadamasa. 1986. "Satchō meiyaku no seiritsu to sono haikei." *Rekishigaku kenkyū* 557:1–27.

———. 1996. *Bakumatsu ishin: honryū no jidai.* Tokyo: Bun'eidō.

———. 1998. "Chōshū to Satsuma: Keiō san nen kōhan no seikyoku." *Bukkyō daigaku sōgō kenkyūjo kiyō* 5:39–57.

———. 2000a. "Kindai nitchō ni okeru 'Chōsenkan' to 'Nihonkan.'" *Bukkyō daigaku sōgō kenkyūjo kiyō.* March 2000 special supplement:207–216.

———. 2000b. *Meiji ishin to kokka keisei.* Tokyo: Yoshikawa kōbunkan.

Arikawa Shōji, Kadota Akira, Uemura Kazunari, Kodama Keisuke, and Matsuda Shūmei. 1964. "The Bombardment of Kagoshima." *Kagoshima kenritsu tanki daigaku kenkyū nenpō* 2:117–162.

Asahi Shinbunsha. 1981. *Nedan no Meiji Taishō Shōwa fūzokushi.* Tōkyō: Asahi Shinbunsha.

Baba Rokurō. 1893. *Sō Gesshō den: ishin chūseki.* Edited by Fukuchi Gen'ichirō. Tokyo: Kōmeisha.

Beasley, W. G. 1955. *Select Documents on Japanese Foreign Policy, 1853–1868.* London: Oxford University Press.

———. 1967. "Politics and the Samurai Class Structure in Satsuma, 1858–1868." *Modern Asian Studies* 1 (1):47–57.

————. 1972. *The Meiji Restoration.* Stanford, Calif.: Stanford University Press.

Berton, Peter, and Paul F. Langer. 1981. "Nobori Shomu: A Pioneer in Russo-Japanese Cultural Relations." In *The Russian Impact on Japan: Literature and Social Thought,* edited by Peter Berton, Paul F. Langer, and George O. Totten, 13–19. Los Angeles: University of Southern California Press.

Bolitho, Harold. 1974. *Treasures among Men: The Fudai Daimyo in Tokugawa Japan.* New Haven, Conn.: Yale University Press.

————. 1977. "Aizu, 1853–1868." *Proceedings of the British Association for Japanese Studies* 2:1–17.

————. 1979. "The Echigo War, 1868." *Monumenta Nipponica* 34 (4):259–277.

————. 1989. "The Tempō Crisis." In *The Cambridge History of Japan,* 6 vols. Vol. 5, *The Nineteenth Century,* edited by Marius B. Jansen, 117–167. Cambridge, Eng.: Cambridge University Press.

————. 1991. *The Han.* In *The Cambridge History of Japan,* 6 vols. Vol. 4, *Early Modern Japan,* edited by John Whitney Hall, 183–234. Cambridge, Eng.: Cambridge University Press.

Borgen, Robert. 1986. *Sugawara no Michizane and the Early Heian Court.* Cambridge, Mass.: Harvard University Press.

————. 1995. "Oe no Masafusa and the Spirit of Michizane." *Monumenta Nipponica* 50 (3):357–384.

Buck, James H. 1959. The Satsuma Rebellion of 1877: An Inquiry into Some of Its Military and Political Aspects. Ph.D. diss., American University.

————. 1960. "Japan's Last Civil War: The Satsuma Rebellion of 1877." *Military Review* 40 (6):22–29.

————. 1973. "The Satsuma Rebellion of 1877: From Kagoshima through the Siege of Kumamoto Castle." *Monumenta Nipponica* 28 (4):427–446.

Calman, Donald. 1992. *The Nature and Origins of Japanese Imperialism.* London: Routledge.

Caron, François, and Joost Schouten. [1663] 1935. *A True Description of the Mighty Kingdoms of Japan & Siam.* Translated by Roger Manley. Edited by C. R. Boxer. London: Argonaut Press.

Chan, Wing-tsit. 1963. *Instructions for Practical Living and Other Neo-Confucian Writings by Wang Yang-ming.* New York: Columbia University Press.

Chang, Richard T. 1970. *From Prejudice to Tolerance: A Study of the Japanese Image of the West, 1826–1864.* Tokyo: Sophia University.

Childs, Margaret H. 1980. "Chigo Monogatari: Love Stories or Buddhist Sermons?" *Monumenta Nipponica* 35 (2):127–151.

Ching, Julia. 1976. *To Acquire Wisdom: The Way of Wang Yang-ming.* New York: Columbia University Press.

Chu Hsi, and Daniel K. Gardner. 1990. *Learning to Be a Sage: Selections from the Conversations of Master Chu, Arranged Topically.* Berkeley: University of California Press.

Conroy, Hilary. 1960. *The Japanese Seizure of Korea, 1868–1910: A Study of Realism and Idealism in International Relations.* Philadelphia: University of Pennsylvania Press.

Cortazzi, Hugh. 1985. *Dr. Willis in Japan, 1862–1877: British Medical Pioneer.* London: Athlone Press.

———. 1994. "Sir Harry Parkes, 1828–1885." In *Britain and Japan: Biographical Portraits,* edited by Ian Nish, 1–19. Richmond, Surrey, Eng.: Curzon Press.

Cortazzi, Hugh, and Gordon Daniels. 1991. *Britain and Japan 1859–1991: Themes and Personalities.* London: Routledge.

Craig, Albert M. 1961. *Chōshū in the Meiji Restoration.* Cambridge, Mass.: Harvard University Press.

Craig, Albert M., and Donald H. Shively, eds. 1970. *Personality in Japanese History.* Berkeley: University of California Press.

Crawcour, Sydney. 1964. "Notes on Shipping and Trade in Japan and the Ryukyus." *Journal of Asian Studies* 23 (3):377–381.

Cua, A. S. 1982. *The Unity of Knowledge and Action: A Study in Wang Yang-ming's Moral Psychology.* Honolulu: University Press of Hawaii.

Daniels, Gordon. 1996. *Sir Harry Parkes: British Representative in Japan, 1865–83.* Richmond, Surrey, Eng.: Curzon Press.

de Bary, William Theodore, and Irene Bloom, eds. 1999. *Sources of Chinese Tradition.* Vol. 1, 2nd ed. New York: Columbia University Press.

de Bary, William Theodore, Wing-Tsit Chan, and Burton Watson, eds. 1960. *Sources of Chinese Tradition.* Vol. 1. New York: Columbia University Press.

Döderlein, Ludwig Heinrich Philipp. 1880. "Die Liu-Kiu-Insel Amami Oshima." *Mittheilungen der Deutschen Gesellschaft für Natur-und Völkerkunde Ostasiens.*

Duus, Peter. 1995. *The Abacus and the Sword: The Japanese Penetration of Korea, 1895–1910.* Berkeley: University of California Press.

———. 1998. *Modern Japan,* 2nd ed. Boston: Houghton Mifflin.

Earl, David Magarey. 1964. *Emperor and Nation in Japan: Political Thinkers of the Tokugawa Period.* Seattle: University of Washington Press.

Edström, Bert. 1997. *The Iwakura Mission in Sweden.* Stockholm: Center for Pacific Asia Studies, Stockholm University.

Ehara Yoshimori. 1973. *Amami seikatsushi.* Tokyo: Mokujisha.

Ericson, Marc D. 1979. "The Bakufu Looks Abroad: The 1865 Mission to France." *Monumenta Nipponica* 34 (4):383–407.

Ericson, Steven J. 1996. *The Sound of the Whistle: Railroads and the State in Meiji Japan.* Cambridge, Mass.: Harvard University Press.

Eskildsen, Robert. 2002. "Of Civilization and Savages: The Mimetic Imperialism of Japan's 1874 Expedition to Taiwan." *American Historical Review* 107 (2):388–418.

Etō, Jun. 1983. "Opening the Nation Again." *Journal of Japanese Trade and Industry* 2 (3):57–58.

———. 1998a. *Nanshū zan'ei.* Tokyo: Bungei shunjū.

———. 1998b. *Nanshū zuisō sono ta.* Tokyo: Bungei shunjū.

Fox, Grace Estelle. 1969. *Britain and Japan, 1858–1883.* Oxford: Clarendon Press.

Fujioka Nobukatsu and Jiyū shugi shikan kenkyūkai. 1999. *Kyōkasho ga oshienai rekishi: Meiji shōwa shoki nihon no igyō.* Tokyo: Sankei shinbun nyūsu sābisu.

Fujitani, Takashi. 1996. *Splendid Monarchy: Power and Pageantry in Modern Japan.* Berkeley: University of California Press.

Fukuzawa Yukichi. 1959. *Fukuzawa Yukichi zenshū.* 22 vols. Tokyo: Iwanami shoten.

Furukawa, Tesshi. 1967. "Saigo Takamori." *Philosophical Studies of Japan* 8:1–17.

Giddens, Anthony. 2000. *Runaway World: How Globalization Is Reshaping Our Lives.* New York: Routledge.

Gluck, Carol. 1985. *Japan's Modern Myths.* Princeton, N.J.: Princeton University Press.

Goble, Andrew Edmund. 1996. *Kenmu: Go-Daigo's Revolution.* Cambridge, Mass.: Harvard University Press.

Gotō Kazuo, and Matsumoto Itsuya. 1987. *Shashinshū yomigaeru bakumatsu: Raiden daigaku shashin korekushon yori.* Tokyo: Asahi Shinbunsha.

Gotō Yasushi. 1967. *Shizoku hanran no kenkyū.* Tokyo: Aoki shoten.

Hackett, Roger F. 1971. *Yamagata Aritomo.* Cambridge, Mass.: Harvard University Press.

Haga Noboru. 1968. *Saigō Takamori.* Tokyo: Yūzankaku.

Hall, Ivan Parker. 1973. *Mori Arinori.* Cambridge: Harvard University Press.

Harada Nobuo. 1989. *Edo no ryōrishi: Ryōribon to ryōri bunka.* Tokyo: Chūō kōron-sha.

Haraguchi Izumi. 1990. "Meiji ishin o sasaeta otokotachi." *Kyōiku tsūshin* 27 (9):1–3.

Haraguchi Izumi, Nagayama Shūichi, Hinokuma Masamori, Matsuo Chitoshi, and Minamura Takeichi. 1999. *Kagoshima-ken no rekishi.* Tokyo: Yamakawa shuppansha.

Haraguchi Kiyoshi. 1968. *Nihon kindai kokka no keisei.* Tokyo: Iwanami shoten.

———. 1996a. "Kinmon no hen no ichi kōsatsu 1." *Meijō shōgaku* 46 (2):1–60.

———. 1996b. "Kinmon no hen no ichi kōsatsu 2." *Meijō shōgaku* 46 (3):1–54.

Haraguchi Torao. 1966. *Bakumatsu no Satsuma: Higeki no kaikakusha, Zusho Shōzae-mon.* Tokyo: Chūkō shinsho.

———. 1973. *Kagoshima-ken no rekishi.* Tokyo: Yamakawa shuppansha.

———. 1980. *Kagoshima-ken nōji chōsa.* Tokyo: Gannandō shoten.

Haraguchi Torao, Robert K. Sakai, Mitsugu Sakihara, Kazuko Yamada, and Masato Matsui, eds. 1975. *The Status System and Social Organization of Satsuma: A Translation of the Shūmon tefuda aratame jōmoku.* Honolulu: University Press of Hawaii.

Haring, Douglas G. 1952. *The Island of Amami Ōshima in the Northern Ryūkyūs.* Washington, D.C.: Pacific Science Board National Research Council.

Harootunian, Harry D. 1966. "Jinsei, Jinzai, and Jitsugaku: Social Values and Leadership in Late Tokugawa Thought." In *Modern Japanese Leadership,* edited by Bernard S. Silberman and H. D. Harootunian. Tuscon, Ariz.: University of Arizona Press.

———. 1970. *Toward Restoration: The Growth of Political Consciousness in Tokugawa Japan.* Berkeley: University of California Press.

Hasanuma Keisuke. 1989. "Shizoku kakumei, aruiha kindai Nihon ni okeru shimin kakumei ni tsuite (1)." *Kobe hōgaku zasshi* 39 (2):269–297.

Hashimoto, Mitsuru. 1987. "Collision at Namamugi." Translated by Betsey Scheiner. *Representations* 18 (Spring):69–89.

Hasunuma Keisuke. 1989. "Shimin kakumei, aruiwa kindai Nihon ni okeru shimin kakumei ni tsuite." *Kobe hōgaku zasshi* 39 (2):269–297.

Hatanaka Akira. 1992. "Kagoshima jō ni tsuite." *Reimeikan chōsa knekyū hōkoku* 6:65–97.

Heine, Wilhelm. [1856] 1990. *With Perry to Japan: A Memoir.* Translated by Frédéric Trautmann. Honolulu: University of Hawaii Press.

Hellyer, Robert Ingels. 2001. "A Tale of Two Domains: Satsuma, Tsushima, and the System of Foreign Relations in Late Edo Period Japan." Stanford, Calif.: Department of History, Stanford University.

Hicks, Nigel. 1993. "Into the Live Lava Lab." *Geographical: The Monthly Magazine of the Royal Geographical Society* 65 (10):37–41.

Hill, George William. 1908. "Biographical Memoir of Asaph Hall." In *National Academy of Sciences: Biographical Memoirs* 6:241–309. Washington, D.C.: National Academy of Science.

Hirao Michio. 1961. *Yamauchi Yōdō.* Tokyo: Yoshikawa kōbunkan.

Hiratsuka Michio. 1937. *Okinoerabujima shasō no enkaku.* Kagoshima: Kagoshima-ken shakai jigyō kyōkai.

Howell, David Luke. 1995. *Capitalism from Within: Economy, Society, and the State in a Japanese Fishery.* Berkeley: University of California Press.

Hoshi Ryūichi. 1995. *Ōuetsu reppan dōmei.* Tokyo: Chūō kōronsha.

Huber, Thomas M. 1981. *The Revolutionary Origins of Modern Japan.* Stanford, Calif.: Stanford University Press.

———. 1982. "Men of High Purpose." In *Conflict in Modern Japanese History: The Neglected Tradition,* edited by Tetsuo Najita and J. Victor Koschmann, 107–27. Princeton, N.J.: Princeton University Press.

Hübner, Joseph Alexander. 1874. *A Ramble Round the World, 1871.* Translated by Mary Elizabeth Herbert. 2 vols. London: Macmillan.

Huffman, James L. 1997. *Creating a Public: People and Press in Meiji Japan.* Honolulu, Hawaii: University of Hawaii Press.

Hurst, G. Cameron. 1998. *Armed Martial Arts of Japan: Swordsmanship and Archery.* New Haven, Conn.: Yale University Press.

Ideishi, Takehiko. [1918] 1976. *The True Story of the Siege of Kumamoto Castle: Kumamoto rōjō no jikkyō.* Translated by James H. Buck. New York: Vantage Press.

Ihara Saikaku. 1972. *Five Women Who Loved Love.* Translated by Wm. Theodore de Bary, Rutland, Vt.: C. E. Tuttle Co.

Ikai Takaaki. 1992. *Saigō Takamori: Seinan sensō e no michi.* Tokyo: Iwanami shoten.

Ike, Nobutake. 1943. "Triumph of the Peace Party in Japan in 1873." *The Far Eastern Quarterly* 2 (3):286–295.

Ikegami, Eiko. 1995. *The Taming of the Samurai.* Cambridge, Mass.: Harvard University Press.

Imura Ryūsuke. 1998. "Shiryō kara mita Sakurajima kazan An'ei funka no suii." *Kazan* 43 (5):373–383.

Inoue Kiyoshi. 1953. *Nihon no gunkoku shugi.* Tokyo: Tōkyō daigaku shuppankai.

———. 1970. *Saigō Takamori.* 2 vols. Tokyo: Chūkō shinsho.

Ishii Kanji. 1989. *Kaikoku to ishin.* Vol. 12. Tokyo: Shōgakkan.

Ishin shiryō hensankai. [1939–1941] 1983. *Ishin shi.* 6 vols. Tokyo: Yoshikawa kōbunkan.

Ivanhoe, P. J. 1990. *Ethics in the Confucian Tradition.* Atlanta: Scholars Press.

Iwata, Masakazu. 1964. *Ōkubo Toshimichi: The Bismarck of Japan.* Berkeley: University of California Press.

Iwayama Seiko, and Iwayama Kazuko, eds. 1999. *Saigō san o kataru: Gishi Iwayama Toku no kaisō,* expanded ed. Tokyo: Perikan sha.

Jansen, Marius B. 1961. *Sakamoto Ryōma and the Meiji Restoration.* Princeton, N.J.: Princeton University Press.

———. 1986. "The Ruling Class." In *Japan in Transition: From Tokugawa to Meiji,* edited by Marius B. Jansen and Gilbert Rozman. Princeton, N.J.: Princeton University Press.

———. ed. 1989. *Cambridge History of Japan.* Vol. 5, *The Nineteenth Century.* Cambridge, Eng.: Cambridge University Press.

Jansen, Marius B., and Gilbert Rozman, eds. 1988. *Japan in Transition: From Tokugawa to Meiji.* Princeton, N.J.: Princeton University Press.

Kagoshima kyōiku iinkai, ed. 1983. *Kagoshima (Tsurumaru) jō honmaru ato, Kagoshima-ken maizō bunkazai hakkutsu chōsa hōkokusho 26.* Kagoshima: Kagoshima kyōiku iinkai.

Kagoshima-ken, ed. [1939–1967] 1974. *Kagoshima-ken shi.* 7 vols. Reprint, Kagoshima: Kagoshima-ken.

Kagoshima-ken ishin shiryō hensanjo, ed. 1975–1980. *Kagoshima-ken shiryō: Seinan sensō.* 3 vols. Kagoshima: Kagoshima-ken.

Kagoshima-ken kyōiku iinkai, ed. [1961] 1985. *Kagoshima-ken kyōikushi.* Reprint, Tokyo: Maruyama gakugei tosho.

Kagoshima-ken rekishi shiryō sentā Reimeikan. 1996. *Reimeikan jōsetsu tenshi zuroku.* Kagoshima: Kagoshima-ken rekishi shiryō sentā Reimeikan.

———, ed. 1983. *Kagoshima-ken shiryō: Nariakira kō shiryō 4.* Kagoshima: Kagoshima-ken.

Kagoshima-ken shiryō kankōkai, ed. 1986. *Katsura Hisatake nikki.* Kagoshima: Kagoshima-ken shiryō kankōkai.

Kagoshima-shi shi hensan iinkai. 1969–1971. *Kagoshima-shi shi.* 3 vols. Kagoshima: Kagoshima-shi.

Kaitei Naze-shi shi hensan iinkai, ed. 1996. *Kaitei Naze-shi shi.* 3 vols. Naze-shi: Naze shiyakusho.

Kanbashi Norimasa. 1980. *Shimazu Shigehide.* Tokyo: Yoshikawa kōbunkan.

———. 1985. Saigōshi: keizu. In *Saigō Takamori no subete,* edited by Godai Natsuo, 289–299. Tokyo: Shinjinbutsu ōraisha.

———. 1992. "Saigō Takamori to Hashimoto Sanai." *Keiten aijin* (10):57–88.

———. 1993. *Shimazu Nariakira.* Tokyo: Yoshikawa kōbunkan.

———. 1994. "Saigō to Gesshō." *Keiten aijin* (12):52–73.

———. 1995. "Saigō no takumi na taiei gaikō." *Keiten aijin* (13):53–75.

———. 1996. "Saigō no takumi na taiei gaikō (sono ni)." *Keiten aijin* (14):69–88.

———. 1998. "Saigō Takamori to Satchō dōmei." *Keiten aijin* (16):57–95.

————. 1999. "Satchō meiyaku teiketsugo no Satsuma han." *Keiten aijin* (17):7–26.

Kassel, Marleen. 1996. *Tokugawa Confucian Education: The Kangien Academy of Hirose Tansō (1782–1856)*. Albany, N.Y.: State University of New York Press.

Katsuta Magoya. [1894] 1976. *Saigō Takamori den*. 5 vols. Reprint, Tokyo: Shigensha.

Katsuta Masaharu. 2000. *Haihan chiken*. Tokyo: Kōdansha.

Kawabata Taihei. 1967. *Matsudaira Shungaku*. Tokyo: Yoshikawa kōbunkan.

Kawaguchi Taeksada. [1878] 1988. *Jūsei nikki*. 2 vols. Reprint, Kumamoto: Seichōsha.

Kawahara Hiroshi. 1971. *Saigō densetsu*. Tokyo: Kōdansha.

Kawasaki Saburō. 1897. *Saigō nanshū*. Tokyo: Shun'yōdō.

Kido Takayoshi. 1983. *The Diary of Kido Takayoshi*. Translated by Sidney DeVere Brown. 3 vols. Tokyo: University of Tokyo Press.

Kihara Saburō. 1977. *Aiganaki*. Tatsugō, Kagoshima: Amami gun, Tatsugō chō.

————. 1996. "Saigō Takamori no shimazuma Aigana no keifu." *Keiten aijin* (14):165–178.

————. 1999. "Saigō Takamori no sannin no tsuma." *Keiten aijin* (17):111–122.

Kim, Key-Hiuk. 1980. *The Last Phase of the East Asian World Order: Korea, Japan, and the Chinese Empire, 1860–1882*. Berkeley: University of California Press.

Kita Heishirō. 2001. *Seisei jūgun nisshi*. Edited by Sasaki Suguru. Tokyo: Kōdansha.

Kodama Kōta. 1995. *Nihonshi nenpyō chizu*. Tokyo: Yoshikawa kōbunkan.

Kokuryūkai, ed. 1908–1911. *Seinan kiden*. 3 vols. Tokyo: Kokuryūkai honbun.

Kosaka Jirō, and Esaka Akira. 2001. "'Kono hito no tame nara' to 'omowaseru miryoku.'" *Rekishi kaidō* (November): 18–25.

Koschmann, J. Victor. 1987. *The Mito Ideology: Discourse, Reform, and Insurrection in Late Tokugawa Japan, 1790–1864*. Berkeley: University of California Press.

Kunaichō rinji teishitsu henshūkyoku. 1968–1977. *Meiji tennō ki*. 13 vols. Tokyo: Yoshikawa kōbunkan.

LaCapra, Dominick. 1989a. "History and Psychoanalysis." In *Soundings in Critical Theory*, edited by Dominick LaCapra. Ithaca, N.Y.: Cornell University Press.

————. 1989b. *Soundings in Critical Theory*. Ithaca, N.Y.: Cornell University Press.

Leibowitz, Joshua Otto. 1970. *The History of Coronary Heart Disease*. Berkeley: University of California Press.

Loewe, Michael. 2000. *A Biographical Dictionary of the Qin, Former Han and Xin Periods, 221 B.C.–A.D. 24*. Leiden, Neth.: Brill.

Lu, David John. 1997. *Japan: A Documentary History*. Armonk, N.Y.: M. E. Sharpe.

Maehira Fusaaki. 1991. "'Sakoku' Nihon to kaigai bōeki." In *Nihon no kinsei*, edited by Asao Naohiro. 18 vols, 1:131–170. Tokyo: Chūō kōronsha.

Matsuura Rei. 1968. *Katsu Kaishū*. Tokyo: Chūō kōronsha.

Mayo, Marlene. 1966. "Rationality in the Meiji Restoration." In *Modern Japanese Leadership: Transition and Change*, edited by Bernard S. Silberman and H. D. Harootunian, 323–369. Tucson, Ariz.: University of Arizona Press.

————. 1972. "The Korean Crisis of 1873 and Early Meiji Foreign Policy." *Journal of Asian Studies* 31 (4):793–819.

McClain, James L., John M. Merriman, and Kaoru Ugawa. 1994. *Edo and Paris: Urban Life and the State in the Early Modern Era.* Ithaca, N.Y.: Cornell University Press.

McLaren, Walter Wallace, ed. [1914] 1979. *Japanese Government Documents.* 2 vols. Reprint, Washington, D.C.: University Publications of America.

McMaster, John. 1992. *Sabotaging the Shogun: Western Diplomats Open Japan, 1859–69.* New York: Vantage Press.

McNair, Amy. 1998. *The Upright Brush: Yan Zhenqing's Calligraphy and Song Literati Politics.* Honolulu: University of Hawaii Press.

Miyaji Saichirō, ed. 1991. *Nakaoka Shintarō zenshū.* Tokyo: Keisō shobō.

Miyamoto Tsuneichi, Haraguchi Torao, and Higa Shunchō. 1968. *Nihon shomin seikatsu shiryō shūsei.* 31 vols. Tokyo: San'ichi shobō.

Miyauchi, D. Y. 1968. "Kokuze Sanron: The Three Major Problems of State Policy." *Monumenta Nipponica* 23 (1–2):156–186.

Miyazaki Michio. 1970. *Aomori ken no rekishi.* Tokyo: Yamakawa shuppansha.

Mizuno Masatoshi. 1978 *Seinan sensō-ki ni okeru nōmin ikki: Shiryō to kenkyū.* Fukuoka: Ashi Shobō.

———. 2000. *Seinan sensō to Azo.* Kumamoto: Kumamoto Nichinichi shimbun jōhō bunka sentā.

Mōri Toshihiko. 1978. *Meiji roku-nen seihen no kenkyū.* Edited by Ōsaka shiristu daigaku hōgakkai. Tokyo: Yūhikaku.

———. 1979. *Meiji roku-nen no seihen.* Tokyo: Chūō kōron shinsha.

Morris, Ivan. 1975. *The Nobility of Failure.* New York: New American Library.

Morse, Edward S. 1917. *Japan Day by Day.* 2 vols. Boston: Houghton Mifflin.

Motobu Hirotetsu. 1996. *Idai na kyōikusha Saigō Takamori: Okinoerabujima no Nanshūjuku.* Osaka: Kaifūsha.

Murakami Sumio. 1995. "Saigō no shi o hōzuru ittsu no dempō." *Keiten aijin* 13: 137–165.

Murano Moriji. 1985. "Seinan sensō no chūritsu-ha oyobi shigakkō-ha no dōkō." In *Saigō Takamori no subete,* edited by Godai Natsuo, 111–138. Tokyo: Shinjinbutsu ōraisha.

Mushakoji, Saneatsu. 1942. *Great Saigō: The Life of Saigō Takamori.* Translated by Moriaki Sakamoto. Tokyo: Kaitakusha.

Najita, Testuo. 1970. "Ōshio Heihachirō (1793–1837)." In *Personality in Japanese History,* edited by Albert M. Craig and Donald H. Shively, 155–179. Berkeley: University of California Press.

———. 1974. *Japan.* Englewood Cliffs, N.J.: Prentice-Hall.

Nakane Sekkō. [1921] 1968. *Sakumu kiji.* Edited by Nihon shiseki kyōka. 4 vols. Reprint, Tokyo: Tōkyō daigaku shuppan.

Nakayama Hiroshi. 1985. "Dai Saigō no shisō." In *Saigō Takamori no subete,* edited by Godai Natuso, 183–198. Tokyo: Shinjinbutsu ōraisha.

———. 1992. "Dai Saigō in okeru Shushigaku/Ōyōmeigaku no juyō ni tsuite." *Keiten aijin* (10):39–56.

Naze-shi shi hensan iinkai, ed. 1963. *Naze-shi shi.* 3 vols. Kagoshima: Naze shiyakusho.

Nihon shiseki kyōkai. [1910] 2001. *Shimazu Hisamitsu-kō jikki.* 3 vols. Reprint, Tokyo: Tōkyō daigaku shuppankai.

———, ed. [1928] 1968. *Ōkubo Toshimichi monjo.* 10 vols. Reprint, Tokyo: Tōkyō daigaku shuppankai.

———, ed. 1931. *Iwakura Tomomi kankei monjo.* 8 vols. Tokyo: Tōkyō daigaku shuppankai.

Nish, Ian Hill. 1994. *Britain & Japan: Biographical Portraits.* Folkestone: Japan Library.

———. 1998a. *The Iwakura Mission in America and Europe: A New Assessment.* Surrey, Eng.: Curzon Press.

———. 1998b. "The Iwakura Mission: Aftermath and Assessment." In *The Iwakura Mission in America and Europe: A New Assessment,* edited by Ian Nish, 188–198. Surrey, Eng.: Curzon Press.

Nobori Shomu. [1927] 1977. *Saigō Takamori gokuchūki: Amami Ōshima to Dai Saigō.* Edited by Sakamoto Moriaki. Reprint, Tokyo: Shinjinbutsu ōraisha.

Nock, Elizabeth Tripler. 1948. "The Satsuma Rebellion of 1877: Letter of John Capen Hubbard." *Far Eastern Quarterly* 7 (4):368–375.

Ochiai Naosuke. 1893. Interview by Yoshiki Takejirō. *Shidan sōkiroku* 12:77–97.

Oguchi Yoshio. 2000. "Satsuma-han to kinsei Ryūkyū-koku no jinkō." *Reimeikan chōsa kenkyū hōkoku* 13:1–42.

Ōhira Yoshiyuki. 1993. "Bakumatsu Satsuma hanshi, Yōmeigakusha: Itō Mōemon Sukeyuki to sono kakei." *Reimeikan chōsa kenkyū hōkoku* 7:13–43.

Ōishi, Shinzaburō. 1990. "The Bakuhan System." In *Tokugawa Japan: The Social and Economic Antecedents of Modern Japan,* edited by Chie Nakane and Shinzaburō Ōishi. Tokyo: University of Tokyo Press.

Okada, Takehiko. 1984. "Neo-Confucian Thinkers in Nineteenth-Century Japan." In *Confucianism and Tokugawa Culture,* edited by Peter Nosco, 215–250. Princeton, N.J.: Princeton University Press.

Okatani Shigemi. 1915. Interview by Yamada Takehachirō. *Shidankai sōkiroku* 265:24–31.

Olson, Lawrence. 1992. *Ambivalent Moderns: Portraits of Japanese Cultural Identity.* Savage, Md.: Rowman & Littlefield.

Pflugfelder, Gregory M. 1999. *Cartographies of Desire: Male-Male Sexuality in Japanese Discourse, 1600–1950.* Berkeley: University of California Press.

Pompe van Meerdervoort, Johannes Lijdius Catharinus. 1970. *Doctor on Deshima: Selected Chapters from J. L. C. Pompe van Meerdervoort's Vijf jaren in Japan [Five Years in Japan] (1857–1863).* Tokyo: Sophia University Press.

Ravina, Mark. 1999. *Land and Lordship in Early Modern Japan.* Stanford, Calif.: Stanford University Press.

Ryū Kazutoyo, ed. 1968. *Tatsugō senkyochū no Nanshū ō jitsuwa denkishū.* Kagoshima: Naze shiyakusho.

Sagara Tōru, Mizoguchi Yūzō, and Fukunaga Mitsuji, eds. 1980. *Satō Issai, Ōshio Chūsai.* Vol. 46, *Nihon shisō taikei.* Tokyo: Iwanami shoten.

Saigō Takamori. 1971. *Saigō Takamori's Poems and Posthumous Works.* Translated by Moriaki Sakamoto. Tokyo: Hyōgensha.

Sakaguchi Tokutarō. [1921] 1977. *Amami Ōshima shi.* Reprint, Tokyo: Daiwa gakugei tosho.

Sakai Kenkichi. 1999. *Satsumaimo.* Tokyo: Hōsei daigaku shuppan.

Sakai, Robert K. 1957. "Feudal Society and Modern Leadership in Satsuma-han." *Journal of Asian Studies* 16 (3):365–376.

———. 1964. "The Satsuma-Ryukyu Trade and the Tokugawa Seclusion Policy." *Journal of Asian Studies* 23 (4):391–403.

———. 1970. "Shimazu Nariakira and National Leadership in Satsuma." In *Personality in Japanese History,* edited by Albert M. Craig and Donald H. Shively, 209–233. Berkeley: University of California Press.

Sakamaki, Shunzo. 1964. "Ryukyu and Southeast Asia." *Journal of Asian Studies* 23 (3):383–389.

Sakamoto, Moriaki. 1971. *Seinan sensō no gen'in to shite no Fukuzawa Yukichi to Ōkubo Toshimichi no tairitsu oyobi Saigō Takamori no kanshi to ikunshū no eiyaku.* Tokyo: Hyōgensha.

Sasaki Junnosuke. 1969. *Bakumatsu shakairon.* Tokyo: Hanawa shobō.

Sasaki Suguru. 1977. *Boshin sensō.* Tokyo: Chūō kōronsha.

———. 1991. "Seinan sensō ni okeru Saigō Takamori to shizoku." *Jinbun gakuhō (Kyōto daigaku jinbun kagaku kenkyūjo)* 68:1–46.

———. 1994a. "Meiji tennō no junkō to 'chūmin' no keisei." *Shisō* (845):95–117.

———. 1994b. "Saigō Takamori to Saigō densetsu." In *Iwanami kōza Nihon tsūshi 16: Kindai 1,* edited by Asao Naohiro, Amino Yoshihiko, Ishii Susumu, Kano Masanao, Hayase Shōhachi, and Yasumaru Yoshio, 325–340.

———. 1997. "Taisei hōkan to tōbaku mitchoku." *Jinbun gakuhō (Kyōto daigaku jinbun kagaku kenkyūjo)* 80:1–32.

———. 1998. *Ōkubo Toshimichi to Meiji Ishin.* Tokyo: Yoshikawa kōbunkan.

Sassa Tomofusa. 1986. *Senpō nikki.* Edited by Takano Kazuto. Kumamoto-shi: Seichōsha.

Satow, Ernest Mason. [1921] 1968. *A Diplomat in Japan.* Reprint, London: Oxford University Press.

———. 1998. *The Diaries and Letters of Sir Ernest Mason Satow (1843–1929): A Scholar-Diplomat in East Asia.* Edited by Ian C. Ruxton. Lewiston, N.Y.: E. Mellen Press.

Schmid, André. 2000. "Colonialism and the 'Korea Problem' in the Historiogaphy of Modern Japan: A Review Essay." *Journal of Asian Studies* 59 (4):951–976.

Schwartz, Henry B. 1908. *In Togo's Country: Some Studies in Satsuma and Other Little-Known Parts of Japan.* Cincinnati: Jennings & Graham.

Senda Minoru. 1979. *Ishin seiken no chitsuroku shobun: Tennōsei to haihanchiken.* Tokyo: Kaimei shoin.

Shiba Ryōtarō. 1975. *Tobu ga gotoku.* 7 vols. Tokyo: Bungei shunjū.

Shibusawa, Eiichi. [1894] 1994. *The Autobiography of Shibusawa Eiichi: From Peasant to Entrepreneur.* Translated by Teruko Craig. Reprint, Tokyo: University of Tokyo Press.

Shimazu Tadayoshi. 1993. *Nisshin kō iroha uta.* Edited by Shōko shūseikan. Kagoshima: Shōko shūseikan.

Shimizu Kōgi. 1975. *Ōyama Iwao*. Tokyo: Shinjinbutsu ōraisha.

Shimodōzono Junji. 1996. "Saigō Takamori to Katsu Kaishū." *Keiten aijin* 14:103–126.

Shindō Toyō. 1982. *Jiyū minken to Kyūshū chihō: Kyūshū kaishintō no kenkyū*. Fukuoka: Koga shoten.

Shinoda Kōzō. 1947. *Meiji shinbun kidan*. Tokyo: Sudō shoten.

Silberman, Bernard S., and Harry D. Harootunian. 1966. *Modern Japanese Leadership: Transition and Change*. Tucson, Ariz.: University of Arizona Press.

Smits, Gregory. 1999. *Visions of Ryukyu: Identity and Ideology in Early-Modern Thought and Politics*. Honolulu: University of Hawaii Press.

Ssu-ma Ch'ien. 1969. *Records of the Historian: Chapters from the Shih chi of Ssu-ma Ch'ien*. Translated by Burton Watson. New York: Columbia University Press.

Steele, M. William. 1976. "Katsu Kaishū and the Collapse of the Tokugawa Bakufu." Ph.D. diss., Harvard University.

———. 1981. "Against the Restoration: Katsu Kashū's Attempt to Reinstate the Tokugawa Family." *Monumenta Nipponica* 36 (3):299–316.

———. 1982. "The Rise and Fall of the Shōgitai: A Social Drama." In *Conflict in Modern Japanese History*, edited by Tetsuo Najita and J. Victor Koschmann, 128–144. Princeton, N.J.: Princeton University Press.

———. 1990. "Edo in 1868: The View from Below." *Monumenta Nipponica* 45 (2):127–155.

Suematsu Kenchō. 1921. *Bōchō kaitenshi*. Rev. ed. 12 vols. Tokyo: Suematsu Haruhiko.

Sugitani Akira. 1962. *Etō Shinpei*. Tokyo: Yoshikawa kōbunkan.

Sugiyama, Shinya. 1984. "Thomas B. Glover: A British Merchant in Japan, 1861–70." *Business History* 26 (2):115–138.

———. 1993. *Meiji ishin to Igirisu shōnin*. Tokyo: Iwanami shoten.

Suzuki Hankyū. 1988. *"Daihyōteki Nihonjin" o yomu*. Tokyo: Daimeidō.

Suzuki Tomokichi. 1928. *Kyōdo senshi*. 2 vols. Kyoto: Kyōto rentaiku shōkōdan.

Swale, Alistar. 1998. "America, 15 January–6 August 1872: The First Stage in the Quest for Enlightenment." In *The Iwakura Mission in America and Europe: A New Assessment*, edited by Ian Hall Nish, 11–35. Surrey, Eng.: Curzon Press.

Tachibana Nankei. [1795] 1974. *Tōzai yūki*. Edited by Munemasa Iso'o. 2 vols. Tokyo: Heibonsha.

Takemitsu Makoto. 1999. *Han to nihonjin: gendai ni ikiru "okunigara."* Tokyo: PHP kenkyūjo.

Takeuchi Rizō. 1983. *Kagoshima-ken*. Tokyo: Kadokawa shoten.

Tamamuro Taijō. 1960. *Saigō Takamori*. Tokyo: Iwanami shoten.

———. 1966. *Seinan sensō*. Tokyo: Shibundō.

Tan'o Yasunori, and Kawada Akihisa. 1996. *Imēji no naka no sensō: Nisshin Nichirō kara reisen made*. Tokyo: Iwanami Shoten.

Tanaka Akira. 1991. "Meiji ishin no sekaishiteki kankyō o dō toraeru ka." In *Sōten Nihon no rekishi 6: Kin gendai hen*, edited by Sasaki Ryūji, 14–25. Tokyo: Shinjinbutsu ōraisha.

Tanaka Niiharu. 1970. "Shigakkō to Seinan sensō." In *Shizoku no hanran*, edited by Konishi Shirō, 183–205. Tokyo: Chikuma shobō.

Tanaka Sōgorō. 1938. *Ōkubo Toshimichi*. Tokyo: Chikuma shobō.

———. 1958. *Saigō Takamori*. Tokyo:Yoshikawa kōbunkan.

Toby, Ronald P. *State and Diplomacy in Early Modern Japan*. Princeton, N.J.: Princeton University Press, 1984.

Tomomatsu Entai. 1961. *Gesshō*. Tokyo:Yoshikawa kōbunkan.

Totman, Conrad. 1967. *Politics in the Tokugawa Bakufu, 1600–1843*. Cambridge, Mass.: Harvard University Press.

———. 1975. "Tokugawa Yoshinobu and Kobugattai: A Study of Political Inadequacy." *Monumenta Nipponica* 30 (4):393–403.

———. 1980. *The Collapse of the Tokugawa Bakufu, 1862–1868*. Honolulu: University of Hawaii Press.

———. 1993. *Early Modern Japan*. Berkeley: University of California Press.

Tōyama Shigeki. 1951. *Meiji Ishin*. Tokyo: Iwanami zensho.

Tsuchihashi, PaulYachita. 1952. *Japanese Chronological Tables: From A.D. 601 to 1872*. Tokyo: Sophia University Press.

Tsunoda, Ryusaku, William Theodore de Bary, and Donald Keene, eds. 1958. *Sources of Japanese Tradition*. 2 vols. NewYork: Columbia University Press.

Tu, Wei-ming. 1985. *Confucian Thought: Selfhood as Creative Transformation*. Albany: State University of NewYork Press.

Uchimura, Kanzō. 1908. *Representative Men of Japan*. Tokyo: Keiseisha.

Ueda Shigeru. 1998. *Saigō Takamori no sekai*. Tokyo: Chūō kōronsha.

Ueki-chō. 2001. *Tabaruzaka no tatakai*. Ueki-chō, Kumamoto: Ueki-chō.

Ujiie Mikito. 1995. *Bushidō to erosu*. Tōkyō: Kōdansha.

Umegaki, Michio. 1988. *After the Restoration*. New York: New York University Press.

Ushioda Akira, and Kihara Saburō. 1990. *Saigō no ango (shimazuma): Aigana*. Tokyo: Mizuumi shobō.

Varley, H. Paul. 1971. *Imperial Restoration in Medieval Japan*. New York: Columbia University Press.

Vlastos, Stephen. 1989. "Opposition Movement in Early Meiji, 1868–1885." In *The Cambridge History of Japan*. Vol. 5, *The Nineteenth Century*, edited by Marius B. Jansen. Cambridge, Eng.: Cambridge University Press.

Wakabayashi, Bob Tadashi, and Yasushi Aizawa. 1986. *Antiforeignism and Western Learning in Early-Modern Japan: The New Theses of 1825*. Cambridge, Mass.: Harvard University Press.

Walker, Brett L. 2001. *The Conquest of Ainu Lands: Ecology and Culture in Japanese Expansion, 1590–1800*. Berkeley: University of California Press.

Walthall, Anne. 1995. "Off with Their Heads! The Hirata Disciples and the Ashikaga Shoguns." *Monumenta Nipponica* 50 (2):137–170.

Wilson, George M. 1970. "The Bakumatsu Intellectual in Action: Hashimoto Sanai in the Political Crisis of 1858." In *Personality in Japanese History*, edited by Albert M. Craig and Donald H. Shively, 234–263. Berkeley: University of California Press.

Wolff, Derek. 1998. "Life with(out) Saigō." Department of History, University of Chicago.

Yamada Jun. [1944] 1997. *Nanshu hyakuwa*. Revised ed., Tokyo: Meitoku shuppansha.

Yamada Seisai, ed. 1939. *Saigō Nanshū ikun*. Tokyo: Iwanami shoten.

Yamada Shōji. 1987. "Kawaguchi Seppō ni tsuite." *Keiten aijin* (5):156–175.

———. 1992a. "Saigō no Kabayama San'en ate shokan." *Keiten aijin* (10):265–269.

———. 1992b. *Saisetsu Saigō Takamori nenpu*. Kagoshima: Saigō nanshū kenshōkai.

———, ed. 2000. *Shinpen Saigō Takamori kanshi shū*. Revised ed., Kagoshima: Saigō nanshū kenshōkai.

Yamada Tatsuo, Iinuma Jirō, and Oka Mitsuo, eds. 1977–1983. *Nihon nōsho zenshū*. Tokyo: Nōzangyoson bunka kyōkai.

Yamaguchi Muneyuki. 1993. *Saigō Takamori*. Tokyo: Meitoku Shuppansha.

Yamamoto Tsunetomo. 1979. *Hagakure: The Book of the Samurai*. Translated by William Scott Wilson. Tokyo: Kodansha International.

Yamamura, Kōzō. 1974. *A Study of Samurai Income and Entrepreneurship: Quantitative Analyses of Economic and Social Aspects of the Samurai in Tokugawa and Meiji Japan*. Vol. 76. Cambridge, Mass.: Harvard University Press.

———. 1986. "The Meiji Land Tax Reform." In *Japan in Transition: From Tokugawa to Meiji,* edited by Marius B. Jansen and Gilbert Rozman, 382–399. Princeton, N.J.: Princeton University Press.

Yates, Charles L. 1987. "Restoration and Rebellion in Satsuma: The Life of Saigo Takamori (1827–1877)." Ph.D. diss., Princeton University.

———. 1994. "Saigō Takamori in the Emergence of Meiji Japan." *Modern Asian Studies* 28 (3):449–474.

———. 1995. *Saigō Takamori: The Man behind the Myth*. London: Kegan Paul International.

Yokoyama Izumi. 1997. "An Interpretation of the 1914 Eruption of Sakurajima Volcano." *Proceedings of the Japan Academy* 73, ser. B (4):53–58.

Yoshimoto Masayuki. 1985. "Saigō Takmori to Shimazu Nariakira." In *Saigō Takamori no subete,* edited by Godai Natsuo, 31–48. Tokyo: Shinjinbutsu ōraisha.

Yui Masaomi, Fujiwara Akira, and Yoshida Yutaka, eds. 1989. *Nihon kindai shisō taikei 4:guntai, heishi*. Tokyo: Iwanami shoten.

Sources

There are two major compilations of Saigō's letters and papers: *Dai Saigō zenshū (DSZ)* and *Saigō Takamori zenshū (STZ)*. DSZ, compiled in 1923, consists of two volumes of letters and a one-volume biography. The letters are annotated and transcribed in the original epistolary form *(sōrōbun)*, and there are some photographic reproductions of the original documents. The biography, however, is of questionable value. It is largely undocumented and includes many well-known but suspect anecdotes. *STZ*, a six-volume document collection completed in 1980, is an exhaustive collection of primary source material. It includes nearly five hundred letters from Saigō, almost two hundred letters to Saigō, public records related to the Saigō family (including census and family succession documents), a collection of Saigō's poetry, a collection of observations about Saigō, a biographical dictionary, a chronology, and a bibliography. The letters are carefully annotated with extensive supplemental material. Unfortunately, the editors of *STZ* did not simply reproduce Saigō's letters but partially converted his original epistolary form into conventional Japanese, a practice called *yomikudashi*. Although the *yomikudashi* is generally easier to read, in some cases it generates ambiguities not found in the original. Therefore, although I have relied primarily on *STZ*, I also have referred to the older collection. Since the completion of *STZ* in 1980 a handful of additional letters have been discovered or retranscribed. See, for example, Yamada Shōji 1992a.

For Saigō's poems I have found Yamada Shōji's recent collection especially useful (2000). Other important documents include *Shushō genshiroku*, Saigō's transcipion of Satō Issai's writings. *STZ* has a Japanese translation of this text, but for tracing classical references I have used the classical Chinese *(kanbun)* in Yamada Seisai 1939, 5–70.

Accounts of Saigō's time in exile deserve special mention because few primary sources survive. The most extensive account is by Nobori Shomu, first published in 1927. Nobori's academic credentials are remarkable. He was one of Japan's leading translators of Russian culture and the author of nearly a hundred translations and studies of Russian literature. He taught

Russian studies at the Japanese Military Academy and Waseda University and served as a special adviser to the Japanese cabinet on Russian affairs. (Berton and Langer 1981). Nonetheless, his study of Saigō is problematic; although reportedly based on interviews, it lacks any scholarly apparatus. Further, as an Amami Ōshima native, Nobori was inclined to indulge the most romantic legends of Saigō's time in exile. Still, the account is valuable as an example of Saigō lore, and parts can be substantiated in primary sources. I also have used a compilation of Saigō lore assembled by one of Aigana's descendants (Ryū 1968).

Glossary

For a glossary and other supplemental resources see www.emory.edu/ HISTORY/RAVINA/lastsamurai.html

Index